THE PAUPER'S FREEDOM

ÉTUDES D'HISTOIRE DU QUÉBEC/
STUDIES ON THE HISTORY OF QUEBEC

Magda Fahrni et / and Jarrett Rudy
Directeurs de la collection/Series Editors

1 Habitants and Merchants in Seventeenth-Century Montreal
Louise Dechêne

2 Crofters and Habitants
Settler Society, Economy, and Culture in a Quebec Township, 1848–1881
J.I. Little

3 The Christie Seigneuries Estate Management and Settlement in the Upper Richelieu Valley, 1760–1859
Françoise Noël

4 La Prairie en Nouvelle-France, 1647–1760
Louis Lavallée

5 The Politics of Codification
The Lower Canadian Civil Code of 1866
Brian Young

6 Arvida au Saguenay
Naissance d'une ville industrielle
José E. Igartua

7 State and Society in Transition
The Politics of Institutional Reform in the Eastern Townships, 1838–1852
J.I. Little

8 Vingt ans après *Habitants et marchands*, Lectures de l'histoire des XVIIe et XVIIIe siècles canadiens
Habitants et marchands, Twenty Years Later
Reading the History of Seventeenth- and Eighteenth-Century Canada
Edited by *Sylvie Dépatie, Catherine Desbarats, Danielle Gauvreau, Mario Lalancette, Thomas Wien*

9 Les récoltes des forêts publiques au Québec et en Ontario, 1840–1900
Guy Gaudreau

10 Carabins ou activistes? L'idéalisme et la radicalisation de la pensée étudiante à l'Université de Montréal au temps du duplessisme
Nicole Neatby

11 Families in Transition
Industry and Population in Nineteenth-Century Saint-Hyacinthe
Peter Gossage

12 The Metamorphoses of Landscape and Community in Early Quebec
Colin M. Coates

13 Amassing Power
J.B. Duke and the Saguenay River, 1897–1927
David Massell

14 Making Public Pasts
The Contested Terrain of Montreal's Public Memories, 1891–1930
Alan Gordon

15 A Meeting of the People
School Boards and Protestant Communities in Quebec, 1801–1998
Roderick MacLeod and Mary Anne Poutanen

16 A History for the Future
Rewriting Memory and Identity in Quebec
Jocelyn Létourneau

17 C'était du spectacle!
L'histoire des artistes transsexuelles à Montréal, 1955–1985
Viviane Namaste

18 The Freedom to Smoke
   Tobacco Consumption and Identity
   Jarrett Rudy

19 Vie et mort du couple
   en Nouvelle-France
   Québec et Louisbourg au XVIIIe siècle
   Josette Brun

20 Fous, prodigues et ivrognes
   Familles et déviance à Montréal
   au XIXe siècle
   Thierry Nootens

21 Done with Slavery
   The Black Fact in Montreal,
   1760–1840
   Frank Mackey

22 Le concept de liberté au Canada à
   l'époque des Révolutions atlantiques,
   1776–1838
   Michel Ducharme

23 The Empire Within
   Postcolonial Thought and Political
   Activism in Sixties Montreal
   Sean Mills

24 Quebec Hydropolitics
   The Peribonka Concessions
   of the Second World War
   David Massell

25 Patrician Families and the Making
   of Quebec
   The Taschereaus and McCords
   Brian Young

26 Des sociétés distinctes
   Gouverner les banlieues bourgeoises
   de Montréal, 1880–1939
   Harold Bérubé

27 Nourrir la machine humaine
   Nutrition et alimentation au Québec,
   1860–1945
   Caroline Durand

28 Why Did We Choose to Industrialize?
   Montreal, 1819–1849
   Robert C.H. Sweeny

29 Techniciens de l'organisation sociale
   La réorganisation de l'assistance
   catholique privée à Montréal
   (1930–1974)
   Amélie Bourbeau

30 Beyond Brutal Passions
   Prostitution in Early Nineteenth-
   Century Montreal
   Mary Anne Poutanen

31 A Place in the Sun
   Haiti, Haitians, and the Remaking
   of Quebec
   Sean Mills

32 The Pauper's Freedom
   Crime and Poverty
   in Nineteenth-Century Quebec
   Jean-Marie Fecteau

The Pauper's Freedom

Crime and Poverty in Nineteenth-Century Quebec

JEAN-MARIE FECTEAU

Translated by Peter Feldstein

McGill-Queen's University Press
Montreal & Kingston • London • Chicago

Published originally under the title *La liberté du pauvre. Crime et pauvreté au XIXe siècle québécois* © VLB Éditeur 2004

English-language edition
© McGill-Queen's University Press 2017

ISBN 978-0-7735-4947-0 (cloth)
ISBN 978-0-7735-4948-7 (paper)

Legal deposit second quarter 2017
Bibliothèque nationale du Québec

Printed in Canada on acid-free paper that is 100% ancient forest free (100% post-consumer recycled), processed chlorine free

This book has been published with the help of a grant from the Canadian Federation for the Humanities and Social Sciences, through the Awards to Scholarly Publications Program, using funds provided by the Social Sciences and Humanities Research Council of Canada.

McGill-Queen's University Press acknowledges the support of the Canada Council for the Arts for our publishing program. We also acknowledge the financial support of the Government of Canada through the Canada Book Fund for our publishing activities.

We acknowledge the financial support of the Government of Canada through the National Translation Program for Book Publishing for our translation activities.

Library and Archives Canada Cataloguing in Publication

Fecteau, Jean-Marie
 [Liberté du pauvre]
 The pauper's freedom: crime and poverty in nineteenth-century Quebec/ Jean-Marie Fecteau; translated by Peter Feldstein. – English-language edition.

(Studies on the history of Quebec; 32)
 Translation of: La liberté du pauvre : sur la régulation du crime et de la pauvreté au XIXe siècle québécois/Jean-Marie Fecteau. – Messageries ADP, 955, rue Amherst, Montréal, QC H2L 3K4. – Montréal: VLB, 2004.
 Includes bibliographical references and index.
 ISBN 978-0-7735-4947-0 (cloth). – ISBN 978-0-7735-4948-7 (paper)

1. Poverty – Québec (Province) – History – 19th century. 2. Crime – Québec (Province) – History – 19th century. 3. Liberalism – Québec (Province) – History – 19th century. 4. Social control – Québec (Province – History – 19th century. 5. Québec (Province) – Social policy – History – 19th century. I. Title. II. Title: Liberté du pauvre II. Series: Studies on the history of Quebec; 32

HC120.P6F4213 2017   362.509714   C2017-900340-2

This book was typeset by Marquis Interscript in 10/13 Sabon.

This book is dedicated to Jérémie, who will, I hope, forgive me for the hours of a father's presence that its writing took from him.

Contents

Foreword by Martin Petitclerc xi

Introduction 3

PART ONE REGULATION AND LIBERALISM IN QUEBEC 7

1 The Concept of Regulation 9
2 Freedom, State, and Individual: The Shifting Patterns of Nineteenth-Century Liberal Regulation 37
3 The Regulation of Crime and Poverty: The Old System in Crisis 66

PART TWO CRIME AND PUNISHMENT IN THE LIBERAL ERA 107

4 The Administration of Crime and the Vicissitudes of Liberalism 111
5 The Regulation of Juvenile Delinquency and Child Protection 137

PART THREE POVERTY AND WELFARE IN THE LIBERAL ERA 163

6 An Ethics of Poverty 165
7 Church and Religion in the Charity Economy 206

Conclusion 263

Notes 279

Bibliography 359

Index 399

FOREWORD

The Freedom of Jean-Marie Fecteau

You hold in your hands an English translation of the final book written by my late friend Jean-Marie Fecteau, emeritus professor in the Department of History at the Université du Quebec à Montréal (UQAM). Beyond the sadness evoked by having to write about a friend in the past tense, the writing of this introduction posed certain challenges. Jean-Marie died too young; he had books left to write. His last project, on which little progress could be made, was the writing of a long introduction to the English translation of his book, now published as *The Pauper's Freedom*. So it is by force of circumstance that I find myself taking stock of an intellectual adventure that was brutally interrupted by a devastating illness in the fall of 2012. That said, in rereading his writings and speeches, it has been a pleasure to renew my acquaintance with the historian and intellectual whom I so appreciated – a man who always preferred the bold pursuit of an intellectual project to the cautious compilation of factual knowledge. It is this facet of Jean-Marie's career, fully in evidence in *The Pauper's Freedom*, that I have sought to present in this foreword.[1]

Born 29 March 1949, Jean-Marie was raised in the working-class neighbourhood of Saint-Roch in the Lower Town district of Québec City. His was a family of very modest means and it was thanks to a scholarship that he gained admittance to the prestigious (and conservative) Petit séminaire de Québec, a private college founded in 1668 and traditionally dedicated to the training of priests. After finishing the classical curriculum, he was admitted to the history program at Université Laval where he obtained his bachelor's and master's degrees, the latter after writing a thesis on the French Revolution. His master's years gave a decisive impetus to his intellectual trajectory. He got involved in the student movement and took part in the student strikes of 1975 and 1976, among whose demands were the inclusion of Marxism and critical theory in the undergraduate curriculum. In parallel, he was hired by the Ministry of Social Affairs to do extensive research on the history of the social question in Quebec.[2] This engagement led him to the works of Michel Foucault and the Marxist political sociologist Nicos Poulantzas, which would deeply inflect his intellectual path. With the support of his master's supervisor, Claude Galarneau, he decided to pursue doctoral studies under the supervision of Michelle Perrot, a professor at the Université de Paris-Diderot and a close associate of Foucault. In 1983, he defended his doctoral dissertation on poverty and crime in Lower Canada.

The following year he was hired, first as a substitute professor, then as a regular professor, in the history department of UQAM. This public university, with its mission of making higher education accessible, had been since its inception in 1969 a hub of left intellectual activity in Quebec. Jean-Marie's colleagues in the department included Marxist-aligned historians such as Stanley Bréhaut Ryerson, Alfred Dubuc, Michel Grenon, Nadia Fahmy Eid, Robert Comeau, and Richard Desrosiers. At this time, he was intellectually aligned with the "socialism and independence" tendency around which many UQAM professors rallied.[3] This ideological and political context would have a significant impact on Jean-Marie's historiographical output, at least until the 1995 referendum on Quebec sovereignty. He subsequently became more discreet in his political involvement, even though a resolute commitment to social justice persisted in his teaching and research. He was inhabited by a free-thinking disposition and a stormy temperament that had never really been dimmed by his rather conservative education. At UQAM, the boy from Québec City's Lower Town found himself right at home.

After 1995, the bulk of his considerable energy was devoted to the development of his research team, and this remained a central preoccupation until the end of his life. In 1990, with the help of Jean Trépanier, a professor in the School of Criminology at the Université de Montréal, Jean-Marie founded and became the director of the Centre d'histoire des régulations sociales (CHRS).[4] André Cellard, a professor of criminology at Ottawa University, and Janice Harvey, a professor of history at Dawson College in Montreal, joined the centre a few years later. A dozen more professors joined his research team in the new millennium,[5] further enriching this vibrant hub of education and research on Quebec history. Some seventy-five students, including myself, obtained master's or doctoral degrees under his supervision during his years as director of the CHRS. His research greatly contributed to the development of various fields of historiography, including political history, the history of law, and of course the history of poverty and crime.

In this essay, whose primary goal is to stimulate discussion of his work, I will outline my colleague's intellectual project – to produce a political history of social regulation – and how it fits into the historiography of the last forty years.

What did Jean-Marie mean by the study of social regulation? Put simply, it involves the writing of a political history of social relations as a means of understanding social change. Bound up with a political consideration of norms, the concept of social regulation obviously includes the legislative, executive, and judicial branches of government as well as its administrative apparatus. But other institutions are also in play: our everyday acts and thoughts are driven, and also constrained, by various norms not directly issuing from these institutions. Social regulation encompasses a wide variety of normative entities, depending on the political forms taken by the "power of constraint and the contours of the collective destiny (Fecteau 1992c, 4)" that characterize a given society. Jean-Marie always held that the study of the administration of crime and poverty was a superb angle of analysis from which to understand the evolution of a "mode of social regulation," and hence social change itself. There, in a few words, is the spirit in which *The Pauper's Freedom* was written.

Since my task is to discuss Jean-Marie's intellectual trajectory, I have opted for an essentially chronological approach to the presentation of his principal research projects, situating them within their historiographical context: his early neo-Marxist work on social regulation; his 1990s involvement in political history; the reformulation of his historiographic project on social regulation, leading to the writing of *The Pauper's Freedom* in 2004; and, finally, his more recent work on the practice of history, written during the closing years of his life.

A NEW (CAPITALIST) ORDER OF THINGS

Un nouvel ordre des choses: la pauvreté, le crime et l'état au Québec, de la fin du XVIIIe siècle à 1840 is the published version of his doctoral thesis, completed under the supervision of the historian Michelle Perrot. Perrot, in a highly productive dialogue with Michel Foucault, challenged the French scholar's thesis that a disciplinary agenda of social control had manifested itself, in the modern period, through the implementation of a "carceral archipelago" made up of prisons, asylums, hospitals, factories, and other institutions.[6] In his dissertation, Jean-Marie revisits this perspective, embarking on a critical investigation of Foucault's arguments that would stimulate his research for the rest of his life. While a study of the discourse on confinement during the modern period might lead one to believe in a bourgeois agenda of social control, as Foucault did, Jean-Marie stressed that "the material circumstances of social control are of another order entirely. It manifests itself in an ever contested, ever-fleeting equilibrium between the logic of class domination and its material conditions of operation. In other words, social control is much more a day-to-day combat, with unequal weapons, than it is a monolithic apparatus operating to effect submission" (Fecteau 1983, 2). This materialist and institutionalist critique of Foucault's intellectual project led Jean-Marie to emphasize the concept of "social regulation." He used this concept to assert that the social order is a fragile, ever-changing product of the dynamic nature and very materiality of fundamental social relations, in this case class relations. This idea reappears in *Un nouvel ordre des choses:* "The social regulation at issue here thus appears as a fragile, perpetually contested compromise between the exercise of domination by the ruling classes and the practice of resistance by the working classes" (Fecteau 1989, 10).[7]

His colleague and friend Jacques-Guy Petit, a professor of history at the Université d'Angers in France, has noted that the concept of social regulation was commonly used in France in the sociology of actors, networks, and organizations (Petit 2005). But more than this sociological tradition, it was Marxism – and especially French Marxist currents deriving from Louis Althusser, including the work of Nicos Poulantzas[8] – that exerted a strong intellectual influence on Jean-Marie in the 1970s. His doctoral thesis draws on early work in a school of thought known today as "political Marxism," developing primarily in the wake of research by the historian Robert Brenner.[9] Jean-Marie was equally well acquainted with the "French regulationist school," a group of neo-Marxist economists that included Michel Aglietta, Alain Lipietz, Robert Boyer.[10] These scholars stressed the historical process of institutionalization of social relations and they popularized the concepts of "mode of regulation" and "regime of accumulation," which had a significant impact in Quebec.[11] Beyond their considerable differences, these Marxian perspectives concurred in their overt critique of economic determinism and their insistence on the importance of class conflicts and institutionalized compromises as determinants of historical change, especially at the level of the state.

Jean-Marie's historiographic project reflected the enduring influence of these currents. While he never considered history "a process without a subject" (Althusser), he paid more attention to shifting institutional forms of power than to the resistance struggles of history's subjects. This observation sheds light on his relative disinterest in "bottom-up" approaches centring around the problem of identity formation in subalterns as derived from the social history work of E.P. Thompson. Moreover, Thompson had vehemently opposed Althusser's structuralist theory of Marxism several years earlier.[12] This Thompsonian approach was at that time much more influential in English-speaking academia, including the Montreal History Group directed by Brian Young at McGill University.[13]

Part 1 of *Un nouvel ordre des choses* focuses on the "feudal mode of social regulation." Jean-Marie contends that Lower Canadian society was feudal because it was still politically structured by "extraeconomic" (institutional and normative) practices of labour exploitation, including seigneurial dues, tithes, *corvée*, forced labour, and so on. For Jean-Marie, this mode of regulation, "i.e., the dynamic of the social relations of domination, is not based on economic control (actual control of production and trade guaranteed by a legal framework) but on observance of a normative and customary framework that stratified and distributed the instruments of control in such a way as to ensure extraction of the social surplus" (Fecteau 1983, 18). His study of this particular form of social relations of domination demonstrated the enduring stability of this mode of social regulation until the mid-1810s. And this stability was explicable as the product of working-class participation in the reproduction of these social relations of domination, which they reinterpreted as forms of wealth redistribution. His analysis of the base-level (community) and institutional (church and state) organization of poor relief in Lower Canadian society prior to 1815 shows that "the hold of the dominant classes over the mass of producers ... is extremely weak. The regulation of relief is primarily a question of a sociability founded on the base community ... The legitimation of this system of relief was essentially based on a customary order often reinterpreted, on the part of the masses, as a social redistribution process" (Fecteau 1989, 74). Even the regulation of crime, according to Jean-Marie, was primarily a function of these underlying solidarities, implying that "the punishment system put in place and controlled by the feudal state was not the primary mechanism by which illegal acts were curtailed" (Fecteau 1989, 77).[14]

This "subtle distribution of autonomies inscribed within tradition" (Fecteau 1983, 18), reflecting the relative leeway enjoyed by the producer classes (habitants, artisans, etc.) under the feudal mode of production, was put under strain by the experience of crime and mass poverty after 1810. What struck Jean-Marie was "the gap between the vigour of the discourse and the timidity of the reforms actually implemented," due to the contradictions of the feudal mode of regulation. This mode was riven by both "the accelerated commodification of social relations and the reproduction of feudal relations of submission based on customary law" (Fecteau 1989, 86). From 1815 to 1840, the customary order associated with the feudal mode of social regulation was no longer able to arbitrate the social conflicts provoked by rising poverty in the context of the capitalist transition. A "great crisis" ensued, auguring the dethroning of a mode of regulation that no longer sufficed to ensure the reproduction of social relations of domination.

Jean-Marie described the emergence of a new political configuration of social relations, a "capitalist mode of social regulation" no longer founded on the customary order of the base communities, but rather on the market and the state norm. The implementation of this mode of regulation was experienced in a particular way in Lower Canada, due to a class structure specific to this colonial society (nobility attached to the land and not to imperial commerce; highly autonomous poor classes). This material structure of life paralyzed the operation of the local institutions and made the numerous attempts at philanthropic reform (schools, hospitals, asylums, houses of industry, prisons, etc.) impracticable. As a result, and especially from 1840 on, the colony saw the timid development of new practices for the administration of crime and poverty, very different (more modest and, importantly, more cynical) from earlier grand philanthropic designs for mass reform. At any rate, these multiple projects, studied by Foucault, were quickly defeated by the actual experience of crime, while the prison became the receptacle of choice (albeit completely overburdened) for the expeditious treatment of vagrancy, homelessness, and drunkenness. In this context, the new, pessimistic observation that reform of the masses was impossible led to a new vision of poverty and crime as unavoidable facts of the "new order of things." For Jean-Marie, "the task then became that of remodeling the charity relation and the punishment relation, and adapting them to the capitalist mode of administration in the process of being uneasily explored and discovered by people in the West" (Fecteau 1989, 250–2, 261).

POLITICAL HISTORY, NATIONAL HISTORY

By the time *Un nouvel ordre des choses* was published, the crisis of the socialist program for the transformation of society had already had a major impact on Marxism's standing among academics. In the mid-1980s, they rejected much more than this worldview and the strict historical materialism associated with it: even much of the historiographic questioning and the methodology of social history, and in particular the reliance on economic explanations of historical change, became suspect.[15] A profound rethinking was underway and a diverse range of new historiographic projects saw the light of day. Beyond the much-discussed "fragmentation of history," a broad consensus gradually formed around the goal of producing a non-determinist, non-materialist analysis of culture and the political realm. Although Jean-Marie had little affinity with this new cultural history, especially as conjoined to a version of methodological individualism, he played an active part in the renewal of political history. He was particularly attentive to the French philosopher Marcel Gauchet's call for a "paradigm change in the social sciences." A few years earlier, Gauchet had posited a close association between historical knowledge and a new reflection on the political, understood here as "the most broadly encompassing level of societal organization" and the locus of "recomposition of the scheme of a total history" (Gauchet 1988).[16] To Gauchet's influence could be added that of the German historian Reinhart Koselleck, whose work in conceptual history was just appearing in English and French translation at the turn of the 1990s.[17]

This holistic conception of the political found fertile terrain in the Quebec of that time, when a vibrant political conjuncture was moving toward the 1995 referendum on sovereignty. For much of the Quebec left, the question was not merely constitutional: in the face of the neoliberal politics and aggressive anti-unionism of that era's governments, a new coalition of nationalist, trade unionist, and feminist movements found itself supporting the Quebec sovereignty agenda. For the intellectuals involved, the conjuncture was conducive to a considerable broadening of constitutional politics, one example being historians' growing interest in the republican intellectual tradition in Lower Canada.[18] This political context was at odds with the Anglo-Canadian and American intellectual worlds, where debate raged around the politics of "identity" and "difference." Beyond the innumerable historiographic points of view raised, involving feminist materialist and post-structuralist perspectives in particular,[19] the effect of this debate was to make it increasingly difficult to fall back on a holistic conception of the political – a fortiori when it resembled what could be called a national political community.

Like the French Marxist tradition from which he drew inspiration, this background offers insight into the difficulty, for Jean-Marie, of integrating an analysis of gender and racial difference into his historical analysis. While he appreciated the critical dimension of these analyses, his conception of the political led him to view difference (increasingly including social class difference) not as a primary (sexual, racial, etc.) experience prior to the political but as one of its consequences. For Jean-Marie, the political sphere had become the place where social, sexual, racial, religious, national, and other differences can be formulated as a matter of importance in a given historical context. In short, he contended that politics underlies experience, not the reverse, echoing Gareth Stedman Jones's suggestion when he broke with the school of social history derived from E.P. Thompson in the early 1980s.[20] Furthermore, this explains why, if Jean-Marie's political history is a national history, it is not because a primary experience of identity is imposed on the political, but because Western liberal democracies had made the nation (rather than social class, gender, or race) the primary locus of the institutionalization of the political sphere from the turn of the nineteenth century: "Since the end of the eighteenth century if not earlier, with the ebbing of Enlightenment universalism, the national community has become the space of experience and the horizon of expectation of historical research on human beings in society, quite simply because it constitutes the (political) locus *par excellence* of the totalization of particular multiple identities. In other words, all history is national history" (Fecteau 1999a).[21]

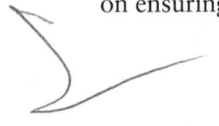

It is in this political and ideological context that Jean-Marie took part, in 1992, in the founding of the Association québécoise d'histoire politique, whose main activities were holding symposia and publishing the *Bulletin d'histoire politique*. He was a linchpin of this effort, to some extent representing the socialist left among this coalition of sovereignist intellectuals aligned with the "socialism and independence" tendency that wielded considerable influence at UQAM. A few years before the founding of the association, he had been active in the Mouvement socialiste, a grouping of trade union leaders and left-democratic intellectuals who had some influence over UQAM. The Mouvement was highly critical of the Parti québécois; it advocated a socialist independence agenda before dissolving at the turn of the 1990s. This political commitment was already apparent in Jean-Marie's work on the Rebellions of 1837–38 at the end of the 1980s. At a roundtable on this topic held at the meetings of the Institut d'histoire de l'Amérique française in 1987, he stressed that "one consequence of the defeat was a formal separation between the discourse on the social and the discourse on ensuring the survival of the nation. Under the aegis of the Church in particular, the years following 1840 witnessed a systematic process of denationalization of the social, in parallel with a desocialization of the national."[22] This line of thinking was to colour his commitment to a renewal of political history.

Thus, Jean-Marie's conception of political history was never a nostalgic appeal for a return to "grand" national history at the expense of the methods and problematics of social history. In 1994, at the time he was tracing the broad outlines of the historiographic project adopted by the *Bulletin d'histoire politique*, he stated that the "facile pointing of fingers at Marxism" by certain political historians was quite simply a theoretical dead end, and that "a vision of the world [Marxism] stressing people's determination of their collective future can hardly be said to be resistant to the collective dimension" (Fecteau 1994d, 5n5).[23] Instead, he attributed the decline of traditional political history to the "timidity of the problematics" and the "conservatism of the methods" used by its practitioners. The worldwide conjuncture after the fall of the Berlin Wall justified the development of a new political history: "In these societies imbued with an ideal of democracy, the political has become the issue driving the ambitions and aspirations of all." For Jean-Marie, it was not so much that "everything is political" as that "the reality expressed by the economic, the social, gender relations, culture – when this reality puts in play the power of constraint and the contours of the collective destiny – is the sum of [the questioning that takes place in the political sphere]" (Fecteau 1992c, 4)

This perspective led to sharp debate on the part of political historians, in the pages of *Bulletin d'histoire politique* and elsewhere.[24] At the very end of his life, "as a historian of politics and a citizen of sovereignist allegiances," he published a diatribe against the recrudescence of a neoconservative nationalist view of Quebec political history.[25] The occasion was the publication of a report by the historian Éric Bédard on the decline of political and national history in Quebec universities (Bédard and D'Arcy 2011). This report, closely associated with the nationalist movement and rather reminiscent of the conservative critique issued several years earlier by J.L. Granatstein (Granatstein 1998), represents precisely the kind of political history Jean-Marie had combatted throughout his career.[26] Bédard's report defines political history as the study of "influential figures and events" with a view to apprehending Quebec as "a [unified national] community of memory and destiny" (Bédard and D'Arcy 2011, 8). Ensuing from this was an attack on social history (ironically wrapped in an appeal to pluralism) for having allegedly made "troubling choices" running counter to the practice of political history and, consequently, to the identity foundations of the national political community.

It would be superfluous to revisit Jean-Marie's critique at length here, for it reiterated the essence of his historiographic approach as formulated up to the early 1990s. Rejecting false dichotomies between social history and political history, he emphasized that social history had served to problematize society as a historical construct in need of explanation. In this process, and contrary to what traditional political history, and by extension Bédard's report, would have us believe, the nation "became less an entity to be historicized than a construct to be comprehended in space and time" (Fecteau 2011, 215). Social history then becomes perfectly compatible with political history, which, rid of its unitary conception of the nation, is capable of problematizing the political dimension of societal existence with renewed vigour: i.e., "the imperatives proper to power and collective decision-making, to the kind of collective agency in which the constraints placed on everyone are central, and in which the future of the collectivity is played out." The historian, "out of a duty to meaning, dismantles the loom in order to better analyze the thread, rebuilding it in its new truth as a historical fact and not as a mere memory referent or primary identity" (Fecteau 2011, 220, 235).

Jean-Marie's new conception of political history led him to reformulate not only the problem of the nation but also that of domination and power relations. In the 1990s, the political was for him no longer just the institutionalization of the social relations of domination, as he had understood it in the 1980s; now, when "perceived as a dimension of the exercise of collectively determined powers, as a space of materialization of both shared and conflicting norms ... the political can take on all the breadth it deserves to be given; i.e., that of a *collective destiny determined by choices* ... Political history, reconciled with itself in a transformed world, resumes being an interrogation of the effectiveness of collective decision-making, the weight of shared norms."[27]

It should be clear that the "interrogation of the effectiveness of collective decision-making" was, for Jean-Marie, a research program in and of itself. From this starting point, he proceeded to isolate various constitutive dimensions of the political: the institutional (state, school, prison, etc.), the behavioural (civic action, protest, etc.), the symbolic (representations and ideologies), the normative (law, customs, etc.), and the "regulatory" (legislation, regulatory affairs, and the power relations they imply) (Fecteau 1998b). For him, political history is not a closed "field" in the domain of history but rather a critical and comprehensive questioning of how a society organizes and transforms itself to confront the challenges it faces. Jean-Marie began work on a number of dimensions of this research program, including history of law, association and company law, prison and reform schools, state formation, transformation of the Catholic Church, and so on.[28]

Beyond the empirical research to which it gave rise, one of the most original and interesting aspects of Jean-Marie's conception of political history is epistemological and ethical in nature. In a two-page manifesto published in the first issue of *Bulletin d'histoire politique* in 1992, he affirmed that history "can once again become a global reading of human beings' fate" via the analysis of the political (Fecteau 1992c, 4). He became critical of historiography's retreat into empirical study of more circumscribed objects after the collapse of "grand theory," a sign of its having given up on the attempt to account for social change and the collective destiny. His conception of political history thus led to a critique of empiricism, not as a method of administration of evidence and validation of hypotheses but as a discourse aiming to justify this "pragmatic" retreat of the discipline, which thereby came to look askance at any effort at theorization based on knowledge of the past. Not only would empiricism's epistemological stance inevitably lead to a naive brand of realism, but the discipline of history would no longer be able to participate in the creation of the "conditions for the determination and realization of collective choices" (Fecteau 1994d, 8). Only by recasting the problem of social change at the political level could history regain its social relevance, which meant posing "the question of the future" (Fecteau 1998b, 8).

Jean-Marie was alone in defending this perspective during a bitter debate among historians over a "revisionist" version of Quebec history articulated by Ronald Rudin in the early 1990s (Rudin 1992). Rudin found it paradoxical that constitutional demands were being made for recognition of Quebec's specificity even as revisionist historians were attempting to "normalize" Quebec's society and past. The historiographic agenda of "normalization" was, he argued, one of the most durable offshoots of the Quiet Revolution. It had, in particular, emphasized the historical study of socioeconomic structures common to the Western experience and downplayed the importance of studying values specific to a French Canada generally mistrustful of the universal values of modernity. A few years later, Rudin published *Making History in Twentieth-Century Quebec*, reiterating the essence of his critique while giving greater prominence to post-Quiet Revolution nationalism in his explanation of the motivations for modernizing revisionism (Rudin 1997, 294).

The debate aroused by Rudin's arguments largely focused on how accurately he had pinpointed this "revisionist" tendency, with most historians refusing to admit that the Quebec political context could have played a significant role in their analysis.[29] Yet few historians stressed, as Jean-Marie did, that Rudin's call for a better balance between values and structures did no damage to the practice of history, even when it took on the hues of relativism with respect to the values of modernity and science. Jean-Marie viewed with a critical eye Rudin's epistemological retrenchment, as the debate went on, into a traditional objectivist stance mistrustful of nationalism and, indeed, of any reference to the nation itself (Fecteau 1999a). He argued that this critical examination of the practice of history had to go much further – among other things, that it had to interrogate the impasse of empiricism. Obsessed with what it could count, Quebec and Western historiography had relinquished the fundamental political dimension of the historical experience; i.e., that which is hard to explain, "the missed opportunities or voices in the desert," "oppression in its most critical manifestations," "crushed aspirations," etc. (Fecteau 1995c). For this reason, the challenges of historiography were much greater than Rudin's appeal for a "more balanced" history led one to believe.

For Jean-Marie, empiricism had won out over the committed practice of history, the ethical search for meaning that had always gone hand in hand with the development of historical knowledge. Whence the silence of the historians, who had become serious and rigid to the point of no longer having anything to say about the "meaning of our present life, our ever more fragile collectivity"; in short, about the global political dimension of human existence. For Jean-Marie, the challenge looming in front of historians was

> to discover a new way of writing the history of our collective existence, one that is not limited to describing the materiality of our lives or the diversity of expressed thought; to discern what was deeply abnormal about our society, not by comparison with other purportedly normal but in fact merely dominant societies, but rather because it uniquely and specifically exhibited multiple forms of oppression. A society whose cohesion ultimately derived from a particular configuration of relations of dependency. The task is to discover, in short, how Quebec, among others, experienced its abnormality, if only in order to better emerge from it. (Fecteau 1995c, 37)

The Pauper's Freedom would take up this challenge. Before presenting the book, however, I must say a few words about how the author's conception of social regulation evolved in the 1990s, for this too is key to an understanding of his project.

SOCIAL REGULATION, MORAL REGULATION

In *Un nouvel ordre des choses*, Jean-Marie pitted his neo-Marxist perspective against the perspective of social control derived from Foucault's work on the "carceral archipelago." During the 1980s, for reasons discussed above, both of these critical theory-linked approaches began to lose steam. Foucault himself had moved away from his carceral archipelago program in the second half of the 1970s. In courses given at the Collège de France, he had begun to problematize power differently, with a view to producing a genealogy of the liberal rationality of government, or what he called "governmentality" (Foucault 2009b, 2010). His thinking on this, although not set down in a major work as the idea of the carceral archipelago had been, slowly diffused through 1980s French- and English-speaking academia.[30] Major works by Jacques Donzelot, François Ewald, Giovanna Procacci,[31] and other French scholars took inspiration from the Collège de France lectures. The lectures likewise had a considerable impact on Jean-Marie's conception of social regulation, although he never explicitly invoked Foucault's thinking on governmentality.[32]

In France, these new ideas about the liberal rationality of government took the form of a historical analysis of the "social question." This refers to a fundamental political debate cutting through the nineteenth and twentieth centuries about the heightening tensions between the citizenship regime and the rise of social inequality. The citizenship regime instated by the French Revolution, based on people's sovereignty, had the potential to effect a radical transformation of nineteenth-century society. To make revolution obsolete, it became necessary to separate the question of social inequality from that of people's sovereignty – whence "the invention of the social" (Donzelot). Such a "genealogical" analysis of the social had important consequences for theory: the "social" lost its status as a primary material reality (as it did in Marxism), becoming instead a discursive category deriving from the political. The problematics and style of *The Pauper's Freedom* are in large part borrowed from these important works,[33] even if Jean-Marie never went as far as to consider the social, or even the political, as mere discursive categories.

Published in French, these works had less impact in English Canada. There, scholars seeking to free themselves from Marxist ideas about the state took a somewhat different theoretical tack, although it, too, was influenced by Foucault's new thinking on governmentality. The most important point of departure in English Canada was probably *The Great Arch: English State Formation as Cultural Revolution*, by Philip Corrigan and Derek Sayer, which introduced the concept of moral regulation. While it evokes Foucault, this book is largely rooted in the Gramscian Marxism of E.P. Thompson as applied to the long battle for cultural hegemony between social classes (Corrigan and Sayer 1985, 268).[34] Briefly, Corrigan and Sayer come at state formation as a cultural revolution in governmental practices that involved "normalizing, rendering natural, taken for granted, in a word 'obvious,' what are in fact ontological and epistemological premises of a particular and historical form of social order" (Corrigan and Sayer 1985, 4). Although it sits within the Marxist tradition, the book signalled a break with historical materialism by giving analytical primacy to the political dimension of moral regulation in explanations of state formation and the capitalist transition.

This line of thinking gave rise to numerous works on moral regulation and Canadian state formation.[35] Following Foucault on some points, these works considerably expanded the domain of concern to all forms of the "conduct of conduct," and hence to regulation practices other than those conventionally regarded as being a function of the state.[36] With the state no longer posited as the locus of institutionalization of class relations, these relations lost their centrality in the construction and reproduction of the social order. A principal consequence has been to open up the analysis to other power relations, including social relations of gender and race.[37] Certain scholars then began to take a greater interest in the political discourse of moral regulation, rejecting the materialist postulate of a match between the nature of this discourse and its material conditions of presentation.[38] Such displacements, among others, fed into intense historiographic debates, at times drawing fierce criticism from materialist historians (Palmer 1990).

Jean-Marie followed the moral regulation debate with great interest, notably at the end of the 1980s when he wrote a laudatory review of Bruce Curtis's book on education in Canada West (Fecteau, 1988; Curtis 1988). Still under Marxism's influence, he stressed the dangers of an analysis that would lead to neglect of the materiality of social relations. A few years later, when he had broken with historical materialism, he formulated what might be called an institutionalist political critique of moral regulation.[39] Jean-Marie contended that the construction, reproduction, and transformation of norms and institutions could not be reduced to a governmental agenda of moral regulation; instead, they should be regarded as the specific political configuration of the multiple conflicts running through a society (with no further presumption that class conflict is the dominant social contradiction).[40] If so, then charity, prison, and asylums must not be interpreted as mere modalities whereby the governmental agenda of moral regulation is put into practice. More importantly, this liberal rationality of government, which assumes the patient construction of an "individualist" subjectivity, is only one of the multiple forms that the exercise of power under liberalism can take.[41]

This leads to a final remark regarding the critical distance kept by Jean-Marie from the moral regulationists. Their approach could not account for the political, at least as he conceived of it in the historiographic project that occupied him from the early 1990s on. Between the moral regulation of subjectivities and the inevitable resistance it aroused among the regulated, scholars had lost sight of what he called "the question of collective agency," or the shared political aspirations that made a particular society not merely the sum of the social (ergo power) relations of which it is constituted; in sum, the kind of collective agency explaining why, since the turn of the nineteenth century, men and women have persisted in believing in the necessity of organizing as a polity despite the conflicts dividing them.[42] In 2007, for example, he emphasized the need to study the state as the basic incarnation of this collective political agency under liberalism: "it is clearly not a matter of denying power, power relations, or structural inequality. It is a matter of observing how they act and are deployed within a space in which 'being-together' is both the lived reality and the desired end" (Fecteau 2007a).

A HISTORY OF FREEDOM

Jean-Marie had concluded his 1989 analysis of the feudal mode of regulation with a preliminary analysis of the emergence of the new capitalist "mode of administration of men and women." During the 1990s, however, while taking up this angle of attack, he no longer conceived of modes of social regulation as politico-institutional configurations of the social relations of class proper to a given mode of production (feudalism, capitalism, etc.). With the historiographic and epistemological turbulence of the 1990s, the concepts of labour and the wage system lost their centrality to his analysis of the regulation of crime and poverty.[43] Divorced from its neo-Marxist origins, the concept of social regulation could now be employed (in a scarcely conducive ideological context) in advocating for a critical political history centring around the global analysis of social change.

In order to tackle this project, Jean-Marie effected a major shift in perspective. In *Un nouvel ordre des choses*, he had embarked on an analysis of the "base organization" and the "institutional network" of regulation, setting the table for a study of how the "discourse of reform" had interpreted the crisis of institutionalized practices of punishment and welfare. The book had closed, moreover, with a discussion of the "passage from discourse to reality," involving the emergence of new welfare practices (Fecteau 1989, 207). The approach was reversed in *The Pauper's Freedom*, where he adopted what might be called a conceptual history approach to social regulation, explained as follows: "The [nineteenth] century's major transformations, whether on the plane of politics, economics, or ideology, were primarily keyed to the idea of freedom. Any historical analysis of [the changing administration of poverty and crime] must stay attuned to the shifting meanings of freedom over time … Beyond rallying cries and ideologies espousing laissez-faire and freedom of thought, the idea of setting the superstructure of society on a foundation of freedom amounted to a complete overturning of the logic of interaction between individuals in society" (37).

Taking the full measure of this radical change called for an in-depth reconsideration of liberalism, a dominant historical category in the historiography of the eighteenth and nineteenth centuries, and of course a central concept of neoliberal politics since the 1980s. In Jean-Marie's view, this historiography had generally reduced liberalism to a bourgeois ideology, centring around individual liberty and battling the powers conventionally seen as threatening to it, beginning with the Church.[44] It was important, he believed, to work back to the original meaning of liberalism – a revolutionary aspiration based on liberty – before it crystallized into an ideology closely associated with the bourgeoisie. In this regard, Jean-Marie also argued against the Marxists, for whom the democratic revolutions were essentially bourgeois and could be reduced to the experience of capitalist exploitation, which would, he argued, only be imposed many years later. Interested in discerning the evolution of collective political agency, he maintained that liberalism must be conceived as the bedrock lying beneath the shared values that arose out of a new relationship to the world, a relationship inherited from the Western experience of democratic revolution. Beyond class, gender, or racial divides, the new common sense that was liberalism manifested itself in "the immensely appealing ideal of freedom running through the nineteenth century," "a freedom-seeking impulse that even now finds expression in our societies" (3).

This is to say that the bourgeois liberal ideology never succeeded in encompassing the totality of meanings, and of societal projects, contained within the revolutionary aspiration toward liberty. Before it was formulated in the terms of political economy, codified in civil and criminal law, configured as a mode of regulation, and embodied by a vision of a bourgeois social order, liberalism was a new way of experiencing and thinking about the relationship between the individual and society. Thomas Haskell, in an important paper on changing societal views of slavery in the mid-eighteenth century, called this a "real change in sensibility," a "cognitive style" stemming from new ways of living associated with capitalist social relations (Haskell 1985). Like the new humanitarian sensibility studied by Haskell, liberalism was, for Jean-Marie, a new relationship to the self and the world based on the deep conviction that each individual is the bearer of an "inner" freedom. Whether or not this freedom is "real" matters little: the important thing is that this conviction has palpable effects in the depths of the contemporary political mind, being directly linked to the principles of agency (will) and individual responsibility that inform all social relations. Obviously, the belief in one's inner freedom did not manifest itself as de facto recognition of this freedom for all individuals; inequality between classes, sexes, and races was very real. That said, what Jean-Marie wanted to emphasize was that henceforth, for all marginalized populations, the nascent struggle for recognition would invariably hinge upon the idea that they too possess the fundamental attributes of the "liberal" individual. The consequence is that power and domination would now have to be justified by stressing the subaltern's incapacity to make proper use of his "inner" freedom.

Liberalism is thus the fundamental category of contemporary politics, encompassing the whole problem of collective agency, which Jean-Marie describes as the need to politically configure "the existential reflex embodied in the will to endure and to make sense of time as it passes," a reflex at the root of "the institutions, norms, and conventions that structure life in society" (11). In this sense, it forms "the undercurrent of Western thought" (45) to the present day. However, there is nothing smooth or continuous about this undercurrent, for there were discernible shifts in the historical manifestations of the concept of liberty. Jean-Marie identifies three major periods forming the scaffolding of his argument: the period of revolutionary aspiration, in which individual liberty found its natural extension in politics and the state (1680–1815); the period of aggressive bourgeois redefinition, in which the political sphere and the state were viewed as a threat to individual liberty (1830–70), and the period marked by a crisis of liberalism, when a new political aspiration emerged, dictating a profound rethinking of individual-state relations (1870–1930).

These periods must not be likened to a sequence of mental frames, analogous to how the Marxists conceived of successive modes of production. For, between the "new freedom-centred relationship to the world" underlying collective agency and the implementation of a mode of social regulation, there was the whole space of politics, power relations, discourses of legitimation, practices of resistance, etc. Recall that for Jean-Marie, liberalism had yet, at the turn of the nineteenth century, to be frozen into a mode of regulation that would soon arbitrarily declare the subject's inner freedom to be that of the property-owning man, while pitting his "individualist" will against people's sovereignty and the state. And while the revolutionary aspiration to liberty, like the new humanitarian sensibility identified by Haskell, was not incompatible with the bourgeois capitalist order, neither did it inexorably lead to it.[45] Jean-Marie argued that multiple avenues remained open in the aftermath of the democratic revolutions, including societal agendas founded on a very different conception of the relationship between the individual and the polity. Examples are the socialist and cooperative ideologies, which likewise arose out of the new relationship to the world inaugurated by the democratic revolutions.

Even though it is the title of his book, Jean-Marie is not asserting that the "pauper's freedom" is fully realized under the liberal mode of social regulation. Rather, this title is to be taken in the sense implied by the following sentence: "The pauper's freedom is *both* a condition of their servitude and a constraint on the powerful. It is not so much the locus of their autonomy as it is the horizon of their poverty" (22). Jean-Marie proceeds to demonstrate the impact of this conception of the "pauper's freedom" on the regulation of crime and poverty. He finds that the modern problematization of crime clearly conveys the central place assigned to liberty in the new relationship to the world. Precisely because it is defined as a "free," voluntary, and deliberate act committed by a person "of sound mind," crime can be punished by state-commanded isolation in the first half of the nineteenth century. And it is also because the inner freedom of the subject is an inviolable personal space that all ambitions of reforming criminals are rapidly abandoned (as recommended by Tocqueville, for example) and a new, vengeful emphasis is placed on incarceration. The moral education of the criminal, as envisioned within the philanthropic ideals of reform of the masses that Foucault analyzed, is no longer under consideration. In the latter third of the nineteenth century, incarceration came to serve as an exemplary punishment, allowing "the liberal prison [to find] its legitimacy in a world in which freedom must reign" (121). Moreover, the promise of parole, not re-education within the carceral space, was now seen as the way to reform, further enhancing the prison's image as an instrument of punishment, and ultimately as the "end of the road" receptacle for human poverty, a position it occupies to this day. No mode of social regulation, in the wake of the revolutions, managed to make of the prison anything other than a place of punishment. Here, then, we find the Foucauldian intuition of a close connection between individual liberty and the carceral archipelago. However, Jean-Marie viewed these developments as the outcome of a fraught historical process that pushed crime to the margins of collective agency, and not the primary locus of the political construction of subjectivities.

Arising out of the same aspiration to liberty, the conundrum of extreme poverty underwent a very different evolution from that of crime. Here the implementation of the liberal mode of social regulation had as its main consequence the increasing separation of poverty from crime. This separation is explainable in the terms of liberalism itself. Despite all the disciplinary utopias of the bourgeoisie, poverty, unlike crime, could never be defined solely as the outcome of a deliberate individual act. In the early nineteenth century, deeply transformed by liberalism, charity – even Catholic charity – no longer sought to restore the old order's relations of dependency. Even though it went hand in hand with intense religious proselytism, Catholic charity stopped trying to transform the masses as per the grand philanthropic reform agenda of the turn of the nineteenth century. At a time when Thomas Malthus (1766–1834) was positing poverty as the natural condition of the people, liberal charity, whether public or private, standardized its methods and adopted as its sole objective that of standing with the poor in their poverty. By the last third of the nineteenth century, hardly anyone was spending time reminding the poor, in ever more elaborate fashion, that they could not elude the burden of their freedom. At that point, charity "appeared to represent an ideal compromise between the dictates of liberty and the necessary response to its social consequences" under the liberal mode of regulation (186). For Jean-Marie, this is one of the keys to understanding the central role of the Catholic Church in Quebec society. Ideologically hostile to bourgeois liberalism, it nonetheless underwent a profound transformation so that it could develop a sophisticated charitable practice that took the "pauper's freedom" as a given, and so play an active part in the development of the liberal mode of social regulation.[46] In this specific sense, the Quebec Catholic Church – even the ultramontane strain thereof that has so fascinated historians – was profoundly liberal.

That said, despite several decades of liberal charity, and unlike crime, which centred around the deliberate act of the criminal, poverty was always susceptible to being politicized so that it could be used to promote grand projects for social transformation. This is what transpires from the great crisis of the liberal mode of social regulation in the early twentieth century, when the extension of suffrage, the development of a science of social relations (sociology), and the rise of nationalism conduced to a profound transformation of liberal common sense. Starting in the 1930s, the welfare state model would shake the liberal mode of regulation in democratic societies to its core, materializing a new political relationship between the individual and society that would be embodied by the granting of a normative quasi-monopoly on the social to the state. In this process, charity lost its normative power and was progressively relegated to the outskirts of social regulation. It was not just a shift from a "private" to a "public" mode of administration. This shift in fact revealed something deeper about liberalism: from this moment, in the political consciousness, individual freedom was no longer so much the cause as the consequence of social solidarity, of a new "collective agency" that made it possible. A whole new way of conceiving of social relations and power came into being, overturning the prevailing mode of regulation and the ways in which poverty had been administered – at least until the crisis of the welfare state in the 1970s, when the problematic of liberty was once again profoundly renewed, legitimizing a much impoverished conception of individual-society relations. I return in my conclusion to the issues raised by this book.

A "NEW POLITICAL HISTORY"?

With the collapse of the socialist agenda for society and the aggressive affirmation of neoliberalism, epitomized by Margaret Thatcher's proclamations that "there is no alternative" and "there is no such thing as society," it became urgent to comprehend liberalism as a historical phenomenon. Jean-Marie was not the only intellectual of his generation to have progressively made liberalism the theoretical horizon of his intellectual project. For example, the neo-Marxist historian Ian McKay put forward a "liberal order framework" as a project of Gramsci-inspired political history rooted in the historiographies of political discourse, state formation, moral regulation, and law developed in the 1990s (McKay 2000). To restore to history its overall intelligibility, to go beyond the fragments produced by prudent empiricism, McKay proposed to deconstruct and redefine the discursive category of "Canada" as something other than, on the one hand, the embodiment of an essentialized national identity and, on the other, the backdrop to the dynamic of social relations (relations of class, gender, race, ethnicity, sexual orientation, etc.). He proposed instead to define "Canada" as an original liberal project of rule in Western history (McKay 2000, 628).

For McKay, this project took the ideological form of liberalism, which, founded on the ontological category of the individual, articulates a particular hierarchy of three foundational principles:[47] property rights, individual liberty, and formal equality. Liberalism is thus analyzed as a coherent, formalized, stable discourse set up against other discourses based on different articulations of fundamental values. A postulate concerning a causal connection between material reality and political consciousness looms behind this conception. Considering property as a primary basic value of liberalism, McKay defines this ideology as primarily that of one social class having specific material interests. Adopting a Gramscian framework of analysis, McKay contends that it is in the "war of position" for cultural hegemony – i.e., the very nature of politics – that social classes come to define themselves politically as representatives of interests much broader than their own. The issue becomes showing how the bourgeoisie and its allies managed, over the course of the war of position running through history, to adapt the core of liberal ideology (property, liberty, equality) to strategic ends. Meanwhile, socialism became the refuge of all those who, denouncing bourgeois hegemony from different standpoints, came together ideologically "outside" of liberalism (McKay 2005). And the historian, too, according to McKay, must study liberalism from this outside position – a process he describes using the military metaphor of the "reconnaissance" of enemy terrain.

Although he devoted little discussion to McKay's historiographic project in *The Pauper's Freedom*, Jean-Marie subsequently published an in-depth critique of it. He found McKay's approach to have great merit. He particularly appreciated that McKay does not stop at affirming the "autonomy" of the political as a field of knowledge (with its own objects, sources, and methods), but goes on to reconceptualize it as an overall questioning of the various dimensions of human existence (economic, social, cultural, etc.) (Fecteau 2009, 2). He likewise appreciated that this historiographic project was conceived as a "political act of research" aiming to transform the neoliberal order and to tie the practice of history to a political reflection on the future (McKay 2005, 83).

Nevertheless, there are significant differences between the two authors' versions of political history. For Jean-Marie, liberalism was much more than an essentially hermetic ideology based on a static hierarchy of the values of "property, liberty, and equality" and articulated as a political agenda of hegemonic domination (by the liberal order). Rather, liberalism refers to a universe of meaning, a "collection of institutionalized social reflexes" forming "the backdrop to a panoply of social prospects and potentialities" (38). To bring out this range of potentialities, it is necessary to reject the postulate of continuity and coherence between the universe of meaning that is liberalism and the implementation of any specific agenda of cultural hegemony, however dominant (Fecteau 2009, 8). Doing so allows for a better understanding of the central role of Catholicism in the evolution of the liberal mode of regulation in Quebec. In contrast, the definition of liberalism adopted by McKay constrains him to presenting Catholicism as a more or less fixed culture at the bounds of the bourgeois liberal order, a strategic territory to be occupied in the war of position driven by the bourgeois will to domination. More generally, it is by restoring to liberalism its full depth of meaning that it can become a concept allowing for a non-deterministic conception of social change, hence equal to the task of creating a political history open to the future. This, however, calls for a profound commitment to a critical examination of a universe of meaning that still broadly structures our relationship to the world and limits our capacity to rethink it (Fecteau 2009, 21). In this sense, Jean-Marie wrote the history of liberalism from within, not from a position of exteriority, as McKay's approach dictates.

Apart from this remark by Jean-Marie, McKay's historiographic project provoked a wide-ranging debate that is beyond the scope of this introduction.[48] In addition to copious discussion as to the putative capacity of the liberal order framework to shed light on various aspects of Canadian history, some authors have questioned the validity of the analysis itself. Bruce Curtis's critique is worth dwelling on, not only for its insightfulness but also because it helps clarify certain aspects of Jean-Marie's intellectual trajectory. Like him, Curtis argues that McKay did not go far enough in rejecting Marxist materialism and was therefore unable to fully understand the historical meaning of liberalism. Rather than adopting a "Thatcherite" definition, Curtis offers a more substantial conception of liberalism as a mode and/or practice of government. On the one hand, and this coincides with Jean-Marie's concerns, Curtis notes that liberalism was never destined to shrink down to a bourgeois ideology pitting individual liberty against social constraint. On the other, the reduction of liberalism to an agenda of domination lends artificial coherence to much more fraught practices of power (Curtis 2009, 189). Curtis calls for a cleaner break with the materialist tradition of social history, recalling that "the popular equation, structural location – defines interest – constitutes identity – determines action, simply doesn't hold" (Curtis 2009, 179). In other words, power is not to be looked for in capitalist relations of production, nor in any primary social reality. Working from the Foucauldian perspective of governmentality, Curtis attempts instead to understand how social reality was defined, by social science in particular, so that it could be acted on by nineteenth-century liberal practices of government.[49] It is on this condition, he believes, that we can understand the complex forms of power and domination associated with liberal governmentality.

Jean-Marie always kept a critical distance from moral regulationism, reformulated here by Curtis in the Foucauldian terms of governmentality. Curtis's perspective, which entails analytically deconstructing the "state" category to take account of the diffuse nature of governmental practices (Curtis 2007), is hard to reconcile with Jean-Marie's conception of the political. In the final years of his life, Jean-Marie believed that this perspective of governmentality is ill suited to thinking about the political. After all, he noted, the political sphere is not only a space in which multiple forms of power are exercised but also one in which a type of "collective agency" is formulated, explaining why these conflicts do not lead to the breakup of society. This collective agency, he argued, had come into being historically with the great democratic revolutions in the form of the nation-state, which "subsumed several modalities of existence of social relations by merging them within a common space: the space of politics" (Fecteau 2007a).[50] Such a conception of politics does not mean denying the power relations in play in the development of a mode of social regulation, as he made clear in important papers on the regulation of crime and poverty published at the end of his life.[51] Finally, in a major work on the census as a practice of power designed to create the conditions of possibility for liberal governmentality, Curtis had, according to Jean-Marie, neglected this aspect of collective agency, consequently underestimating the "diverse political potentialities" made possible by the birth of the census-taking state.[52]

Beyond their differences, Fecteau, McKay, and Curtis all held that the political is not an autonomous field of historical inquiry, but rather the intellectual act of posing the fundamental question of social change. This question was reformulated in the context of the ideological and historiographic upsets associated with the crisis of Marxism. While taking their distance, to varying degrees, from historical materialism, these authors have remained loyal to the intellectual project associated with it: that of creating the conditions for a body of critical historical knowledge of the social order. There are certain indications that this latter conception of the political, rooted in the debates aroused by the crisis of Marxism, has been falling out of fashion in the neoliberal context.[53] I discussed earlier the periodically heard appeals for a return to a political history with a simpler national narrative, centred around a linear presentation of "important events" and "great men." This traditional conception of political history can take on a more sophisticated mien, as it does in the work of Michel Ducharme. Revisiting liberalism, Ducharme has put forward a new intellectual history of the concept of liberty in the Canadas between 1776 and 1838.[54] In a work first published in 2010 (with the English translation appearing in 2014), he analyzed the clash between two opposing conceptions of liberty: the classical republican liberty upheld by the Patriotes and the modern constitutional liberty characteristic of British rule. For Ducharme, the Patriotes, like the historians they influenced, never understood that British rule was not a corrupt authoritarian social order but a fundamentally legitimate one based on the core values of "liberty, property, and security." Ducharme, unlike Fecteau, McKay, and Curtis, ultimately adopts the vantage point of the established social order.

This work perhaps attests to a major shift underway in Quebec and Canadian intellectual life and historiography. In this regard, where one stands on the "Quebec national question" is not decisive, since essentially the same perspective is found in a work by sovereignist historian Éric Bédard that forthrightly states its "epistemological bias" in favour of the autonomy of actors and the power of ideas (Bédard 2009, 319). According to Bédard, French-Canadian political reformers of the mid-nineteenth century, who may be described as inhabited by the principles of Ducharme's "modern liberty," succeeded in inoculating the French-Canadian nation, as a community of memory and destiny, against the dangers of excessive "republican" democratization of the social order.

It is not my intent here to deny Ducharme's or Bédard's genuine contribution to the study of liberal and reformist ideas but rather to underscore the great divide between this so-called "new political history" and the political analysis of power put forward by Jean-Marie and others. "Denouncing power where it acts as a vector of domination remains," he writes in *The Pauper's Freedom*, "the goal of any history that refuses to be more than a tedious compilation of past occurrences" (18). Until the end of his life, Jean-Marie remained convinced of the need to develop critical historical knowledge of the social order.

CONCLUSION

The Pauper's Freedom is a book by an important historian whose intellectual trajectory bears witness to a firm anchoring in the issues of the present. In conclusion to this lengthy introduction, I would like to make some brief additional remarks about the book you are about to read.

First, this book does not deliver what might be expected from a conventional historical monograph. The discipline of history has in general trained us in patient, meticulous research as a prelude to the publication of more or less definitive results, accompanied by the standard precautions on the (generally spatiotemporal) limits of their validity. This book charts a different course. It is an intellectual exploration of the changes undergone by Western liberalism that proceeds by bringing the power issues revealed through the administration of crime and poverty in Quebec to bear on that history. Not only does the book not provide definitive results – concerning crime rates or working-class standards of living, for example – but it also refuses to isolate the space of Quebec (or Canada) from a much broader (in fact Western) experience of liberalism. Consequently, it rather unusually juxtaposes quotations from the Patriote Amury Girod, the Bishop of Montreal Ignace Bourget, the English philosopher Jeremy Bentham, and the French political thinker Alexis de Tocqueville, to name just a few. In bringing together the ideas of such different figures, Jean-Marie is not trying to isolate the putative cultural specificities of Quebec so much as to show that beyond their major differences, the ideas of these figures take on their full meaning when they are thought of as different versions of "liberal common sense." Such an approach certainly has limits vis-à-vis the traditional monograph, but it has the great advantage of getting away from typical discussions of Quebec's specificity (backwardness, Catholicism, nationalism, ruralism, etc.) to explore the foundations of what we might call a comprehensive history of liberalism.

If a consistent concern emerges from this research-focused career, I would say it is that of nesting theory and empirical research within an open-ended, ever-revised practice of historical study. Here again, the classical monographic model has accustomed us to the presentation of research results within what is generally termed a "theoretical framework," cursorily presented at the beginning of a work and just as soon set aside. Here, by contrast, theory is only a group of propositions comprising a framework that may be able to make sense of a confusion of events awaiting empirical study. Like the Marxist perspective that provided him with early inspiration, Jean-Marie's regulation-based approach in *The Pauper's Freedom* remains profoundly dialectical. The approach attempts to grasp historical movement itself. Theory and empirical fact are two moments of a single intellectual act of analysis, itself performed within the onward flow of history. Jean-Marie sketches out this dialectic – inseparable from a demanding practice of historical study – in his first chapter. He does not present a definitive theoretical framework (contrary to his initial neo-Marxist formulation) to be mechanically applied in other "regulationist" studies, but instead embarks on an open-ended discussion of the capacity of "regulation" to become a dynamic historical concept, "a way of conceiving of the passage of time and how time acts on the substance of reality" (12). This chapter, moreover, ends with a detailed presentation of the key historical periods at issue, reminding us that there cannot be a social regulation approach that ignores the time factor. This treatment, continuing throughout the rest of the book, is certainly unfinished. Still, it points toward fundamental issues in the study of history, and particularly the need for a political history that takes up the (theoretical, empirical, ethical) challenge of comprehending social change after the breakup of "grand theory."

I will conclude with a more personal appreciation of *The Pauper's Freedom*. You will have gathered that for the most part I share Jean-Marie's critical historiographic project.[55] That said, like other scholars, I believe that he did not always succeed, once he began serious work on it in the early 1990s, in accounting for the diversity and specificity of the forms of domination and resistance running through any given society. But it would be unfair to claim that he denied the existence of these social relations of domination. It is quite simply that his approach to political history is possible only if it systematically refuses to assign these relations an existence prior to the political organization of society. This is why, in contradistinction to the approach taken in *Un nouvel ordre des choses*, *The Pauper's Freedom* does not begin by analyzing a primary conflict around the redistribution of the product of labour and asserting that it structures the mode of social regulation. It begins instead with a type of collective agency that takes the form of "liberalism," engendering a new kind of political organization and a new pace of social change that will constitute the conditions of possibility for the materialization and transformation of power relations themselves. In short, if this book is titled *The Pauper's Freedom,* it is to remind us that the multiple forms of domination, resistance, and emancipation are to be looked for in the political sphere, in the collective agency found in the "liberal" depths of our historical consciousness.

The perspective is stimulating, but doesn't it risk meeting an impasse if it does not succeed in discerning, in the dynamic of power relations, the historical and political conditions under which liberalism can be put behind us? Despite the quantity of criticism levelled at Marxism, it at least had the merit of bidding historians to ask the fundamental question of the historical conditions under which capitalism and liberalism might give way to another system. In this regard, despite its appeals for an exploration of unexplored potentialities and its allusions to a "welfare state [that] would ultimately reconfigure this freedom and place it on a sounder footing" (278), Jean-Marie's historiographic project seems to me to give out onto a paradoxical political history, in which human societies find themselves more or less condemned to seeking "liberal" solutions to social problems defined in the terms of liberalism. It is here, I think, that we can measure the considerable consequences of Jean-Marie's relative disinterest in studying forms of resistance to power. Even if we accept the postulate that practices of resistance, in the context of a liberal mode of regulation, must take the form of liberalism itself, doesn't an analysis thereof allow us to think about the historical conditions that will let us go beyond the present social order? Jean-Marie was aware of this issue, as is clear from the foundational role played by the great democratic revolutions in his analysis of the regulation of crime and poverty. Still, his relegation of these democratic revolutions to a kind of symbolic founding moment of liberalism adds weight to the idea that he never really succeeded in pairing his critical analysis of power with an examination of the politics of resistance.

In the end, Jean-Marie, like many Marxist-influenced scholars of his generation, perhaps failed to gauge the full impact of the abandonment of political thinking about capitalism on the study of history.

With the fall of the Berlin Wall, it became urgent to understand liberalism and make it a principal category of historical analysis. After all, it was not at all clear that the totalitarian states of Eastern Europe would follow a transition leading straightforwardly to globalized capitalism. Perhaps this explains the interest shown by contemporaneous social scientists in a basic distinction – of great interest as part of a critique of neoliberal politics – between liberalism and capitalism. For Jean-Marie, one form this took was as a need to distinguish the liberal "mode of regulation" from the capitalist "mode of production"; on this basis, he could assert the autonomy of the political as a level encompassing the organization of life in society. The historiographic gains to be derived from such a theoretical distinction were numerous, and there is clearly no question of a return to a simplistic historical materialism. Still, twenty-five years after the fact, it seems to me that the consequence of such a theoretical distinction was to marginalize the project, seen in embryo in *Un nouvel ordre des choses*, of a political history of capitalism as "a mode of administration of men and women." If the intellectual act of resistance that is political history is still relevant today, is it not precisely because of its capacity to problematize the long and fraught history of the naturalization of capitalism as an insurpassable limit on what Jean-Marie called our "collective agency"?

Martin Petitclerc
Professor of History, Université du Québec à Montréal
Centre d'histoire des régulations sociales

THE PAUPER'S FREEDOM

Writing is the power to transmit love not only to one's nearest and dearest, but also, through the next person encountered, into the unknown, distant, future life.

Peter Sloterdijk, *Rules for the Human Zoo*

Introduction

This book is a continuation, and also a beginning. It follows on an analysis I began many years ago (Fecteau 1989) of the administration of crime and poverty in Quebec from the late eighteenth century to the 1840s. I wanted to extend this analysis by studying how these approaches changed up to the start of the twentieth century. My previous book ended with the hypothesis that, contrary to the interpretation popularized by Foucault, the reformist logic attendant on the invention of the prison and other institutions of social regulation at the turn of the nineteenth century differed profoundly from the logic that characterized their effective expansion. But it left unexamined the assumption that the liberal mode of regulation implemented in the mid-nineteenth century would dominate the regulation of crime and poverty more or less uncontested until the arrival of the welfare state with the Keynesian legislation of the postwar era, and even perhaps thereafter.

This book does away with this overly gradualist account. Paradoxically, however, to do so necessitates restoring to the liberal mode of regulation all its breadth and logic. Liberalism cannot be reduced to the radical ideologies of combat raging in the mid-nineteenth century, which would leave traces up through the 1930s; or, worse still, be brought down to the holy trinity of liberty-equality-property espoused by businesspeople everywhere. Its bourgeois form – and in fact even its radical form – offers a narrow, scaled-down, self-conflicting version of the immensely appealing ideal of freedom running through the nineteenth century. For the purposes of this book, liberalism is defined as a particular approach to the construction of the social fabric that serves as the basis for a wide array of ideologies. It is the multifarious embodiment of a freedom-seeking impulse that even now finds expression in our societies. In the nineteenth century, the bourgeois elites succeeded in reinterpreting this basic impulse by whittling it down to the bare bones. As the new century got underway, this reductive enterprise came under fire from reformers, while other societal agendas strained toward the light within bourgeois hegemony itself.

The study of the treatment of crime and poverty in this context is a particularly fruitful line of inquiry. The ideal of freedom being concretized during the nineteenth century bore within it the genetic material for a society in which the rejection of social norms represented by crime, like the structural inequalities represented by poverty, had to become inconceivable. At its very core, liberalism as a world view, a conception of the spatiotemporal existence of societies, implies a relationship of individuals to the social whole in which such phenomena cannot exist. In this conception, crime and poverty cease to be unchanging features of an immanent social order; they are no longer inherent to an imperfect world born in original sin. They become social *problems*, clues to a basic dysfunction in a nascent social order. Especially after mid-century, the dominant bourgeois version of liberalism would strive to defuse the revolutionary implications of this vision of crime and poverty by attributing their occurrence to the individual responsibility of the people involved. I examine the coherence of this individualistic, apolitical view and elucidate the profound crisis it underwent in the face of criticism from the new social sciences, from workers' struggles, and from reform elements of the elites in the early twentieth century. This leads us to see this variant of liberalism for what it is and was: an instrument of domination in the service of self-interest, one that perverts the ideal of freedom by rebranding it as the law of the jungle. Staunch anti-statism, contempt for the labouring masses, and fear of the implications of extended suffrage were only a few manifestations of a freedom-centred world view that quickly degenerated into a conservative ideology aghast at what the future seemed to portend. It was left to a few radicals, often in conjunction with trade unionists or feminists, to strive for the creation of new institutional and legal forms, which would become the earliest avatars of twentieth-century social policy.

But in sketching out the liberal view of crime and poverty, this book is also a beginning. It is not and should not be regarded as a descriptive history of penal and welfare institutions. Instead, the task of this book is to attend to the discourse used to legitimize policies and institutional innovations – a discourse that forms an integral part of the larger debate on crime and poverty taking place throughout the West. It is not, of course, that discourse precedes or determines practice, but that its analysis can shed light on the galaxy of representations lying beneath the policies and institutions responsible for welfare and punishment, as well as the fundamental changes that took place therein.

This galaxy of representations is a legacy of Western thought. A comparative history of national discourse and practice, while undoubtedly necessary, is not my focus here, for it is first necessary to drill down to the common intellectual bedrock lying beneath all these various national experiences. The specific case of Quebec sits comfortably within this common heritage, even though most of the debate took place in Western Europe and very little, at least broadly and explicitly, on the periphery (with the partial exception of the United States). I have therefore had to rely to a great extent on French and British documents for the generalized and often verbose expression of the liberal ideal of crime, poverty, and their administration. Because of this methodological choice, this book becomes a cross between, on the one hand, a general history of the representations and modes of administration of poverty and crime, and, on the other, a local history that strives to grasp the specificity of Quebec's experience with the liberal regulation of these phenomena.

This study unashamedly assumes certain analytical postulates that it would be vain to seek to demonstrate with the classical approach to empirical "proof" in history.[1] Instead, this book presents what should be considered as a set of analytical hypotheses, illustrated by excerpts from the writings and speeches of figures from Quebec and elsewhere in the West, that point toward a different history of crime and poverty and of the specific guises in which liberal regulation appeared in Quebec.

Part 1, then, begins by clarifying the basic methodological premises of my analytical approach (chapter 1). It goes on to examine the fundamental postulates and world view of liberalism (chapter 2), and it ends by recapitulating the principal forms exhibited by the transition to the liberal mode of regulation of poverty and crime (chapter 3). Part 2 analyzes the shifting vantages from which crime has been viewed. It strives to illustrate how the liberal approach to the regulation of deviance constituted a major break with the penal model inherited from the Enlightenment (chapter 4). It then studies the specific and, in my view, exceptional case of juvenile delinquency (chapter 5). In part 3, I consider views and approaches to the treatment of poverty. Chapter 6 analyzes how, in this case too, liberal regulation represented a fundamental break with the reform-mindedness that prevailed at the turn of the nineteenth century. Chapter 7 focuses on the religious sphere of influence in Quebec – a must for anyone wishing to understand the charitable economy of Quebec – and elucidates its far-reaching influence over the administration of poverty. Throughout parts 2 and 3, I pay attention to the crisis of the liberal mode of regulation in the late nineteenth and early twentieth centuries and how reform movements affected the course of this mode of regulation.

The analyses and conclusions presented in this book are and could only be my own, but its writing would have been inconceivable without the sustained and particularly stimulating contributions of the professors and students of the Centre d'histoire des régulations sociales at the Université du Quebec à Montréal (UQAM). I owe them an immense debt, and thank them warmly for their work and our fruitful discussions. I would be remiss if I did not mention the constant and sympathetic support of my friend and former colleague Jean-Paul Bernard, who read an early version of this manuscript and managed (at least partially) to assuage my anxieties and doubts as a historian. Finally, the direct and indirect assistance of granting bodies such as the Social Sciences and Humanities Research Council of Canada and the Fonds québécois de recherche sur la société et la culture was equally essential.[2]

PART ONE

Regulation and Liberalism in Quebec

Michael Walzer (1984) has remarked that liberalism is an "art of separation," and so it is. Liberalism effects a separation between the private and public spheres, of course, but also between roles assigned to genders, classes, and ethnicities; between new social categories – of clienteles, users, and rights-holders, for example – that were taken up with gusto by bureaucrats; and between different modalities of intervention depending on the category of problem at issue – legal versus illegal, normal versus pathological, criminal versus charitable, responsible versus irresponsible, adult versus minor, and so forth. Liberalism also entails a separation between disciplines, categories of knowledge, ways of apprehending reality; between science and non-science. And finally, it entails a division of the infinite manifestations of reality – the empirical profusion of things that happen, things that exist – into classes. Between the claims of relativism, the simplistic certainties of positivism, and the invitation of postmodernism to contemplate this profusion in all its intricacy, how can anyone hope to conceptualize the global? How can we put together the pieces of what presents itself pragmatically as the ultimate reality, the existing world?

I begin this book with a discussion of regulation, freedom, and liberalism because I harbour the conviction that the meaning of things can be arrived at in practice through the use of a criterion, or a method, that transcends them. It is a rather unfashionable conviction, I know: that the past (like the present, in fact) presents itself to our human consciousness for the meaning that can be derived from it – if only fleetingly, if only for an instant, even with the knowledge that this meaning will be rethought and reworked by those who follow us. But at least those future generations will have a meaning on which to cut their teeth, like mine did with Marxism and structuralism. In this precise sense, the search for meaning is, in effect, an ethics of becoming.

The postulate that the search for meaning is both possible and necessary applies not only to the nineteenth century in general but to the specific case of Quebec in particular. The nineteenth century birthed our democratic societies – societies of people free to think, produce, and live their lives while striving to survive the often dangerously unpredictable consequences of a new form of freedom. The social structures emerging from this process are expressed here in terms of *regulation*, and the purpose of chapter 1 is largely to explain what I mean by this concept. It will also be necessary, in reflecting on the mode of regulation put in place in the nineteenth century, to define the societal reflexes or basic representations underlying the idea of freedom and the reality to which this idea gave birth (and from which it almost died): this is the work of chapter 2. With these premises established, chapter 3 goes on to discuss the changes that occurred in the administration of crime and poverty within the broader framework of the transition from the Enlightenment to liberalism.

I

The Concept of Regulation

It might be said that history is above all an exercise in comprehending changes in lived experience through time and space; a fraught search for meaning beyond individual agency yet outside the overdetermining structures that have long towered over history and its cliffs (Chartier 1997). Indeed, a fundamental task of historians is to acknowledge the fragility of the societies they strive to comprehend; the fragility of the modes of coexistence enacted by every society. If so, then we must become accustomed to apprehending this fragility from two angles:

- *Fragility in space*, where identity is unceasingly recomposed through multiple allegiances, endless forms of reciprocal recognition. So much is this the case that at the end of the day, many historians are no longer able to view any society as anything other than an abstraction more harmful than it is useful. The profound crisis of the humanities is a manifestation of the deep-seated malaise that grips the social scientist when the task at hand is to embrace, within a single analytical quest, the stochastic proliferation of lived experience, the thousand and one segmentations of the social fabric, the endless recompositions of people's sense of identity – so much so that one wonders how, beyond discourse, symbolism, and the signified, societies can actually "hold together" within the social space.
- *Fragility in time*, as societies teeter equivocally between the weight of the past and people's aspirations for the future; or, in the felicitous formulation of Reinhart Koselleck (1985), between their space of experience and their horizon of expectation. Fragile from the outset because of their complex relationship to the space of lived experience, communities watch as time inexorably assails their frail

conventions, the endless compromises that make social cohesion possible. Time is the number one threat to the perpetuation of societies, if only because it renders their reproduction quickly incongruous, soon obsolete, and ultimately unviable.

It is with this consciousness of the fragility inherent in human works that the history set out in this book has been understood. More precisely, by x-raying the failures and aporias of life in society, it seems possible to get a better handle on what I would call the texture of this fragility. Every society is subjected to the tensions engendered by the inequalities it allows to exist, or actively brings into existence, particularly as regards the distribution of material and cultural wealth. Every society is also confronted with the culture of rejection that goes by the name of crime. Poverty and crime form a pair of age-old companions whose existence marks out the limits of the social fabric and its reproduction. A study of these phenomena serves to trace the contours of the possible alternatives that a given social formation allows itself, by elucidating what it rejects as well as what it too indulgently accepts. I have assigned myself the additional goal of elucidating these dimensions during a time of upheaval, when they were profoundly redefined; when, in the aftermath of the great revolutions, new modalities of the social fabric were being invented, throughout a nineteenth century whose influence remains with us to this day.

SOCIAL REGULATION

How do societies "hold together"? How is it possible to reconcile that logic of minimal harmony, whereby social formations do not fly apart into constellations of individualities, with the reality of conflict at the core of their daily existence? How can we make sense of the necessity of any given form of social cohesion, what with the inevitability of its ultimate dissolution? Of course, a certain species of postmodernism dodges these questions, first by denying their pertinence, and then by casting silence over the issues they imply. Everything is a "discourse," is it not? All is culture. At a time when the grand, more or less self-contained systems of interpretation have noisily collapsed, it seems as though all that remains is the capillarity of the infinite forms of relationship among individuals.

And yet thoughts, discourses, representations, and systems of ideas have to be taken seriously, as must those individual and collective *acts* whereby humanity transforms time into reality – the sum total of the gestures made by those who actually live history. The social sciences have tried to make sense of these palpable marks on the surface of the real. They have shown how even the most minute and ephemeral human acts fit within specific operative frameworks. Indeed, the birth of modern knowledge about our societies is to be located in the excitement experienced by social scientists at the discovery of these "structures" underlying human action. It was tempting indeed to regard this set of invariant – or at any rate enduringly stable – facts or states of affairs as the firm foundation of reality, perceptible behind the superficial profusion of events. This temptation was soon yielded to, and it became fashionable to contrast individual with society, agent with structure, freedom with determinism, and, on the methodological plane, methodological individualism with holism (Caillé 1986; Villeval 2002). The locus of society came to be defined as being in tension between these two dimensions of reality.

The question became: What exactly does this tension consist of? Taking a stab at an answer, it can be said that if we must try to grasp the meaning of this concomitant presence at the core of the social – the determinism of structures and the randomness of individual and collective acts – then that meaning cannot be found in some vague contradiction between the general and the particular, but rather in their dialectical presence at the heart of action and practice.[1] In their formal agency, men and women confront time, grab it up – in an effort as essential as it is futile – to fix its form, or at least make it predictable. With the concept of *regulation*, I am attempting to capture this unending quest for fragile regularities in the hope of containing, albeit to a small extent, the chaos of time as it acts on the various loci of the social. Driven by the existential reflex embodied in the will to endure and to make sense of time as it passes, the institutions, norms, and conventions that structure life in society come into being.

I posit that there exist modes of social regulation whereby people in society learn to organize space, confront time, and express these efforts in perpetually threatened – yet perpetually pursued – formal regularities enacted in real time. This is not, of course, to deny the fundamental contribution of individuals, acting alone or collectively, to the forms that this regulation will take. Likewise, there is no question of ignoring the reality of class and gender relations as primary modes of social segmentation, or of setting aside the essential impact of power relations and hegemonies on the construction of these regularities. What must be done instead, taking account of all these facts that make the social a field of constant struggle, is to come up with a flexible, heuristic means of apprehending the delicate, uncertain passage of social formations through time. Between social structures, which have lost favour as an object of study, and the countless ways in which agents think and act out their lives, which have attracted increasing scholarly interest, what I am striving to understand here is how *institutions* are formed. I want to elucidate the regulating logic whereby agency always takes place *within* a framework (normative, institutional, conventional) even as it *transforms* that framework. Consequently, I see no point in positing some precedence or prevalence of discourse over practice, framework over implementation, thought over life, or norm over act,[2] or in the opposite stance of lazily giving up on making sense of the profusion of social phenomena and falling back on the complacent observation of diversity as an empirical fact.

In my conception, regulation is a *historical* concept: a way of conceiving of the passage of time and how time acts on the substance of reality.[3] From this vantage, any static analysis of the organizational or normative structures of societies can only be a preliminary step in the analysis of a mode of regulation. Rules must be comprehended, that is, with reference to those who break them as much as to those who administer or are ruled by them; conventions must be analyzed from the standpoint of those who render them obsolete as much as those who act within them; and institutions and their import must be gauged with reference to those who contest them as much as those who give them life. For this reason, what I term "regulation" is not to be regarded as a *state*, a passive description of a given societal structure, or a *relation*, a bond between elements, individuals, or groups. Rather, it is a process enacted or in action, a logic of *movement* that impels a society from one point in time to another.

The concept of "social control" was long employed to express this insistence on the meaningfulness of societal evolution. At an early stage in the progress of Western democratic thought, doubts were expressed about the perfect continuity posited by Enlightenment-era liberalism between the free development of individual wills and the sociality deriving from the confrontation among individualities. Could the happiness of all, the general interest, actually transpire as a straightforward function of the sundry passions engendered by social life, the expression of each person's interests?[4] It hardly seemed likely that a government of free people could amount to nothing more than a collection of political wills squaring off in enlightened debate. Society was increasingly portrayed as much more than the sum of its parts, and some observers

– Auguste Comte, for a prominent one – began to perceive the necessary existence of a general order, a normative substrate surpassing and imposed upon individuals:

> Although it may be useful and, in certain cases, even necessary to consider the idea of *society*, abstracted from that of *government*, it is universally recognized that these ideas are in fact inseparable. In other words the lasting existence of every real association necessarily supposes a constant influence, at times directive, at times repressive, exercised, within certain limits, by the whole on the parts, in order to make them converge toward the general order from which they always naturally tend to deviate, more or less, and from which they would deviate indefinitely could they be entirely left to their own impulses. (Comte [1826] 1877, 629)[5]

With the burgeoning of the social sciences at the turn of the century, in large part based on a critique of liberal postulates (see chapter 6), Comte's intuition was formalized:

> The passions first must be limited. Only then can they be harmonized with the faculties and satisfied. But since the individual has no way of limiting them, this must be done by some force exterior to him. A regulative force must play the same role for moral needs which the organism plays for physical needs. (Durkheim [1897] 2005, 209)

The American sociologist Edward Ross gave the name "social control" to this "force exterior to the individual" (Ross [1901] 1970). In reaction to liberal formalism, which posited that order arose out of the normal obedience of free citizens to the laws they collectively adopt through the intermediary of the democratic state (even though it means entrusting that state with the responsibility of punishing violators), the "social control" approach was intended as a scientific reflection on the modalities according to which individuals are made to adjust to the social organism in which they find themselves.[6] Order, the stable reproduction of society, no longer transpired from the aggregate of individual wills but as a complex construct presupposing both a coercive apparatus and a logic of voluntary allegiance.[7]

It was not long before the meaning of this concept – one of the most popular sociological concepts of the years 1900 to 1950 – shifted, under the influence of 1940s functionalism in particular, toward a search for the conditions making social conformity possible.[8] Even in the late

1940s, a broad definition of the social control concept still held sway; the concept was regarded as a tool for apprehending the constituent parts of individuals' integration into the social whole.

> Social control can be defined as the sum total or rather the whole of cultural patterns, social symbols, collective spiritual meanings, values, ideas and ideals, as well as acts and processes directly connected with them, whereby inclusive society, every particular group, and every participating individual member overcome tensions and conflicts within themselves through temporary equilibria and take steps for new creative efforts. (Gurvitch 1945, 290)

However, further to new critiques of the dehumanizing effects of bureaucracy and of the normalizing processes entailed by the development of the welfare state, the concept of social control would increasingly be saddled with a pejorative connotation. The turning point came with the simultaneous publication, in 1961, of Michel Foucault's *History of Madness* in France and Erving Goffman's *Asylums* in the United States. Now madness, and soon other manifestations of illness (see, e.g., Foucault 1963) or deviance, were analyzed not as social problems standing in the way of successful social integration, but as intellectual constructs serving as a justification for the construction of a space (of asylum), with the desired outcome being that the specific power dynamic in which this all took place could operate without hindrance.[9] From that moment, social control was increasingly thought of in critical, even libertarian terms as a tool used by the dominant classes to consolidate their power.

The task then became to describe and analyze the strategies of coercion and power adoped by the elites, and largely directed at the dominated classes, with a view to the reproduction of unequal societal arrangements. This way of framing the issue had the additional effect of redirecting analytical work toward the main instruments of coercion: prisons, asylums, hospitals, and other custodial institutions.

This evolution of the concept of social control, perceptible by the late 1940s, led to the rejection of the collaborative interpretation prominent in early research in favour of an approach giving pride of place to conflict and power relations. In the work of a precursor such as Georges Canguilhem, normality ceased to be equated with the dominant form of reality or the law of averages;[10] it became what remains once the bounds of abnormality have been marked out – a normative construct whose borders are methodologically discernible as the negative space of abnormality.[11] From that point on, the study of modes of punishment, forms of refusal, procedures of exclusion, and "accidents" of history found new heuristic validity.

But a very high price had to be paid for the fecund insights delivered up by a critical approach in which class conflict is considered central to any analysis of social conformity. For a given instance of domination, it was necessary to posit not only a victor but also a process whereby this victor managed to consolidate and reproduce that victory. In an ironic twist, an analysis that once sought to denounce enterprises of power and control over the masses ended up postulating the inevitable success of those enterprises.[12] The very concept of "control" implied a manipulation of behaviour, whether voluntary or otherwise,[13] that left little room for the initiative of the dominated, the response of those who, being controlled, found themselves at best in the role of victims, at worst in that of power's playthings. Some social control theorists grudgingly admitted the relevance of Gramscian analyses of hegemony and how it comes to be accepted as the societal norm,[14] but most ultimately wanted to know *how* power (be it psychiatric, moral, penal, or sexual) operates and not *why*, under what circumstances. The underlying postulate was that domination produces conformity and normality; or, in a more simplistic version, that they happen as byproducts of the dominant ones' striving to fulfill their own interests. A hypothesis of this nature always risked becoming an all-purpose response, in which the multiple manifestations of control are reduced to the instruments of repression or discipline. Control ruled the school as much as it did the prison; the difference, for many authors, seemed to lie only in the degree of coercion permitted.

Given the rather Manichean mould in which social control came to be cast, it is no surprise to find such approaches coming under virulent attack, especially in the last twenty years. It has become common to criticize them for oversimplifying a complex state of affairs, to strive for a sharper understanding of how the dominant exert their dominance, and to rehabilitate the agency of the dominated.

One kind of critique challenges the relevance of any generalization based on the social control model.[15] The model, it is claimed, inaccurately posits the existence of a control procedure followed by a social group (the bourgeoisie) or institution (the state) under the guidance of a coherent plan and an intent to put that plan into practice. In arguing against this residue of outmoded functionalism, these authors emphasize that any policy, any program of "control," is shot through with contradictions, that the principal agents of such control are deeply ambivalent or even divided among themselves, and that the efficacy of such control endeavours has been greatly exaggerated.

> The "social control" model ... assumed that capitalist society was systematically incapable of reproducing itself without the constant interposition of state agencies of control and repression ... The punitive sanction of the state need not be regarded as decisive in the reproduction of exploitative and unequal social relations. (Ignatieff 1981, 180, 182)

Incapable of capturing reality in all its complexity,[16] this approach is alleged to cultivate confusion between the putative intentionality of the control agents and the tangible results of the measures they implement.[17]

But the main critique directed at the social control approach is that it has grossly neglected the purported victims of control procedures. This is said to be so in that the "real" social control is that which is enacted by the very logic of the social system in which they live out their lives.

> A close examination of the historical evidence also raises the question of whether the activities of the state make much difference to social change at all, and whether the kinds of social regulation sociologists criticise are better understood as based in the economic relationships and structures of market capitalism, or perhaps in the particular cultural patterns of Western societies. (Van Krieken 1991, 9)[18]

It is also said to be so in that this approach always posits some degree of passivity on the part of the masses targeted by control procedures and policies. This objection to the social control approach arose quite early.

> It is not only that "social control" ... has been so overused that it is frequently applied carelessly, or that the "order-disorder" formula has become trite through excessive use. It is rather that even the most sophisticated social control arguments ... tend to exaggerate the novelty of nineteenth century perceptions of disorder, to reify the "controllers" to the point that they become ... a homogeneous elite ... indistinguishable from society as a whole, and to assume that institutions are imposed by that elite or that society upon passive, malleable subjects. (Fox 1976, 204)[19]

A bottom-up history, an analytical endeavour undertaken from the perspective of the masses, would serve to identify the false postulates of both the traditional historiography, with its admiring emphasis on reformist humanism, and the social control-based version of elites' hunger for power and control.

> There is no "new social history" of deviance; no reexamination of institutionalization "from the bottom up" ... The theoretical ferment in social history has been pre-empted in the history of deviance by a stylized contest between the twin perspectives that dominate analysis in this field: consensus-oriented "humanitarianism" and conflict-oriented "revisionism" ...
> The protagonists share an underlying domain assumption that client populations are passive objects of administration. (Bellingham 1986, 533)

This critique proved highly effective in that it took aim at a whole set of weaknesses in the works of the social control theorists. The very history of the concept, its "erratic genealogy" (Cohen 1989, 348), was such that its usage had long oscillated between a vague striving to apprehend the conditions under which individuals are integrated into society and a more focused attempt to discern the conditions under which deviance is taken in charge.[20] The fact that the concept of social control is hardly ever used anymore outside this second, more restrictive sense is symptomatic of its limited analytical effectiveness and its inability to account for a more general order of things.[21]

Another basic limitation has to do with the fact that the definition of an institution or policy is not reducible to its function, which is only one of its dimensions. The search for meaning inherent in any study of the social fabric is in no way limited to this function: to speak of "control" implies that a prior definition has already been assigned to this relationship between the dominant and the dominated, the agent responsible for integrative and/or repressive procedures and the citizens targeted by these procedures.

Finally, the postulate inherent in this approach – namely, that the putatively one-way operation of "control" produces conformity as an effect, no matter how much that effect must be placed in perspective – does not help at all to grasp the complexity of the social practice thus enacted, in that the targeted masses do not just react to policies and control measures: at times they initiate them, and more often they transform or divert them.

In sum, the concept of social control came under sustained attack from interactionist currents more sensitive to the complex dialectic arising when controller and controlled come into contact on the actual field of institutional practice. The dominance achieved by the interactionist perspective goes far in explaining the rapid decline of social control in recent years,[22] so much so that a sociologist such as Robert Van Krieken has sought to reject its heuristic pertinence outright, invoking the analytical imperatives imposed by any attempt to understand the interaction between an agent and an institution:

> It is essential to develop a sensitivity to the ways in which particular patterns of family life and social interaction have developed in relation to a given economic and cultural environment, independently of, as well as in response to, state action and attempts at social and psychological regulation ... The kind of explanatory logic which responds to this requirement is not one based on concepts like control, regulation, repression, domination or administration, but one of asymmetrical negotiations, alliances and compromises occurring within structured fields of power relations. (Van Krieken 1991, 17)

In the wake of this critical enterprise, however, it is important to look at what is at stake, and also what has been lost. The concept of social control was, fundamentally, a critical reflex that sought to lay bare the relations of power and domination lurking under the surface of what was presented as a mission of progress and humanization, and thus to ascertain the deeper meaning of the countless attempts undertaken throughout the ages to "reform" popular habits and practices. This critical perspective was also intended as an instrument of struggle, a tool for resistance placed in the hands of the dominated. And indeed, denouncing power where it acts as a vector of domination remains, I believe, the goal of any history that refuses to be more than a tedious compilation of past occurrences.[23]

Too often, the approach that gives precedence to the actions of the "agent" over the operation of the system lapses into narrow empiricism. This occurs because this approach arose in a context in which deep doubts were being expressed about the great explanatory paradigms that had hitherto dominated the humanities. An early critique of social control expresses this mistrust:

> How then are we to think through a theory of the reproduction of social life which would give relative weights to the compelled and the consensual, the bound and the free, the chosen and the determined dimension of human action in given historical societies? Contemporary social theory is increasingly aware that it has been ill-served by the grand theoretical tradition in

its approach to these questions – a Parsonian functionalism which restricts human action to the discharge of prescribed roles and the internalization of values; a Marxism which in its hostility to the idealist account of human subjectivity went a long way toward making the active human subject the determined object of ideological system and social formation; and a structuralism which likewise seems to make individual intellectual creativity and moral choice the determined result of cultural and discursive structure. (Ignatieff 1981, 184–5)

Appeals to empirical fact create a strong temptation to keep to the level of description, to devote meticulous analysis to the daily lives of agents. If there is no great bourgeois conspiracy, no carefully planned attempt to work a massive transformation of popular habits and practices, it is still possible to describe the myriad interactions taking place within the contingent loci of situations and institutions. After all, history can surely (goes the argument) make do with describing past events while remaining sensitive to the never-ending specificity and uniqueness of historical situations, as long as they are mapped out at ground level, in the spontaneity of the moment. But this approach too is problematic:

There has emerged a "third way," a new counter-revisionist paradigm grounded in the precepts of the "new social history." This "new consensus," as it might be called, while undoubtedly more nuanced, more balanced, and more solidly anchored "in the archives" than earlier progressivist or revisionist paradigms, is itself highly problematic. It offers no convincing synthetic overview of the nineteenth-century asylum experience. Baldly stated, asylum studies in the 1980s retreated into a "timid empiricism," meticulous and solidly researched case studies of individual (most often private) asylums replacing the bold and sweeping national surveys of the "New Left" generation of the 1960s and 1970s. What has been lost in all this archival fact-grubbing is precisely what made the work of Foucault, Rothman and Scull both so provocative and seminal: their open engagement with "the theoretical"; their insistence that at the heart of the nineteenth-century asylum experience lay the fundamental question of power; that, ultimately, the asylum should be studied not in and for itself but for what it reveals about the nature and meaning of the wider nineteenth-century social order. (Brown 1994, 268–9)[24]

If social control theories do not fit the realities of families and individuals interacting with the institutions responsible for the administration of poverty and crime, must it follow that there is no way to cognize the relationships arising between agents and institutions in their totality?[25] Despite the best of intentions, the bottom-up approach often remains captive to the profusion of popular reactions and initiatives vis-à-vis the nominal control agents and the institutions they put in place, yet the diversity of cases that might be studied is near-infinite. How can historians make sense of this diversity (assuming that making sense of anything is their primary duty) without framing it within the operational logic of the institution; without measuring the regulating effect of the constraints entailed by the resort to that institution, without evaluating the capacity of the norms by which it is governed to impose a stable order? Interactionism resonated with the increasingly dominant pragmatism of the humanities in response to the decline of grand systems of interpretation. Its focus on the initiative and autonomy of the agent frequently renders it unable, however, to grasp the global or the general except more or less contingently as a kind of frame or "field" constituted by the dynamic of negotiations, alliances, and compromises that characterize individual agency. The meaning of agency is thus brought down to the concrete experience of agents: it coalesces out of the activity in which they engage. No structure, then, has any logic of operation outside of the logic deriving from the concrete experience of its operation.

These considerations clearly apply to the notion of power as well. The social control perspective was built out of a search for the conditions of production of power and its effects, up to the point of its sedimentation and capillarization at the core of the social, as described in the major works of Foucault. It was an impassioned search for all forms of power and especially the most subtle ones, those that diffuse into the social body as the scattered particles of inegalitarian relations. It becomes so difficult to make sense of such complexity that power itself is reduced to an "interaction."

> One cannot properly realize the notion that power is not a thing which some people, groups or institutions possess, but rather a social relationship, without also jettisoning the zero-sum logic which lies at the heart of notions not just of social control, but also of policing, regulation and colonisation, and perhaps ultimately the very notion of the dissolution of the distinctions between state and civil society. Those who are disadvantaged in a power relation continue to act and have agency, even domination is a process of interaction. (Van Krieken 1991, 17)

In this conception, power is not a thing that can be possessed, not even a strength with which one can be endowed as a prior characteristic, but the product of an interaction. It is indeed utterly remarkable to observe the extent to which historical approaches focusing on the agent's point of view are devoid of any discussion of power, much less domination. At best, power is merely assumed, relegated to the background like a discreet backdrop for agency. At worst it is trivialized, if not denied as one of the multiple circumstances attendant on individuals' interactions with the institutions of social regulation. By the magic of the agent's autonomy, institutions become "service centres" essentially at the disposition of their clienteles. Consider, for example, this description of the nineteenth-century insane asylum:

> The community perceived the hospital as an institution that offered medical and social services in addition to its psychiatric and custodial functions ... It is not so much that custodialism did not exist in late nineteenth-century asylums ... But to imply that this very element of custodialism was an attempt on the part of middle-class doctors to exercise social control over the lives of their working-class patients is simply too easy and, indeed, misleading ... Both the increased use of the hospital by the families of Norristown's female patients and the greater reluctance of men's families to commit them to an asylum illustrate the exercise of considerable choice on the part of the so-called victims. It is time to shed social control interpretations. (McGovern 1986, 15–16)[26]

The margin of freedom left to the families or individuals facing the institution is claimed to have dissipated the power inherent in the institution, diffusing it into the banal mundanity of interactions between institutional agents and their "clientele."[27] In a fascinating paradox, an approach historically rooted in a critique of the rationality, intentionality, and effectiveness of social control measures takes up the same postulates, but this time assigning them to the agent.

Some authors liken the agent's autonomy to a "strategy," suggesting that an ad hoc rationality characterizes the acts of an individual or family group. Following this logic, one could just as arbitrarily posit the intentionality of the agent's initiatives faced with what the institution has to offer. As the authors cited above would have it, this set of actions has an inherent effectiveness in that any possibility of conceptualizing the specific development of the institution is now predicated on this interaction. For here again, the agent's autonomy is conceived as a form of *freedom*, a locus of personal or collective initiative in which the action of constraints and structures appears only as a backdrop or pretext to agency. Yet as David Garland notes:

> The imposition of a compulsory structure which requires an agent to behave in particular ways – or to choose within a predetermined range of possibilities – is not synonymous with the creation of new "freedoms," even if it does involve the agent in new forms of choosing and deciding. To talk of this as "freedom" is highly misleading. The chains of interaction along which power flows are made up of a dense entanglement of freedoms and coercions, choices and constraints, and the exercise of "voluntary choice" is itself entangled in calculations of interests, patterns of habits, and emotions of love, fear and obligation. Analysis must eschew the rhetorical tendency to talk about "freedom" in oversimplified ways, not least because it tends to repeat the propaganda of the advocates of neo-liberal reform. (Garland 1997, 197)

The "freedom" of the nineteenth-century poor cannot be conceived as a space of autonomy filled by the strategic rationality of the agent. Not, of course, that the rational act was off-limits to the working classes, that the expression of free will was always denied them, or that they were incapable of initiative, innovation, and world-changing action. Quite the contrary: our history can very much be conceptualized in terms of their agency, their resistance, their inventiveness in the face of adversity, the power of their hopes, and the breadth of their expectations. But this history cannot ignore domination, inequality, and the power of the dominant. It is true that history is at times put into overdrive by the thrust of revolution. But this change, this freedom to act, this upthrust of resistance, this appearance of the new where it is no longer expected, all these tangible manifestations of the life of societies are only thinkable if the conditions for their possibility, their conceivability, are in place. This structural logic gives meaning to the upwelling of the new; it tempers the surprise of change with the perception of what makes it possible.

In this book's field of interest, the pauper's freedom is both a condition of his servitude *and* a constraint on the powerful. It is not so much the locus of their autonomy as it is the horizon of their poverty. Again, it is not that the poor are passive, or that the unavoidable representation of poverty under liberalism is one of miserabilism woven from noble sentiments. Still, the institutions by which poverty was administered must be taken seriously, and they rarely afforded the poor opportunities to essay their particular survival strategies; too often these institutions were inescapable repositories for their despair. The essence of modern poverty is not need as such: it is the powerlessness that accompanies need. This powerlessness is the product of a societal logic that I term liberalism, for want of a better word (see chapter 2).

But to comprehend the specific contours, constraints, and possibilities of this societal logic, it must be considered as a whole. The concept of regulation is intended here to express the necessity of this holistic approach. Regulation as a concept strives to make up for the analytical deficiencies of social control while preserving its critical dimension.[28] Arising from cybernetics and often likened to the systemic approach,[29] regulation serves to take the measure of an entity, the interrelations among its elements, and the effect of time upon it. As Canguilhem defines it, "Regulation is the adjustment, in accordance with a rule or norm, of a plurality of movements or acts and their effects or products, which their diversity or succession at first makes alien to one another" (Canguilhem 1990, 711).

The *dynamic* dimension of regulation is thus central: the term applies not to a static network of relations so much as a process of social reproduction and transformation.[30] A close kinship is evident between this early conception of social regulation and cybernetics, or the related discipline of systems theory. The emphasis is on the relatively stable reproduction of a closed system over time.[31] As soon as it is noticed that the system reproduces itself, the stable cohesion of its fundamental elements can be presumed. This stability is achieved by the processes of adaptation and adjustment, whereby the system makes the changes necessary to provide for its permanence and integrity.

In my view, however, this strictly systemic account of regulation is incapable of making sense of the processes at work when societies change. For one thing, society is actually not a "system" but a fabric of heterogeneous relations informed by an operational logic. For another, the social "whole" is not a prior unit whose endurance one seeks to understand, but the partially contingent outcome of individual and collective agency inscribed within given conditions of coherence.[32] Put another way, the social logic implied by the concept of regulation has nothing to do with the maintenance of any system and everything to do with the relative endurance of ways of doing, living, seeing, and thinking that are inscribed within a set of norms and institutions from which they derive meaning. By acting or reacting, alone or in groups, men and women weave themselves into a normative and institutional fabric even as they transform it by their actions or reactions. Social action becomes comprehensible either by manifesting itself under conditions of relative predictability or, on the contrary, by setting itself apart from standard patterns of behaviour. In this sense, individuality, freedom, contingency, uniqueness, accidents, and revolts are not obstacles to the coherent functioning of a given social formation; on the contrary, they constitute its mode of operation, even its vital substance. In fact, their existence or prevalence gives clues to the depth and the fragility of the norms and institutions undergirding them.[33]

It should be obvious that the concept of regulation used here has little to do with control, if only because it does not even remotely imply a conscious agenda of domination (without, of course, denying the historical possibility of such an agenda) or any functional correspondence between a norm or institution and a given social "need." Furthermore, it does not presuppose that social relations, and the ways in which they change, are under the control or supervision of a given group. And finally, despite the ambiguity created by another meaning of the word "regulation," the concept cannot be reduced to an analysis of the regulations or rules governing a given social action or reality. A description of normative structures is only one dimension of a much more complex process of regulation of the social.

In sum, regulation is an intransitive concept: no one "regulates" anything; instead, a process occurs whereby a set of actions takes place within a set of norms even as it transforms them. A mode of regulation, then, is an analytical construct denoting the historically specific social logic whereby great numbers of individuals fit dynamically into social reality as they obey (well, badly, sometimes not at all!) the norms, rules, and institutions structuring it. The mode of operation of this social logic can be discerned by analyzing its regularities and constancies as well as its weaknesses and variations.

To illustrate what is at stake in the concept of regulation, take the example of car traffic. What would a regulation-based analysis tell us about this phenomenon? It should be obvious that traffic regulations do not tell the whole story! The analysis must also consider how thousands of individual vehicle movements, not coordinated by a higher authority (or functionally organized according to its needs), not connected by membership in a particular group or shared convictions, can result in a remarkably stable and predictable state of affairs without anyone's individual freedom being infringed or anything other than sporadic control being posited. The task is not to describe traffic (that is relatively easy) but to understand it. This of course means knowing something about the road network, traffic regulations, car manufacture and maintenance, driver habitus, and car use patterns. It also means accounting for the impact of economic structures (market production, wage relations), political structures, and social structures that serve to explain why people have to be on the road at a given place and time.

Traffic emerges from this analysis as a peculiar relationship among individuals. But it is a living relationship, a relationship in motion and transformation – in short, a process. There are accidents, events, and experiences that do not obey the rules. Traffic jams, frequent accidents on some sections of roads, protests (e.g., against pollution), and other contingencies point to deficiencies in the structure or weaknesses in its regulating logic. Furthermore, the practices of agents, as distinct from the rules they are supposed to obey, point to a lived reality quite different from the official reality: thus, in Quebec, the common practice of driving at 120 kilometres per hour despite the official 100 km/h highway speed limit. Finally, any number of phenomena (e.g., the growth of cycling and alternative modes of transport, an oil crisis, the redesign of a downtown area, the decline or growth of suburbs, telecommuting and variable work scheduling, pollution) can profoundly alter a mode of traffic regulation to the point that it ceases to operate as before.

Traffic, then, is not a "system" but a mode of relation among individual agents understandable in terms of its formal structure and gaps – and, most importantly, knowable *by and through* the changes it undergoes. The fact that traffic is not a fleeting event, that it involves a set of relatively predictable behaviours, that it takes place over time without losing its recognizable configuration, makes it explainable in terms of regulation. A regulation-based analysis can produce a dynamic picture of the changing relationships among individual actions and the structures in which they are embedded. Whereas the notion of control is clearly inadequate to an understanding of a phenomenon such as obedience to traffic regulations, bound up as it is with complex processes of buy-in, rejection, and ambivalence, regulation theory makes these considerations a central part of the analysis.

To think of society in terms of regulation is to rethink social relations as a shared and sometimes adversarial construct set within an overall logic of societal reproduction and change. There is no question of denying the general characteristics induced, in a given society, by prevailing systems of production and consumption, or by the ways in which cultural and ideological representations are constructed and communicated. But all these dimensions[3] of life in society are also structured according to a *political* logic.

"Political" can be taken in the primary sense of the organization and administration of collective decision-making, the choices and actions that enable social formations, as established collectivities, to survive over time (or cause them to perish). But here the term refers to a deeper logic according to which certain types of social relations generate a set of responses by institutions (and not only the state) to their evolving internal contradictions. This structuring of the modes of resolution of societal tensions (as improvised, temporary, fragile, or ineffective as these modes may be); the adversarial, disputed character of this structuring; the way in which it is altered, eventually breaks up, and is replaced by another type of societal organization, are what the concept of "mode of social regulation" seeks to capture.

This structuring is clearly not to be conceived of as a "system" because there is no posited automatic response to the contradictions running through modes of regulation, and these contradictions are internal as much as they are generated by external pressures (wars, natural disasters, etc.).[34] But in fact, a general logic is posited, a logic not flowing from the various "functions" that some institutions are reckoned to take on, or from some "structural" effect conjectured to explain the regularities that underlie individual agency.[35] The rationality at play here is a limited one, in which the agent's behaviour constitutes this reality even as it leads to its fragility, changeableness, and contingency.

The limited rationality of the social logic expressed by the concept of regulation can be grasped by analysing the effects of *institutionalization*. The concept of institution (Chevallier 1981) is indeed central to any discussion of regulation in that it reflects the structure of the agency possessed by the men and women who operate within a given regulatory logic. By virtue of the institution, this agency is inscribed in time; it acquires a collective meaning beyond the spontaneous, repetitive, or routine acts of individuals. Following the same logic, institutions help categorize certain acts and give them a shared meaning, beyond individual wills. In either case, institutionalization[36] is a key modality of the endurance of societies and the regulating logic that undergirds them, for two reasons.

The first is that an institution is self-legitimizing and produces meaning autonomously:

> Any institution that is going to keep its shape needs to gain legitimacy by distinctive grounding in nature and reason: then it affords to its members

a set of analogies with which to explore the world and with which to justify the naturalness and reasonableness of the instituted rules, and it can keep its identifiable continuing form. Any institution then starts to control the memory of its members; it causes them to forget experiences incompatible with its righteous image, and it brings to their minds events which sustain the view of nature that is complementary to itself. It provides the categories of their thought, sets the terms for self-knowledge, and fixes identities. All of this is not enough. It must secure the social edifice by sacralizing the principles of justice. (Douglas 1986, 112)

This process also implies a complex dialectic that institutes a two-way relationship between individuals and institutions. Revel describes this phenomenon well:

People need institutions, which is another way of saying that they make use of them as much as they are used by them. Within a given configuration, institutions are not conceptualized as existing as such, above society or encompassing it: they embody and bring out forms of reciprocal dependency that constitute the mould in which social interplay is cast and that are constantly being actualized among those who participate in that interplay ... One tends toward an open-ended, supple, relational definition of institutions. This definition formalizes a set of conventions that are the settled forms of the exchange (of which coercion and conflict form a part). (Revel 1995, 81)[37]

Second, institutions are more than a mere (and at times a highly contingent) effect of consensus and interaction; they are a locus of relative stability that establishes a specific relationship between human agency and time. They provide a framework for this agency, enclose it within a physical and temporal space of regularity or predictability. In so doing, they impose specific constraints on people's impulses or, on the contrary, compel them to act in a given manner. In either case, they generate a sort of injunctive language composed of norms and rules.

The inescapable polysemy of the concept of institution becomes clear: it is intended to account for the structuring of human agency in all areas of social reality. Institutions, that is, can interpenetrate with social reality to widely differing degrees, inasmuch as the regulated space they express and concretize can be either extremely diffuse (e.g., the literary institution [Robert 1989]) or, on the contrary, contained within a well-delimited space (e.g., prisons and asylums as institutions).

But the institution is not just the product of an instinct for survival in the face of change. It is also a site at which key contradictions are expressed, in two main respects. First, it must be said that the sense of permanence in which institutions are draped is in fact just a self-generated illusion, a sham. From their inception, institutions work to obscure their origins. What Lepetit says of norms and conventions applies a fortiori to institutions:

> Objects' detachment from the moment of their production does not have as its only result, by an almost mechanical effect, that of rendering norms more stable. Because they withstand the disappearance and renewal of the circumstances and people who instituted them, they lose their initial signification and help make the convention opaque for those who participate in it. The weight of the past becomes all the more extreme in that it derives its force from its own oblivion. (Lepetit 1995, 282)

The trick played by the institution is to incorporate and consolidate whatever changes are made to it into an illusion of endurance, putting forth the perception that it has always been thus. The reality is, of course, that institutions change continually in response to the very practices of the people they nominally govern.

> Objects, institutions, and rules only exist insofar as they are put to use, and, moreover they do not draw a mere frame around agency, but configure the resources, changed by practice, that are available to the agents. The past, refigured in the present, takes on a hypothetical status since it is perpetually open to revision. The future, projected in the image of today, remains unforeseeable; a present yet to come will endow the social space with new meaning and a new configuration. (Lepetit 1995b, 297)

Second, institutions represent a false consensus, an illusion – continually created and then shattered – of a world view shared by those who act under their governance. They do not merely fix certain acts into a stable form for the long haul: they also structure power relations that are all the more powerful if the institution's mission is one of coercion (or strong persuasion). For there is nothing in the definition of institution that precludes its being a site of *forced* agreement, of a vision one is given no choice but to share. Institutions are not just the spontaneous creation of human agency: as Foucault demonstrated so well, they can also carry an agenda[38] or serve as vehicles for the implementation of power techniques.

The space thus institutionalized gives rise to classification and marking procedures that are central to modern forms of power.

> On the parade ground, in the factory, in the school, and in the hospital, people are gathered together *en masse*, but by this very fact may be observed as entities both similar to and different from one another. These institutions function in certain respects like telescopes, microscopes, or other scientific instruments: they establish a regime of visibility in which the observed is distributed within a single common plane of sight. Second, these institutions operate according to a regulation of detail. These regulations, and the evaluation of conduct, manners, and so forth entailed by them, establish a grid of codeability of personal attributes. They act as norms, enabling the previously aleatory and unpredictable complexities of human conduct to be conceptually coded and cognized in terms of judgments as to conformity or deviation from such norms ... The development of institutions and techniques which required the co-ordination of large numbers of persons in an economic manner and sought to eliminate certain habits, propensities, and morals and to inculcate others, thus made visible the difference between those who did or did not, could or could not, would or would not learn the lessons of institution. These institutions acted as observing and recording machines, machines for the registration of human differences. These attentions to individual differences and their consequences spread to other institutions, especially those which had to do with the efficient or rational utilization or deployment of persons. (Rose 1988, 187–8)

To be sure, not every institution is an instrument for the compulsory inculcation of values and behaviours. Here, to a great extent, lies the central semantic ambiguity of the concept of institution – a term that can, after all, designate a spoken language just as well as a prison. But the idea here is to point out the fundamental homology according to which certain institutions of regulation are inscribed within a broader conceptual framework. Prisons, hospitals, houses of industry, and poorhouses are not merely "establishments": they are also instituted practices. The narrowness of the space of their deployment, and the intensity of the resulting power dynamic, only strengthens the institutional effect.

Ultimately, a study centring around regulation rests on the postulate that each social formation harbours institutional forms – norms, conventions, rules, institutions – that give each society a particular experience, a characteristic texture. The institutional stratum of social reality is situated below the grand forces determining life in society (gender and class relations, political structures, modes of production, etc.) but above the quotidian, contingent practices of agents, and it imparts a particular configuration to the overlying and underlying strata. I posit as well that the sum total of these realities (structures, normative and institutional parameters, social action) is organized according to a particular logic possessing its own historicity, and I refer to this logic as a "mode of regulation." The particular social configuration of capitalism, for example, can be conceived of as a mode of regulation; it is not just a societal form, mode of production, or transhistorical economic formation.

The concept of regulation corresponds, in fact, to analytical dictates that have been expressed rather explicitly by what has been called the "regulation school."[39] A good part of the work inspired by this group (particularly that of Michel Aglietta and Robert Boyer) partakes of an economics-centred perspective of little interest to us here.[40] However, the integration of a dialectical-cum-critical dimension into the regulation-based analysis of societies, brilliantly effected by Alain Lipietz (1979), gives the concept its full heuristic relevance.[41] Regulation, for Lipietz, is a conceptual tool designed not to analyze the persistence of systems over time but rather the play of *contradictions* leading every system to be transformed, and eventually to disappear.[42] A mode of regulation endures over time as long as it does not fly apart under the pressure of its internal contradictions and the structural crisis to which they may give rise. Again, the effectiveness of the social cohesion engendered by a mode of regulation can be assessed not by its regularities so much as by the discontinuities, accidents, revolts, and dysfunctions that act on it. The dynamic stability of a mode of regulation is a function of its capacity to handle both exogenous developments and the consequences of its endogenous contradictions.[43]

The operation of a mode of regulation over time is also affected by the relations of production and exchange and the gender relations obtaining in the society in question. In particular, societies based on class and gender inequalities consistently feature three crucial social dysfunctions:

1 Poverty, or structural inequality of access to essential resources.
2 Illness, or the temporary or permanent physical or mental incapacity to take on the tasks and responsibilities necessary for survival in society.
3 Crime, or the deliberate, premeditated transgression of the societal rules.

In the present day it has become a truism that poverty, illness, and crime are *constructed* categories, and that the treatment of these phenomena will be fundamentally conditioned by the specific social order in which they occur. Furthermore, a deeply inegalitarian society will – regardless of its operative mode of regulation – tend to treat them differentially, to the detriment of the dominated social strata, as a function of its prevailing power relations and especially its class and gender divisions. It remains that the persistent occurrence of these phenomena affords a commanding vantage from which to analyze the contours and contradictions of a mode of regulation.

This is true if only because the manifestation of these phenomena, although it transcends specific modes of regulation and constitutes one of the long-range constants of inegalitarian societies, gives rise to specific symbolic constructs, and to specific modes of administration, as a function of the regulatory logic in place. That is, the ways in which poverty, illness, and crime are defined and administered within a given spatiotemporal context open up a privileged window on what constitutes normality within that context.

A mode of regulation reveals its structure, its contradictions, and its fragility or endurance only when it is studied under tension, up against the actions of human beings and the imponderables of time. Poverty, illness, and crime are universal features of inegalitarian societies; they are like the scum forming on a sea of social relations. But they also have the power to elicit contingent or even stubbornly persistent reactions by the social order. Each mode of regulation constitutes, in effect, a specific way of responding to these fundamental contradictions, of laying them out within a minimally coherent framework.

This is why, as in every history, it is important to specify the spatiotemporal setting on which this study of regulation will focus.

THE DEMOCRATIC CAPITALIST TRANSITION IN QUEBEC

This book studies the regulatory logic taking shape in Quebec during that uncertain era when democracy and capitalism were being put in place as the dominant modes of social organization. Of course, as discussed above, a mode of regulation undergoes permanent transformations as a result of the social practices arising within it. And it is equally true that each element of this mode, each institution or system of norms, possesses its own time scale, sometimes reaching far into the past.[44]

But in times of great crisis or structural upheaval, the societal logic in which men and women have always lived may suddenly break apart. A whole set of institutions, norms, and conventions emerges with remarkable concomitance, materializing a new order of things. The resulting changes interweave, and a titanic remaking of the bedrock of social life takes place. The transition to capitalism, which Karl Polanyi termed "the great transformation" in a justly famous and forward-looking book (Polanyi 1944), is one such time.

Although it may seem strange, historians have become increasingly allergic to discontinuity and ever more satisfied with the static empirical descriptions to which their instruments of measurement and analysis permit them to aspire. By the same token, they have become disillusioned scientifically with the relevance of global analysis and politically with the possibility of revolutionary change. Too often they are content to pursue small shifts in "concrete" reality, scattered amid the multiple "temporalities" to which they have submitted since Fernand Braudel (when not gazing lazily into a fool's mirror at the fixed images and afterimages of their particular object of study). The search for the basic features of the transition to capitalism, and the transformative logic thus enacted, has yielded to isolated inquiries into specific aspects of this transition, if not outright rejection of the potential heuristic value of a synchronic analysis of its dimensions.[45] Drawing parallels and connections is a job for a philosopher or a social scientist, not a historian. The best the historical discipline has to offer is a set of "syntheses" – insufferable conglomerations of factual certainties designed to initiate novice readers to the events and reforms of a given period. Historical pragmatism is the order of the day.

But all the Braudelian levels of time that run through reality are lived at the same time. The great historical disruption represented by capitalism was experienced in the form of fear and expressed in the form of acts; these were objectified and reified in institutions, which proceeded to channel the possibilities that arose into circumscribed futures. The time when capitalism and democracy became the two pillars of a new mode of regulation is a unique time, one deserving to be analyzed as a whole and not chopped into little isolated temporalities. From the end of the eighteenth century to the start of the twentieth, the mode of regulation we still live under was put in place. Pregnant with new possibility, it was also enriched by the sediments of history that it dragged along with it. Between nostalgia for what was being lost and dreams of what was being created, the world was overturned on a scale and with an abruptness rarely equaled before then. Looking back at this era, we must strain to discern the new peering through the cracks in the old, while avoiding the teleological temptation to speculate about the effects of what was to come. For the period in question was marked by profound ambivalence. Not the kind that typically precedes a choice, nor the structural indecision constitutive of people's powerlessness in the face of a history over which they have little control. No, I speak here of a kind of creative seesawing between freedom as a dream and a horizon and domination as the common denominator of societies in transition. I refer to a hope, perhaps never before felt so strongly, that men and women could be freed from the bonds that prevent them from inventing a just and egalitarian society, squaring off against a shrunken version of that hope, an ethic of social egoism posing as "realism"; a pragmatism of small advances and grand ethics, drained of content by bourgeois liberalism.

The implications of this nascent democracy, this freedom to create a better world, were foreign to mechanistic determinism. They constituted impulses of struggle and resistance that would eventually help to overthrow, or at least strongly modulate, the bourgeois logic of regulation that nearly extinguished the humanist hopes of the eighteenth century.

The geographic focus of this study is Lower Canada and its successor jurisdiction, Quebec. I see this political and social nexus as offering relevant terrain for an analysis of how the prevailing mode of social regulation shifted in the nineteenth century. Any national territory is unique, of course, and it would be pointless to look for precisely the same set of social relations in another setting. Nonetheless, my hypothesis is that the democratic revolutions of the late eighteenth and early nineteenth centuries created a zone of influence occupied by societies that underwent the transition to the modern-day mode of regulation at roughly the same pace. If so, then it seems likely that a study of one particular manifestation of this transition would tell us much about the others.[46]

But this hypothesis poses some difficult problems. To what extent is it in fact proper to posit the synchronicity of these various transitions? The notion of a "delay" or "time lag" has tended to dominate historical accounts of the influences exerted by some national experiences upon others. In particular, colonies are assumed to have followed the lead of the motherland. But apart from the political impasses to which imperial domination may lead,[47] there are no grounds for finding that any given society has lagged behind any other. Such a notion derives from a deeply wrongheaded, Whiggish conception of comparative history; as if typical institutional configurations and patterns of social relations originate with the dominant, "advanced" countries before radiating out to the more backward ones. Within the polity determined by a set of borders, each nation passes laws and creates institutions corresponding to its own social realities. It does appear nonetheless that many nineteenth-century national configurations shared a mode of regulation and some of its characteristic institutions. Examples include fundamental political liberties, the abolition of slavery, the existence of a labour market, confinement (prison) used as a mode of punishment, and the spread of a personal ethics based on individual autonomy. Concomitant with these developments was the rise of a particular conception of philanthropy, along with the notion that individuals are or can be amenable to therapeutic reform. Each of these features of the mode of regulation in question undoubtedly had its own historicity from one country to another; still, one is struck by their remarkably synchronous development throughout the West.[48] It appears that beyond the specificities of institutional configurations, class dynamics, and legal frameworks, one mode of regulation succeeded in extending its logic across much of the nineteenth-century world. The manner in which this process took place largely remains to be elucidated, but it is clear that the conceptual explanations propounded to date – invoking cultural influence or transmission, the dissemination of ideas at international conferences, institutional mimicry, the exemplary value of "models," ideological domination, and so on – are far from sufficient to account for the phenomenon, and so to escape the "analytic cage" of the nation-state.[49]

Given these considerations, it can be said that the case of Quebec is well suited to an analytical study of the transition between modes of regulation in the West. But again, there is no reason to assign an ideal type to the society of Quebec and Lower Canada – to appeal, for example, to its "Americanness" or to the relative recency of European colonization. The concept of "new society" (Bouchard 1999), derived from a rather dubious classification of societal types, is of little value here. It seems more pertinent to consider any society, any social formation, as a *singular* recomposition of social relations, a unique totality. If this uniqueness is recognized, then a national specificity can be ascribed to certain phenomena without ignoring the existence of supranational regularities. Comparative history must not be confused with co-occurrence;

it is inaccurate to juxtapose national spaces as comparable totalities, subjecting them to an exercise of categorization that turns them into reified entities.

It is, however, possible to compare frameworks of thought, structures of aspiration, ways of relating to the past, and the normative and institutional stratifications through which they are materialized. From this standpoint, the nation (here, Quebec[50]) is not a relation itself but a *space* in which relations between individuals are instituted. What happens in this space can only be usefully compared and contrasted with what happens elsewhere if the terms of the comparison have some common basis. In that case, comparison serves to elucidate the ways in which institutions, norms, schemes of thought, or social relations are manifested within different national spaces; it sheds light on the meaning and historicity of these phenomena.[51] But merely drawing parallels between entire social formations whose only point in common is that they constitute national spaces is bound to result in vague, generalized analogies of highly dubious heuristic import.

One could, of course, express doubts as to the "representativeness" of the Quebec case. Would it not be preferable to study the mode of regulation as it occurred in European societies, rather than its pale colonial "copy"? Apart from the dubiety of the notion of "borrowing" – which, in the historiography of Quebec, too often stands in for a serious analysis of institutional forms – the colonial status and small scale of Quebec society afford a number of analytical advantages. The great debates raging across the Atlantic are found here in capsule form, often purged of the needless repetition and logomachy found in Europe. In the more limited context of colonial society, it is as if the cream of the discourse has been skimmed off, making the argumentation simpler and more trenchant. Better still, it becomes possible to compare the whole of the discourse with the actual set of initiatives undertaken. Allowing for regional specificities and colonial constraints, Quebec society can serve as a "scale model" from which the basic traits of the transition between modes of regulation can be discerned. A systematic comparison of reform-oriented debates and discourses as well as institutional innovations does, after all, indicate a remarkable homology and synchrony between Europe, the United States, and the Canadian colonies. Developments relating to correctional practice, charitable associations, capital punishment, and criminal law reform generally occurred with a time lag of only a few years. And the same goes for subsequent developments in the liberal era, which are discussed in the following chapters. Moreover, this time lag is not solely attributable to the colonial condition: internal constraints on decision-making, local perceptions, and real needs have just as much or more explanatory power in this regard.[52]

* * *

During the great transition, a new mode of regulation was instituted in Quebec. Based on the fundamental postulate of human freedom, the implementation of this mode was modulated by the fact of unequal access to societal resources. Before exploring the primary loci at which the new regulatory logic was manifested, it is necessary to examine the paradoxical and changing representation of the world that underlay it: liberalism.

2

Freedom, State, and Individual: The Shifting Patterns of Nineteenth-Century Liberal Regulation

Any research on the ways in which crime and poverty were dealt with in the nineteenth century must account for a basic fact: that the century's major transformations, whether on the plane of politics, economics, or ideology, were primarily keyed to the idea of freedom. Any historical analysis of these transformations must stay attuned to the shifting meanings of freedom over time.

At first sight, this statement sounds like a mere truism. However, in the era when it was coming into being as a political, economic, and ethical construct, freedom was not just an aspiration; it was also, and to an even greater extent, an immense problem. Beyond rallying cries and ideologies espousing laissez-faire and freedom of thought, the idea of setting the superstructure of society on a foundation of freedom amounted to a complete overturning of the logic of interaction between individuals in society that had formerly prevailed – and this in two respects.

First, it meant that there was now room, deep within conceptions of life in society, for a culture of time and potentialities to develop. There was room for a conception of individual agency that could form the bedrock of the future society to be built. In this sense, liberalism was and is much more than just another ideology: it is the ever-expanding horizon encompassing a whole range of possibilities available to modern societies.

Second, freedom as a political construct gave rise to a fundamental redefinition of the relationships between particular and general, individual and society, citizen and state. This long and complex labour of rebuilding the social fabric in the political sphere may be gauged by the widening distance between the concepts of private and public.

FREEDOM, WILL, AND RESPONSIBILITY: A NEW CULTURE OF TIME AND SPACE

Liberalism can be characterized by the ever-more explicit content of the arguments it has put forward for freedom since the eighteenth century.[1] However, at least in the sense in which it is construed here, liberalism is not reducible to some kind of "ideological" content, and the task at hand is not to discern that content in the discourse of an era. Discourse here is only an instrument – always falling short, at times leading us astray – that opens the door onto a larger realm made up of beliefs, aspirations, and ethical assumptions, all of which form the backdrop to a panoply of social prospects and potentialities; they are the condition for the possibility of a variety of isolated projects, or perhaps agendas, for social change.[2] In particular, liberalism presents itself as a particular way of setting the relations between the social whole and its constituent parts in their spatiotemporal context. It expresses that moment in history when the market, as a mode of regulation, demanded that the political sphere be rebuilt according to the logic of democracy.[3] In this sense, liberalism has to be construed much more broadly than as just another ideology. It is a veritable mode of existence that wraps the individual within a specific *ethic* of personhood. It lays out a framework for behaviour that constrains and channels agency even down to its ethical dimension. Until now, the discipline of history has devoted very little study to these ethical frames of reference, yet beyond the conscious and rational expression of ideas, they define a space for the expression of the values, aspirations, and ethical precepts that underlie discourse and practice.[4]

At the root of liberal agency, then, one finds a set of ethical prenotions and behavioural techniques arising from market practice, as well as a renewed faith in the power of reason.[5] A set of fundamental values is applied to rebuilding the notional scaffolding attendant, in any society, upon the conception of social time and space. In the case at hand, these pre-notions consist, for example, of personal responsibility for the consequences of one's actions, the ethics of keeping a promise, the ability to devise plans for the future and strategies to carry them out, and the positing of the individual as the basic unit of the social relation. Once freedom of thought and action becomes the principal element of the social fabric, and once the individual will is conceived of as the ultimate standard against which the validity of social action is measured,[6] it becomes possible to envision people's trajectory through time as the complex outcome of this will and hence – inasmuch as the free expression of this will can only be consistent with the social good – as *progress*. Likewise, the social space becomes the terrain for the free and reciprocal exchange of goods and ideas, a space of fruitful confrontation among individuals.[7]

In this context, it becomes germane for people to think about relationships to the Other, and to the future. The liberal universe is one of movement and diversity, two dimensions of reality whose existence as social attributes is predicated on individual liberty. In this universe, reality is constituted, things happen, through constant contact between differences, through conflict (whether dialectical or otherwise) between extremes. The confrontation between units unfamiliar to each other, who ideally lack motives other than those of self-interest rightly understood and the need to keep their promises, appears as an eminently creative process, the moment when sociability is brought into being. The workings of the market as observed by David Ricardo, the political universe defined by Benjamin Constant, even the ethics of John Stuart Mill, are nothing more than domains in which this fundamental rule holds.[8]

Of course, there is no question of portraying freedom as an invention of the nineteenth or even the eighteenth century, or of denying the possibility of prior sporadic occurrences of liberal attitudes. But when "liberal" attitudes appeared in the feudal context, for example, it was within a social construct fundamentally hostile to them, a construct founded on other principles of coexistence – personal dependency, tradition, honour attaching to status, conformity, and so forth. Freedom, in all its existential complexity, did not become a model of social organization, a regulating principle, an instrument for societal reproduction and evolution, until economic and political institutions (and the dominant discourse associated with them) were seated on the bedrock of liberalism. That moment came to pass only when the nineteenth century was half over. But it was concomitant with a major reconfiguration of the givens of economic, social, and political reality as well as of the ideological schemas superimposed on that reality. From then on, liberalism became a sort of hypertext of the sayable whose importance can hardly be overestimated.

It is true that this development had long been on the horizon. The eighteenth century had witnessed the accentuation of a set of fundamental historical phenomena that gave rise to a new "ethics of self"[9] (and other). At least four of these phenomena can be named:

1 The first was, of course, the market.[10] The world of trade is an opportunity to discover the Other while also discovering the power of one's own agency. Profit, the accumulation of possessions, happens *as a result* of interaction with the Other, in a process in which consent to trade and absence of constraint constitute the indispensable preconditions for the relation.[11] The growth (or decline) of one's fortune is determined by one's dual capacity to participate in the temporal process of history and to establish social relations with the Other.

2 The second was a sort of historical pedagogy of revolt that coalesced as the result of the numberless uprisings and occasional revolutions (against the Dutch Republic, for example, or in Cromwell's England) that punctuated the modern era, leading up to the revolutionary cataclysm of the late eighteenth century. All this turmoil amounted to a historical demonstration that the alternative of fighting the immanent order of things is both thinkable and possible. These revolts were initially carried out in an effort to reinstate that same immanent order, which the rebels believed to have been betrayed by the dominant classes.[12] Ultimately, however, they constituted the historical model for its overthrow.

3 The third was a similar pedagogy of intellectual and moral dissidence. A legacy of the Reformation, it showed that one's relationship to God, and one's conception of how good can triumph over evil, can take a number of paths from which men and women are free to choose.

4 Finally, the evolving heritage of rational thought from Erasmus to Descartes and on to Kant revealed reality to be a complex compound and not a simple metaphysical creation. An ethics founded on reason set the stage for the "discovery" of the self, the Other, and history:

Discovery of the self: Where conformity to the natural order of things had once been a matter of faith, it now became a matter of construction of the self. Personal ethics and civic virtue were not givens but had to be actively cultivated. The self, in its new guise, was thus eminently reformable, ideally by a labour of self-construction or self-discipline, or if not, then by an effort exerted by others. I come in due course to this ideal of reformability and its far-reaching consequences for the management of poverty and crime.

Discovery of the Other: From ideas of the "noble savage" to the anthropological gaze on foreign civilizations inaugurated by the

Enlightenment, the encounter with the Other became, ipso facto, a source of self-knowledge. The humanitarian ideal is but one facet of an upended mental world in which confrontation and comparison with others became an essential means of building one's own identity.

Discovery of history: History became an open-ended temporal process, and the continuity implied by the movement of things and people through time appeared – truly for the first time – as a fragile and perpetually renegotiated equilibrium between the field of past experience and people's aspirations for a better future.[13]

In sum, what was being invented were the new mental reflexes and conceptual frames of a world learning to live with the Other as a mirror of the self and with time as movement toward the better. It was an extraordinary shift that has yet to be fully elucidated by historical research; the result was the formation of a substrate of sorts, constituting the precondition for the existence of the modern world.[14]

It is worth dwelling a bit longer on the content and implications of this substrate. It was not simply made up of shared "values," however universal. Thus, the deathless triptych "liberty-equality-property," to which liberalism is too often reduced, could and did undergo innumerable adjustments and restrictions in response to contingencies, circumstances, and short-term allegiances to any of numerous versions of liberalism. At best, what were laid down were the outlines of a program of social organization that would undergo several profound transformations – as I shall show with respect to the systems responsible for the administration of crime and poverty.

No doubt, liberty as a primary existential condition, formal equality as the normative basis for relations with the Other, and property as the essence of one's relationship to things constitute the core principles of liberal sociability. But much more fundamentally, the liberal universe represents a tectonic shift in the foundations of the social fabric, for it has been recentred around the individual or citizen. He or she is henceforth at the centre of the social nebula, is guided primarily by his or her will, and operates according to the principle of responsibility for one's actions.

Will The primacy of the will is the gauge of freedom's presence and its essential precondition. The will is that basic impulse that corresponds to what is free in an act or thought. In Thomas Haskell's conception, it is the point of origin from which humans are able to inflect the temporal continuum with their willed behaviour.[15] More, the expression of the will makes it possible to transform one's desires into reality, or at least to modify reality by this outward manifestation of desire:

> The heart of personhood lay in the will, and the will, though not necessarily supernatural, was uncanny. The self formed as pure point of origin through its mysterious capacity of "willing," of almost magically transmuting the evanescent, inward, and private experience of desire and choice into the concrete, outward, and public phenomenon of action. More mysterious still, the resulting external acts produced consequences that corresponded with, or satisfied, the internal desires – or, at least, could do so if the will allowed itself to be guided by the dictates of reason and knowledge. (Haskell 1987, 874)

The expression of "free" will is thus an act essential to one's confrontation with other individuals/citizens of a given social whole. The deliberate act, the overt, tangible expression of one's inner desires and aspirations, takes its place in a vibrant "commerce" of ideas and practices.[16] In this competitive realm, success and truth are the collective sanction by which the good is determined as the product of the free intermixing of thoughts and actions. They are the outcome of a screening process made possible by unfettered confrontation among the profusion of sentiments, gestures, and acts that form the substance of life in society. But all this is possible only if freedom is not distorted by arbitrariness or undue coercion; if the will is authentic and not simulated; if it emanates from a "self" fully conscious of its desires and aspirations. This means, further, that the will is not only a fact and a requirement but also a self-transformative process. Its possession authorizes the individual to claim the title of citizen.

Responsibility The freedom and power to act thus become primary attributes of the individuality that ultimately constitutes true sociability and that now seeks to replace older forms of community solidarity. But this happens at a cost: an unprecedented extension of the principle of responsibility.

> What people are responsible for extends no farther than our causal perception – that is, our way of sifting through the virtual infinity of consequences flowing from a person's acts and omissions, classifying only a small fraction as truly *belonging* to the actor in a morally relevant way and thus qualifying

for praise or blame. At most, we hold people responsible only for evils over which we believe they have significant causal influence – ones about which they "can" do something. Even this is only an outer limit, a prerequisite that is necessary (but not sufficient) for blameworthiness, for there are many evils that people obviously *could* do something to alleviate for which we do not hold them responsible ...

Causal relationships are something we *impute* to the people, events, and things around us, and we do so in ways shaped by social convention. (Haskell 1998b, 298–9)

Acknowledgment of the sway that individuals can have over (individual and collective) destiny means that it is necessary to impute a larger share of responsibility to the deliberate, willed act. This becomes the ethical principle governing the use of the transformative power ascribed to such an act. More precisely, each person, by virtue of being a citizen, is in some manner "accountable" for what transpires and whether or not it is desirable.[17] Responsibility is another way of expressing the deeply human character of the causality associated with things that happen. Its assertion invalidates the divine causality formerly considered to be basic to human agency (or at least displaces it to another level of understanding of the world).[18] The best characterization of freedom, after all, involves regarding someone who makes use of it as *causing* what transpires, rather than this being a passive consequence of that which determines her. "To be 'free' instead of determined is to perceive oneself, or one's choices and actions, as causes instead of effects, as origins that reach creatively into the future, rather than terminations foreordained by antecedent events. It is, at least provisionally, to perceive oneself as an uncaused cause" (Haskell 1998c, 319).

The principle of responsibility thus establishes a causal link between reality and the will, and it situates this causal link *inside* the individual, ascribing to her not only the capacity to change reality but also the ethical obligation to effect this change for the good. In short, responsibility is the ethical requirement for the individual to be a dynamic force within the social, someone who can both initiate change and answer for its desirability.

Will and responsibility are the basic elements of the self that make freedom both possible and efficient as a mode of regulation. Together, they constitute a new ethic of self that helps to explain the emergence, in the eighteenth century, of a deep-seated human impulse to change the world for the better. Haskell clearly shows how the ever-widening influence of this ethic explains the rise and persistence of humanitarian thought. If the world and its fate ultimately depend on what humanity makes of them, it becomes both possible and necessary, materially feasible and ethically paramount, to eliminate misfortune and, as Saint-Just put it, to realize the "new idea" of happiness.[19] The fact that this altruistic quest for others' happiness is not only compatible but closely concomitant with the market economy should not be surprising. It is Haskell who once again points out the structural homology between the two:

> Capitalism and humanitarianism seem antithetical – and their concomitance puzzling – because of the divergence of the sentiments on which each rests. Capitalism fosters self-regarding sentiments, while humanitarianism seems other-regarding. What can account for the parallel development in history of two such opposed tendencies? The mystery fades considerably once we recognize that, in spite of their divergent properties, capitalism and humanitarianism also have something important in common: both presuppose the existence of wide causal horizons. Both depend on people who attribute to themselves far-reaching powers of intervention. Neither can flourish unless it can enlist the energies of people who display a strongly self-monitoring disposition, people who routinely allow their behavior in the present to be shaped by obligations incurred in the distant past and by anticipations of consequences that lie far in the future. People who dwell only in the present and attribute to themselves little power to alter the course of events live in a world that cannot sustain either a market-oriented form of life or the acute sensations of moral responsibility that Nietzsche derisively associated with the "bad conscience" of the humanitarian reformers. (Haskell 1987, 853)

This universe of aspirations, this faith in the future, this belief in the possibility of controlling one's destiny, this acute sense of broad personal responsibility, this whole constellation of feelings and ethical choices entailed by the new, freedom-centred relationship to the world – all this is still with us. Liberalism in the "bourgeois" sense is but one way in which the spirit of freedom was materialized in history (alongside socialism, corporatism, communitarian solidarity, or even anarchism).

For there is no question of returning to a simplistic causal version of liberalism's rise. It is important to emphasize the historicity and contingency of the culture, or the ethics, constituted by the collection of principles and values described here. The initial manifestations of this culture, in terms of both democratic demands and humanitarian or reform projects, can be located in the eighteenth century; it forms the undercurrent of Western thought to the present day. But the ways in which this culture might have been concretized are near infinite. In the name of the individual will, one can draw up societal blueprints running the gamut from bourgeois liberalism to communism (as ideal conditions for the full expression of this will and its aspirations). In the name of personal responsibility, one can equally well justify a systematic policy of state-dependent solidarity or a system in which the negation of such a policy makes it possible for that same responsibility to be borne by others. And who would dare to ignore, in this era of brutal globalization, that it was once quite possible to imagine a world of inequality and oppression in the name of freedom?

What makes for the complexity of the liberal constellation is that it constitutes all at once a culture, a galaxy of representations and aspirations constructed around the idea of freedom, and a specific political agenda underlain by a restrictive interpretation of freedom, equality, and property. It is not enough to state that a society is organized around the will as a source of change and decision, and around responsibility as a relational principle. This leaves open the question of which adjustments to these fundamental axioms of the social fabric are permissible. What, for example, are the outer bounds of the willing faculty? To what extent can people be accountable for their actions? These are crucial questions to which a panoply of answers can be given. Political liberalism carefully marked out the bounds of will and responsibility with reference to age, mental capacity, respect for others' freedom, conformity to a particular ethical and legal framework, and so on. As necessary, it also placed specific conditions on their expression in certain realms of social life (restrictions based on sex, congenital deficiencies, race, general interest, access to property, etc.). Liberalism was constantly torn between the ideal of a world built on human freedom and the narrow, impoverished approach to social organization with which the bourgeois elites sought to actualize this ideal.

Liberalism, in short, was a new and extremely powerful modality of relation to the self and the Other, and for this reason history has nothing to gain by portraying it as just another "ideology." More than an ideology, more even than a world view, liberalism corresponds to a mad desire in the entrails of humanity, a faith in the creative continuity between what we can do and what we are entitled to do, between the control we can exert over our lives and the norms that are set out as positive values of community life; a faith that there can be compatibility, if not felicitous complementarity, between the happiness we build within ourselves, through our acts and thoughts, and the happiness of others. Around this faith, this vital reflex, this mental universe, a restrictive mode of social regulation was built – in my terminology, the liberal mode of regulation.

Of course, other ways of realizing the ideal of freedom have been invoked and declared possible, most of them in reaction to liberal regulation (socialism, corporatism, solidarism, anarchism, Catholic social teaching). Bourgeois liberalism in fact interposed itself between a conservative constellation of ideas and a sort of macrocosm of progressive forces that would constantly challenge this mode's fragile hegemony. The whole history of the nineteenth century can be read as a continual recomposition of social forces in which conservatives, liberals, and radicals kept reinventing the ideal of freedom and change central to the liberal worldview in accordance with each one's societal agenda. From utopian socialism to international communism, various successors to classical liberalism were envisioned. Similarly, from conservatism to fascism, different types of reticence and nostalgia – even outright desires to reinstate the past – were thinkable and indeed thought. But in the immense majority of cases, such ideas crystallized into societal agendas centring around a conception of the will and of personal responsibility that places the individual at the centre of history – whether he feels enjoined to adhere to tradition and obey the transcendent will of a supreme being; whether, on the contrary, he is encouraged to pursue his own interest above all and to give free rein to his spirit of initiative, or whether his creativity is to be subsumed within the life of the group or class.

Thus, the broad space of politics stretches out between freedom as an organizing principle and society as a tangible form of organization. A whole century, the nineteenth, would discover how long and tortuous is the path from the thought of personal freedom to its collective expression. If the rationalist dream of the Enlightenment was that of the social fabric expressed as a harmonious, uninterrupted continuum between the individual and the whole, the actual construction of modern societies was to reveal the contradictions and impasses that rendered this idea utopian. Freedom offered new horizons, yes, but the ultimate form taken by the relationship between the individual and the polity (and its avatar the state) remained very much subject to historical contingency.

LIBERALISM, THE STATE, AND THE INDIVIDUAL

The fundamental political dimension of the changes taking place in the administration of crime and poverty during the transition to capitalism can best be discerned in the form taken by the relationship of the part to the whole – the individual to the social whole symbolized by the state. More precisely, the place assigned to the individual in the community, the continuity or lack of continuity between his and the community's interests, and the relative separation between the private and the public suggest the political conditions under which social problems were taken in charge in the nineteenth century.

When interrogating the history of the relations between the individual and the state – the ultimate symbol of the national community – it is necessary to begin by identifying and analyzing the points of contact between them. As a first approximation, three dimensions of the political can be distinguished: the ways in which individuals are represented in the collective, the effectiveness and breadth of executive and bureaucratic power, and the organization of dispute settlement mechanisms under the judicial system (Fecteau 1986a). These distinctions entail that the state be conceived essentially as a means of materializing sovereignty, public regulations, and the power to judge. To this essentially functional definition of the state corresponds an understanding of the individual as the primary unit of sociability, as the elementary particle of the social whole who becomes, throughout the history of democracy and liberalism, the bearer of civil, political, and finally social rights.

A logical sequel to this exercise entails an analysis of the points of contact between the individual and the state. An initial angle of approach is to consider those points where the individual is the *active subject* of the relation: in this category are constructs of political legitimacy as determined through *representation* procedures (elections, parties, decision-making rules, etc.), as well as the multiple types of *recourse* that citizens have to the state, either in its judicial form (litigation) or as a provider of goods and services (grant applications and other forms of assistance, use of public utilities, etc.) (Fougères 1992).

In a second angle of approach, people are the *object* of the relationship. State action on the individual ranges from modes of behavioural supervision (from national identity to civil and criminal codes) to the expansion of regulatory logic throughout various spheres of social life (hygiene, work, commerce, consumption, recreation, etc.). Also included are the organization and administration (direct or private sector-mediated) of basic services such as transportation, currency, or health and social services.

Historical studies of state-individual relations focusing on these points of contact are of great value, to be sure, and in the case of Quebec remain few and far between. But such an analytical enterprise, although it produces a wealth of useful empirical knowledge, oversimplifies the problem and ultimately falls short. It is also necessary to conceptualize the logic underlying these interactions, the manner in which the *connection* between the individual will and the expression of the collective good is made.

One is inevitably struck by the relative linearity of the historical work done on these interactions. Both received wisdom and scholarship hold that a slow erosion of individual autonomy in favour of burgeoning bureaucracy has occurred since the eighteenth century. This process is variously attributed to the ascendancy of bureaucratic rationality (from Hegel to Weber), the implications and imperatives of capital accumulation (from Marx to Gramsci), or the functional needs brought on by the increasing complexity of social life (from Durkheim to Parsons). Whatever the case, we remain face to face with one of the most enduring truisms of the social sciences. Even the "deconstruction" of the concept of the state and the rediscovery, by Foucault and his followers, of the capillarity of powers beyond the state's monopoly on legitimate force, as expressed, for example, in the problematics of "governmentality" (Foucault 2009), succumb to the appeal of linear – or worse, teleological – history. The analytical poles of individual and state are too often deconstructed within a deeply gradualist and formalist framework, and a search for origins or a tracing of genealogies wins out over a careful study of discontinuities. In studies covering a wide range of historical periods, in which the state is variously viewed as a bureaucratic or military apparatus (J. Meyer 1983), a democratic organization (Bénoit 1978), or even an instrument of social regulation (Ewald 1986) or a cultural form (Corrigan and Sayer 1985), the state evolves gradually into a mature form perceptible from the time of its origins. Similarly, the conceptualization of the individual/subject subordinated to state authority is taken to be an invariant historical fact that need never be examined.

My contrary argument is that the history of the state implies above all a history of the diverse, historically changing forms taken by the political organization of human communities. The state is only one possible structural form of the political relation, and even this form undergoes a series of critical transformations throughout its history. Moreover, these transformations are not exhausted by the great radical shifts represented by monarchy, democracy, and contemporary administrative bureaucracy. The contemporary state itself, beyond the apparent continuity suggested by an overly perfunctory analysis of growth patterns derived, perhaps, from statistics on public finances or the civil service, actually undergoes profound changes – so profound that they may lead to a redefinition of how the state is embedded within liberal society.

But there is more. To apprehend individual-state relations demands the identification and study of the conjunctural shifts that upend people's vision of the individual/society relation and the ways in which it is materialized within the social space. As simplistic as it would be to speak of "an" individual grappling with the state since the earliest days of political rationalization, it would be equally reductive to posit "a" state, however "governmentalized," that gradually extended its multiple ramifications over civil society and the individuals of which it is composed. Instead, we must speak of fragile and changing *conjunctures* at which the discourse on the individual and the state is transformed by its confrontation with concrete action and historical modes of state organization, and in each such instance the power dynamics between the social groups in play must be accurately assessed. In other words, the history of individual-state relations exemplifies the complex and changing dialectic woven between discourse and social practices.

Put differently, this history poses the question of the *economy* of relations between the whole and the part, the individual and the collective, within a given society. This economy rests on an ever-problematic encounter between a hegemonic worldview (in the case at hand, the liberal worldview) and the concrete problems posed by the government of men and women. These two poles of reference (worldview and political system), one inscribed within discourse, the other within government institutions and practices, both underwent profound changes in the nineteenth century, driven by the dynamic and dialectic interaction between them.[20] It is necessary to understand these changes and their implications in order to acquire the tools needed to fix the backdrop to the multiple types of relations between individual and state. More specifically, it is necessary to elucidate the variety of ways in which a state can be enmeshed within a market-regulated civil society,[21] as well as the vagaries of the liberal discourse on the individual. To do so is to gain clarity on the lability of the boundaries between private and public.

The Institutionalization of Community Life

The liberal state is not and never has been the supreme reflection of the unity of individuals in a nation. Within the social space thus delimited are a host of sectoral crystallizations, *institutions*, each constituting a socialization mechanism and a pole of community identification unto itself. The state has a monopoly on the legitimate use of force, but it is only one manifestation of the far-reaching institutionalization of the social that epitomizes the development of capitalism. It exists alongside a host of associations, each possessing its own organizational structure and capable of instituting collective action durably over time, and this complex configuration of institutions of different dimensions is central to the political problem of liberal societies. A great many nicknames for the liberal state have been propounded (the minimal, philanthropic, solidarist, corporatist, Keynesian, or neoliberal state, to name several), each representing a different understanding of this complexity and how the state fits into it.

Another way to say this is that the entities created by citizens cannot be viewed as merely intermediate between the state and the individual.[22] Rather, they constitute more or less hierarchical, autonomous groupings which, taken together, provide a framework for social life and inscribe it idiosyncratically in time.[23] Under specific historical circumstances, institutions such as churches, trade unions, or businesses can even present themselves as competitors of the state. They can claim to do better at manipulating meaning, shaping identities, or simply meeting certain collective needs over the long haul. Seen from this angle, the institutions of "civil society" (Rangeon 1986b) can become frankly political from the moment they can claim to administer certain areas of community life in place of the state – education, welfare, and production, for example. The state then has no choice but to reckon with them. The extent to which a government finds itself in this position is closely tied to the historical conjuncture of the corresponding society, and this partly explains why, even given the notably synchronous economic development of Western societies from the mid-nineteenth century onward, such a diversity of models for the organization of the state (compare Germany with the United States, for example) should exist.[24]

The Liberal Discourse on the Singular and the Collective

It becomes important here to delve further into the nature of liberal discourse. The liberal ideology as such is generally defined as a dynamic amalgam of three basic values: freedom, individualism, and property. In classical treatments of the topic from Locke to Mill, the advent of these values thoroughly subverted the feudal order, clearing the way for the rise of the modern world. It was only with the rise of socialist and collectivist ideologies in the second half of the nineteenth century that liberalism finally encountered a worthy adversary, or so it seemed. Suddenly placed on the defensive by the rise of class struggle (or, according to a more "neutral" version, by the contradictions inherent in the industrial era), it soon found itself fighting on two fronts: against communism, and against various forms of corporatism presenting themselves as a third way between capitalism and communism. The Keynesian revolution allegedly consecrated the victory of liberalism, but only to thrust it into even more glaring contradictions, which explains the emergence of neoliberalism in the 1970s. This standard interpretation forms the backdrop to a heroic saga of struggle by individuals against an enterprise of subordination running from monarchic power through to the welfare state. (Indeed, in some versions, it is "freedom" itself that fought this battle.) In this way, the history of state-individual relations becomes, through successive shifts in perspective, the history of liberalism.

A number of things are wrong with this interpretation. First, as shown in the first part of this chapter, the aspirations and values at the root of the modern ethos of progress and liberty are much broader and deeper than the word liberalism can contain. Second, beyond its apparent transhistoricity, liberalism exhibits a particularly problematic and changing relationship to the social whole. It presents itself as a peculiar historical conception of the relations between the whole and its constituent parts, one that is particularly sensitive to the fluctuations of societies making the transition to capitalism.

The Boundaries between Private and Public

On the one hand, there is a state in constant confrontation with other forms of collective social organization; on the other, a liberal discourse varying in synch with the historical construction of individuality in modern societies. Both poles of the confrontation between state and individual, as it is standardly presented, raise difficult analytical challenges, which coincide when considering the "boundary" that would come to separate the private from the public in liberal society.

First, an observation: the democratic struggle against the *ancien régime* was waged in large part by carving out spheres of pertinence, zones of jurisdiction, or spaces of competency from which the fight against what was increasingly perceived as monarchic arbitrariness could be waged.

The distinction between public authority and the individual was henceforth expressed in the form of a clear demarcation between the private and public spheres, a demarcation that quickly became the starting point for thinking about power and the state in these societies. This division was, however, both theoretical and practical, absolute and relative, principial and historical. Even though it underlies the whole galaxy of political representations in the nineteenth century (not to mention the twentieth[25]), it took on an infinite number of changing forms depending on the context. Although the public-private distinction is essential to the world in which modern freedoms were constructed, it never took the form of a sharp, definitive, empirically verifiable dividing line according to which contemporary social formations were structured. This may be why a *spatial* dimension was brought into the discussion.

In discussing this dimension, a degree of terminological ambiguity must be noted. The private/public dichotomy ebbs and flows according to the peculiar rhythms of the societal context in which these domains are embedded. This dichotomy can take three forms.

1. It can be based on a distinction between the intimate and the collective. The construction of the bourgeois ethos in the eighteenth century crucially involved the delimitation of a private realm, a place of intimacy sheltered from the ambient social environment. A barrier of this kind was seen as necessary to protect the individual from the frenzies of public life. The concept of fundamental rights thus came into being as a means of preserving the resulting zone of freedom and safety, and hence the integrity of the person, from society's encroachments.
2. It can also refer by extension to that sphere in which the free pursuit of human interaction, delimited by personal interest, must be sheltered from interference. Adam Smith and the proponents of laissez-faire would invoke this basic distinction in prescribing what they saw as the optimal conditions for national prosperity. Commerce between people, they said, should be maximally unhampered by publicly imposed proscriptions.[26]
3. Finally, during the nineteenth century, this distinction came to correspond to the dividing line between civil society and the state.[27] In a fascinating process, the public space built in the eighteenth century as a bulwark *against* monarchic sovereignty – a locus of debate in which citizens took positions on public affairs[28] – shrank to make room for the implementation and operation of state sovereignty.

> This entailed the emergence of a private sphere that was neither intimate nor exclusively commercial – a sort of depoliticized collective sphere based on the free market in goods and ideas, on a capacity to act that could be viewed as being "outside" the public authorities, or in parallel with them.[29]

But beyond this dividing line central to liberal discourse, beyond the ever-open question of which tasks should be assigned to the democratic state, the distinction between the private and public spheres does not imply any necessary or unavoidable *opposition* between them. The opposition would come to appear unavoidable with the expansion of the state and the broadening of suffrage. At length, liberal thinkers began conceiving of public power as a threat as much as (or more than) a natural expression of the collective will. Particularly after 1850, the private-public divide became a basic axiom of liberal thought.

However, the foregrounding of this divide by the historiography tends to obscure the deeper logic of the liberal distinction between the two spheres, and especially the basic and necessary *continuity* between them. From the outset, the whole idea of a society based on respect for individual liberties is predicated on such continuity. The properly socialized individual, making use of his will in the service of his self-interest rightly understood, will freely enter into a set of emotional or rational, practical or symbolic interactions with others. The sum total of these relations, in their infinite diversity, spontaneously gives rise to an equilibrium forming the very texture of the society. The market is but one of the manifestations of this logic in which all is the outcome of confrontation between free units, but there are many others: to wit, all the forms of association that develop in liberal society, as well as the polity itself, which is an expression of the diversity of freely expressed opinions about the destiny of the whole. The community always transpires as the result of the interindividual relation; it is the expression, in another dimension or on another plane, of the same logic of competition between wills.[30] The state, too, is just an extension of the logic of freedom and competition that structures the private sphere, and for that reason constitutes the supreme collective body, the level at which problems are solved when individuals, acting alone or in association, are unable to solve them without help. In this sense, the state is always fundamental, sometimes "minimal," sooner or later "interventionist," but never superfluous. It is situated both upstream and downstream of the private relation. Upstream, it provides individuals with basic civic education and implements the collective infrastructure necessary for private exchanges to take place. Downstream, it arbitrates disputes through the civil courts, punishes individual excesses through the criminal justice system, takes charge of personal deficiencies through the health and welfare system, and ultimately intervenes wherever private initiative is powerless to handle a problem threatening the survival of the whole.

Given this logic, the liberal imagery of private and public "spheres" inadequately describes the true state of affairs; in fact, this imagery reflects a *crisis* in liberal representation provoked by the crystallization of late-nineteenth-century anti-statist discourse. Classical liberal thought would have spoken instead of areas of jurisdiction, shifting with the evolution of a social formation in time and space.[31] There is nothing essentially minimal about the liberal state, and there are times and circumstances when even a liberal ideologue would countenance a high degree of intervention on its part. A fairer description of it is as a barometer of the health of civil society: the room taken up by the state is inversely proportional to the vigour of private relations within a given collectivity. The private-public distinction, then, becomes primarily a *criterion* for the allocation of responsibilities. State intervention conforms to an internal operational logic rather than a rigid allocation of roles.

That said, certain basic rules cannot be broken. Most importantly, state intervention is to be *general* in scope, applying to every member of the social formation. Only in exceptional cases can it focus on particular situations or individuals. Relatedly, it will always be more fully justified where it involves establishing a *prior* (or if absolutely necessary, a preventive) container for the expression of private initiatives, without supplanting them. Civil and criminal codes, public health regulations, and basic education policies are examples of this kind of intervention. Curative and a posteriori measures are to be reserved for exceptional cases only. Finally, state intervention will tend to take a *normative* and *regulatory* form. Routine management can be entrusted to private initiative, under the watchful eye of the authorities. The state will administer a service only where it is well established that to entrust it to the private sphere would be impossible or dangerous.

HISTORICAL RHYTHMS OF STATE-INDIVIDUAL RELATIONS

The liberal discourse on the individual and the state has played a central, even a hegemonic role in the various modalities according to which aspirations to freedom have been realized since the eighteenth century. But this discourse has changed over time, as illustrated by the lability of the boundaries between private and public. I now look a little closer, diachronically, at the stages in the evolution of state-individual relations, including those moments when conceptions of this dyad changed quite radically.

The Liberal Utopia and the Changing World (1680–1815)

At the risk of profoundly misconceiving it, historians have often depicted the eighteenth century – from Locke to Smith and from Rousseau to Condorcet – as the time when liberalism in its standard sense was rolled out over Western societies. However, important scholarly work has been done in recent decades on a thorough reinterpretation of the classics of seventeenth- and eighteenth-century political and economic thought.[32] The primary contribution of this work has been to show how the undeniable and growing place of the individual in economic and political thought does not at all suggest that these thinkers had, at this early stage, arrived at a concept of "individualism." Their worldview was not one in which the "individual" is an irreducible unit having primacy over society or the community. On the contrary, the fate of the polity was always their primary concern. While the monarchic state may well have been an impediment to individual liberty, the more pressing problem was that the existence of monarchy precluded the possibility of creating a perfect polity into which the new individual could merge. The forces pitted against the monarchy were not motivated by self-interest[33] but by the civic virtue of the subject in the face of monarchic corruption (Pocock 1985, 50–71; Thompson 1975), or by the posited existence of a prior contract founded in nature and reason (Sledziewski 1989, 39–62; Lessnoff 1986). The idea that there could be an opposition between a tutelary state and the private sphere would have seemed outlandish even to Adam Smith, for whom the virtues of the market and the "invisible hand" were in no way inconsistent with the state's ultimate power to regulate economic actors. Smith actually spent more time attacking what he regarded as obstacles to the free circulation of goods and people – most notably, monopolies and corporations of all sorts (Tribe 1978, 80–146).

For certain Enlightenment philosophers, the critique of the state was first and foremost a critique of the arbitrariness represented by its absolutist form, not a fundamental challenge to its pertinence as a regulating mechanism. Their appeals to liberty were aimed at restoring *civic virtue* as the perfect mode of community existence. They sought not to diminish the state but to promote a set of individual attributes essential to the construction of the new society. The individual did not precede the whole; he was subsumed within it. The basic postulate was that civil society, made up of selfish individuals in thrall to all the passions, is an artificial and fragile construct as long as the union of these wills is not postulated by the idea of an initial social contract (Rousseau) or guaranteed by a moderate oligarchic government (Hume), or, for the more radical thinkers, a republican government. The great discovery of the Scottish school of political economy spearheaded by Smith was that these "selfish passions," bolstered by self-interest rightly understood, produce prosperity when they regulate the circulation of goods (Hirschman 1977). It was only a short step to turning this into a principle of political organization – a step taken with the great revolutions of the late eighteenth century. With their arrival, the question of liberty and its tangible political expression was abruptly restored to the centre of political debate. The task at hand was to reconceive the state so as to provide the institutional foundation for the civic virtue vaunted by the Enlightenment.

The most radical forms of revolutionary thought descried artificial obstacles to the natural continuity between virtuous citizens and the collectivity (the state): ministerial corruption, despotic arbitrariness, corporate privilege, and irrational customs inherited from tradition. All these "nuisances" had to be eliminated.[34] In the event, the revolutions took the form of practical enterprises that ultimately laid bare the fragility of this new political realm, as well as the need to contain individual initiative within a codified set of rules. The Napoleonic Code of 1804 can be construed as an attempt to control the excesses of individuals henceforth considered to be free. The market, in particular, had the potential to interfere with the political stability of the nation,[35] and it is in this context that the immense and systematic effort expended to reform the masses in the aftermath of the great revolutions (see chapter 6) must be situated. The task at hand was to cast the individual within the mould of classical civic virtue, a utopian construct to which philanthropy in particular made a major contribution. It had very little to do with individual liberty vis-à-vis the state. This phenomenon sheds light on the notable affinities between modern social policy and one strain of revolutionary thought.[36] It also explains how the utilitarianism of someone like Jeremy Bentham, although firmly founded on the promotion of self-interest, could accommodate a wide-ranging program of state regulation (Bentham 1830). When attained according to the ideal of revolutionary democracy, people's sovereignty appears as both an individual *and* a collective totality, in which there is seamless continuity between the citizen and the polity: as if that unique entity, the individual, found the elements of the polity within himself, in the terms of his own virtue.

The Uncertain Apogee of Liberalism (1830–70)

The Industrial Revolution, the burgeoning nationalitarian movements, and the implementation of censitary democracy formed the backdrop for a massive reconfiguration of political thought. Not only did political economy schematize Smithian thinking; it extended it to the domain of production. It thereby created a comprehensive economic science potentially capable of including the problem of sovereignty and the state within its epistemological frame. More pointedly, a far-reaching reinterpretation of state legitimacy was looming, in the terms posed by the logic of the market economy. This was an inversion of analytical priorities that gave first priority to the individual, rationalized by his awareness of his own interest, and second priority to political organization and the construction of the social.

The capacity of Western governments to adjust to the new logic of the liberal political economy can thus be read as a political choice aimed at "depoliticizing" the social by containing it within the dynamic of civil society.[37] The hegemonic position of liberal discourse in the aftermath of the revolutions not only served to render politics secondary; it also "naturalized" politics, as it were, by making the political sphere a dimension of individual liberty, by making politics subservient to the expression of self-interest. In this sense, the political sphere became not only the logical outcome of a society founded on competing freedoms: it provided for the reproduction of that society by making sure that its basic rules of operation were obeyed.

At that moment when triumphant liberalism redefined its relationship to the state, and thereby to the political sphere, the social relation became a naturalized (and secularized) process in which the individual and not the nation is primary and "sovereign": he must be protected from the collectivity, not the reverse. The space containing the whole profusion of interpersonal relations and sentiments can be defined as primary and prior to the political relation, while also remaining external to it: in this way, it can make a legitimate claim to being "private." But the private as understood here is not a withdrawal from the collective and a retreat into the sphere of the intimate and personal: it *is* the collective, or rather its condition of existence, its constituent unit. Defined in this way, the private sphere includes the worlds of both intimacy and sociability. Meanwhile, a parallel tendency emerges in which the public space is conflated with the domain of state jurisdiction.[38] The only measures that can henceforth be defined as public are those designed to implement formal frameworks for individual liberty and guarantee its full realization and protection. The stewardship of this collective interest clearly rests with the state, the only structure possessing legitimate authority as a result of the democratic manner in which it is constituted. In this ideal world, then, freedom is limited only by the framework collectively placed around it in order to regulate its excesses. Relations between civil society and the state, central to eighteenth-century political thinking, are now to be reinterpreted as relations between two complementary spheres: the private and the public.[39]

Such, at least, is the ideal construct of interindividual relations found in the liberal thought of the day. But already the harsh realities of the transition to capitalism and its social effects were summoning other, more threatening visions of the future onto the horizon. The revolutionary excesses of 1789, and much later the political and workers' revolutions of 1848, suggested the possibility of using the political sphere for purposes other than the promotion of individual liberties and the smooth operation of the market. The democratic legitimacy of the state, and also its social influence, were being called into question by a whole host of phenomena: the breakup of old social relations under the impact of industrialization, the emergence of the "social question" as people scrambled to find a response to rampant poverty, and the promotion by certain radical thinkers of a state-driven policy for administering the masses. With its new democratic legitimacy and concomitant power, the state was also proving itself a potentially major *actor* with the capacity to weave itself into the fabric of social relations to a hitherto unseen extent.[40] The question was now being openly posed as to *how much* intervention was the right amount, and how much would bring on conflict between the state – however democratic – and civil society. It was at this precise moment that the private-public conundrum was clearly stated as a divide between respective (and potentially conflicting) spheres of action.[41]

To posit this dichotomy is, of course, to raise the question of where and how civil society groups and associations fit into it. In this model, the only permanent and ultimately legitimate collectivity is the nation, the polity emanating from the political will to coexist in society. Any other grouping can only result from the contingent acts of free agents operating within civil society. The *association* is the perfect model of this temporary and voluntary coming together of social actors. Any attempt to railroad individuals into an association would be tainted by memories of slavery. Similar distrust was aimed at certain institutionalized components of the social fabric that had been founded on any criterion other than voluntary association (e.g., race, religion, language, or older community forms[42]). Right at the time when association was being acclaimed as the form of sociality of the future, these institutions came to be perceived as potentially lethal forms of social coagulation.[43] The state found itself with no competition as it presided over the establishment of the conditions necessary for the expression of private initiative. In liberal discourse, the state became an instrument whose expansion might be feared but whose legitimacy could never be contested, for it was seen as the political outcome of the liberal market in opinions and desires.

Emerging from this liberal construction of private-public relations in the mid-nineteenth century was a linear historiography of the continual expansion of state power. This historiography depicts the expansion as having occurred at roughly the same pace as the expansion of democratic suffrage and the perception that industrialization was provoking an ever-worsening social crisis. The *boundaries* between private and public shifted, with public interest gradually gaining ground at the expense of market anarchy. Working within this paradigm, some historians attempted a cumulative history of the growth of the state in which the welfare state is the inevitable heir of this process of expansion.[44] Implicit in this history is the postulate of the largely irreducible character of the private and public spheres, the existence of an oppositional dynamic between them, and the resolution of this opposition in favour of the public sphere through the growth of the state. An analysis of what took place after 1870 will serve to ascertain the validity of this historical account.

The Crisis of Liberalism and the Emergence of Critical Discourse (1870–1930)

As the nineteenth century drew to a close, the liberal thinkers' preoccupation with state intervention turned, for many of them, into outright hostility. By then the ideal of liberty had been concretized hegemonically (although only partially, need it be said) for over a century in the form of liberal democracy and the free market in goods and ideas. But by the latter third of the century, the liberal institutions were generating major impasses and contradictions as a result of social conflict and their own basic logic – that of profit and the market. Free enterprise was well on the way to evolving into monopolistic hegemony; the "voluntary" association of citizens had become a necessity, given the need for isolated workers to unite in self-defence; formal equality before the law could not hide the fact that mass poverty had become a chronic condition. The bourgeois ideal of the nuclear family had butted up against the imperatives of the urban labour market, which employed women and children. Liberal individualism, betrayed by the civil society it had done so much to birth, could hardly find consolation in its control over public institutions. The extension of suffrage now gave a voice to the losers in the competition, or at least some of them: they would from now on be addressing their demands directly to the state. Given these developments, what prevented the state from transcending its formal status as the collective expression of individualities to become a major *social actor* in its own right? The revolution of 1848, by initiating a debate over the right to welfare and by implementing important social measures (the public workshops), had already demonstrated how the locus of liberal democratic legitimacy could be transformed, under pressure from the masses, into a tool for action. That tool could be turned to purposes very different from the promotion of the sovereign individual.

To assert in this context that liberal ideology found itself on the defensive would be a euphemism. It would be more accurate to say that in the wide-ranging debate over what the new society should look like, liberal discourse rapidly ceased to be a central point of reference for the future of humanity. It was increasingly reduced to a personalist ideal with no global positive program – a mere personal ethics with claims to represent a political agenda. At a time when the future seemed profoundly in question, the ideal of societal harmony arising as the ineluctable historical product of free rivalry between individuals was unmasked as a utopian fantasy. A future in which self-seeking behaviour risked turning into ceaseless societal conflict was a future to be feared. Reeling from the blows, liberal discourse was transformed into anti-statism. In defiance of the entire liberal tradition, it turned to promoting the individual *in opposition to* the state and denouncing the weaknesses of democracy.[45]

This shift is fundamental enough to be dwelt on for a moment.[46] It could be demonstrated, for example, that what remained of liberal discourse at this juncture rested on postulates antithetical to the liberalism of everyone from Constant to Mill. Individual liberty was being dressed up as a biological law of the species, with Darwinism drawn on to provide pseudoscientific validation for the ethic of competition. Praise for freedom of association gave way to warnings of the potential for various groups to impose constraints on the individual. Trust in the infinite possibilities of freedom, in human progress, became profound skepticism as to the perfectibility of the individual, under the influence of genetic theories in particular.[47]

But the clearest indicator of the decline of classical liberalism was arguably its profound *depoliticization*. As already stated, the political dimension is central to the liberal worldview. It constitutes this worldview not merely as a discourse but as a societal agenda, one that gives out onto a collective vision for the future. Several developments, however, were combining to consign the liberal ideal of a polity strictly derived from market forces to oblivion – most notably, the extension of suffrage (with the onset of political demands by feminist movements) and the intensification of pressure from the working classes (in organized or unorganized form) for a more active state role in resolving social problems. In reaction, many liberal thinkers turned to critiquing not only the state but politics per se. They decried the political sphere, denounced it as a field of struggle open to every power instinct – every abuse and instance of favouritism on the part of irrational, ignorant profiteers and strivers.[48] Some even began to question majority rule, the sacrosanctness of legislative acts, and ultimately the very sovereignty of the democratic state – "the great political superstition," in the words of Spencer ([1884] 1969, 151–83).[49] The basic political rationale of liberalism was overturned: no longer the outcome of free deliberation by property owners, nor an exclusive arena for the nation's elite and its political parties, the state had to be regarded with suspicion.[50]

Two sets of discourses and social practices sprouted up on the ruins of liberal ideals, on the unresolvable aporias of a discourse on the individual that no longer had any use for the collective. These two alternatives prospered and achieved widespread currency.

The first was socialism, whose discourse on the state is oddly parallel to that of liberalism.[51] In its great political and social struggle against liberalism, socialism (in all its various guises) adopted and assimilated its adversary's unproblematic postulation of complementarity between community and individual, though changing their order of primacy. Community became synonymous with class, transcending both the individual and the associations of civil society.

The second, gathering steam in the 1880s, was a renaissance of communitarian thought, a vast discursive universe that would generate a host of proposals presented as a "third way" between socialism and liberalism, communism and capitalism. From the communitarianism of Ferdinand Tönnies to that of Otto Friedrich von Gierke; from the solidarism of Léon Bourgeois to the organic solidarity of Émile Durkheim and the "new liberalism" of the English reformers; from the institutionalism of Maurice Hauriou to the social Catholicism of *Rerum Novarum*, and from the social economy of Charles Gide to the cooperativist ideal, a whole profusion of models ushered in what Jacques Donzelot (1984) has called the "invention of the social." Too little study has been devoted to this often contentious buzzing of ideas and projects born out of the "crisis of liberalism."[52] Certain scholars have perfunctorily depicted it as the relatively fertile soil from which the various forms of corporatism emerged, while others have identified it with the emergence of the welfare state (Ewald 1986).

What was really going on was a relentless search for ways to actualize the collective within a given social space. Put another way, it was the end of the peculiar Western episteme in which the problem of individual/society relations had been inscribed since the end of the eighteenth century if not earlier. The (re)discovery of the group as an autonomous, politically viable means of constituting the social would have a profound impact on conceptions of the social order. It would first lead to a radical critique of individualism: Durkheim's whole oeuvre (but especially *The Division of Labor in Society* [1893] 1984) is erected on the postulate that there exists a social superstructure above the individual, and strives to elucidate the ways in which community life is structured. Sociology, as a new science of the social, was thus built on a critique of the primacy of the individual[53] and on a search for a more or less organic logic to life in society.

These various schools of thought were not content to critique individualism. They challenged all the other tenets of liberalism as well, including its conception of the workings of society and the construction of the social fabric. They countered the constraints of competition with the imperatives of solidarity as a mode of social organization. Likewise, they rejected the generativity of conflict between extremes in favour of an affirmation of *consensus* as a mode of conflict resolution and a precondition for freedom.[54] Finally, the emergence of statistics and actuarial science, the appearance of what might be called a "logic of the mean,"[55] served gradually to replace the principle of personal responsibility with that of professional or social risk (Ewald 1986, 229–348; Fecteau 1994b).

Crucially, the discovery of the "social" did not just imply a redefinition of individual-community relations, with a consequent remaking of the rules of society. This discovery also called the role of the state into question. History, always prone to teleology, has portrayed the period from 1870 to 1920 as the one that witnessed the rise of the welfare state.[56] I maintain, on the contrary, that its emergence necessitated a fundamental reconciliation between liberalism and the state, which would have to await the great crisis of the 1930s and especially the Second World War. The postulate underlying this analysis, which must remain a hypothesis at this stage, is that the emergence of the welfare state is to be distinguished from the general increase in state intervention.[57] The years 1880 to 1930 must be understood as a unique period of radical change that only a simplistic teleological (or genealogical!) analysis could designate as the beginnings or origin of the welfare state.

Throughout these years, the alternatives proposed to the abusive operation of the market, beyond the mere suppletive expansion of state power, generally share a *critique* of the state that revoiced the old liberal mistrust even as it went beyond it. Solidarism, corporatism, Catholic social teaching, and fascism all regarded the ongoing transformation of the mode of regulation as a renaissance of the social in opposition to both the individual and the state, the two dominant and complementary poles of the liberal world view. While the logic of the welfare state entailed giving the state a central managerial role in social affairs, the "discovery" of the social in the late nineteenth century – even though it went along with a significant degree of politicization – also implied the relegation of the state to secondary status. The theories of jurists such as Maurice Hauriou (1909) and Léon Duguit (1908) were typical in arguing that the law should allow other bodies constituted within the nation, *in parallel* with the state, to participate in the production of rules. As an example of this approach, this era witnessed the first appearance of social law, a body of law that, although collective, was not exhausted by state-generated legislation; it acknowledged the social and indeed political legitimacy of other types of association. Catholic social teaching, and the social entities to which it gave rise, partake of this logic.

For these thinkers, when society is approached as a conundrum, a difficult problem to be solved, the state represents only one legitimate form of the collectivity, albeit the farthest-reaching and most powerful. Government intervention in social affairs is only legitimate to the extent that "intermediate" bodies (not "civil society" in the liberal sense) prove powerless to intervene. The whole debate over social insurance, for example, reveals this tension, or competition, between autonomous social organization and the role of the state. It was not until the Keynesian revolution that the state's role as the sole provider of welfare was recognized. This historical moment would, moreover, correspond to the rehabilitation of the individual and the expansion of his rights, henceforth redefined as social rights. But that is another story.

* * *

The ideal of freedom forms the foundation for all the competing ideas about society that emerged in the wake of the Enlightenment, including the liberal worldview and its alternatives. This chapter has retraced the corresponding interpenetrations between discourse and practice, in the process analyzing how the discourse reveals an inventory of sorts in which it is possible to imagine, as regards the social fabric, the logic according to which the part is nested in the whole, and how this logic changed throughout history.

As a necessary prior step, it has been important to grapple with the fundamental values structuring representations of time and agency in the embryonic democratic capitalist societies, as well as the liberal discourse that was the hegemonic expression of these values. This discourse was central to the transformation of individual-society relations in the nineteenth century and to the instatement of a new mode of regulation, some of whose manifestations are examined in what follows. Moreover, the presence of the liberal conception of the world in the field of analysis constitutes a major epistemological obstacle. For those who idealize it and those who criticize it alike, the bourgeois version of liberalism is the unavoidable horizon of any analysis of individual-state relations in the nineteenth century. It is almost as if the big question of the organization of political life in modern societies (for that is what is at issue) can be reduced to a comparison between a discourse seen as hegemonic and the social reality underlying it.

I have tried to demonstrate – rather summarily no doubt – that liberalism, as the apotheosis of a yearning for freedom, forms the common substrate and the condition of possibility for the shifting forms taken by the social fabric in the nineteenth century. But this common substrate could and did manifest itself in a wide variety of ideologies, institutions, and concrete realizations. Furthermore, it rendered increasingly fragile and disputed the restricted, narrow version of liberalism preferred by the mid-century hegemonic bourgeoisie. The ideal of freedom could not, in the end, find full expression in that kind of liberalism.

For this reason it has been crucial, in retelling the history of the dialectical relationship between liberalism and the nineteenth-century evolution of Western societies, to situate the disruptions that took place within a *diachronic* analysis; these disruptions show that if each era defines its own logic, it does so not in a search for origins so much as in an ever-renewed, always fraught rereading of systems of thought and practices of the past. As has often been the case, the many different ways of *avoiding* writing the history of our era – genealogical research, the cult of origins, teleological analysis, lazy postulates about the endurance of ideological forms – become evident in this connection.

3

The Regulation of Crime and Poverty: The Old System in Crisis[1]

The ways in which poverty and crime are dealt with are among the main indicators of the principles on which a given mode of regulation rests. Thus, any discussion of the liberal logic of regulation calls for careful study of the transition toward this logic with respect to the conception of both crime and poverty. This transition was not a gradual shift, a more or less contingent modernization of the administration of the new social problems. A simplistic historical chronology might lead one to believe that a whole set of institutions and corresponding policies was implemented in a steady continuum as new functional needs arose. But that was not at all the case. In general, the transition to a new order is an eminently fragile and fraught process with a regulating logic of its own – a logic whose deep meaning will be betrayed when it is deformed by future occurrences.

In Lower Canada (as elsewhere), in the half century running from the Constitution Act of 1791 to the Act of Union of 1840, the traditional modes of poverty and crime regulation went into profound crisis as a result of harsh criticism levelled against them, and also because of ongoing economic, political, and social transformations. An analysis of this crisis with reference to the discussion so far presented in this book leads to two preliminary remarks.

The first concerns the notional space of crime and poverty. These phenomena (like the state, the family, etc.) are long-range historical constructs, and their historical analysis can easily accommodate all manner of anachronisms and teleologies. For example, the persistence of certain words (such as "deserving poor," "work," "moral reform," "treatment," "crime," or "imprisonment"), their use over long periods of historical time, renders their meanings deeply ambiguous and ultimately largely dependent on the peculiar logic of charity or punishment in which they are embedded. And, from the Middle Ages to our day, that logic has been utterly transformed – not once, but several times. Consequently, it is important to study synchronically, in their historical context, the ways in which these various notions intertwine with the dimensions of a complex historical phenomenon such as poverty or crime.

The second remark relates to the apparent paradox that while a diverse range of modes of administration of crime and poverty have existed throughout history, they have generally been channelled into a relatively limited repertoire of "solutions."[2] Consider crime: how should it be punished? By locking up or physically punishing the criminal, by banning the crime? Is it enough to punish, or is it also important to try to prevent recidivism? Or consider poverty. Anyone wishing to help the poor has to answer or at least reckon with a set of long-running questions. Who is poor? To what extent do poor people deserve the help given them? Who is responsible for organizing and providing that help? Should it be given in the form of money, employment, or perhaps some form of temporary or continuing moral support? Should poor people be institutionalized? What is the goal: eliminating poverty, preserving an immutable social rank, personal sanctification, altruistic solidarity? Inasmuch as the treatment of crime and poverty is always a reflection of the inequalities that structure a given polity, the different manifestations of those inequalities may crystallize in a specific economy of measures whose origins often date far back in time. It becomes difficult to grasp the meaning of the changes that have swept through the modes of regulation of crime and poverty throughout history, particularly in the tumultuous nineteenth century.

Another good example of this methodological problem concerns the notion of reforming the criminal, which is found in Western thought from the fourteenth century (if not earlier) to our day. On a rather trivial level, reform means erasing the stigma brought by the perpetrator upon himself. But a whole set of questions then arises. How should the crime and its perpetrator be dealt with? What constitutes an offence, and what are its effects? How is responsibility to be assigned? What are the causal processes at play? Who should punish each particular crime; in other words, what is the jurisdictional hierarchy of punishment? What methods should be used to punish criminals, and what is their underlying rationale? Can criminals be reintegrated into society, and if so, how? While each of these dimensions has its own temporality, they tend to come together within a given space and time, thus imparting a historical structure, a tangible manifestation, a meaning, to the idea of reform. The notion of reform, then, is devoid of analytical relevance unless it is understood within a specific historical logic of punishment.[3] The same is true for the concept of charity, which can be found in such a variety of normative economies that the utterance of the word itself poses more problems than it solves.[4]

Likewise, since the elements of any given system of punishment or welfare belong to a specific economy of regulation, they must not only be studied synchronically but also set within the overall context of the society in which they exist. This means not only the existence of an identifiable, historically specific logic articulating and merging the various aspects of these systems but also the existence of what might be called a *political economy* of punishment and welfare: *economy* because modes of intervention and institutions are configured in a particular manner as a function of the class, gender, and race dynamics structuring the society and the material conditions of the era; *political* insofar as this configuration is primarily dictated by modes of collective organization and conceptions of how individuals are or should be integrated into the whole. Therefore, only a precise, rigorous analysis of discourse on poverty and crime, combined with a careful study of welfare and punishment practices, has any hope of assessing the effectiveness and evolution of a mode of regulation.

These two remarks point to the difficulty of analyzing *change*, transition, between different historical approaches to poverty and crime. In order to write the history of the prison or of welfare, the shifting logic of regulation in which they are inscribed must be historicized. This means grasping the contradictions experienced by the system existing at any given time, the structure of the critiques levelled at it, and the paths leading to the deployment of a new logic of punishment or charity.[5]

In line with these analytical constraints, this chapter begins by briefly studying the essentially feudal mode of crime and poverty regulation that existed in Lower Canada up to the early nineteenth century, its general structure, and the state's role in its operation. The chapter goes on to consider the ways in which that system went into crisis and how various changes were made in an attempt to resolve it. It concludes by evaluating the limits and constraints specific to the transition between modes of regulation in Lower Canada.

A FEUDAL LOGIC OF REGULATION

In late-eighteenth-century Lower Canada, crime and poverty were still being dealt with according to an essentially feudal logic of regulation. In this area as in numerous others, the trauma of the conquest had left this logic largely intact – at least temporarily. Crime, poverty, and mental illness sat ensconced within a social dynamic essentially contained within urban and rural communities. Municipalities, villages, trades, and religious orders were primary points of reference. Each individual had his rightful place or *status* within this dense network of social hierarchies.[6]

When anyone deviated from the established order, their behaviour was handled by the various forms of collective organization existing within society. In feudal systems, crime in particular was primarily a private affair, a disruption of acceptable relations between individuals; only secondarily was it a matter for the sovereign's exemplary justice, and that only after the historical moment when his power became durably established. Similarly, poverty was merely the lot of the immense majority of people. If a person found himself disabled or in dire straits for reasons beyond his control, his peers, relatives, or community were expected to look after him. In all but the gravest cases, the community took charge of administering the relief or the sanction.[7] This model presupposed the stable reproduction of the communities in question. Things changed, however, as the economy was steadily monetized, feudal and dynastic wars disrupted normal life, and epidemics swept over Europe. An increasingly dense stratum of people subsisted at the margins of society, eking out a living from precarious urban trades, begging, or petty theft, detached from whatever community might once have been theirs.

Against this backdrop, and particularly in response to the great crises of the fourteenth century, the power of the state began to take shape. The feudal state (or the urban patriciates in some countries) gradually acquired and made increasingly frequent use of its capacity to repress the extreme manifestations of this endemic crisis of feudal regulation. Most prominently, the first vagrancy and wage labour laws were enacted, and institutions specifically directed at certain categories of marginal people and societal rejects were established.[8] General hospitals and beggars' prisons were built in France, houses of correction and workhouses in England and (shortly afterward) the United States. The feudal-mercantilist state thereby sought to increase the collective wealth of the kingdom by forcing the idle poor and "vagabonds" (as they were called) to work, thereby also resolving its problems of poverty and mendicancy. These policies were, however, an abject failure, and the critical reception they were often accorded was indicative of a logic of regulation relying entirely on community control. The vagrant or troublemaker, the outcast par excellence, deserved nothing from the community he had rejected (and/or been banned from). Daniel Defoe wrote:

1. There is in England more labour than hands to perform it. And consequently a want of people, not of employment.
2. No man in England, of sound limbs and senses, can be poor merely for want of work.
3. All our workhouses, corporations and charities for employing the poor ... are, and will be public nuisances, mischiefs to the nation which serve to the ruin of families, and the increase of the poor.
4. That it is a regulation for the poor that is wanted in England, not a setting them to work ...
   'Tis the men that won't work, not the men that can get no work, which make the numbers of our poor; all the workhouses in England, all the overseers setting up stocks and manufactures won't reach this case; and I humbly presume to say, if these two articles are removed, there will be no need of the other. (Defoe 1704)

Meanwhile, the king's criminal justice continued to be based on exemplary public punishment, which doubled as a deterrent to others contemplating the same crimes and proof of the sovereign's power to preserve the immanent order of things.[9]

In this context, the public authorities were slow to curtail disruptive phenomena that exceeded the self-regulating capacities of local communities. Beyond its narrow insertion into the local community dynamic (a matter to which I return), the central state possessed neither the financial wherewithal nor the administrative staff necessary to implement a "national" network of correctional and welfare institutions, and thus to make good on its ambitions. It had to rely heavily on the local authorities, and in some instances the church, for assistance. The monarchy was in essence a minarchy before that term existed. Outside the big cities, state-run institutions of confinement, including prisons, houses of correction,[10] and workhouses, were relatively modest.[11] The great majority of studies show, moreover, that these institutions were simply repositories and had no bona fide treatment policy. They were places where the bodies of those who "have no purpose"[12] could be warehoused en masse, thus providing a makeshift solution to a glaring problem.[13] As for persons who found themselves isolated in the community due to illness, infirmity, or insanity, the churches could take care of them. Certain religious congregations were founded specifically for this purpose, while some pre-existing congregations created institutions to suit the purpose.[14] There was no question of a "rational" or functional division of responsibility for the management of these populations. This treatment of bodies was simply incorporated into a communitarian worldview in which, from the family to the sovereign, every state, every social body, bore the consequences of the inequality arising from immutable differences in status.[15]

Once detached from the community, whether because of extreme poverty, an accident, a catastrophe, or by being banished, these nameless members of the masses were often parked in Church-based institutions (lazarettos, hôtels-dieu, etc.) or, later, in institutions run by the monarchy or the municipalities (general hospitals, beggars' prisons). Thus assembled, these persons lived the life of the shut-in. Abandoned children, elderly people without families, vagrants, the sick, the incurable, the insane: all were locked up according to a logic in which care, custody, and quarantine were inextricably bound together. Exclusion from family or community networks led to a non-space, a nowhere land administered by religious or lay staff possessing varying degrees of specialization.

In fact, the mercantilist view of poverty that went along with the earliest institutions of systematic confinement may be seen as the final version of an older economy of the poor founded on a perpetually entertained confusion between the poor and the masses in general. Poverty was less a regrettable lack of something than the inescapable condition of a world predetermined by an immanent order of things. The anthropologist Bartolomé Clavero has studied this unfamiliar-seeming world, in which charity was but another name given to a relationship of reciprocity and deference between people of different social status. Charity, in this sense, was not a *policy* intended to restore a measure of equality among individuals, much less a pursuit of any kind of solidarity, but a *custom* whose existence reasserted the immutable, paternalistic distance between people of different status.

> Neither did law occupy the whole terrain and it was not sufficient unto itself. An order of charity preceded and guided it ... The relative absence of juridical treatises on whole areas of social life is striking ... The law hardly concerned itself at all with domestic forms of the *oiconomia* and with familial forms of wealth creation. It is not so much that there existed a vacuum: the problem in this area is that virtues were paramount and charity took precedence. (Clavero 1996, 142)[16]

This mode of regulation subsisted largely unaltered in certain colonial societies, although it was inflected by the specific features of the societal formation in which it was embedded. Early on, New France had the traditional charitable institutions: the hôtels-dieu of Quebec City (1639) and Montreal (1644), to which two general hospitals were added in 1642. The hôtels-dieu mainly took care of the sick poor while the general hospitals housed invalids, mental patients, beggars, and a few pensioners paying for their room and board. As of the 1680s, an ephemeral poor relief office and a few ordinances banning begging filled out this minimal structure of welfare and control. Meanwhile, the king's criminal justice dealt out the ultimate exemplary sanction to those committing the few offences considered particularly disruptive to public order (Lachance 1984).

Once again, what is notable here is the *thinness* of this bureaucracy. Just a few dozen cases were housed in any given institution or processed by the criminal courts each year. The small size of the colonial population was obviously a factor, but even more important was the prevailing feudal logic of welfare, in which access to the hôtels-dieu and general hospitals was a "privilege" reserved for certain people excluded from community-level assistance.[17]

The English conquest changed nothing about the situation. The charitable institutions, like the religious congregations administering them, survived the surrender of Montreal and the Royal Proclamation of 1763. Despite threats of suppression, these religious communities quickly made themselves indispensable to their new masters, who would subsidize them before long. The fact that these institutions were already fulfilling basic charitable functions in an almost exclusively Catholic society explains in part why the British Poor Law system was not introduced into Quebec after the conquest.[18]

The criminal justice system underwent a similar evolution. If much has been made of the transition to English criminal law, it is because the institutional and legal disruption that it occasioned was an important feature of the abrupt substitution of one colonial power for another. Nevertheless, the basic logic of operation of the penal system remained unchanged, with British penal structures being swapped in for French ones in relatively short order.[19] A striking continuity is observable into the early nineteenth century as regards both the populations concerned by the penal system and its primary function.

This continuity is notable in terms of how local power was exercised. Here, the work of Donald Fyson is indispensable. Significantly inflecting my older thinking on this subject,[20] Fyson highlighted the peculiar workings of the old regulating system at the local level:

> The criminal system [was] one of several primary tools in the regulation of community disputes, rather than an instrument of last resort ... going before a justice to make a complaint, far from being a last resort, was one of several primary mechanisms which people used in response to aggressions against them. (Fyson 1995, 401, 404)

The development of a radical critique of the old justice system, to which I return in part 2, might give one the impression that punishment was organized in such a way that it had an extremely limited effect on most interactions between individuals. This is certainly the case, for example, for the highly centralized and formalized superior courts, which judged only a miniscule proportion of offences. Most of these were crimes that, because of their gravity or the status of the person committing them, outstripped local communities' capacity for self-regulation, especially in the cities. In Quebec after the conquest, the Court of King's Bench was disproportionately called on to judge British colonists, who accounted for at most 5 to 10 percent of the population but 50 to 60 percent of convicts in the years 1764 to 1791. The criminal justice system was clearly handling the exceptional, the excluded. The fact that French Canadians were not found in these courts testifies less to a boycott of the legal system on the part of that community than to its remarkable capacity to deal with crimes at the local level.[21] The individuals who found themselves facing this tier of royal justice were those beyond the reach of community conflict resolution. Thus, our analysis of cases heard by the Court of King's Bench in Quebec City from 1791 to 1815 shows that of eighty-one cases in which the defendant's profession is identifiable, 25 percent were British soldiers.

But the situation was very different at the local level, where the operation of the justice system revolved around that central personage known as the justice of the peace. He was responsible for exercising another age-old function of the king's justice: the arbitration of conflicts occurring within the communities of the realm. Recent historiography has done much to highlight the peculiar dynamic in which the operation of justice was intimately connected with the customs, traditions, practices, and strategies of the families and social groups who made up the fabric of village or artisanal communities.[22] Terms such as "infrajudicial" and "internormative" have been used to describe the phenomenon at play here, which reflects the peculiarity of the "state" arising out of the feudal mode of regulation; to wit, that it partakes of both a coercive (or suppletive) logic in which the state's power comes down (inadequately and very partially) on the marginalized *and* a communitarian logic in which the king's justice is deftly integrated into the community itself, into the social regulation of conflicts between subjects.[23] Fyson has shown how the complaint process was used in Quebec to bring community conflicts before justices of the peace. The cases heard by the local justice system fell into two main categories: assault and other violence, and contravention of local police regulations (especially as regards permits). Noteworthy here is the extremely limited extent of the law enforcement *initiated* by local authorities. The criteria, timing, and conduct of a prosecution were all under the plaintiff's control. This system often proved remarkably efficient, its agents perfectly competent – provided that they were permitted to regulate social relations on the basis of tradition and local custom, without interference from a central government which, for the time being, made no attempt to impose a more all-encompassing normative system. When the rise of democracy and liberalism created a pressing need to formalize and centralize this normative logic, the old regulating system would quickly come to appear outmoded and ineffective.[24]

TOWARD A NEW MODE OF REGULATION

Insofar as the old forms of community solidarity were torn down with the decline of feudalism, one might try to argue that the feudal mode of regulation contained within itself the structural conditions of its own crisis. The relative fragility of this regulatory logic is further highlighted by the limited intervention capacity of the monarchic state (beyond its capacity to pass laws) or even the local authorities (apart from their arbitration functions), as well as the overlapping or duplication of penal or welfare measures (since royal initiatives only supplemented or added to traditional measures). The fragility is misleading, though, in that the breakup of regulatory entities, their dissemination to the local level, and the large measure of autonomy thus granted to those who intervened directly gave this system for the management of poverty and crime a remarkable degree of efficiency and longevity. The crisis manifested itself with increasing regularity when endemic poverty took forms that could no longer be handled by the traditional institutions, whether community-based, local, or monarchical, and when ever-present crime began to pose a systematic threat to public order. The crisis centred, of course, on the cities, those places of freedom and licence that served as a catchment for the many people excluded from rural employment. These people flowed into and merged with the existing population of people plying obsolete trades, soldiers and sailors who had basically deserted their companies, beggars, vagrants, people selling various wares on the street. Here, in the vibrant, teeming activity of these unhygienic, ill-lit neighbourhoods and streets, the elites' fears mushroomed. The upper classes feared these dank cesspools where moral injunctions met their end, where the strong arm of the king's law enforcement groped around in a void – where all hopes for a well-policed, well-regulated society evaporated. It was a very old fear, as old as the big feudal cities. But as the nineteenth century got underway and the revolutions taught people to expect a better world, as the initial stages of the Industrial Revolution consigned old ways of producing and living to the past, the endemic crime and poverty of the big cities began to look intolerable. For some people, these evils – in their hideous ordinariness and their suspiciously frequent cohabitation with each other – epitomized a world well on the way to losing the bearings that made it possible for the traditional social fabric to reproduce itself. For others, they were the deplorable signs of a world incapable of taking up the challenge of modernity and its auspicious horizons. This implicit alliance between conservative nostalgia and liberal aspiration yielded a novel consensus among the dominant classes, beyond the various solutions and reform proposals to which we shall come. From this moment it was possible to envision comprehensive administrative models as alternatives to the old system, whose structural weaknesses were becoming clear, in Lower Canada as throughout the West.

These developments help explain the intensity of the criticism of penal and welfare approaches heard throughout the West in the late eighteenth century, and in Lower Canada in the first decades of the nineteenth – criticism that would not cease until the modern institutions of punishment and welfare were finally in place. Even in the early days, some observers were aware that far more than mere institutional reform was needed. The first thing to note is how the tenor of the criticism shifted during this period. What had begun with Henry Fielding, Cesare Beccaria, and Voltaire as a critique of penal *procedure,* for example, became – with Jeremy Bentham and John Howard in England and with Benjamin Rush in the United States – a defence of a systematic model of punishment by *confinement.*[25]

Conceptions of how to address poverty evolved in parallel. In the classical era, the mercantilist notion of the poor as an immanent and necessary social category had led to both local management of contingencies (the English Poor Laws being an extreme example) and the brutal internment and repression of people falling into the most extreme categories of poverty – beggars and vagrants – who were often locked up willy-nilly with invalids, old people, abandoned children, and prostitutes. These holding pens served to rid the realm of surplus members of the population not dealt with by local regulating mechanisms. In the waning years of the eighteenth century (and in parallel with Howard's humanistic campaign), a completely different idea appeared: that it was possible to design institutions in the interests of reform and rehabilitation, of saving lost souls, and that the enlightened elites could use these institutions to promote a mass transformation of public morals. This notion found form in a far-reaching societal endeavour in which penitentiaries, workhouses, and other institutions became the tools of choice for the transformation of the people. The critical discourse in question was recurrent and supranational in scope because it was believed that the birth of the modern nation required nothing less. The inadequacies of the old mode of regulation were pointed out for the sole purpose of building a new and comprehensive one.

One important feature of this new mode is that it ultimately treated poverty and crime as two aspects of a single societal dysfunction. Poverty and indigence among the masses – in the increasingly hideous, socially intolerable guise of "pauperism" – could also manifest themselves as crime. Both could be construed as the ultimate expression of a profoundly maladaptive character trait identifiable not just at the outer margins of society but in the whole working class. The distinctions among these institutions – e.g., between the house of correction and the workhouse, the house of refuge and the prison, the hospital and the insane asylum – were more a function of the specific conditions of confinement (criminal or charitable) than of any essential difference thought to exist or be necessary at the level of problems, clienteles, or programs. In short, poverty, illness, and crime were henceforth apprehended as constituent parts of a general phenomenon of societal disruption. This was well expressed by Pierre-Jean-Georges Cabanis, who proposed that prisons and hospitals be incorporated into a single policy:

> The suppression of begging is so closely tied to the organization of public relief that it is doubtless quite impossible to separate them. How indeed

can one pronounce begging to be a crime if the public authority has not, on behalf of the nation, provided relief sufficient to prevent or alleviate poverty; if it has not provided work for every individual who has or claims to have none? (Cabanis 1798, 2)[26]

POVERTY AND CRIME AS A SOCIETAL CHALLENGE

The initial stages of the transition to capitalism were therefore a time of both grand utopian reform schemes and deep-seated nostalgia for a past soon idealized. How could it have been otherwise when centuries-old political systems collapsed in the space of just a few decades, leaving the stage empty for unknown and untried democratic aspirations; when new methods of production herded an impoverished and marginalized population into the cities even as these same techniques yielded wondrous technical innovations and commercial exploits; when the eternal values of tradition were struck with the full force of desires for change and progress? Even political economy, that science of hard-headed certitudes, had yet to acquire the hegemony it would soon enjoy in the academic world and among the captains of industry.

People hadn't yet learned how to conjugate society in the singular. Given the (apparently) solid foundational status of Enlightenment thought at this time, the construction of new societies (or the reconstruction of old societies) was bound to appear as a *collective* challenge. There was no way of starting from the individual and arriving at a complex society, whether structured by a democratic state or by divine right. The power of the polity could be conceptualized in only two ways: as the expression of the common will of citizens or the undivided loyalty of subjects. Everyone – monarchists and republicans, legitimists and democrats, conservatives and liberals alike – could agree at least that the social upheavals associated with the transition to the new order were a concern for the political authorities first and foremost. Power, whether conceived as a cause or a result,[27] was directly implicated in the resolution of these problems.

This principle was especially applicable to poverty. Dean (1991) and Procacci (1993) have shown how social inequalities in a society claiming to be democratic can be reconceptualized as a *political* problem. Beyond "natural" variation in talents, poverty in Enlightenment-era societies was bound to be an obstacle to de facto equality. Society is what citizens make of it, provided they are given the chance to realize their potential and aspirations. Already, Enlightenment-era thought, and especially the revolutionary variants thereof, postulated the administration of poverty as a primary responsibility of the state. Montesquieu wrote:

> The alms given to a naked man in the street do not fulfil the obligations of the state, which owes to every citizen a certain subsistence, a proper nourishment, convenient clothing, and a kind of life not incompatible with health ...
>
> The riches of the state suppose great industry. Amidst the numerous branches of trade, it is impossible but some must suffer; and consequently the mechanics must be in a momentary necessity.
>
> Whenever this happens, the state is obliged to lend them a ready assistance; whether it be to prevent the sufferings of the people, or to avoid a rebellion. In this case hospitals, or some equivalent regulations, are necessary to prevent this misery. (Montesquieu [1748] 1777, 2: 156–7)

In England, Adam Smith was saying basically the same thing:

> No society can surely be flourishing and happy, of which the far greater part of the members are poor and miserable. It is but equity, besides, that they who feed, clothe and lodge the whole body of the people, should have such a share of the produce of their own labour as to be themselves tolerably well fed, clothed and lodged. (Adam Smith, *The Wealth of Nations*, quoted in Himmelfarb 1984, 52)

The French Revolution would add the obligation of civic solidarity to the reason of state:

> In a well-ordered Republic, each citizen has some property, alms do not wither courage; the aristocracy disguised as public charity does not command servitude, the beggar's name is unknown, and the Republic alone can enforce the great law of universal beneficence, by means of wise regulations and a rational economy. Yes, I speak of their rights, because in a democracy under construction, *everything must conduce to the elevation of each citizen above his primary needs* – by means of labour if he is able-bodied, education if he is a child, or relief if he is infirm or elderly. (*Rapport Barère*, quoted in Hatzfeld 1989, 280)[28]

One could hardly find a better encapsulation of the continual reference to "happiness" that appears in the founding texts of the epoch[29] and underlies a philosophy eminently optimistic about the future of human society, once liberty has been won.

But Enlightenment humanism does not boil down to humanitarian lip service. Too little note has been taken of the relatively large sums of money deployed to fight poverty in the late eighteenth century. The French Revolution, for example, confiscated clergy property and attempted, in an effort without historical precedent, to implement a national welfare system. In England, the cost of enforcing the Poor Laws skyrocketed, reaching 4 million pounds by 1800 (Innes 1996, 144), while the Speenhamland system amended the Poor Laws to cover the able-bodied unemployed. Moreover, the currents of thought developing in the early nineteenth century must be understood in reaction to this development. The same analysis holds for prisons. The ideas of Beccaria and especially Howard were aimed not only at rationalizing the penal system but also at improving the lot of prisoners languishing in the dank, insalubrious jails of the *Ancien Régime*. Howard devoted his whole life to this effort.

REFORM OF THE MASSES: THREE APPROACHES

Once the revolutionary ferment had abated, the failure of welfare policy became evident, and it was time for some serious rethinking. In the early decades of the century, and especially after the Napoleonic Wars, three major visions of the transition to the new world took form. Each engendered a specific approach to poverty and crime.

The Philanthropic Tendency

Early nineteenth-century philanthropists and reformers in general made the moral reform of the masses one of their primary objectives. For some, the motive was to restore paternalistic ties between the dominant and the dominated; for others, it was to inculcate the new society's values into the putatively ignorant masses. All of them set about this vast undertaking – that of *transforming* the people to fit the ideals of the elites – by attempting to rally the ruling classes around the implementation of the necessary institutions of reform: schools, prisons, and so forth: "Stretching out ahead of the reformers was a vast enterprise of socialization. The purpose of this undertaking was the construction of a subject different from the productive subject: namely, a subject conscious of his social duties, a civic subject" (Procacci 1993, 228).[30]

From schools for the poor to hospices for the elderly, from home care to prisoner rehabilitation, philanthropic initiatives in general flowed directly out of a form of Enlightenment optimism which held that the "people," given resources and proper training, could adapt to the new society and, in so doing, open the door to progress.[31] The right to happiness was not extinguished with the dying hopes of the revolutions; in fact, it finds an echo in the writings of certain economists to this day.[32]

But the philanthropic tendency did not by any means imply a strictly private philosophy of welfare. Quite the contrary. Many philanthropists were conscious of the limits of private initiative in this area and the need for state involvement: "Indigence, in its sufferings, calls upon these two forms of support: it is the common object of public and private charity. As personal misfortune, it solicits the latter: as a scourge, it calls for the former. From the one it demands personalized care; from the other, extensive planning and powerful protection" (Gérando 1839, 1: 2).[33]

The role of philanthropy in the implementation of penal reforms since the late eighteenth century reflects with equal eloquence the opening up of a renewed regulatory role for the state. There is in fact no inherent contradiction in philanthropic thought between state intervention and civil society initiatives. Any properly constituted society must marshal all its forces to fight poverty: the acculturation of the working classes is too big a project to be left to individual initiative.

The Malthusian Tendency

Malthusianism was a direct reaction to the philanthropists' optimism. The idyllic future made possible by people finally free to use their reason had found its consummate expression in the works of Thomas Paine (1791), Nicolas de Condorcet (1793), and William Godwin (1793). This boundless confidence in human reason was the target at which Thomas Malthus's famous pamphlet took aim. It was both a blunt challenge to mercantilist claims about population and a radical reinterpretation of the nexus between nature and reason postulated by the Enlightenment. For Malthus, the working classes' propensity for rapid reproduction when their passions are not controlled leads to overpopulation, condemning those same classes to an ever-precarious existence. To ignore this law of nature only makes the situation worse. His is a dark, pessimistic view of a future of humanity[34] that forever subjugates human ambitions to the inexorable operation of economic and demographic laws and holds that only "moral restraint" and private charity can hope to mitigate their effects. Systematic welfare legislation such as the Poor Law leads this class into indolence, encourages vice, and hence increases the pressure on resources already barely sufficient.

With Malthus, political economy became an economy of scarcity. Just as Edmund Burke had tried to show that experience and tradition could prove better guides than people's desires for change (Burke [1790] 1955),[35] Malthus told of a sordid, frightening world in which individuals are tripped up by nature and their propensity to sin; a world in which compulsion is more powerful than human freedom. Men and women are always prone to sin; nothing guarantees that reason will naturally and inherently drive them toward good. Looming hunger and hardship, an uncertain future: fear of these is what spurs human beings to obey the unyielding laws of survival.[36] Progress is always in danger of giving way to vice and indolence. It follows that any institution that exempts people from fulfilling their obligations through virtue and work, even on the pretext of philanthropy, encourages vice and is therefore fundamentally harmful. Anyone resorting to being housed in such institutions must be regarded as morally bankrupt, and must acutely feel the shame associated with this status.

In Malthusian philosophy, crime and poverty are complementary. Both sit on the same slippery slope of immorality – the one a little further downhill than the other. The "solution" becomes self-evident: if these phenomena are just the manifestation of weak morals and insufficient self-restraint, then morality and self-restraint must be shored up by making the experience of obtaining public relief, and a fortiori of going to jail, as humiliating and degrading as possible. Any member of the lower classes contemplating such solutions must apprehend them to be less desirable than resigning himself to his daily life.[37]

The impact of this thinking was everywhere in evidence at the start of the nineteenth century. A particularly eloquent statement is found in French minister of the interior Adrien de Gasparin's recommendations to Louis Philippe I in 1837:

> While we must keep our distance from that excessive form of philanthropy which creates beggars with the very relief it provides them, it would be even more regrettable to see no other cure for these excesses than in the contrary excess, and to remain insensitive to the most genuine suffering out of a fear of bringing fake suffering into being. While continuing to provide relief to the pauper, we must show him that it is unreliable and precarious; it must be discredited in his eyes by associating it with a feeling of shame. No one

must believe that he is entitled to be assisted, and holding out one's hand must always be a degrading act. (Gasparin 1837, 32)

With the failure of the rationalist utopias, the misuse of freedom was now perceived to be an option that the poor could exercise. The French Revolution had demonstrated the political excesses of a logic of reason; the new imperative was to avert the social and economic excesses stemming from that logic. Economic wisdom, like political wisdom, is not an inherent trait of individuals artificially freed of the imperatives of survival. David Ricardo wrote:

> By gradually contracting the sphere of the poor laws; by impressing on the poor the value of independence, by teaching them that they must look not to systematic or casual charity, but to their own exertions for support, that prudence and forethought are neither unnecessary nor unprofitable virtues, we shall by degrees approach a sounder and more healthful state ...
>
> If by law every human being wanting support could be sure to obtain it, and obtain it in such a degree as to make life tolerably comfortable, theory would lead us to expect that all other taxes together would be light compared with the single one of poor rates. The principle of gravitation is not more certain than the tendency of such laws to change wealth and power into misery and weakness; to call away the exertions of labour from every object, except that of providing mere subsistence. (Ricardo [1817] 1911, 63)

In this way, poverty was construed as the *condition* for a well-built society, rather than a scourge.[38] The abject poverty found in the industrial cities would consequently be analyzed by the Malthusians not as a brutal outcome of industrialization but as an effect of overly permissive policies.

The Christian Tendency

It tends to be forgotten that interpretations of poverty in the vibrant intellectual context of the early nineteenth century are not exhausted by the two tendencies just discussed, for a sophisticated school of Christian social thought had emerged out of the religious awakening that followed the end of the revolutionary period in Europe. At the crossroads between philanthropic optimism and Malthusian moralistic pessimism, Christian theorists believed in the possibility of a societal renaissance in which the masses would learn discipline under the guidance of a renewed religious ethics. The work of the Noetics in England[39] and of Alban de Villeneuve-Bargemont in France laid the groundwork for a full-fledged Christian political economy[40] with a strongly conservative cast.

This political economy rested on two postulates: the immutability of poverty and the central role of religion in cementing the social fabric. Unlike the philanthropists, the Christians rejected reason as a guide to personal action; they were skeptical of secular attempts to instill morality in the masses.[41] But they did not conclude that poverty was the outcome of unbending economic laws, much less the effect of the vice ascribed to the masses. Contra Malthus, Christian political economy conceived of poverty and crime as the pernicious outcome of uncontrolled industrialization and the loss of the old social and ethical bearings. It emphasized benevolent paternalism as an important component of social policy on poverty.

The key was to restore the bond of authority and mutual deference by which rich and poor had once been united:

The poor must have need of a charity of the rich, and the rich must be unable to do without the industry and activity of the poor. There must be a commerce in services and benefits; in dependency and goodness, work and reward, in order for the members of society – bound to one another, necessary to one another, like the members of a single body – to form but one family in the eyes of the common father, while awaiting the perfect order in which the poor man will be compensated for the suffering inseparable from his condition, in which no inequality other than that of merits and virtues will remain. (René-Michel Legris-Duval, quoted in Villeneuve-Bargemont 1834, 2: 187)[42]

However, it was not necessarily the old order that needed to be restored. Christian thought held out the hope of a future in which the guiding ethical principles would be provided by religion:

If the lower classes are stirred to action before Christianity has been reconstructed in people's minds, Europe will witness horrifying conflict the like of which may never have been seen in the annals of the world. This is what religious men everywhere must understand today ... If they want to spare religion and society unparalleled calamities, it is not enough for them to take their distance from the political order of the past ... they must stake out a position in the future, setting themselves up all at once as the defenders, the moderators, and the guides of the interest of the masses, the truly popular interests, whose inevitable triumph, bound up with that of charity, will end the social cycle of which humankind has already traversed several stages. (Philippe (Abbé) Gerbet, quoted in Villeneuve-Bargemont 1834, 2: 214–15)[43]

Until the end of the 1840s, the Christian tendency was continually tossed between the temptations of conservatism and aspirations toward Christian modernity, this latter being championed by a small minority who laid the foundations for early social Catholicism (Duroselle 1951).

SHARED POSTULATES

Unsurprisingly, the three tendencies just described[44] engaged in ideological and tactical clashes that could at times be quite harsh. Yet they were in enduring agreement on certain postulates relating to the meaning of poor relief, the kinds of individuals who should receive it, and the type of society in which they are enveloped.[45]

The Meaning of Charitable and Penal Intervention

All observers, whether enthusiastic or reticent about the ongoing process of industrialization, agreed that charity must aim to develop the *autonomy* of members of the working classes, to guarantee that they can thrive, or at least survive, in the modern economy. The idea of inculcating people with a spirit of providence thus became central in Western thought:

> Thus was this world ordered, that the providence of the working classes is necessary to combat misery, and that, when misery arrives, resulting from some unavoidable accident or from one of those sins which human frailty is unable to elude, first family relief, and then the charity of our fellow men, supports our existence and provides for our needs … Thus political economy and morality, the rules of beneficence and the interests of society, agree as to the importance of proscribing any public institution whose apparent liberality dispenses man from providence. To promise relief from any misery in the name of the state is to encourage vice and imprudence, to produce excess population, to call down the scourge of poverty, to degrade the moral character and to corrupt the sentiments of the lower classes; it is finally to oppose in every way the improvement of humanity and the march of civilization. (Duchâtel 1829, 190–1)

But providence, in this view, was a seed that had to be sowed in untilled soil; or, for the Malthusians, a culture that had to be forced upon people universally prone to immorality. Even the prisons were to become convents of moral reform.

Malthusian conclusions about the necessary withdrawal of the state from social affairs were far from unanimous, as Joseph-Marie de Gérando noted: "The system of public charity has nothing in common with that which has been designated as legal charity; or rather, they are mutually exclusive. One of these two systems is governed by strict and absolute rules; the other is inspired by humane intentions" (Gérando 1839, 492).

Whether exclusively private or combined with public welfare, charity was fundamentally a *relation*, a consolidation of ties between classes. It always, in one way or another, reflected the guardianship of the rich over the poor: "The essence of a good administration of public charity, then, is the art of creating a voluntary, immediate, and individual guardianship of the prosperous over the unfortunate" (Gérando 1832, 11).[46]

However, this guardianship was no longer a simple affirmation of authority, a reassertion of the inferior status of the poor under the *Ancien Régime*. It was now a tool that could be used for the improvement of the working classes, a method for initiating the peasant and the worker to the values necessary to survival in the modern world.

Charity was also an exchange, in that it bound the poor closer to the rich. It implied a form of reciprocity in which the poor must prove themselves worthy of the relief they receive. For some observers, this was because poverty is inextricably bound up with vice; for others, it was simply to ensure that the relief granted actually had its intended effect. The necessary consequence was more systematic control over the granting of relief, including the possibility of investigating denizens of the poorhouse.

> Charity was not a duty performed as a result of holding resources on trust for communal benefit: it was an act of mercy performed as a result of morally refined sensitivity in the giver to the sight or knowledge of human suffering. Because the act of giving was now voluntary in a moral as well as legal sense, it was reasonable for the donor to expect the recipient to conform to certain continuing standards of deservingness – chiefly to strive to restore and retain a self-supporting position in society by participation in the labour market. Because the act was to benefit society as well as the distressed recipient, the donor *also* had a duty – the duty to ensure that the gift was properly bestowed and applied. (Roberts 1998, 70)[47]

While strident debate took place about the meaning and goals of penal confinement and the state's role in the distribution of relief, these diverse currents of thought all bespeak a complex enterprise of rebuilding a social fabric threatened by the ongoing upheavals. All concerned came to believe that systematic, targeted control over the distribution of relief (whether "outdoors" or in institutional settings) was desirable.[48]

The Meaning of the Individual

A second area of agreement among these different tendencies has to do with a posited trait of human nature: namely, that the poor are *capable* of changing – in fact, that they can be *made* to change, either by the unforgiving laws of nature and economics, the paternalistic intervention of the dominant classes or, *in extremis*, by confinement in a charitable or penal institution. This was a prerequisite for well-structured charity and the consolidation of the bond between rich and poor that it made possible. The poor man and the criminal, under the influence of their superiors' or guardians' objurgations, can *learn* to be provident, to survive life's ups and downs by dint of honest toil. It was thought possible, using methods ranging from education to institutionalization – not to exclude the morality-inducing rounds of the "visitors of the poor" – to instill noble sentiments in them, to teach them moral restraint, religious submission, providence, and the value of work.

If so, then the poor man's autonomy, such as it is, must be subordinate to his conformity to his social condition and the fundamental laws according to which society is constructed. His freedom is not a freedom to act, but a freedom to conform to the new order.[49] And "progress" is, as ever, predicated on mass adherence by the working classes to the values of the elites.

But this ability to change, to "reform" or better oneself, entails an effort of the will, a freedom to make decisions that rests fully and centrally with the individual. Mass-scale reform is contingent on individual action, in the sense that each person's active buy-in to the desired adjustment of mass values is needed. Paternalism still rules, but no longer works by the mere assertion of authority: it is enlisted in a missionary crusade to mobilize the people, which means mobilizing each and every individual.

The Organization of Society

In the purest Enlightenment tradition, seamless continuity between the state and civil society remained unquestioned by all tendencies. Even the

Malthusian critique of the Poor Law, and of "legal charity" more generally, did not call for the abolition of state intervention unless it proved counterproductive, thus constituting bad policy. What the critics objected to was not so much the public provision of relief as the prospect of that relief being given out indiscriminately.[50]

So, the two areas of general agreement just discussed – that it was indispensable to strengthen the social fabric during this period of crisis, and that the working classes were morally malleable – led to a third: that the inculcation of morals, of proper ways for the masses to behave, had to be a collective endeavour. Everyone, whether progressive or conservative, secular or religious – whether they invoked the power of human reason or urged humankind to surrender to the transcendent laws of nature – viewed poverty as the strategic locus for the remaking of the world. This task could not be accomplished without the expression of some kind of solidarity. And the task was urgent, for the new world stretching out before these various observers appeared to be in imminent danger of crumbling if nothing was done to shore up its foundations.

THE SHOCK OF PAUPERISM

The currents of thought just analyzed were all born during the European revolutionary era and derived from a vision of society in which poverty was inseparable from membership in the undifferentiated masses. True, a degree of decision-making autonomy, of free will, was ascribed to each individual member of these masses – thus constituting an implicit acknowledgment that the masses *are*, in fact, composed of individuals – but only as necessary to secure each person's willing conformity with the new social order. All these "free" individuals were expected to subscribe to the same values, to unite under the same rules, and to aspire to the same version of happiness.

This broad-brush view took on special relevance when applied to that portion of the masses that had yet to rally to the philanthropists' values. These authors give the impression of a shapeless mass of people always prone to slipping into abject poverty or turning to crime, whether out of vice, improvidence, or lack of the cultural attributes necessary to survive the transition to modernity. The people may be portrayed as incapable (at least for the moment) of shouldering the great expectations riding on the future or, on the contrary, as ever likely to succumb to the sirens of modernity. Neither liberal nor conservative commentators, however, evince much inclination to classify poor people or criminals according to any system resembling those in use today. At most, they divide up the clienteles by sex, age, or gravity of the person's condition or offence.

This primitive view cannot and does not survive the advent of the Industrial Revolution. It is scarcely possible to overestimate the impact of the rise of mass urban poverty, in lockstep with industrial progress, on the social thought of the day. The term "pauperism" will henceforth serve to focus the gaze on the outer fringes of poverty and to distinguish it from the "ordinary" poverty of the masses. From the 1830s, this extreme poverty, developing in the heart of the most advanced centres of industry, comes to be viewed by many observers as an anomaly specific to capitalism. The shock felt by Engels ([1845] 2009) reverberates throughout the elite classes. For the misery that strikes the "industrial class" has very specific features: it is concentrated in the cities where the new factories are located; it affects a population made vulnerable by its relative newness to the urban setting and by a precarious wage relationship; and it takes extreme forms that prove resistant to traditional methods of providing relief.

> It must be admitted that the lack of work and the insufficiency of wages are the most general causes of indigence among the able-bodied. Whether the lack of work or the inadequacy of the day's wage derive from industrial circumstances beyond anyone's power to control, or whether it is a function (unfortunately the most ordinary case) of the worker's lack of skill, his indolence, or his misbehaviour, charity is nearly powerless to fight these incessant causes of pauperism. (Rémusat 1840, 48–9)

Pauperism was a new and strikingly noticeable kind of poverty. It was found in those noisome locales where extreme dependency and criminality cohabited, and it posed a special challenge to all the tendencies discussed above, for it shook the consensus on which they rested. After all, how much autonomy was possible among people living in such a state of destitution? Was there a cure or even a salve for this condition?

Two reactions were possible. Conservative observers such as Villeneuve-Bargemont faulted the "industrial system"; for them, the new pauperism only reaffirmed the need for a restoration of traditional values, including the entrenchment of elite paternalism toward the poor. Others, including the foremost liberal philanthropists, regarded pauperism as an infantile disorder that capitalism would one day outgrow. But, for these different reasons, both groups believed in some form of systematic public intervention as a means of alleviating the problem.

If civilization, in the course of its advances, increases the inequality of conditions and renders it more appreciable; if, in so doing, it occasions varying degrees of misfortune, and renders their outward image more grievous; if, in calling men on to higher and stronger destinies, it leaves in distress those whose weakened or paralytic faculties cannot answer its call; if, in its ascendancy, it meets some obstacles, causes some friction, and increases the likelihood of accidents, even as it holds out prospects of success, would it not be right for it to show concern for the victims sacrificed as the very result of the labour that helps it achieve its ends, and for it to indemnify those whom it runs over along the way? (Gérando 1839, 1: 464)[51]

Most commentators, however, found the Malthusian view an easier way out of their anxieties. Industrialization, they believed, had done no more than lay bare the maladaptive nature of a portion of the working classes. Those who fell into pauperism were said to lack "moral restraint," that inner quality which enables people to face the future by making provision for its vagaries. Pauperism thus afforded a striking practical demonstration of Malthusian theory and the effects of vice.

There are those who still speak and write of pauperism as one of the greatest evils of society, and as generally implying crime, if not inseparably connected with it; and yet are perpetually confounding pauperism, in this view of it, with poverty; and use the terms a pauper, and a poor man, as if the distinctions were few and small between the classes and characters of dependents upon alms. This is grossly wrong ... By leading to an indiscriminate treatment of the poor, as if they were of course vicious, it becomes a means of making them vicious ... Let pauperism then, I would say, have its recognized technical sense, and be understood to imply a preference of support by alms, to support by personal labor. (Tuckerman 1838, 291–2)

Based on what he observed in London, Patrick Colquhoun laid down the new and basic distinction between the "ordinary" poverty of labourers everywhere and the mass destitution or "indigence" characteristic of industrial society:

Poverty ... is the state of every one who must labour for subsistence ... Indigence therefore, and not poverty, is the evil. It is that condition in society which implies want, misery, and distress. It is the state of any one who is destitute of the means of subsistence, and is unable to labour to procure it to the extent nature requires. (Patrick Colquhoun [1806], quoted in Himmelfarb 1984, 78)

Gérando in particular dwelled on the distinction at length:

> The terms poverty and indigence, employed as synonyms in everyday language, are far from expressing the same idea and depicting the same situation. Poverty is the middle degree between difficult straits and destitution; it leads and confines to indigence, but it is not by any means indigence itself; it is a danger as much as a hardship. He is poor who does not have enough of the necessities of life, who has only a part of them, who has them but only barely; he is poor who lacks enough to live on decently, given his condition. Indigence is extreme poverty. It is deprival of the essentials; it is sheer destitution. To be poor, it suffices to have nothing of one's own, or even to possess very little; to be indigent, one must be unable to obtain for himself what he lacks. The poor man has only his hands to provide for his subsistence; the indigent has nothing to live on at all. The poor man suffers hardship; the indigent risks perishing. What the poor man chiefly needs is support; what the indigent needs is relief. The situation of the poor man must be prevented from worsening; that of the indigent must be alleviated without delay. (Gérando 1839, 1: 5–6)

As soon as this specific category of poverty – indigence, or pauperism – had been isolated, the way was clear for a systematic process of stigmatization to begin.[52] Edwin Chadwick's celebrated *Report on the Sanitary Condition of the Labouring Population of Great Britain* (1842) would describe this population in language more typically applied to industrial pollution or unsanitary urban living conditions.[53] Eight years earlier, the Poor Law Amendment Act had provided an even better illustration of how the demarcation between indigence and ordinary poverty would soon have a deeply disruptive impact on welfare practice. From 1834 on, able-bodied men were almost entirely excluded from any possibility of public relief outside of being interned in workhouses. These institutions, which spread throughout England in short order, served as a tangible manifestation of the stigma attaching to indigence. A person would have to feel exceedingly desperate to apply for housing in institutions ruled by compulsory labour and separation of the sexes; therefore, to make such an application was ipso facto to admit one's membership in the class of the indigent. The social and moral scourge of pauperism was thus channelled into and contained within the workhouse system. By process of elimination, those left outdoors belonged to the "deserving" poor. This physical distinction between the two groups was mapped onto a distinction between areas of responsibility. Indoor relief – and hence indigence – was the province of the state, while outdoor relief – and hence ordinary poverty – belonged to that of private charity. Various nations devised different systems for the management of pauperism, most often under public auspices. The extreme form of these institutions was the penitentiary.

Thus it was no accident that the penal laws were overhauled in the same general thrust. The French revolutionaries had made prison the principal form of penal sanction, and this trend was only accelerated with the rise of the pauperized masses throughout Europe. In England, the laws passed by the government of Lord John Russell in the 1830s, following upon Sir Robert Peel's reforms, standardized confinement as the principal mode of sanction for most criminal offences. From then on, the penitentiary and the jail became the mainstream approach to crime management.

The first-priority resort to institutionalization was also evident in the area of poverty. With the Poor Law Amendment Act, philanthropic aspirations to reform, Malthusian moral pessimism, and the conservatism of most protagonists of the religious awakening came together in a single amalgam.[54] Mass confinement in workhouses now targeted a stigmatized population, serving as both the expression of and the therapy for their moral decay. The distinction between the poor in general and the denizens of the workhouse had less to do with each person's objective poverty than with his capacity to bear up under it.[55]

But the stigmatization of the indigent and the suppression of pauperism, undergirding a broad social consensus among the elites,[56] do not sum up the transition to liberal charity. For one thing, the fixation on pauperism went along with the positing of a fundamental link between the extreme poverty covered by the term and the general condition of the working classes. For another, the observation of the impoverished masses' cultural and moral failings, and the consequent need for the elites to reform them, remained fundamental to welfare policies in the 1830s. An even more fundamental shift was soon to come.

CRIME AND POVERTY IN THE COLONIES: THE CASE OF LOWER CANADA

These debates and issues found an echo even in the remotest colonies. It is true that Lower Canada, with its small and widely dispersed population, its nascent industry, and its largely autarkic agriculture, felt the social effects of the great political and economic transition in Europe to a very limited extent. Quebec City and Montreal had so far been barely grazed by the phenomenon of proletarianization, and the problems associated with pauperism would only make themselves felt with the mass arrival of British immigrants in the 1830s. Nevertheless, the colonial elites had their gaze fixed on what was happening in Europe. They could see that it was only a matter of time before they too would have to modernize their approach to managing crime and poverty; moreover, the example of the great American cities was already bringing this realization closer to home.

The Critique of the Old System

This attention to developments in Europe led to an embryonic critique of charitable and penal institutions in Lower Canada, especially after 1810. The criticism was all the more remarkable in that the institutions targeted were relatively young, or at any rate recently remodeled. One example was the state-run system for the care of abandoned children, which dated from 1801.[57] Another was the prisons: while the earliest had been built in 1805 on the model proposed by John Howard,[58] many were considered outmoded only a few years later. What bothered the reformers was not the chronological age of some of these institutions but the perception of their having been tacked on to the old system of punishment and welfare. The criticism of these institutions took issue with three basic features of that system.

The first was a model of charity based on alms doled out at the whim of the traditional elites, including the religious communities, often to people perceived as least deserving of relief.[59] Charity, it was argued, should be a systematic effort to raise up the poor with the generous support of the rich.[60] Indiscriminate assistance was viewed as counterproductive; whence, for example, the criticism of government-subsidized institutions that cared for abandoned children. This amounted to "a tax upon the virtuous, for the support of children of the vicious and unfeeling."[61]

These charges soon gave rise to a critique of the amateurism that seemed to pervade the whole system. The numerous deficiencies in the treatment of the insane and the ill, as well as those affecting the policing system, were laid at the door of an unsystematic and unprofessional approach. This charge was levelled at religious communities[62] and other benefactors[63] as well as at the constabulary system for the apprehension of criminals.[64]

Corresponding to the new professionalism being demanded was a desire to subject punishment to the dictates of *treatment*. This was the deep meaning of criticism lodged against British criminal law, which was implemented in Quebec mainly after 1815. Note that this criticism did not concern procedure but rather sentencing. Capital punishment in particular was seen as being meted out too indiscriminately under the "Bloody Code."

> Our Criminal Legislation in fact has remained nearly stationary, notwithstanding the example of the United Kingdom, and the existing Establishments, more suited to new Countries, of the neighbouring States of *America*.
>
> The natural consequences of this state of the Criminal Law have been aggravated by the encreasing reluctance evinced by the Provincial Executive and influential Inhabitants to enforce a Penal Code extremely severe ... all which circumstances tend to shew that the public Mind is ripe for some modification in the treatment of Prisoners and in the Punishment of Convicts.[65]

Reform of the penal system thus came to be regarded as the prerequisite to a systematic approach to the administration of justice. Blind cruelty had to give way to clinical treatment of what was henceforth perceived as a social evil.[66] The critique of sentencing, then, was soon augmented by a critique of the old model of confinement: "The great amount of crime in Lower Canada has its principal source in the absence of all discipline in the Prisons, and the faulty construction of the Buildings in which the Prisoners are confined in common, and more particularly in the inefficiency of the English code of punishment introduced into this Province."[67]

Arbitrariness, amateurism, inefficacy, gratuitous violence: the delicate balances characterizing the administration of both poverty and crime increasingly looked obsolete, irrational, wasteful of resources. For reformers and philanthropists, the task at hand was huge: to build a new mode of administration of crime and poverty from the ground up. As in Europe, the door was now open in Lower Canada to every species of utopia.

Utopian Thinking about Confinement

Institutional renewal schemes proliferated in Lower Canada in the years 1815 to 1840. Proposals included a new provincial public hospital, a penitentiary, a public insane asylum, a provincial house of correction, and houses of industry for Montreal and Quebec City. Beyond what was actually accomplished (a matter to which I return), this reformist zeal itself deserves to be examined. Everyone proceeded as if, beyond the specific features of each type of institution, the solution to the societal problems of poverty and crime necessitated the *confinement* of the individuals concerned. Confinement was presented as an all-purpose intervention with the capacity to curtail all the various disruptive phenomena at work within society. For this reason, there are some striking homologies among the discourses used to justify the building of hospitals, asylums, houses of industry, and prisons. These homologies, however, cannot be reduced to the formal resemblances inherent in the practice of confinement itself; rather, they are more evocative of the social constraints in which a certain practice of power was coming into being. In sum, confinement, in its multiple dimensions, was at this period a *social project*. This project comprised three basic dimensions: prophylaxis, knowledge, and power.

1 *Prophylaxis* Confinement was first and foremost a matter of *isolating* a certain group of people from the rest of the community. It could be justified by invoking the threat they posed to society and also by the need to protect the target "clientele." While this argument seems straightforward in the case of hospitals,[68] it was used for all the other institutions of control as well, from the asylum[69] to the prison[70] and the house of industry.[71] The medical metaphor evident in a concept such as "moral treatment" should be construed in the strict sense that once the limits of the community and the customary norms structuring it had broken down, men (and women) lost their natural immunity to crime and indigence. Apart from a few nostalgic traditionalists, everyone assumed that the dissolution of the old social fabric was an inexorable process. Therefore, an environment conducive to the teaching of a new form of urban sociability had to be created, even if artificially. Isolation was the main prerequisite to rehabilitation, and its extensive application held out the hope of mass reform somewhere down the road: "The morals particularly of the inferior orders of society are of the highest importance to the country and to the whole of its population and whatever tends to preserve them from being contaminated must necessarily tend to prevent the increase of crimes."[72]

2 *Knowledge* Institutionalization fulfilled another essential function, which was to provide for the possibility of *systematic* treatment. Treatment entailed the development of new knowledge and the implementation thereof. The treated population was not the only

beneficiary of treatment, since these people thereby also participated in the accrual of knowledge and the refinement of therapeutic techniques. This imperative underlay thinking about the conditions for the establishment of modern hospitals. For example, the author of an 1818 "Essay on the Establishment of Hospitals in the Province of Lower Canada for the Sick Poor" envisioned a whole network of hospitals, an immense pyramid of institutions with the public hospital at the summit:

> [Hospices for the insane, pregnant women, the elderly, the infected, the scurvy, and the venereal] must be regarded as private rather than public institutions: only the large hospitals are worthy of being built, operated, and paid for by governments ... These private institutions must only be envisaged as *nurseries* for the raising of those individuals who will be found deserving of being transported ... to the hospitals, *those great national reservoirs and laboratories*.[73]

Dr William Hackett, in charge of the mentally ill at the Quebec City General Hospital, similarly stated his belief in the importance of applied research. He feared that the institution would remain "what it has been in the past: a dumping place for lunatics, making it impossible for the members of the profession to put into practice, within its walls, those methods which practice and experience recommend as a cure for this terrible sickness."[74]

The expertise acquired through research also implied a *distance*, a clear distinction between the pauper or criminal being subjected to treatment and the specialist who treated them; a distance between the person of the philanthropist and the social body on which he operated. Both the helping relationship and the act of punishment became transformative techniques. Indigence, now a general malady of the social body, served as the birth certificate of the philanthropic machine for the processing of the masses.

3 *Power* In this context, the delicate question of power must be posed. Not the many pervasive forms of domination present in social interactions, which form the substance of inequality – these have been well elucidated by Foucault. Perhaps more fundamentally, the power of interest here is that which makes coercion possible at a societal level. The historiography has often ignored a central problem in this connection:[75] that the power to confine had to be based on some sort of legitimacy. Under the feudal mode of regulation, the problem seldom arose. There, forced confinement was based on the power of the parent (*lettre de cachet*) or the need

to detain a defendant even before his punishment was handed down. Likewise, there was never any sophisticated legal procedure governing the confinement of vagrants, mental patients, and the infirm in general hospitals, beggars' prisons, and workhouses.[76]

In a democratic system, the game was changed. The concept of the individual as citizen achieved central status, and a fundamental right to protection from excessive state coercion was recognized. The legality of any coercive measure, even if motivated by an intent to reform someone or do her good, lost its presumptive character. It became common to legitimize the resort to confinement by legislating the prohibition of certain acts and associating them with terms of imprisonment.

How else could the mass confinement of the targeted populations be legitimized, if not by invoking a personal deficiency serious enough to justify their isolation? This conundrum was to waylay the best of philanthropic intentions. While insanity and criminality did afford the needed justification,[77] no other social condition gave rise to a legitimate power of detention; social welfare institutions had no legal basis on which to coerce and control the populations in question.[78] This maddening limitation is evident in the frustration expressed by the directors of the Quebec City house of industry in 1836: "What will be wanted is legal control over persons who, being able to work, do not support themselves, but become burthensome to their neighbours. If the House of Industry could be placed within the limits of the Gaol, these vagrants might be committed and held to labour. Out of it there is no legal power of detention."[79]

The Ambiguity of the Philanthropic Critique

From the hospital to the penitentiary, sites of confinement seemed to promise the long-sought panacea for society's ills,[80] but there was deep ambiguity in this state of affairs. Historians have traditionally considered early nineteenth-century philanthropic and reformist discourse to be the precursor of the modern institutions of social control. Such studies do at times note the naive optimism of the founding fathers of modern charity and punishment, their unquestioning belief in the efficacy and reform potential of the institutions they proposed. What these studies tend to neglect is that the gap between the era's reform discourse and the form these institutions took in the latter half of the nineteenth century – their principles of organization and social validation – was much more than an understandable time lag between ideal and reality, theory and practice. In fact, the social ideals of the time would have to undergo a radical transformation in order for the modern institutions to come into being.

That is because the discourse of the day was the variegated product of the conflicting fears, nostalgia, and aspirations of the elites. The world they lived in was, in their eyes, falling apart. It was a world in which what had once been a distressing exception seemed to have become a widespread pattern; in which poverty was always in danger of slipping into unutterable misery, while crime had become a way of life and a means of survival in the grimy, overpopulated cities. Looming on the horizon was a world haunted by endemic pauperism, in which poverty and deviance symbolized a total breakdown of societal mores. Against this backdrop, the population of indigents and criminals became a monster dimly perceived through the haze of the elites' own fear and confusion. That the institutional utopia birthed by the era's philanthropists should, in some respects, come to resemble a microcosm of a lost world – a world in which the impoverished masses could be put to work at the behest of the landlord and the industrialist, the belongings of the propertied classes protected by their injunctions – is hardly surprising. And if so, then democracy and burgeoning industry could be seen as obstacles or constraints as much as promises. What emerged from this fraught process was an ideal of the asylum and the penitentiary that represented both a desperate striving to recreate traditional ties of deference and – although it seems contradictory – an attempt to invent people worthy of the new era.[81] Facing an uncertain future in which everything had become possible, torn between the ecstatic optimism of the Enlightenment and the jaded pessimism of the Malthusians, the elites began to think of the (idealized) historical deference of the masses as a possible option for the future. The modern correctional and philanthropic universe was erected on this profoundly shaky foundation. The future would, of course, betray the elites' aspirations even as it calmed their worst fears. And a more pragmatic use would have to be found for the cathedrals of confinement left behind by these reformist utopias.[82]

A striking example of the ambivalence of reform discourse is to be found in the Lower Canadian debate over the building of a penitentiary. The historiography has generally described the birth of the modern penitentiary as an enterprise aimed at overhauling the old prison. In this approach – systematized in the work of Foucault – the generalized softening of criminal law is said to go hand in hand with the replacement of capital and corporal punishment by detention, which became the primary means of dealing with crimes against people and especially property.

This, however, is just another example of the gradualist approach in which reform discourse is seen as the precursor to future transformations. For how are we to explain that the early avatars of the penitentiary primarily contained a population that had never been subjected to the strict sanctions of the Bloody Code? The main target, after all, was the mass of petty criminals, and the methods included the application of vagrancy laws and the use of summary convictions by justices of the peace. The answer is that the real function of the early penitentiary was to take over from the house of correction as a better means of systematizing and standardizing the treatment of the masses.

In Lower Canada, the campaign for a penitentiary was initially justified by the need to punish small-time criminals. This was clearly stated by a Montreal grand jury in September 1826:

> The Grand Jury are convinced that now is the time for providing an extensive and well regulated Penitentiary, in which Persons convicted of the less formidable and atrocious species of Crimes could be employed in such a manner as would be useful to themselves and render their Imprisonment less expensive to the Public.[83]

This wish soon turned into a proposal for the penitentiary confinement of all convicts:

> a general Penitentiary for the whole Province, where Convicts could be compelled to labour, would be a most important step towards the diminution of crime and classification of Criminals; ...
>
> ... such an Establishment would render the present Gaols ... permanently adequate to the confinement of *the accused* ...[84]

Abruptly, the existence of a conviction replaced the gravity of the crime as the main criterion used to distinguish among the individuals of interest. The way was clear for the philanthropists' carceral utopia to be put in place. From now on, the penitentiary was to be the site for the treatment of the convicted criminal, in a functional division of labour that would leave the old jail in charge of preventive detention, as it always had been. But it would not be a straightforward matter to convert this dream into a reality.

INSTITUTIONAL INERTIA AND ISOLATED REFORMS (1815–40)

The reality in Lower Canada was as disappointing as the reform discourse just discussed was nominally rational, systematic, and comprehensive. Reform efforts were characterized by fits and starts, trial and error, abortive legislative measures and timid reconfigurations. Moreover, the role of the state was not nearly as central as the reformers surely wanted. The state alone possessed the wherewithal to implement a systematic policy for reform of the popular habitus, yet it accomplished little during the years 1815 to 1840. In the areas of care for the poor and abandoned children, state support remained remarkably traditional in approach. A more innovative project, the building of an insane asylum, would continue to be a pious hope throughout this entire period. As to the extent of state funding for institutions, it actually declined relative to population.[85]

Only the onslaught of British immigration, starting in the 1810s and reaching a peak in the 1830s, would force the authorities to take large-scale measures (although these were always presented as exceptional). Thus, for example, the establishment of the first immigrants' hospital in 1816, which would soon come under government control; or the Marine Hospital inaugurated in Quebec City in 1834.[86]

The penal system remained relatively intact as well. Apart from the timid acts of 1824 abolishing capital punishment for three types of offences,[87] criminal law remained practically unchanged.[88] The policing system was only modified in any notable way by the implementation of night watch in the big cities after 1818.[89] A somewhat modernized police force would not be implemented in Lower Canada until the Rebellions and Lord Durham's mission, and then only ephemerally.[90] Even the operation of the criminal courts stabilized rapidly, although there was a marked rise in prosecutions around 1815. The most notable change here was the relative decline in prosecutions of crimes against the person before the Court of King's Bench.[91] At the local level, the profile of prosecuted offences remained quite stable, and apart from a peak number of convictions occurring between 1815 and 1825, the number of cases heard at trial in Montreal decreased as a percentage of population.[92]

All in all, the instruments of social regulation exhibited remarkable continuity with the past. New institutions and measures were merely superimposed, often in a contingent and disorderly fashion, on the old system, at times to relieve the older institutions of overload. The logic of state involvement in these areas remained unchanged. Even much of the judicial responsibility continued to be exercised locally, in the villages as in the cities. The reformers' calls for more systematic government action went largely unheeded.

There are a number of explanations for this state of affairs, including the relatively insignificant demand for relief in Lower Canada, at least until the crisis of the 1830s; the enduring conflict between the House of Assembly and the Legislative Council;[93] and the underfunding of the colonial government. Perhaps most fundamental was the structural weakness of the colonial state.

This weakness was a function of three factors. First, the essence of colonialism was thoroughgoing political dependence on the interests of the empire. In Lower Canada, welfare policy often faced resistance, and often micromanagerial oversight, from the British authorities.[94] Second, the colonial government had great difficulty asserting its authority over all the inhabitants of the colony. So limited was its ability to provide for the well-being of the whole population that the Patriotes, during the Rebellions, were able to set up a veritable parallel network of authority.[95] Third, the government tried to make up for its organizational failings at the local level with overly centralized decision making. Its unwillingness to implement municipal institutions – an indispensable precondition for the delegation of judicial and welfare powers – attests to a clear democratic deficit in the colonial political system. In the short term, this deficit made it impossible to rethink the role of the state in these areas.

Nevertheless, these structural impediments did not stop significant changes from taking place. Notwithstanding the discourse of reform, the period running from 1815 to 1840 augured a fundamental division which, in the capitalist mode of regulation, would separate the management of poverty from the punishment of crime.

CIVIL SOCIETY AND THE EMERGENCE OF PRIVATE WELFARE INITIATIVES

The gap between the utopian thinking of the reformers and the timid structural reforms undertaken by the government tells only part of the story about the changes taking place in Lower Canada. Other developments important to the transition to liberalism relate to the on-the-ground organizational practices of civil society, and to the novel uses to which certain institutions, held over from an earlier era of state power, were put.

> It ought to be impressed upon the minds of the people, that there are no means of preventing the evil of poverty but a general dissemination of habits of industry and moral restraint, no relief to be expected from charity, which when these habits are general, will always be amply sufficient.[96]

A parallel discourse, emerging in conjunction with the grand projects of public institution-building put on the table after 1815, implied an essential retreat from the philanthropic ideal of treatment of the masses, and this in two respects: first, it betrayed a thoroughgoing distrust of state intervention,[97] and second, it stressed the *voluntary act* as the basis for the provision of relief as well as for assessing the merits of each potential charity case. Some observers had always held the view that traditional private charity, despite criticism from the proponents of grand, state-sponsored reform projects, had lost none of its relevance. But something very different had been afoot since at least the late eighteenth century: a remarkable unfolding of secular private initiative in the field of charity, driven by the feverish mobilization of the elites. The old forms of charity were giving way to a more or less standardized practice of giving, a genuine political economy of charity distributed through a plethora of philanthropic associations, each with its own specific mission.[98] This rejection of state involvement was an initial manifestation of the strength of the liberal discourse on the administration of societal problems. It bespoke a new confidence in the capacity of civil society to take on this job, without the necessity of state involvement. And it asserted, in this connection, the pre-eminence of free enterprise, the precepts of which would be violated by any systematic attempt to organize public relief for the poor.[99] In a world succumbing to Malthusian pessimism, the political necessity of mass therapy, the need for mass reform of mores and behaviours, looked to many observers like a meritless project, even a danger to liberty. Poverty had reasons (even a rationality) of its own. Its existence poured cold water on the ambitions issuing from the Enlightenment. The harsh law of supply and demand could be tempered but not ignored. The profusion of human potentialities opened up by the Enlightenment and the revolutions ebbed into a resigned observation that poverty, in the economy of scarcity and exploitation then being dissected by Ricardo, was an inescapable fact of life. It followed from this observation that people of good will could and should organize to counteract, insofar as possible, the most deleterious effect of this scarcity: mass poverty.

The stigmatization of pauperism, that widespread form of extreme poverty characteristic of the industrial era, could initially be used to justify intervention by the public authorities. But it also had the effect of circumscribing the sphere of necessary state intervention. Outside that sphere lay the vast field of "ordinary" poverty, which was thereby defined as an inherent and unavoidable fact of the new civil society, and hence as a matter within its purview. In response to this realization came a period of intense mobilization on the part of civil society: an explosion of Protestant revivalism, especially in the United States; a rapid rise in recruitment by the Congregation of France; the enlistment of the Catholic faith by militant ultramontanism; and a proliferation of workers' cooperation and mutual aid initiatives. These efforts at orchestrating what presented itself as a brand-new system of solidarity by the rich toward the poor blossomed on the ground, under the often powerless and at times indifferent gaze of the authorities.[100]

This new type of charitable institution made its entrance into Lower Canada around 1820. Such institutions shared a certain number of features: they were unabashedly private, targeted a specific clientele, were often nondenominational[101] and multiethnic,[102] and were formed, generally on an ad hoc basis, by members of the urban elites, particularly the wives of merchants or seigneurs. Notably as well, these associations strove to implement more or less permanent structures, supported in some instances by institutional intake systems.[103] It is easy, even tempting, to regard these associations as the precursors of modern charity, especially since several of them exhibited remarkable longevity or influence. But, as discussed in part 3, there were significant differences between these charities and the charitable network that would develop after 1840. Moreover, many of these initiatives were quite timid or small-scale; they were in many cases the work of just one or two people, and their survival was never a certainty. Many factors hampered the operation of these associations, including the difficulty of establishing and maintaining them; the extreme scarcity of competent employees who could administer them; the dire living conditions of their target clienteles; and the lack of a powerful, well-established network of patrons in this time of transition. It was evident that these initiatives lacked the breadth and depth necessary to serve as a cohesive structure for the management of endemic pauperism, and it is indicative of their inadequacy that they continually appealed for state support. In the early 1830s, the government enacted a policy of annual subsidies to private institutions. The funds were distributed in response to applications submitted to the House of Assembly at the start of each session.

At this transitional moment, then, privately organized welfare was still looking to the government for the means to ensure its long-term existence.[104] For Lower Canada, a crucial turning point came in 1836 when a House of Assembly committee tabled recommendations to the effect that these institutions should be denied any entitlement to public funds.

> [The Committee] think it right to remark that the greater part of the applications made to Your Honorable House, which form the subject of this Report, have been made by divers Societies formed under peculiar circumstances, and for the purpose (a laudable one no doubt) of affording relief to the indigent and unfortunate of all classes. These several Societies, supported in the first instance by the voluntary subscriptions of individuals, have by degrees acquired the habit of applying to the Legislature for aid ... Your Committee are of opinion that the several Institutions and Societies aforesaid, (to whom the Committee are ready to pay the tribute of praise due to their merits,) ought to be informed that they must not reckon upon the aid of the Legislature for their future support, but must limit their charities and their expenses according to the funds they can raise from voluntary contributions made by the generosity of individuals.[105]

Thus emerged, in the midst of the social crisis of the 1820s and especially the 1830s, and in the crucible of day-to-day practices, the constituent principles of private initiative in the field of welfare. In the embryonic division of labour between the public and private spheres, private associations were coming to constitute an important form of action, manifesting the vibrancy of civil society. In the field of aid to the poor, the implications of democratic legitimacy and market constraints resulted in a fundamental separation between the duty of charity and the responsibilities of government, which would crystallize at mid-century.

THE PRISON TRANSFORMED

Of course, the devolution to private initiative of primary responsibility for poverty was not paralleled by a similar development with respect to crime. Quite the contrary: in the new division of labour, the state's jurisdiction over penal affairs was universally acknowledged.[106] More specifically, the dividing line was drawn between those functions whose exercise required the use of *coercive power* – which only the state possessed – and those in which relations between the parties in play were strictly voluntary. This explains, for example, why the state played a crucial role not only in policing and punishment but also in the establishment and administration of asylums.

But the prison, too, had to be transformed. The management of crime had to be rationalized, bent to the juridical and systemic constraints imposed by liberal democracy and the marketplace. In this process, the reformers' dream of standardized treatment of offenders came up against the hard realities of liberalism. The first indications that this process was under way in Lower Canada can be seen in the remarkable changes made to the prison system starting in the 1820s – when it acquired the features it still possesses today.

In one thrust, and without any significant modification to the justice or administrative systems, the prison became both a key instrument of *punishment* and a site of mass *detention* – a repository for the many vagrants and itinerants subjected to summary detention. Quebec City prison records show the extent of this phenomenon. Within a space of twenty-five years starting in 1815, the prison population grew by a factor of twenty. Annual incarceration skyrocketed from 65 new inmates in 1814 to 570 in 1830, 824 in 1836, and 1992 in 1840. Concomitantly, there was a relative decline in the number of francophones incarcerated,[107] a significant rise in the proportion of female prisoners,[108] and a marked lowering of the average age of new prisoners.[109]

These demographic numbers do not fully capture the portentous, qualitative shift taking place in the use of the existing facilities. During these years the Quebec City prison became predominantly penal in nature, with a majority of its inmates convicted to terms of imprisonment.[110] This specialization is all the more interesting in that it had nothing to do with amendments to the criminal code: not until 1841, with the passage of Sir Henry Black's bills to consolidate and codify criminal law for the Province of Canada, did incarceration replace capital punishment for the majority of serious crimes.[111]

This shift in the essential functions of the prison system makes more sense when analyzed in terms of the main grounds for detention. It was essentially due to an explosion in imprisonment for vagrancy and other minor infractions against public order, with the number of new inmates of this kind jumping from 293 in 1814–17 to 1329 in 1832–34 (from 40 percent to 65 percent of grounds for imprisonment).

What had happened was that justices of the peace had suddenly begun to use their power of summary conviction to orchestrate an all-out hunt for vagrants and itinerants. The notable rise in the imprisonment of British nationals after 1825 seems to indicate that this was in part a spontaneous reaction to the waves of immigration breaking over the colony throughout these years.[112] But whatever its cause, this development was to fundamentally and permanently modify the carceral dynamic of Lower Canada. For the first time, and for much time to come, the prisons and the justice system coincided in a systematic effort to convict and incarcerate those whose chief crime was often that of being inconvenient to society at large.[113]

* * *

The liberal mode of regulation of crime and poverty was definitively established in Canada starting in the 1840s, in the shadow of the great utopian schemes immediately preceding it. Its establishment parallels early experiences with the application of punishment in a democratic system as well as the first stirrings of the philanthropic impulse in liberal civil society, and it necessitated a reckoning with the troubled heritage of the prison through its reinvention in practice. A new societal division of labour was necessary for the proper administration of crime and poverty in all their manifestations, and this took the form of an increasingly sharp separation between penality and charity. The capitalist mode of regulation primarily depends on the individualization and standardization of behaviour; as soon as this procedure becomes a criterion for the differentiation of behaviour, this mode may be said to have come into existence. From then on, the administration of the masses is inevitably predicated on normative evaluation of individual action. And it is against this backdrop that the modern system of control and punishment begins to take shape.

For one thing, crime was looking less and less like an extreme form of deviance that beckoned to the working classes in general, and more and more like a behavioural deficiency ascribable to the (defective or depraved) individual will. The elites' fears of crime had hitherto tended to focus on the outer fringes of poverty and deviance, where – in their minds, at any rate – the two melded into one under the concept of pauperism. From now on crime would largely cease to be a class attribute, becoming instead an unsound, contingent mode of action. The word crime could still be applied to various categories of delinquents; however, its primary meaning would now be the deliberate, premeditated perpetration of a prohibited act.

In a similar way, society learned to distinguish "ordinary" poverty from the stigma of pauperism. Beyond the extreme forms of poverty that were the unfortunate legacy of an untidy industrial transition, poverty could take the more benign form of occasional want. It formed a kind of trough whose contours were defined by the peaks of others' success, a liability recorded on the balance sheet of life. Reformers and philanthropists conceived of this sort of poverty as a core characteristic of the popular masses, but it could now be set down to life's travails, to personal misfortune, or to isolated cases of unfitness or waywardness. Poverty became in large part privatized, not only because civil society's voluntary organizations were entrusted with its management but more profoundly because it was now regarded as a bona fide mode of existence in society.

Each person's fate was now subjected to the anonymous, ineluctable forces of the market. Poverty reflected failure, crime miscalculation; the one would be handled by civil society and its more or less organized network of solidarity, while the other would be punished by the state with imprisonment. Between the two, a fundamental distance set in, and this distance is central to the logic of regulation in Western societies. I now turn to a consideration of what took place on either side of the dividing line.

PART TWO

Crime and Punishment in the Liberal Era

Since the 1960s or earlier, the "social control" approach discussed in part 1 has been most assiduously developed in the field of historical studies of crime and punishment. As soon as punishment ceased to be defined as a mere societal reaction to the wrongful acts of certain citizens and became instead a political act enmeshed with the inequality and domination that are structural features of many societies, a critical analysis of the emergence of modern modes of penality, and particularly the prison, finally became possible. Of course, the traditional historiography that devoted itself to analyzing crime-fighting efforts survived and produced notable works,[1] but the definition of crime as a social construct opened up new possibilities for heuristic analysis. The best-known works in the field, from labelling theory to Foucauldian critique, sit within this critical perspective.[2]

Obviously, Foucault's *Discipline and Punish* (1975) remains the touchstone of any historical analysis of the penal system. Not so much for its oft-contested historical accuracy[3] as for its pioneering analysis of the processes of power at work in the invention of the modern prison: the processes constituting the substance of contemporary punishment, whereby bodies are controlled and minds conditioned. Since Foucault, studies of prisons and sentencing have come to be enduringly bound up with broader inquiries into power. But this approach has come at the cost of some dangerous historical shortcuts. The Foucauldian hypothesis of a revolution in modes of punishment occurring in the eighteenth and nineteenth centuries is undergirded by two major postulates: first, that this revolution is still alive and well today, in all its tragic repetitiveness (the prison as impossible reform);[4] second, that what is primarily at stake is a practice and a power dynamic between jailer and prisoner, operating on both body and mind, and that this dynamic constitutes the quintessence of the power relations of which society is woven as well as one of their extreme manifestations.

My view, which I shall defend here, is that these postulates are eminently debatable. For one thing, the invention of the prison was only the first act in a fitful, complex, two-hundred-year history of modes of punishment that underwent subsequent and equally far-reaching transformations. For another, the power relation made possible by the prison is a part of two major phenomena never truly analyzed by Foucault: the variable inscription of the phenomenon of crime within the historical evolution of modes of regulation, and the structural logic underlying the political and institutional response to the fact of crime. In other words, it is impossible to conceptualize the history of the prison as a punishment without understanding the place of the criminal act within the societal order, without grasping that this punishment – although undeniably the privileged site of a particular power dynamic – is also part and parcel of a complex strategy for getting to grips with a phenomenon whose definition has changed throughout the history of capitalism and democracy.

What distinguishes crime from poverty, madness, or sickness as an object of regulation – and what dictates that its treatment will be increasingly differentiated from other domains of regulation under the liberal regime – is that crime is always and above all a voluntary and deliberate *act*, not a state undergone or incurred. Early custumals often indiscriminately included civil and penal provisions governing the various acts of daily life. Only when acts defined as criminal came to be seen as breaches of public order coming under the king's jurisdiction did an initial construct of crime as a particular social phenomenon come into being. In the same thrust, the deliberateness of such acts was ever more systematically taken into account in the case law (minimum age of responsibility, self-defence, insanity defence, etc.). Crime was special by the very fact of its existence, which posed the problem of how behaviour defined as wrongful on the scale of a whole society should be treated and sanctioned. It became a specific social problem assignable not to a given group but to the immense group of individuals prone to committing it. But this rather trivial view of crime becomes more complicated when three other phenomena are considered: first, that the *prior* definition of what constitutes a crime is historically variable and always socially determined; second, that the *reaction* to a crime is not uniform either, and differs according to the gravity assigned to a given criminal act; and third, that there exists a practice of *stigmatization* connecting crime to other structural phenomena that relate to either society (e.g., poverty) or the individual (e.g., psychological predisposition).

Insofar as certain offending behaviour (vagrancy, drunkenness, theft) came to be associated more or less systematically with certain classes or groups of people, striking homologies or even at times amalgams appeared, linking the phenomenon of crime by way of analogy to other societal problems. We have just seen an example from the period of transition to capitalism, when the elites' perception of the masses led to crime and poverty being collapsed into a single fear of the "dangerous classes."[5] Crime became a social phenomenon, an extreme manifestation of a structural state ascribed to the poorest of the poor. Even at liberalism's height, this societal reflex of exclusion is consistently in evidence, irrespective of the specifics of penal policy. This is not especially surprising in that the populations on the receiving end of both punishment and welfare were, in fact, one and the same.

The history of the management of crime as a phenomenon is thus much more than the history of a power relation or a logic of discipline. It is the history of a *social* construct of exclusion attaching to classes as much as, or even more than, to individuals. This history shows how it was possible to reconcile the definition of crime as a freely committed act with the stigmatization of extreme poverty. A social and political history of the inscription of crime within a mode of management of inequalities makes it possible to grasp this phenomenon not just as the expression of a power relation but also, and even more so, as an indicator of the modalities according to which the social order of that society was built. And again contrary to Foucault's argument, I contend that this history underwent at least two major transformations before our day. The first, in the mid-1800s, brought about the invention of the modern prison (and the crimes it punished) by making it a core component of liberalism, while the second, in the mid-1900s, inscribed punishment within a dynamic of deinstitutionalization and welfarism. This part of the book concerns itself with the mechanics of the first transition. Beyond the utopianism attendant upon the birth of the carceral archipelago, how was this transition enacted within the realm of liberalism? Its major characteristics are briefly discussed in chapter 4. Chapter 5 puts a finer point on this analysis by focusing on the example of juvenile delinquency. The goal is to show that the invention of the prison and the liberal regulation of crime are two contrasting moments: the peculiar way in which the liberal carceral archipelago operated led to its very underpinnings being called into question at the end of the nineteenth century.

4

The Administration of Crime and the Vicissitudes of Liberalism

In 1843, the Canadian government enacted legislation to reserve penitentiaries for convicts sentenced to more than two years in prison. This important decision, inspired by British precedent, consecrated the decline of philanthropic ideals. The ideal of systematic treatment of criminals gave way to a functional division of labour within the prison system. The most sophisticated type of facility and the one best suited to long-term detention – epitomized by the brand-new Kingston Penitentiary – was henceforth given over to the punishment of the most serious crimes. The jailhouse continued to play its multifarious role as a holding pen for vagrants and petty criminals, a temporary destination for a transient population. Given the precepts of the liberal legal system – i.e., that only the commission of a serious crime, not a misdemeanour, can justify the long-term deprivation of liberty – this division of labour was inevitable.[1] In the expressed rationale for the prison, the problematic of treatment gave way to a discourse on dangerousness as determined from the seriousness of the criminal act. Thus was the logic of today's carceral hierarchy put in place.

The 1843 act illustrates the main argument of this chapter: that the 1840s saw the instatement of a logic of crime regulation that continues, in significant measure, today.[2] But that in no way implies that the changes undergone by the penal order in the nineteenth century exhaust the history that can be written of it. True, the institutionalization of penality took characteristic and stable forms that it is important to describe in brief (first section). These characteristics were made possible by the radical departure represented by liberal logic as it was applied to punishment under democratic rule (second section). But this logic came under sustained attack in the latter third of the nineteenth century; it is essential to analyze this attack in order to grasp the basic contradictions experienced by the liberal management of crime in contemporary societies (third section). The case of the Montreal prison serves to illustrate this evolution (fourth section).

THE ADMINISTRATION OF CRIME AFTER 1840

With a few exceptions, the historical study of nineteenth-century prisons and punishment has, in the wake of studies by Foucault, Michael Ignatieff, and David Rothman, focused on the years before mid-century. With the prison "born," it was as if the writing of its subsequent history could only focus on detailing the subsequent expression of its primary essence.[3] And since the genealogy has varied according to the observer, several have pushed the "birth" of prisons and punishment back in time, positing a gradual evolution already underway in the seventeenth century.[4] Whether conceptualized in Foucauldian terms as a radical departure with long-lasting effects, or in those of the subtle evolutionism entailed by Norbert Elias's "civilizing process," historians of the mid-nineteenth-century prison seem to have been able to understand it only in terms of continuity.

This unspoken gradualism is exacerbated by what I would call the particularism of the discipline of historical criminology. After new areas of research in the social sciences are inaugurated, suddenly blossoming into fields of knowledge about particular aspects of the historical continuum, they then tend to coagulate into rather rigid subfields of specialization. In the field of interest here, some scholars have sought a way out of such scientific dead ends either by widening the survey to take in other disciplinary or institutional techniques (Goffman, Foucault) or by assuming an isomorphism between the logic of punishment and the logic of production in a given society.[5] In my view, it is necessary to go further in this direction;[6] to comprehend the history of modes of punishment as a particular manifestation of the complex, arduous, trial-and-error process that gave birth to modern democracy.[7] More specifically, the consolidation of liberal democratic societies in the mid-nineteenth century, contemporaneous with the first mass workers' revolts, was a crucial moment in the transformation of the punishment system, in three main respects.

1   The first task was to implement a far-reaching *rationalization*[8] and *standardization* of the justice system. Once the criminal laws had been "modernized" (particularly via the abolition of corporal and

capital punishment for the large majority of offences) and prison firmly established as the main mode of punishment, it became necessary to ensure that *all* crimes would in practice be punished; or at any rate, that it could realistically be anticipated that they would be.

But for this to happen, it was not sufficient to "invent" the prison or to rationalize punishment, or even to step up law enforcement. A more fundamental reconception, involving the points of contact between civil society and the judicial system, was necessary. Until this time, beyond penalties (partial, sporadic) for violations of certain municipal bylaws, and the maintenance of a semblance of order in the cities, the operation of the judicial system had depended on the propensity of the king's subjects to sue.[9] It was they who had control over much of the judicial process, for they could choose the criteria, the timing, and often even the outcome of prosecutions. A free society necessitated a different kind of justice, one that could react efficiently and rapidly to its citizens' misconduct while remaining indifferent to their countless lawful initiatives. It would have to standardize both the definitions of crimes and the punishment assigned to them. Only under such a system of law enforcement could the myriad interactions and dealings among the citizens of a modern city be expected to prosper.

Martin Dufresne (1997), in a fascinating study, shows how this large-scale cultural shift took place, homing in on the specific ways in which the justice system was reorganized. At issue here is a set of discrete yet fundamental reforms that would forever change the operation of criminal justice. One was the increasing application of summary prosecution in lieu of the cumbersome and uncertain process of trial by jury. This development had been in progress since the late eighteenth century (Fyson 1995), but by the middle of the nineteenth it had taken on unparalleled importance, if only because it arose in conjunction with other, equally effective measures, such as the devolution of summary jurisdiction to local police chiefs (and soon to local courts such as the Recorder's Court), the radical sanction of malicious or frivolous suits, and police responsibility for complaints.

Another crucial reform was the consolidation and rationalization of policing, mainly in the larger cities, through the implementation of a sizeable, salaried constabulary force. Its members were quickly inculcated with a pronounced esprit de corps and military discipline, concentrated at certain sites (stations), and given uniforms to signal their distance from the rest of the population.[10] The phenomenal rise in arrests and imprisonments after 1840[11] transcended the mere quantitative facts. It denoted a fundamental, qualitative change: from this point on, the likelihood of punishment was increased with an enhanced police presence, a greatly expanded capacity to process even minor violations, and methodical targeting of the urban criminal element.[12] To these measures must be added the rationalization of the court hierarchy (and in particular the reform of the appeals system) as well as an improved spatial distribution of the penal system through the creation of many new judicial districts.[13]

2   Added to this far-reaching rationalization of crime processing procedures was an important dynamic of *institutional specialization*. The functional division of labour between the penitentiary and the jail that came into being in the early 1840s was only the initial manifestation of a process of specialization that would become increasingly pronounced within the correctional system. Enthusiasm for classification of the prison population – a cornerstone of the treatment philosophy espoused in those modern cathedrals of punishment – quickly gave way to disillusion, if only because of the practical difficulties of devising classification criteria that could be shown to be both stable and consistent.[14] Classification came to look like a primitive, awkward, and above all ineffective way of dividing up the different manifestations of crime and criminals, even within a single facility.

The inadequacies of the classificatory impulse would soon lead to institutional specialization, the two main criteria employed for this purpose being age and sex. The first timid attempts to create penal institutions for juvenile offenders (e.g., La Petite Roquette in France) had appeared in the West shortly before 1840, but it took ten more years for the movement to gather momentum on both sides of the Atlantic.[15] In Canada, the reformatories at Île-aux-Noix and Penetanguishene were founded in 1858 and 1859, respectively.[16] While women had long been given special quarters in penitentiaries and prisons, Canada's first women's prison was not built until 1876 (in Montreal, although it was in fact one of the earliest to appear in North America).[17]

Institutional specialization as a function of the convict's degree of criminal responsibility proved much more difficult. The logic governing the choice of sentence length (more or less than two years) as the primary criterion for assignment to either the penitentiary or the jail soon appeared deeply suspect, for this criterion did not actually serve to distinguish petty criminals from felons. The jailhouse housed all manner of petty criminals along with drunkards and vagrants – the population who would soon become known in law and common parlance as "habitual offenders." For this population of recidivists, a special prison on the Irish model – alternatively known as a "central" or "intermediate" prison – was soon proposed. The stated purpose of this prison was to house and isolate criminals sentenced to terms ranging from one or two months to three years. In their annual reports from 1862 to 1894, the Quebec prison inspectors harped incessantly on the need for such an institution and trumpeted its advantages, especially its capacity to isolate hardened petty criminals from the motley population of the local prisons. This proposal never found a receptive ear with the federal or Quebec prison authorities.[18]

Still, this episode reveals a prevailing tendency to strive for what Foucault called a "carceral archipelago," a configuration that could accommodate and sort out specific clienteles and criminal behaviours. In its mature phase, prison diversity was presented as a rational and durable institutional response to the multi-faceted nature of crime.

3   Of course, all these changes – the rationalization of the justice system, its recentring within a logic of mass administration of crime, institutional specialization – would have been unthinkable without considerable *state* control and increasing *bureaucratization*, based in particular on centralized production of knowledge and supervision. The Crown Law Department, Canada East, which became the Department of Justice after Confederation, exerted increasingly tight control over judicial and penal functions.[19] The major stages in the public authorities' adoption of this managerial logic included systematic and periodic reform of the criminal laws until their codification in 1892; the 1857 creation of the Board of Inspectors of Prisons and Asylums, with extensive powers of investigation and supervision; and tighter control over policing and certain lower courts (e.g., the Recorder's Court) by municipal governments. The concomitant decline of the justices of the peace and the sheriffs, the old local authorities, facilitated these developments.

The inescapable conclusion is that the state took near-total control over everything relating to penal administration, even though (as shown in the next chapter) a segment of it relating to juvenile delinquency was entrusted to the private sector.[20] The great departure discussed above was most strikingly materialized here: in the liberal worldview, crime now partook of a specific set of issues and was ever more rigorously distinguished from poverty.[21] The liberal view gave rise to a form of public sanction that clearly sat outside the purview of civil society, as it still does today.

But can the history of the prison and the penal administration be summed up by these structural changes? Certainly not. First, these changes would enable the penal institutions to adapt quickly to changes in the definition of crimes and in the philosophy of penal administration. Second, other transformations were to follow. Between the prison at birth and the prison in adulthood, society's views of the criminal would also be thoroughly transformed.

PUNITIVE REASON REGAINED

Where is the nodal point of the complex interface between the dictates of freedom, the necessity of punishment, and the will to reform? In 1836, during tumultuous debate that would soon degenerate into the Rebellions, a special committee of the House of Assembly of Lower Canada gravely discussed crime and prisons. Members John Neilson and Dominique Mondelet had published an enthusiastic report of their trip to the United States the previous year (Mondelet and Neilson 1835). Among the witnesses heard by the committee was Amury Girod, a staunch Patriote and reformer and a disciple of Philipp Emanuel von Fellenberg, the great Swiss educationalist. Girod's audience of legislators were in thrall to the grand principles of reform that had given rise to the penitentiary, which they were now intending to implement in the colony. He was not at all encouraging:

> The social body decides ... whether one of its members has become the enemy of the whole by his crimes; if so, he is expelled from the community or otherwise punished; but it is the judge and the arbiter of his external actions alone; as far as regards the internal man[,] his conscience and his belief, society has nothing and can have nothing to do. I do not mean to infer from this that society ought to take no interest in the moral reform of the criminal, but simply to assert the right of every man, whether free or a slave, to hold God to be the sole judge of his thoughts, his conscience and

opinions. Doubtless, it would be desirable that we should be able to reform the hearts of perverse men, and doubtless it is necessary to adopt all legitimate means of doing so; but the probability of success in such an undertaking, appears to me not so great as we are disposed to believe it ...

Each member of society must submit to the Law which is the will of the whole, and society has no right to exact any thing further from its members. If a man obeys the Laws, his obligations towards society are fulfilled. If society can accomplish the conversion of an individual imprisoned for crime, into a moral and virtuous being, so much the better; but I have as yet seen no instance of it.[22]

Contra Foucault, the logic of reform – that intimate power dynamic operating between the reformer and the criminal in the silence of the prison – is not a historically stable constant, and one illustration was that the liberal discourse on crime was to become notable for a renewed emphasis on *punishment*. By the same token, it would firmly renounce the reformist philanthropic utopias of Howard, Bentham, John Ruskin, David Livingston, and other sons of the Enlightenment, tossing them onto the heap of good but misguided intentions.

Penitentiary isolation had, after all, aimed to penetrate minds and recapture hearts. The moral treatment and reform of the offender necessitated action on the *soul*; it demanded a borderline totalitarian obsession with changing him *from within*. Liberal discourse sounded the death-knell of this ideal. It insisted that the inner space from which the will emerges, and where responsibility rests, should be free from interference. A custodial sentence is merely that: a loss of one's physical freedom. It does not imply that any learning is being done. And, in a world where regulation is a function of the market, the only thing confinement *can* accomplish is to *punish* prisoners by excluding them from the market's operational logic. Individuals are to be judged by their acts. They will be held accountable only for the outward, explicit manifestations of their will. In this view, crime is not so much an indicator of societal decadence as an individualized form of defiance. In the great liberal transition, the individual has regained responsibility for his actions, whether good or bad, and must bear their consequences.

Girod's opinion, then, was not a dissident, backward voice struggling to be heard amid the clamour of reformers; on the contrary, it was forward-looking, betraying the influence of two Frenchmen whose ideas were to have a major impact on penality in the latter half of the nineteenth century: Gustave de Beaumont and Alexis de Tocqueville. By 1833, with the publication of *On the Penitentiary System in the United States and Its Application in France*, these two thinkers had already laid out the clearest and most coherent expression of the liberal philosophy of crime and punishment. Subsequent works by Tocqueville would merely refine this philosophy.

It is has too rarely been stressed that this philosophy marked a profound departure from the convictions and principles of the reformers who had created the modern prison. It was based not on faith in the possibility of reform but on the principle of freedom of choice implied by the criminal act; not on the pertinence of therapy but on the consequences of freedom for the management of crime in the social order under construction in the West. Reasonable adults were at all times masters of their own reason, if not their own morals. Their power to choose, to apply the will to their own ends – even bad ones – engendered and justified society's right to punish. As Tocqueville put it, "Man in free society can choose between good and evil; evil is on one side, good on the other, virtue is here and vice there. Man has received from God the ability and the right to choose between them" (Chambre des députés, 2 May 1844, in Tocqueville 1984, 2: 244–5).

A corollary was that the misuse of this freedom constituted an indelible stain on one's inner being that made the ideal of reform even more difficult, if not illusory.

> It will be necessary to settle the meaning attached to the word *reformation*.
> Do we mean by this expression the radical change of a wicked person into an honest man – a change which produces virtues in the place of vices?
> A similar regeneration, if it ever take place, must be very rare … It would have been much easier for the guilty individual to remain honest, than it is to rise again after his fall. It is in vain that society pardons him; his conscience does not. Whatever may be his efforts, he never will regain that delicacy of honour, which alone supports a spotless life. Even when he resolves to live honestly, he cannot forget that he *has been* a criminal; and this remembrance, which deprives him of self-esteem, deprives also his virtue of its reward and its guaranty (Beaumont and Tocqueville 1833, 55).[23]

Crime is no longer the mark of corrigible deviance, or perhaps a curable malady of the soul: it is an indignity, the sign of a wayward will, a lack of self-restraint, which deprives the individual of the self-esteem central to liberal agency. In this sphere of the private and the intimate, society's rights give way to more transcendent powers.

> How can we prove with ciphers the purity of the soul, the delicacy of sentiments, the innocency of intentions? Society, without power to effect this radical regeneration, is no more capable of proving if it exists. In the one and the other case, it is an affair of the interior *forum*; in the first case God alone can act; in the second, God alone can judge (Beaumont and Tocqueville 1833, 56).[24]

Where human science cannot aspire to knowledge of the soul, the legitimacy of punishment remains grounded in formal recognition of guilt,[25] prior to any hope of reform.

In light of these fundamental beliefs, Tocqueville's intense hostility toward philanthropy, which he shared with other liberals of his generation, begins to make sense. I am not talking of the science of charity in gestation during this period, which I discuss in part 3, but the deep humanitarian belief in the possibility of reform which dominated the thinking of the modern prison's originators.

> There are in America as well as in Europe, estimable men whose minds feed upon philosophical reveries ... they consider man, however far advanced in crime, as still susceptible of being brought back to virtue. They think that the most infamous being may yet recover the sentiment of honour; and ... they hope for an epoch when all criminals may be radically reformed, the prisons be entirely empty, and justice find no crimes to punish.
>
> Others, perhaps without so profound a conviction, pursue nevertheless the same course; they occupy themselves continually with prisons; ... Philanthropy has become for them a kind of profession; and they have caught the *monomanie* of the penitentiary system, which to them seems the remedy for all the evils of society. (Beaumont and Tocqueville 1833, 48)[26]

But although it was not (or not very) realistic to suppose that an in-depth reform of the criminal could be effected,[27] it was still possible to force him into superficial conformity. If he could not be won over philosophically to the social order, he could at least be compelled to obey it out of self-interest.

> We have no doubt, but that the habits of order to which the prisoner is subjected for several years, influence very considerably his moral conduct after his return to society ...
>
> Perhaps, leaving the prison he is not an honest man; but he has contracted honest habits. He was an idler; now he knows how to work ... and if he is not more virtuous he has become at least more judicious; his

> morality is not honour, but interest. His religious faith is perhaps neither lively nor deep; but even supposing that religion has not touched his heart, his mind has contracted habits of order, and he possesses rules for his conduct in life; ... if he has not become in truth better, he is at least more obedient to the laws, and that is all which society has the right to demand. (Beaumont and Tocqueville 1833, 58)[28]

Criminals, otherwise infirm of conscience and self-esteem, could still acquire ethics by force of habit. Habit did not require active participation as much as passive acceptance, the capacity of the prisoner to be worn down into obedience, to knuckle under, and to carry this submissive attitude forward into his extramural life.[29]

The conception of crime expressed here can be seen to imply the existence, in the liberal worldview, of a criminal population that, to a great extent, eludes the will/responsibility duality discussed above.[30] Improper use of their free will has made them outcasts; it also disqualifies them as objects of pity and legitimate recipients of public charity.[31] Reformist paternalism meets its end at the outermost fringes of vice. Crime involves one of the most lethal sicknesses of the social body: the diversion of the will to selfish and illegal ends. As such, it is a specific blot on society and must be differentiated from poverty with ever greater care.

Moreover, endemic crime has become a social ill. Criminals form a specific society, or rather counter-society, that threatens to poison the society of free citizens. Tocqueville expressed this situation and his proposed solution as follows:

> It must be acknowledged that there exists among us at this moment an organized society of criminals ... It is this society whose members must be dispersed today; it is this benefit derived from association that must be taken away from the evildoers, so as to reduce, if possible, each one of them to being alone against all the honest people united to defend order. The only means of achieving this result is to hold each convict in isolation; so that he makes no new accomplices, and completely loses sight of those he left outside the prison walls. (Chambre des députés, 5 July 1843, in Tocqueville 1984, 2: 135)[32]

Beyond reformist utopias, the prison thus becomes an instrument of social prophylaxis, a place where the society of criminals is destroyed by isolating it from the honest folk. We see here in embryo the theory of "social defence," in which punishment is regarded as a way of immunizing society. Once the criterion distinguishing the criminal from the honest citizen is clearly specified (and that criterion is simply guilt), the prison is freed to become a place of exception where the violation of fundamental rights is permissible:

> We believe that society has the right to do every thing necessary for its conservation, and for the order established within it; and we understand perfectly well, that an assemblage of criminals, all of whom have infringed the laws of the land, and all of whose inclinations are corrupted, and appetites vicious, cannot be governed in prison according to the same principles, and with the same means, as free persons, whose desires are correct, and whose actions are conformable to the laws. (Beaumont and Tocqueville 1833, 44)

In a single thrust, the prison becomes the modern form of a logic of example and deterrence that, *pace* Foucault, has lost none of its social relevance. Obviously, this form of punishment is no longer the brutal pedagogy of the example that once instilled fear and conformity in the king's subjects. It is now a never-ending spectacle embodied in the walls of an institution whose existence illustrates the consequences of abusing one's freedom. The message is conveyed to potential wrongdoers, and indeed to all citizens, that they must make reasoned, prudent use of their ability to choose good or they will be liable to the surrender of their freedom: "The first object of punishment is not the reformation of the convict, but, on the contrary, to give a useful and moral example to society: this is obtained by inflicting upon the guilty a punishment commensurate to his crime" (Beaumont and Tocqueville 1833, 87).[33]

The die is cast: the liberal prison has just found its legitimacy in a world in which freedom must reign. The new punishment paradigm does not, of course, abolish the hope, much less the rhetoric, of prisoner reform.[34] But the prison, the supreme visible symbol of punishment, can no longer focus on reform; its main function from now on will be quite simply to instill in all citizens a fear of being confined within its walls. Here again the principle of less eligibility, which underlies the whole discourse of institutionalized reform during this era, is expressed:

> To prevent a repeat of the offence, to erect a barrier to the increase in the number of criminals: such is the goal pursued by society when it inflicts punishment on the guilty. For such punishment to be effective, the ensuing inconvenience and pain must be obvious to all and must unequivocally win out over the enjoyment or benefit which one may expect to derive from

crime. This idea is summarized with perfect accuracy when we say that punishment must be both afflictive and exemplary. (Astor 1887, 3)

Prison's primary function, on this view, is as a place to be avoided. Although the physical and mental integrity of its population cannot be improperly abused, neither can this institution be turned into a refuge from poverty, or worse, a place where criminals can get temporary respite until they catch their breath. It became a commonplace of the era's discourse on the penitentiary to express the deep-seated worry that prison might become a palace for its denizens – a fear encapsulated in one Quebec prison inspector's remark that "a gaol ought to be a gaol."[35] The conditions were now in place for the emergence of a discourse in which prison is an unavoidably necessary institution whose role is nonetheless to drive away the destitute, even as it too often becomes a place of refuge for them.

> If the diet in our prisons be dreaded, the idlers will not direct their steps so often towards these establishments. There are in the cities of Montreal and Quebec a certain number of rogues who quit the prisons to return to them, after an absence of a few days; for these miserable wretches – the greater number of whom are without any home – like to establish their abode at the common jail, where they find clean beds, an agreeable temperature, chiefly in winter time, and a certain abundance of food, comparatively speaking, all of which induce them to consider the prisons as palaces.[36]
>
> Before building [the central prison, for which the inspectors have been making the case for twenty years], it must be borne in mind that it is intended for all classes of criminals; that it will have to shelter the scum of society, wretches, who, half the time, have neither home, nor food, nor clothing, picked up by the police in the filthy streets and in the haunts of vice and infamy in our cities; and that, accustomed as they are to every misery and privation, it would not be right to lodge them in a palace, in a building which would create a desire to remain in it and return to it, in a word a dwelling affording more comfort than the dwellings of half the honest people in the country ... The inhumanity and barbarity of by gone ages must be carefully avoided; but on the other hand we must not be carried away by a ridiculous and dangerous philanthropy.[37]

Does this mean that the prison can now be summed up in terms of its repressive function and that the discourse of reform no longer has any role to play in this connection; that liberalism has given up thinking of prison and punishment as anything more than a deterrent? Not at all. The foundational reformist discourse associated with the institution cannot succumb so easily. Imprisonment requires the disposition of prisoners' bodies within the spatiotemporal setting of the prison, and there is still some hope of seizing the opportunity of their time in custody to improve them.

This diffuse hope found expression in the recurrent debate over the cellular system. A strange trajectory indeed, that of the cell. In early times, during the glorious epoch that saw the birth of the penitentiary, cells were regarded as the paradigmatic instrument of reform, settings in which the prisoner's mind could be systematically worked on without undue interference from other prisoners. But the cell did not fade into a memory along with the decline of reform sentiment – quite the contrary. Tocqueville, for one, strongly approved of the cell as a key instrument for isolating the prisoner from the society of his congeners:

> We have pointed out the inconvenience of absolute solitude, the deficiency of which is, that it deprives the prisoner's submission of its moral character; but we must at the same time acknowledge its advantages in respect to discipline; and the facility of ruling an establishment of this nature, without the application of severe and repeated punishment, is certainly a very great advantage. (Beaumont and Tocqueville 1833, 40)

In this discourse, the cell becomes the preferred instrument of *management*, an administrative cure-all making up for the notorious insufficiencies of classification.[38] However, while most observers agreed on the advantages of solitary confinement over differential treatment by category or class, they differed markedly on the value of confinement as a *treatment*. Here again, the waning of reform as a purpose of imprisonment is evident. Even Charles Lucas, Tocqueville's staunch adversary, criticized twenty-four-hour solitary confinement only because he favoured more humane treatment for criminals; he continued to believe that nightly lockup was necessary. Some observers argued that total isolation drove prisoners insane. Reform had to rely on other methods such as supervised parole. Moreover, a notable semantic shift was taking place among the advocates of the cellular philosophy, which was now regarded as contributing to a new form of *socialization* (rather than isolation) of the prisoner.[39]

> We do not believe that the prison ... can vanquish the antagonism existing between these two fractions of society, who fear one another and coexist without intermingling ... To prepare the prisoner for life in society, what is needed is to lower the barriers separating him from the honest population, to snuff out the mutual mistrust that is the most serious obstacle to his rehabilitation ... Around the prisoner, we want to see only that honourable portion of society whom he has hardly known thus far, who alone are able to offer him good examples. But the action of this portion of society can only be exerted within the cell. (Astor 1887, 41)[40]

Here we come to the essential feature of the liberal gaze on the prison: from the moment when it becomes an unabashed instrument of punishment, its reforming function is moved out to the *periphery* of the prison, to the space that extends and connects it to civil society. The criminal's salvation now lies outside the prison; rehabilitation must now be cognized in terms of the multiple strategies attendant upon a proper release from prison, not the exercise of power for therapeutic purposes inside its walls. And so the cell is no longer viewed as isolating the prisoner but as putting him in contact with upstanding members of society.

The same holds for prison labour. In the reformist ideal integral to the invention of the prison, work was a pedagogical tool essential to reform. Its power to compel prisoners to observe regularity and order was thought to imprint on their minds, if not a love of work, at least an acceptance of its inescapability. As soon as this ideal began to fade, and concomitant with the progressive abandonment of attempts to transform prisoners' minds, penal work had to take on a whole different meaning. Until the end of the century, philosophers of penitentiary confinement vacillated endlessly between the punitive function of work and its educational value. For example, a British Empire circular dated 16 January 1865 recommended that prisoners serving short sentences perform strictly penal labour, with "productive" work being reserved for longer-term inmates.[41] The punitive function was clearly stated by Terence Joseph O'Neill, inspector of prisons for the Province of Canada:

> It will hardly admit of a contradiction that in Canada, Gaol imprisonment has been received with too little dread by evil-doers. Punishment, in any form, being unknown, the Gaol could scarcely be expected to be deterrent ... If, in addition to this confinement, some species of labour were adopted, not of the remunerative kind, but simply "hard labour," thoroughly objectless except as a punishment, as is, for instance, the tread-wheel and shot-drill, the

Gaol would assuredly have fewer occupants; and much shorter and, of course, less expensive imprisonments, would be found to suffice.[42]

But work could also have a pedagogical function. Increasingly, the idea gained credence that prison work could be made into a trade (rather than a therapy) that would favour a successful release from prison. The prison inspectors, for example, wrote, "Labor being the real instrument of order and progress, to lower it in the eyes of the condemned would be unwise."[43]

Thus, although the liberal discourse was built on a critique of the "totalitarian" reformist utopias of the modern prison's inventors, the expectation of reform nonetheless found new life in this model, albeit indirectly. While it was no longer possible to claim that prison alone could reform criminals, it was still possible to reconfigure the spatio-temporal context of detention in such a way as to provide, as much as possible, for a successful release. That context was reconfigured with reform in mind: the cells separated prisoners from each other, either at night or at all times,[44] but allowed for contact with good Samaritans outside the walls; workshops were offered in which prisoners could learn a trade, and they could earn time off for good behaviour – assuming that there was any hope of their eventually being released.

THE DECLINE OF LIBERAL FORMALISM

Divested of its reformist illusions, the prison was now free to adopt the mission of punishing criminal acts ensuing from a citizen's wayward use of reason. Crime became in effect merely this: the result of a misuse of the freedom to act, punishable by time in prison on the order of a court. Thus the halcyon liberal optimism of the classic period, when law and legality were enthusiastically taken up as instruments for telling good from evil, legal from illegal, honesty from crime – and when prison housed all those caught on the wrong side of those dividing lines.[45] Now that the rational capacity to *desire* evil was established as the basic formal characteristic of the criminal act, and the justice system's unfailing ability to distinguish guilt from innocence and mete out the proper punishment was recognized, crime could be presented in all its positivity. It became possible, in a formal procedure leading from arrest to court to prison, to conceive of its regulation within the inviolable framework of personal liberty. It was a new world of transparent causes, suitable methods, and relevant solutions; a world in which crime, by the visibility of the act through which it is expressed, is precisely what it appears to be – and this is of course the world we still live in today. In its Manichean simplicity, this worldview reassures the honest and law-abiding citizen with the visible, tangible spectacle of that which is presented as his opposite.

The Radical Critique

But things are not and can never be so simple. This conception of crime and its treatment would, without question, enjoy hegemonic status under liberal regulation. Crime, as the wayward product of liberal democratic society, was inseparable from it. It was an ineluctable phenomenon, perhaps even an incurable illness, and so any hope of eradicating it could be no more than a utopian daydream. Yet the basic stance of someone like Tocqueville, which soon entered the canon of received wisdom about prisons, came up against a contrary discourse which, although radically marginalized, was no less revealing for that.

> To train the mind upon those things with which the heart is taken; to light the fraternity's way with the torch of science; to think and feel all at once; to combine in a single effort of love the vigilance of the mind and the powers of the soul; to have a confidence so brave in the peoples' future and God's justice that it becomes possible to combat the permanence of evil and its supposed immortality: is there a more worthy use of one's time and one's life? (Blanc 1845, vii)

The odd admixture of paternalistic nostalgia and Enlightenment humanism that had attended the birth of the prison in the early nineteenth century now reappeared in a progressive version that took its place as an alternative to bourgeois liberalism. It was a different kind of faith in progress,[46] one predicated on hopes of collective emancipation more than on faith in the possibility of individual improvement, and it found its most coherent expression among the socialists. It retained the idea of reform, but now the role of the community took centre stage. Neither the causes of crime nor its cure were a function of the individual will, for crime was a mirror of the wayward society that produced it, and could fade away only in a reformed society:

> There is but one penitentiary system that is both effectual and reasonable: a sound organization of labour. We have in our midst a great school of perversity which is always open, and which must be closed at once: I refer to

poverty. As long as we fail to attack the root cause of evil, we will squander ourselves in a fruitless attempt to prevent the inevitable consequences. Veiled but not destroyed, evil will sprout, and grow under the outward appearance of good, blending disappointment with every advance, and hiding a pitfall under every benefit. (Blanc 1845, 38–9)[47]

Implicit in this discourse is a radical overturning of liberal assumptions. Crime is not the inevitable outcome of the misuse of free will but a contingent and predictable product of social disorder. Prison is thus a symbol of societal failure more than an instrument of visible punishment.[48]

Furthermore, how could anyone suppose that the effects of societal dysfunction can be overcome by simply isolating those in whom that dysfunction is manifested? How can this procedure be in any way presented as the antidote to a misbegotten society?

Unimaginable though it seems, our legislators had faith in the power of solitary confinement to inculcate morality, and this is how they avoided seeing the horror of it. They believed, in their nearly unexampled blindness, that a man can rise to a feeling of duty towards his peers, if he lives apart from them; that it is possible to reform and guide the convict's sociable instincts by violently repressing them, by wasting them away through disuse and inertia of the will; that, in a word, to raise up the fallen one, all that is needed is to lock him up alone with his crimes! (Blanc 1845, 37)[49]

Just as Tocqueville was putting in place the modern principles of liberal penality, a rejoinder came from the radical and republican left, which was quick to notice the cynical withdrawal typical of this worldview:

You endeavour to replace rehabilitation with neglect; thus you do not believe the criminal can be reformed. The honourable men to whom I speak … have the misfortune to despair at the non-existence of goodness in human nature … For our part, we do not despair of the possibility of moral reform, because we firmly believe that, when addressing the human heart, no labour is impossible … Moral problems are more complicated, and more mysterious to us. There is no circumstance in which one is not entitled to expect miracles as great as those formerly worked by religious faith.[50]

It was indeed possible to penetrate into the bottomless recesses of the soul, which the liberals had declared to be out of reach, but through education and socialization, not confinement and deterrence.[51]

In this critique, criminals were no longer members of an ill-defined yet unshakably labelled class of people. The hope of social change at the core of socialism countered liberalism's sharp distinction between illegality and good society with a view of crime as a temporary manifestation of incomplete, deficient socialization. Liberal penality thus, even at its apogee, faced challenges to its most deeply espoused principles. But the greatest threat to its hegemony was yet to come.

Investing in Conscience and Will

By its very success, the liberal conception of crime paved the way for its own obsolescence. In the mid-nineteenth century, the prison had become the most widespread form of punishment, and solitary confinement the standard method for managing the penitentiary population, at least at night. But this situation soon met with a critique of some of the most basic assumptions of liberal penality.

The critique began as an implicit question: Prison is an instrument of punishment, no doubt – but is it no more than that? Is it merely a method of forcibly inculcating honest "habits" – that varnish of conformity with which Tocqueville was perfectly satisfied? Even if it is agreed that crime is first and foremost an act, does it necessarily follow that such an act constitutes a one-way crossing of the border between honesty and crime? Are the mind and the soul of the criminal completely impervious to influence? The science of motivation, emerging from the practice of routine prison management, would soon be making a contrary claim.

The idea was to act upon the criminal's free will, the capacity for reason abiding deep within him; to pluck the subtle strings of desire and hopefulness that kept this capacity alive. The prison, the locus of punishment, would now turn to the business of motivating prisoners to do better in life. The horror it inspired in potential criminals, its fearsome reputation as a place to be avoided, would catalyze a rebirth of the will and a renewal of self-esteem. Yes, the habits prescribed by Tocqueville and his followers would have to be acquired. The key difference was that they would now be acquired willingly, progressively, and with the prisoner in control of the pace of change.

This reconciliation with the prisoner's agency, this faith in his capacity to regain the self-esteem denied him by Tocqueville, was expressed by the Quebec prison inspectors in the following terms:

> The cultivation of pride and self-esteem in the prisoners is a great moral strength to them. Pride is the most powerful sentiment of humanity, for it

is the most purely personal. From this is drawn the principle that we should not degrade those coming to prison and already blighted by crime.[52]

Investing in motivation as opposed to coerced submission became the cure-all applied by the liberal prison. This approach accorded with the primary values of liberalism in that it recognized the operation of the will as primary even in criminals, yet remained compatible with the imperatives of prison management, and especially cell-based confinement. The Irish model[53] and early parole were the very quintessence of this development. Other examples were indeterminate sentencing and the use of merit systems in reformatories. In its new incarnation, prison was at worst a purgatory, one whose duration could be shortened by good behaviour.

But how then was it to play its punitive role, now that it was also saddled with the job of instilling motivation in inmates? Here, ironically, in the marrow of the criminal personality, was the substance of the liberal ethic of will and responsibility. The hope of improvement and personal progress at the heart of liberalism collided frontally with the need to punish deviations from legality by stigmatizing their perpetrators.

Return to the Social

The radical critique of liberal penality held out the hope that the problem of crime could be solved by improving life in the community, thus rendering the criminal act unnecessary. Faced with this critique, liberals had devised a system of crime management centring around legalistic processing of the criminal, leaving reform initiatives to the philanthropists or the prison directors. The prison remained, at its core, the prime expression of the state's power to punish.[54] However, the late nineteenth century saw a radical revision of the basic postulates of liberal penality. The social dimension of the problem was rediscovered, and the idea of treatment was once again envisaged. To be sure, the operative model was not to be that of utopian socialism. The criminal was not to be viewed as just another member of the unhappy masses, labouring and sometimes rebelling within the dysfunctional system of capitalism; nor did it follow that societal change was the only way out. Crime was still to be considered a phenomenon in its own right, but it was now to be treated according to the dictates of science.

Two overarching phenomena are at play here. First, the development of the social sciences, psychology, and social statistics ushered in a new hope that human beings could be intimately and precisely *known*, and that such knowledge could be acquired not through the vague and subjective mechanism of philanthropic or religious empathy, and not only within the liberal framework of universal rights and duties, but according to the precise parameters of an accrued body of scientific knowledge. Science offered the putatively objective possibility of intervening to rectify both the person and the social organism in which he lives.

Second, and simultaneously, the logic of liberal penality was coming in for profound revision. These changes came about in response to the expression of popular and feminist demands, the appearance of the first mass workers' parties, and the extension of the franchise. The result was an enhancement of democratic regulation.

> This drastic revision of penality's logic occurs precisely at the historical moment when the political franchise is being extended to include the mass of the (male) working class within its terms for the very first time ... At precisely the same time a whole series of institutions and regulations are put in place which are designed to identify all those legal citizens (or prospective legal citizens) who lack the normative capacity to participate and exercise their new-found rights responsibly. Once identified, these deviants are subjected to a work of normalization, correction or segregation, which ensures one of two things. Either they become responsible, conforming subjects, whose regularity, political stability and industrious performance deems them capable of entering into institutions of representative democracy; or they are supervised and segregated from the normal social realm in a manner that minimizes (and individualises) any "damage" they can do. (Garland 1985, 249)

Faith in science henceforth made it possible to distinguish the fit from the unfit, the efficient from the deficient, the working masses finally acknowledged as an integral part of the democratic polity from the lower strata incapable of holding that status. The dividing line was no longer between the bourgeoisie and the working class, or even between honest people and criminals as defined by the formalistic criteria of liberal penality. For liberals, a criminal was simply a person who committed a crime. For the new social sciences, crime was an organic deficiency, and it was the scientist more than the judge who could differentiate normality from deviance.

The message now becomes that beating back crime no longer depends on some vague philanthropic enterprise of personal improvement but on the prospect of *finding a cure*. Crime, in this view, is an indicator of personal deficiency rather than endemic societal dysfunction. Consequently, the formalistic treatment of crime begins to look starkly outdated. To look at the *act*, not the person, when determining how to deal with a criminal case is to disregard the unique and peculiar data that the case has just revealed to science; it is, furthermore, to banish the possibility of solving crime through suitable treatment.

> We endeavor to cure crime by a system childishly futile. As well might we sentence the lunatic to three months in the asylum, or the victim of smallpox to thirty days in the hospital, at the end of these periods to turn them loose, whether mad or sane, cured or still diseased ... Offenders must be dealt with as individuals, not as a class. (Roland Molineux [1907], quoted in Rothman 1980, 69)[55]

After legal formalism and the sacrosanct principle of proportionate sentencing, the next basic postulate of liberal penality to be called into question was criminal responsibility.

> Progressives were certain that an environmental interpretation of crime made a mockery of personal culpability. No one who was raised in a slum could be held strictly accountable for his actions. The wretchedness of the social setting was so great that responsibility could not be assigned in uniform and predictable fashion. (Rothman 1980, 53)

If crime was an indicator of sickness, its therapy had to begin with a consideration of its peculiar genesis and etiology in each individual. A case-by-case approach became necessary.[56] Ultimately, doubt was cast on the prison itself – the institution symbolizing the characteristic formalism and standardization of liberal penality: "It has been said that in prison all men are equal; but their natural inequalities are not removed by putting men in custody; they are only ignored; and prison treatment, being uniform, is therefore unequal treatment of individuals" (James Devon, quoted in Garland 1985, 86).[57]

This being the case, the prison suffered from the structural defect of being incapable of providing for individualized treatment: "It became increasingly apparent that the continuing problems of imprisonment – its failure to deter, to reform, to reduce criminality, etc. – were characteristic of the prison itself and not merely accidents of a flawed administration"

(Garland 1985, 60).[58] One way of making up for this failing would be to make the prison a faithful replica of society: "Rather than serve as a model to the society, the penitentiary was to model itself on the society; it was not to be an antidote to the external environment, but a faithful replication of it" (Rothman 1980, 118).

The institution of parole provided for a fraught but manageable coexistence between punishment as an obligation and reform as a desideratum, in particular by making prison a double deterrent. But the concept of prison as a reflection of society heightens the contradiction between punishment and reform, a contradiction formerly resolved with notable effectiveness by the assiduous application of classic liberal penality. In an odd echo of earlier times, the hopes placed in scientific therapy recall the original utopian designs for prisons as instruments of reform, although the terms have changed completely. Prison can now effect reform only if it resembles society, where once it had to do so by providing the antidote to it. Understandably, this approach soon proved a total disappointment to its adherents. Rothman cites a jaded remark from 1933 by Howard Gill, director of the "model" Norfolk Prison Colony in Massachusetts, the most advanced expression of the reformists' hopes for penitentiary science: "It seems impossible that prisons will ever serve as an adequate means of handling the problems of crime ... The thought that we can build a community prison which approximates the normal is faint hope" (quoted in Rothman 1980, 413).

THE CASE OF THE MONTREAL PRISON[59]

The history of the Pied-du-Courant prison in Montreal clearly reflects and illustrates the ongoing changes in liberal penality while highlighting its practical advantages and limits. The discourse on punishment methods in the democratic era was not static or repetitive; it was, rather, quite responsive to the vagaries of the liberal worldview and the contradictions inherent in it, as well as to the challenges to liberalism that arose in the late nineteenth century. But just as the utopian ideal of reform through imprisonment ebbed back into a punitive reflex, turn-of-the-century hopes for the scientific treatment of crime would not have much effect on penal practice.

The reason was very simple: the liberal worldview was the only viable one in a society based on individual liberty. It alone acknowledged the primary purpose of penal justice (punishing crime) while satisfying the demands of basic humanism (not mistreating the prisoner), leaving reformist reveries to the penitentiary managers and philanthropists. Its agenda was simplicity itself: let the prison do what it does best. Let it lock up criminals under conditions suitable for their punishment, and thereby deter honest folk from taking the road to crime.

Given this situation, a science-driven revolution in prison management was not to be expected. Once the West's imposing penitentiary system was put in place after the 1830s, it remained only to manage it in all good conscience, as the liberal philosophy of punishment required. The sombre confines of the modern prison remained impervious to challenges from the new science of criminology; penal formalism was not to be subordinated to case-by-case treatment. Only on the treatment of hardened criminals and recidivists did criminologists and prison authorities see eye to eye. The discourse of eugenics was invoked to justify the indefinite or permanent isolation of this group of people deemed beyond rehabilitation, incapable of life in society. Confinement became the end of the road, a dumping ground for these new wretched of the earth, for whom science had found no better solution than to lock them away in the darkness of the cell. In Canada, the penitentiaries had played this role since the mid-nineteenth century, with the workaday silence of the federal prison administration being periodically disturbed by the occasional prison riot and the commission of inquiry which inevitably followed.[60]

But what of the jailhouse? A revolving door for petty criminals, caught up in the busy administration of everyday violations and misdemeanours, it meted out a kind of haphazard mass punishment without enjoying the luxury of engaging in speculation about the possibility of reform. The Montreal prison is a particularly striking example of this dynamic.

Yet at its inception in 1836, in the heyday of utopian penality, it had been thought capable of rising to the highest challenges, and even one day serving as a penitentiary, following the lead of the one just opened at Kingston in the neighbouring colony. Its designer, the architect Henry Musgrave Blaiklock, seems to have been inspired by the Pennsylvania model (twenty-four-hour solitary confinement) in his design for rather spacious cells arranged in wings looking onto a central corridor.[61]

After 1843, however, when the Kingston penitentiary was assigned the role of housing Lower Canadian criminals sentenced to more than two years,[62] the Montreal prison was confirmed in its role as a holding pen for petty criminals. Thus began a long history of lamentation, in which both prison managers and inspectors deplored the facility's overpopulation, outdatedness, and inadequacy for purposes of rational treatment, as well as the structural impossibility of adopting an effective classification of its inmates. Solitary confinement at the facility came in for special condemnation.

And yet despite all these deficiencies, the Montreal prison did the impossible: it endured. From 1840 onward and throughout the whole period under study, it remained by far the largest penal institution in Quebec.[63] Moreover, all things considered, it evinced a remarkable capacity for adaptation. In fact, all the issues of liberal penality discussed in this chapter can be found encapsulated in its history.

Consider, for example, the principle of functional specialization. Starting in earnest in the 1870s, specific institutions would be built for girls (1870), boys (1873), and women (1876), leading to the disappearance of these populations from Pied-du-Courant. Moreover, efforts were made to convert it into a more modern, cell-based facility. The 1897 inspectors' report states that 227 individual cells had been built in this relatively modest building, along with 84 three-person cells and 4 "open quarters" (Bessière 1997, 35).[64] Even the endless debate over penal labour (work as punishment or work as a means of improvement) was enacted within these old, overpopulated walls. Prisoners had initially been assigned to breaking rocks and beating hemp. In 1839, however, after an abortive project to put them to work under a contract with the City of Montreal, the new prison governor, Charles A. Vallée, commissioned a building in the prison yard to house new workshops.[65] The implementation of these workshops attests to the transition from purely penal work to work designed to provide some form of training.

Obviously, the biggest obstacle to the "modernization" of the Montreal prison related to its role as a local facility for a transient population of petty criminals. The prison inspectors' inability to convince the provincial authorities to build an "intermediate" prison to house "habitual criminals" (vagrants and beggars who used the prison as a short-term asylum) for longer intervals gave way to a realization that the prison could be neither deterrent (in the liberal sense of the term) nor reformative. Even the prospect of early parole was a relatively meagre incentive for a person serving only a month or two in prison, as was the case for the large majority of the facility's population.

Yet there is some evidence that the institution was permeable to developments in late-nineteenth-century criminology. From 1883 to 1903, in marked contrast to the city's fast demographic growth, the population of the Montreal prison underwent a relative decline, stabilizing at around 300. It is not that the facility was losing ground to other institutional alternatives, or that it was saturated, unable to absorb any new prisoners from the burgeoning extramural population, because the number of new inmates resumed its rapid growth after 1905, soon necessitating the building of the Bordeaux prison, which opened in 1913.

It is hard to avoid the impression that the Montreal prison, as outdated and inadequate as penal specialists argued it was, played its role of handling the day-to-day inflow and outflow of petty criminals quite well. It served its purpose as the punitive instrument of first resort. The time was long gone when the authorities were enthusiastically building great shrines to the ideal of reform,[66] yet the prospect of a comprehensive therapeutic solution to crime sat somewhere off in an indistinct future. Only legal formalism remained: punishment in response to violation of the formal injunctions contained in the Criminal Code. Seen in this way, the Montreal prison and its history encapsulate rather well the limited ambitions of liberal penal philosophy. The fact that it also served as a refuge for the poorest citizens – a situation decried throughout the period – constitutes another important dimension of this institution, and one to which it will be necessary to return.

* * *

In 1904, Adolphe Prins, a proponent of the theory of "social defence," proposed to "substitute the positive concept of dangerous states for the classical juridical notion of recidivism," thus marking "the passage from a classical logic, in which punishment is a reaction to an act, to a positive logic in which the goal of punishment is the scientific treatment of a person from whom society has to defend itself" (Debuyst et al. 1995, 288).[67] David Garland has brilliantly described this sweeping revision of the liberal view of crime and its treatment, as well as the effect of this revision on penal practice (Garland 1981 and 1985). The idea was to circumvent, if not to eliminate, the formalism of the liberal legal corpus so as to render better treatment possible. The cardinal objectivity of bourgeois law was to give place to the positivity of modern science.

Of course, nothing like this happened, and science had to look within institutions other than the prisons for terrain where it could be practised.[68] This was because the body of law in question was grounded in principles of equity far more vital to liberal regulation than the fate of the prisoners who had fallen under its authority. At stake were the basic rights guaranteed to every citizen, including due process, proportionate sentencing and legal formalism (i.e., the necessity for an offence to be defined in law before anyone could be prosecuted for it). The constraints imposed on punishment by these dictates made it extremely difficult for anyone – even a criminologist or a social worker – to decide another's freedom without his consent, even for the sake of treatment or rehabilitation. And anyone who sought to violate this logic would have to invoke exceptional circumstances (legal or mental incapacity, dangerousness, imminent risk to society, etc.).

Liberal law proclaimed that only crime and its corresponding punishment could justify the restriction of civil liberties. In so doing, it detached crime from the more general, ill-defined category of mass poverty, making it an individual trait rather than an extreme manifestation of an ambient societal dysfunction. By the same token, it instituted an enduring distinction within liberal regulation between the right to punish the criminal and the need to assist the poor.

5

The Regulation of Juvenile Delinquency and Child Protection

> Were I to fix the date of completion of the carceral system, I would choose not 1810 and the penal code, nor even 1844, when the law laying down the principle of cellular internment was passed ... [but] January 22, [1840,] the date of the official opening of Mettray ...
>
> Why Mettray? Because it is the disciplinary form at its most extreme, the model in which are concentrated all the coercive technologies of behavior.
> (Foucault 1977, 293)

Thus begins the concluding chapter of Foucault's magisterial work on the birth of the prison. For Foucault, the Mettray farm colony for young offenders embodies the very essence of the disciplinary power of normalization central to the invention of the prison.

This event sets the stage for all the ensuing power dynamics, and all the small and oppressive ways in which knowledge is used as a complement to and a justification of that power. For anyone interested in the history of how power has been wielded over human beings, Mettray ushers in a new refinement to the art of punishment through education. But as such, it is a beginning,[1] not a final destination. To call Mettray the culmination of the modern prison is not only, as I showed in the preceding chapter, to arbitrarily minimize the sweeping changes made to the regulation of deviance from the mid-nineteenth century onward, but also to posit an arbitrary continuity between the foundational logic of the prison and the opening of the first institutions for young offenders. For Mettray is notable not so much because it extended and furthered certain techniques of power but because it *broke*, in significant ways, with the penal order then being put in place.

Even as the divide instituted in the liberal order between punishment and reform hardened into its procrustean form, and even as Enlightenment-era utopian aspirations to rebuild the human being faded, there was one group for whom even the most cynical observer still thought reform had a chance of success: children. The Patriote Amury Girod, speaking before the Assembly of Lower Canada, expressed skepticism about the idea that prisoners could be reformed. But he immediately added:

> Take a youth who has reached the age of fourteen years, and then for the first time commits some crime from thoughtlessness, or perhaps even from necessity; confine him in an Asylum for that purpose, educate him, teach him some trade or art, entrust the care of rendering him virtuous to a liberal and enlightened Minister of the Gospel, and out of 100 you will find 80, perhaps 90, young persons of good dispositions and imbued with virtuous principles.[2]

In this too, Girod was a worthy disciple of Tocqueville, who likewise expressed faith in the possibility of reforming children:

> If it be possible to obtain moral reformation for any human being, it seems that we ought to expect it for these youths, whose misfortune was caused less by crime, than by inexperience, and in whom all the generous passions of youth may be excited. With a criminal, whose corruption is inveterate, and deeply rooted, the feeling of honesty is not awakened, because the sentiment is extinct; with a youth, this feeling exists, though it has not yet been called into action. (Beaumont and Tocqueville 1833, 123)[3]

The mind of the child is a *tabula rasa*: it is still possible to make an impression on that mind, indeed a frighteningly educational one, and so to nip in the bud the first stirrings of the wayward will that leads to crime. The treatment accorded to young offenders and children at risk thus constitutes a specific case of the penal logic of institutional specialization being instituted at this time. The idea was to differentiate populations by their particular treatment needs or by the need to isolate them from the mass of ordinary criminals. Children, like female prisoners,[4] were hived off from the adult male prison population.

Adult men bore the brunt of punishment, and it was primarily at them that the liberal conception of crime was directed. Children represented an important exception. In their case it was acknowledged that the strict liberal regulation of crime, based on the proportionate sentencing of deliberate illegal acts, could not apply. Children, being still under the guardianship of their parents, were not "free" in the legal sense. Furthermore, the degree to which a child's act was premeditated, the conditions under which it amounted to an exercise of her free will, had to be determined with reference to her greater or lesser capacity to tell right from wrong. And finally, this being the case, the exigencies of punishment might have to be subordinated to the imperatives of reform. In the case of children, then, the foundational principles of the liberal legal order – free will, the strict indexation of the severity of the punishment to that of the acts committed, the primacy of punishment over reform – came to look like *obstacles* to the effective management of crime. From the outset, the treatment accorded young offenders partook of a different penal philosophy from that which applied to adults.[5]

This abrupt break with liberal tradition is often masked by the gradualist approach criticized in the previous chapter. Most historical studies of the question describe the nineteenth-century evolution of policies on young offenders and children at risk as being divided into two eras. First came a set of children's institutions, complemented or in some cases replaced by foster homes. Following that, and especially from 1880 on, came a broader policy of judicial interference in family life, spearheaded by the enactment of laws governing parental inadequacy and the creation of youth courts. Historians have generally plotted these developments along a temporal continuum, positing a gradual evolution from correctional institutions (reformatories, farm colonies, reform or industrial schools) to youth courts in a process whereby the target clientele was gradually broadened and the treatment of children was standardized.[6]

Yet here, as in the treatment of adults, a precise chronological account will capture some of the qualitative shifts taking place, and hence reveal the issues underlying the regulation of young offenders and children at risk in the nineteenth century. This chronology, focusing on the Quebec experience, is the subject of the following discussion.

The perception of juvenile delinquency and children at risk as constituting a *specific problem* entailed a sequence of ruptures of largely unequal importance and having effects at several different levels, in terms of both how children were regarded and the strategies deriving from that regard. The fact that children were regarded as deserving of special treatment says nothing about the modes of treatment applied, the manner in which the state was involved, or even the specific target populations.

1 From the late eighteenth century to the 1830s, philanthropists increasingly regarded children as a specific category among the masses of the poor, a component of the broader problem of poverty. From the poor schools to the charitable institutions for abandoned children, from the Sunday schools to the first orphanages, one segment of European and American philanthropy focused on vocational training and education for children of paupers. These initiatives were timid and rather sporadic, due to the limited resources available for charity and – as one may imagine – to parents' reluctance to give up their children. The legal vacuum prevailing in those times meant that the institutions in question generally had to obtain parental consent before children could be left in their care. A pioneering provision in the United States allowed certain foundling asylums and institutions for young offenders (e.g., the New York House of Refuge, founded in 1825[7]) to include compulsory powers in their charters. The emerging poor children's aid movement made inroads in Quebec only with the first waves of Irish and English immigration. The province's first orphanages, the Montreal Protestant Orphan Asylum and the Asile des orphelins catholiques, were opened in 1822 and 1832, respectively.

As was the case with criminal matters, the people nurturing these regenerative ambitions found themselves wrestling with the magnitude of the task before them. Nevertheless, a reform discourse specifically focusing on children was soon in evidence.[8] This discourse would provide the justification for all the political and philanthropic initiatives to follow.

The distinction attaching to children at this juncture rested on the belief that their young age necessitated differential treatment. In parallel, Calvinist (or Catholic[9]) morality vehemently reaffirmed the necessary submission of the child to the parents' authority. This initial differentiation of children from adults was therefore embodied in a set of measures designed to provide for the consolidation of traditional family authority.[10] Most of the institutions founded at this time were ephemeral, small in scope where they arose from private initiative, and intended as surrogates for the family.

Childhood was not just another dimension of family misfortune, however. In the cities especially, the problem of young offenders gave particular visibility to the broader problematic of childhood under construction.[11] There was still little in the way of legally mandated philanthropic endeavour vis-à-vis children.[12] An initial policy on children in general became conceivable only as and when the state, in view of the characteristics of its judicial system, found itself facing a mass of young people for whom philanthropic practice had resulted in differential status and treatment. A child's perpetration of a criminal act came to serve as the central criterion for state intervention in this area: the state stepped in to correct for the loss of familial control that the act represented.

As one example, the Napoleonic criminal code of 1810 permitted a judge to rule on a child's degree of "discernment." A child held to lack discernment would be acquitted but could, at the judge's discretion, be placed in a house of correction. Beyond this peculiar provision of Western European legal systems, the general softening of criminal codes during this era made it possible to prosecute children without the risk of a sentence disproportionate to their age.[13] The first physical manifestations of this policy on young offenders took the form of youth blocks in prisons as well as a few specialized facilities (Petite Roquette, Parkhurst). By the late 1830s, a sensitivity to the fate of children in the Industrial Revolution was in evidence throughout the West. But philanthropic initiatives remained scant, as did government commitments of resources.

2 In the latter half of the century, juvenile delinquency and child protection became generally recognized as major societal problems. No longer was it enough to make up for familial deficiencies with ad hoc charity. The task was now to create the conditions under which this class of social misery could be systematically taken in charge. The Mettray farm colony, which opened its doors in the 1840s, was an important step. Although it borrowed the "family" system – in which the population of the colony was divided into houses under the supervision of "parents" – from previous experiments (Hofwyl in Switzerland, Rauhe Haus in Germany),[14] it was state-funded and housed both convicted offenders and children with behavioural difficulties placed by their parents. Mettray brought to the fore the idea that all children at risk, with or without a criminal record, needed special treatment, with a greater emphasis on reform than punishment. This was now to be accomplished by targeting the inadequacies of poor or failing families. A charitable undertaking, no doubt, but one that also bespoke a kind of social prophylaxis in which state power plays a central role.[15] Here is Inspector O'Neill describing these families:

> The harrowing spectacle of the innocence of childhood degraded, through the example of the parents, to the level of brutality, may be witnessed on walking through the slums inhabited by this wretched class,

in the vagrant of some seven or eight summers, the tyro drunkard, proud of mimicking, in its little maudlin swagger and hiccup, the daily action of the miserable parent.[16]

As soon as child poverty is problematized in this way, it becomes possible to invoke the need for public intervention in a broader range of cases – not just for young offenders and abandoned children but for children neglected by unfit parents.[17] This is a remarkable, cascading development that sets the stage for the systematic implementation, throughout the West, of child welfare and correctional systems consisting of prisons and reformatories,[18] farm or penitentiary colonies, reform and industrial schools, and so on. Foster placement went hand in hand with these 1840s developments, paralleled by the development of the penitentiary system. From the 1880s on, new child protection associations sprang up in an effort to systematize the offensive against "unfit" or deficient families, a movement that would be supported, in countries such as France and Belgium, by legislation providing for loss of parental rights in such cases.[19]

In Quebec, this problem gained sporadic public attention starting in the 1830s. The debate around the implementation of public institutions truly got going, however, only after the Act of Union of 1840. This debate, where it touched on young offenders, pitted proponents of punishment against theorists of reform.[20] In 1851, the reformers won a resounding victory with the passage of a series of resolutions by the House of Assembly of United Canada:

> 1st. That it appears to this Committee to be established by the evidence, that a large proportion of the present aggregate of crime might be prevented, and thousands of miserable human beings, who have before them, under our present system, nothing but a hopeless career of wickedness and vice, might be converted into virtuous, honest, industrious citizens, if due care were taken to rescue destitute, neglected, and criminal children from the dangers and temptations incident to their position.
> 2nd. That a great proportion of the criminal children of this country, especially those convicted of first offences, appear rather to require systematic education, care, and industrial occupation, than mere punishment.
> 3rd. That the Common Gaols and Houses of Correction do not generally provide suitable means for the educational or corrective treatment of young children, who ought, when guilty of crime, to be treated in a manner different from the ordinary punishment of adult criminals.

4th. That Reformatory Schools should be established for the education and correction of children convicted of minor offences.

5th. That such Reformatory Schools should be founded and supported partially by local rates, and partially by contributions from the State ...

6th. That the delinquency of children, in consequence of which they may become subjects of penal or reformatory discipline, ought not to relieve parents from their liability to maintain them.

7th. That it is essential that power should be given to detain children placed in such Institutions, so long as may be necessary for their reformation; provided always that no child be so detained after the age of sixteen.[21]

In 1858, Lower Canada got a "reformatory," or reform prison, at Île-aux-Noix on the Richelieu River, built in a clumsy effort to imitate Mettray. The terrible condition of the facility and the frequent instances of children running away across the nearby United States border led to its being moved to Saint-Vincent-de-Paul in 1862.[22] Île-aux-Noix housed youths sentenced for serious crimes. It was clear soon after its opening, however, that it would not suffice. It made no provision for the incarceration of the juvenile petty criminals who still languished in the jails, much less for the housing of street children or abandoned children. It was unclear what was to be done with these

"City Arabs," as they have been termed, who are found in such large numbers in all our principal cities. For this large class of children, our admirable and costly Common Schools are perfectly useless. They will not attend them; they soon, however, find their way into our Common Gaols, and there, their ruin and degradation is rapidly completed.

The statistics of our Gaols shew, what common sense would lead us to expect, that these vagrant and neglected children, form the "raw material" out of which our dangerous criminals are, in due course, manufactured.

Nor do our Reformatory Prisons, admirable and useful as they are, meet the wants of this class, inasmuch as they only receive those who have passed through the Common Gaols; those, in fact, who are already *criminal*.[23]

At the dawn of Confederation, when the Catholic bishops, the St Vincent de Paul Society, and the Montreal city government were all becoming concerned about the issue of abandoned children, Quebec adopted the British system of child protection. Two bills, passed in 1869 with the firm support of the prison inspectors, created reformatories for young offenders and industrial schools for abandoned children and children at risk. These largely state-funded institutions were strictly denominational and administered, on the Catholic side, by various religious congregations.[24] This was the bedrock for the gradual construction of a child protection policy that increasingly saw fit to intrude into the lives of "unfit" families. By virtue of successive amendments to the industrial schools legislation in particular, not only abandoned children but also those who had "unworthy" or "vice-ridden" parents were likely to find themselves locked up in these schools.[25]

The creation, in 1882, of the Montreal Society for the Protection of Women and Children, a cousin to the multitude of similar associations then cropping up in North America, further heightened the pressure in favour of measures designed to take charge of the children of deficient families. The rise of the eugenics movement and the stigmatization of certain populations as deficient and unfit would only encourage this tendency.

3   The early twentieth century saw the inception of a third phase in the evolution of societal perceptions of young offenders and children at risk. Until that time, the operational logic of criminal law, despite the extension of the target population to non-delinquent children, had attended a degree of institutional separation between young offenders and children in difficulty. The division adopted in Quebec between reform schools and industrial schools clearly illustrates this phenomenon.[26] But the further exploration of the issues relating to children at risk, as well as the fact that differences between young offenders and abandoned children were more formal than real, dictated that this dividing line be redrawn. The creation of courts for young offenders, which would soon make their appearance throughout the West, marked a significant change, not so much in the treatment of children as in the role allotted to poor families in the context of reform strategies. The first of these courts were indeed set up primarily as instruments for disciplining unfit or deficient families and for standardizing intervention in their affairs.[27] These courts made it possible to treat each case as a specific problem, thus relegating the offence as such to a position of secondary importance.

But as these courts gradually revealed themselves to be relatively flexible instruments for evaluating the multiple issues surrounding children in distress and not merely for interning or placing children, they came into the vanguard of a major transformation of child welfare policy. This transformation was closely contemporary with the reaffirmation of the working family. A host of phenomena – the expansion of an organized workers' movement, the extension of political suffrage, the urban reform movements, the growth of a reformist or "maternalist" feminist movement,[28] the growing awareness of social problems on the part of both governments and churches (church social doctrine and social gospel), the professionalization of children's aid, and the rise of new sociological and psychiatric knowledge of children and the working family[29] – strongly contributed to a rethinking of the issues surrounding children at risk and to the promotion of a set of measures intended to provide for a healthier urban and familial environment:[30] playgrounds, youth clubs, and family support policies.

As these trends gathered force, they were accompanied by an increasingly virulent critique of custodial institutions and even the foster care system, with a concomitant desire to take account of the diversity of "cases" and the family's history when intervening in parent/child relations. Consequently, the separation between the penal and charitable registers in this area came to seem increasingly unproductive and inapplicable.[31]

In Quebec, the first of the youth courts contemplated in the federal act of 1908 opened in Montreal in 1912 (Trépanier and Tulkens 1995). But feminist groups (notably the Montreal Women's Temperance Union and the Fédération nationale Saint-Jean-Baptiste) and reform-minded elites had been actively calling for this reform since the turn of the century (Dubois and Trépanier 1999). The use of probation and psychological analysis of children opened up a new space of treatment possibilities (Quévillon 2001; Pelletier 2000). However, custodial institutions for youth continued to prosper, with the existing system being augmented by a new protestant reform school, the Boys' Farm and Training School, which opened in Shawbridge in 1908.[32]

Views and policies on children can be divided into three major phases. From the penal and philanthropic outlook to the borders of the sacrosanct nuclear family, the scope of intervention was enlarged to include care for children at risk, even within their own families. This intervention initially centred around repressive sanctions imposed on unfit families, and later, conversely, on the affirmation and promotion of family ties.

As the transformations just outlined continued, a bona fide policy on the regulation of problem children began to come into view.

This policy stemmed initially from the characterization of juvenile crime as a conundrum unto itself. The question of childhood now posed a clear challenge to the basic features of regulation in liberal democratic societies, in terms of the dividing line between the penal and the charitable, the relationship between the private and the public, and the specific modes of intervention essayed.

FROM PUNISHMENT TO CHARITY: THE CONFUSION OF REGISTERS OF INTERVENTION

The liberal logic of regulation effected an increasingly strict separation in the penal order between the necessity of punishment and the desirability of reform. In so doing, it made it possible to reconcile the principle of individual culpability with a modicum of respect for physical and mental integrity. The legitimacy of the penal order came to revolve around punishment of the deliberate act, which was to be governed by strict rules of due process and proportionate sentencing.

These principles of regulation entailed two important operational constraints. The first was that punishment was unequivocally predicated on the offender's free will, so that persons defined as lacking this capacity – the insane, or children under a certain age, for example – were not subject to it. The second was that the principle of proportionality implied a gradation of punishment corresponding, at least in part, to the gravity of the offence. The worse the offence, the greater the legal power of detention (and hence the possibility of prolonged treatment). This led to a fundamental paradox: the conditions for the effectiveness of punishment (and the prisoner reform expected to flow from it) were in stark contradiction with the dictates of *prevention*. The latter, after all, necessitated *prior* intervention, before the irremediable occurred. Moreover, prevention is unable by definition to react *ex post facto* to tangible acts; its whole logic of operation consists of a focus on certain factors that define a social or human condition rather than a particular act.

This demarcation between the right to punish and the need to prevent – blurred in the case of adults by waning enthusiasm for the ideals of criminal reform – came fully into play in the case of children. Here, hopes of reform had remained alive[33] and had indeed begun to take priority over the imperatives of punishment. The discourse of the developers of child reform institutions depicts reform as inextricably linked to the notion of prevention.

> The work is not to cleanse the polluted stream after it has flowed on in its pestilential course, but to purify the fountain whence it draws its unfailing supply. What we have to do is to devise and carry out such measures as shall take possession of all juveniles who may be placed in such circumstances as to be evidently precarious for a life of crime, or who may already have entered upon it, and keep hold of them until they have been trained in the knowledge of the right way and fairly started in a course of well-doing.[34]

Where children were concerned, the liberal legal order was regarded as a constraint that need not be obeyed with any great strictness. Tocqueville admits this candidly when he describes the first institutions for the welfare of abandoned children to be established in the United States.

> Some objections have been made ... against the right granted to the houses of refuge to receive individuals who had neither committed a crime nor incurred a conviction. Such a power, it was said, is contrary to the Constitution of the United States ... It would have been difficult to refute theoretically these objections; but the public saw that the houses of refuge alleviated the fate of juvenile criminals, instead of aggravating it, and that the children brought into it without being convicted, were not the victims of persecution, but merely deprived of a fatal liberty. (Beaumont and Tocqueville 1833, 113)

As it happened, the fraught relationship between the penal and the charitable developed, in the case of children, in two stages. In the first, continuing until the mid-nineteenth century, the distinction between young offenders and abandoned children became increasingly clear, with the penal law applicable to the first giving the state the legal means to justify incarceration, while the tendency was for abandoned children to be entrusted to the care of private initiatives, subject to the rules governing parental responsibility and custody.[35] In the second, the fate of children, runaways in particular, was to inspire state measures to provide for their welfare. There ensued a gradual enlargement of compulsory powers beyond the domain of criminal law. In this process, the power to remove children from their homes was extended to cases beyond the bounds of classical penal law. Thus, runaways and abandoned children who kept company with criminals, or whose parents were in prison, could be legally confined (in the Quebec schools of industry after 1869, for example). The government justified such measures on the basis of de facto or implied abandonment of parental responsibility. Subsequently, and especially after 1880, it became necessary to extend judicial intervention to cases in which a family proved itself unfit to provide for a child's welfare. Compulsory powers over children whose parents were declared "unfit" were extended and, more formally, measures were adopted to provide for a declaration of parental incapacity.[36] The third important stage was the establishment of youth courts and the adoption of measures leading to social worker intervention in problem families. Thus, in the case of children at risk, the initial separation between the charitable and the penal increasingly gave way to legally mandated therapeutic intervention in the family.

In parallel, the penal rules covering young offenders were softened. In Quebec, the opening of the first reformatory was accompanied by legislation making the procedure governing criminal prosecution of minors more flexible[37] even as it authorized exceptionally long periods of incarceration even for minor offences.[38] As this exposition shows, the establishment of youth courts was merely the final stage in a process whereby the rules governing the punishment of crime in the liberal legal order were circumvented.[39]

PRIVATE AND PUBLIC

How does the history of intervention in the case of children at risk square with the traditional historiography according to which the private sector took on the lion's share of welfare-related responsibilities in the nineteenth century? Private philanthropists certainly made a notable effort, as attested by the development of orphanages and other charitable institutions for children.[40] But the state's role was far from negligible. Public assistance in France, or workhouses in England and much of the United States, accounted for a considerable proportion of the housing provided to abandoned children.[41] Moreover, as a consequence of criminal sentencing, a large number of children, convicted or imprisoned with their parents, became de facto wards of the state. And when it became necessary to develop a network of institutions specifically designed for the custody of young offenders, it was most often the state that took charge of these institutions. In fact, it is scarcely an exaggeration to say that the development of a large-scale child welfare movement after 1840 came largely at the impetus of the authorities. So much so that when liberal elements in society did mobilize around child welfare issues in the nineteenth century, their thrust was generally against the growing involvement of the state.[42]

Starting in the 1840s, a whole battalion of philanthropists took it upon themselves to rethink child welfare policy, often reacting not only to the existence of abandoned children but also to the state's approach to child welfare, and particularly the reformatories and workhouses. Charles Loring Brace, Mary Carpenter, and Frédéric-Auguste Demetz[43] based their ideal of reform on the capacity of philanthropists to offer this population suitable treatments. The argument for private-sector involvement was not predicated on the putative superiority of the market,[44] or the supposedly natural capacity of private initiatives to answer public needs.[45] Rather, these observers functionally associated private initiative with the warmth of human contact, with its "natural" capacity to bind child and philanthropist in a helping relationship. Starting from the postulate of a perfect match between love and voluntarism, between personal motivation and effectiveness, a whole policy on child welfare could be envisioned.

> We are all perfectly aware that whatever we do of our own free will, throwing our heart and soul and strength into it, we accomplish far better and more effectually than we do compulsorily ... No mere official, however well paid by their superiors, will ever toil by night and by day, in season and out of season, like those who, animated by the love of God and of man, voluntarily devote their powers to their work, and are willing, if need be, to sacrifice themselves to it. (Carpenter 1862, 440)[46]

But private initiative, in the liberal mode of regulation, did more than merely match the supply of child welfare services with the demand. The liberal vision of childhood far surpassed the charitable dimension, for it was fundamentally concerned with deconstructing and reconstructing children's individuality based on a particular version of *morality*. Yet both the tenor of moral values and the effectiveness of their transmission were as much a matter of personal conviction and edifying example as of normative education. In the volunteer's abnegation, the philanthropist's boundless devotion, lay the essential condition for such access to morality. Unsullied by self-interest, in touch with the eternal values of morality, the free and voluntary individual came to represent the ideal instrument for the transformation of young offenders and children at risk.

This combination of faith in the intrinsic virtue of private initiative with the posited structural incapacity of the state and its functionaries to include the moral dimension of children's aid – helps to explain the process whereby *religion* came to play a central role in this field. It is too often forgotten that in liberal regulation, liberty presupposes an ethic which constitutes the cement by which freedom is normalized. This is accomplished not by indoctrinating the citizen, or the child, into a cult or a hierarchical structure of any kind, but essentially by placing present or future liberty under the aegis of fundamental and eternal values capable of transcending both private passions and collective instincts. In other words, the more private intervention conforms to religious ethics, the more valuable and effective it will be.

> There is besides a deeper and even more important element in voluntary and benevolent effort ... – the religious element. This is not an inculcation of creeds, or even the communication of religious truth ... But we mean that awakening of the religious principle within, which is effected through Divine Grace, by the spiritual action of one soul upon another: that Divine sympathy which, viewing in every human being, however mean or low to outward view, however young or however old, an immortal soul, and a child of the same Father, will be ready, following in the steps of the Saviour, to feel his weakness and bear his burden, and to draw him towards holiness. (Carpenter 1862, 441–2)

In sum, the religious dimension is an essential feature of the privatization of welfare that was underway in the second half of the nineteenth century. This tendency could undoubtedly go as far as an outright division of services along denominational lines, as it did in Quebec,[47] but what remained fundamental was the inseparability of religion and ethics in the liberal mind. This explains the remarkable unanimity of Quebec prison and asylum inspectors, whether Protestant or Catholic, on this matter.

> The prospects of success would be a thousand times greater with the clergy, than with any others. For the position of the former involves their devoting all their energies to the promotion of the spiritual and temporal welfare of those entrusted to their care. They inspire confidence and respect; they are usually better qualified than laymen to gain the affections of youth; they make themselves so intimately acquainted with the characters of the young, and penetrate so deeply into their inmost thoughts, that they know the exact course, which the various dispositions of their pupils require. They

reprove with mildness, punish with love, instruct with kindness, amuse with cheerfulness, and lead to the pursuit of the paths of virtue by friendly offices and touching narratives; in a word they make unremitting appeals both to the heart and to the mind.[48]

That said, the necessity of entrusting the immediate management of juvenile delinquency and child protection services to the private sector in no way implied that the state would withdraw from this domain. Rather, it would instigate a *sharing* of responsibilities in which state funding and even administrative control remained possible, albeit at a higher level. The interlinkage between the public and private spheres would take a variety of forms as a function of the private sector's fundraising capacity, the specific history of church-state relations within each social formation, and the pace at which governmental expertise developed in the areas of financial control and inspection.[49]

Thus, in Quebec, when insistence on children's religious education led to many reform and industrial schools being farmed out to the Catholic congregations, this policy met with strong resistance from the Protestant elites.[50] The Brothers of Charity, a religious institute placed in charge of male young offenders, would be accused of proselytism;[51] more generally, the province of Quebec would be suspected of becoming a culture medium on which old superstitions could grow.

> The public mind in the Province of Quebec, in fact, seems to have fallen into a sort of mania. As a political and social change, the system is, in its root, the sickly fruit of a temporary disease, which threatens to become permanent and to invade the whole body. The Province of Quebec has assumed the condition of a green house, or hot bed, of that clerical supremacy which the remainder of the world have thrown out with disgust. Canada is now the receptacle where renovating and reviving nations vomit the rubbish of the past ...
>
> By appealing in [sic] the Friars to take care of the young delinquents, civil society declares itself incompetent in fulfilling its functions, and if our legislators are consistent with themselves, they must go on with this work, as they have already begun in other directions.[52]

In its emphasis on the need for personalized care and moral education, state child welfare policy in the West afforded various possibilities for private-public collaboration. Drawing cannily on British precedent, the Quebec model – for reasons I analyze later – afforded ample space for religious influence.

DEBATES OVER TREATMENT ALTERNATIVES

The development of systematic child welfare measures did more than call into play a set of relations between the penal and charitable registers, or between the private and the public sectors. Reform in this context essentially meant youth education, and the conditions under which this education took place matter as much as, if not more than, its goals. In contrast to the incarceration of adults, the treatment of young offenders and child welfare cases, whether under charitable or penal circumstances, gave rise to a range of alternatives. From the moment when reform was deemed to take precedence over punishment, the problem of methods was posed, giving rise to frequently virulent debate. Three aspects of the problem are particularly relevant.

Institutions or Foster Homes?

For centuries, placement in foster care or apprenticeship had been the usual procedure with young children; institutionalization had been regarded as a preliminary step only. The development of the earliest institutions for the treatment of young offenders and child welfare cases set up a dynamic, however, in which intramural education could be provided for a relatively long period of time, and in a collegial setting. Pedagogical initiatives from Fellenberg to Hofwyl set out to demonstrate that it was possible to recreate broken family ties in institutional settings. In many cases, such as those of the first American orphanages and houses of refuge, strict group discipline was imposed under the authority of matrons or nuns; in others, the children were organized into small subgroups under the guidance of "parents" (a practice for which Mettray became famous, soon to be copied throughout the West). But in every case, the rhetoric justifying the establishment of child welfare institutions – reformatories, industrial schools, or farm colonies – from the mid-nineteenth century onward put an emphasis on recreating the family environment in the institutional setting.

Confinement of children was not, however, perceived as an unavoidable solution to the failures of parents. Quite soon – indeed, in near-perfect synchrony with the development of the major welfare institutions in the mid-nineteenth century – an alternative solution was developed: placement in foster homes. The idea was to find a substitute family for the abandoned child, or even for the juvenile delinquent, that would raise the child in exchange for payment. This child welfare mode is distinguished from apprenticeship in two respects: the child is integrated into a familial rather than a service setting, and she remains, at least in theory, under the constant supervision of the placement agency. This model, epitomized by the New York Children's Aid Society in the mid-nineteenth century, developed in response to a virulent critique of institutional education in general. The removal of children from working-class families thus took two competing but durable forms, with each social formation adopting a particular configuration thereof. The familial model became the standard of reference for most child welfare practitioners, regardless of the preferred intervention strategy.[53]

In Quebec, a specific statute passed in 1871 provided for the placement of institutionalized children in apprenticeships, including reform and industrial schools.[54] Little is known about these practices and the role of religious congregations in putting them into effect. Given the palpable emphasis on the development of custodial institutions from 1850 onward, it may be assumed that such apprenticeships were relatively few in number. The truth is that Catholic Quebec unabashedly took the road of large-scale institutionalization.[55] Later, in the early twentieth century, as criticism of confinement grew increasingly harsh, institutionalization came to be largely reserved for "intractable" or particularly difficult cases, with the development of youth courts and probation henceforth offering other options.[56]

The extensive institutionalization of Catholic children undertaken by the religious communities of Quebec did indeed come in for increasingly sharp criticism, even (although timidly) from French Canadians. A good example was the opening, at the Armoury on Craig Street in October 1912, of a major "child welfare exhibition" modeled on those held shortly before in several American cities. It was one of the rare occasions when Catholics and Protestants worked together to maximize the impact of an event.[57] This exhibition sought to address the whole panoply of child welfare-related issues (hygiene, urban life, school, play, philanthropic works, religion, child labour, juvenile delinquency, etc.), and it was one occasion when criticism of the Catholic child welfare institutions was openly expressed. These critiques typically emphasized the need to provide assistance to poor families, rather than to preserve children from the harmful influences of an immoral environment.

> Why are children placed in institutions? ... Most of the time it would cost much less to leave these children with their mothers than to entrust them to the care of charitable institutions ... If a mother of five children needs only

an extra $10 per month to keep her family by her side, how are we helping children, and do we really believe we are saving money, when we put them in institutions at a cost of $36 per month? ... A good mother should never be forced to leave her children when it is better, and costs less, to keep the family together ... Where it is necessary to take children out of the home, whether due to the parents' death or for any other reason, why don't we place them with families rather than overload our charitable institutions? The family makes the best citizen. (Anonymous 1912, 29–30)

This criticism would in fact have very little resonance in that era, for the dominance of the religious communities was much too strong. But its existence shows how attitudes toward children and their environment were changing.

City or Country?

Another component of the child welfare debate in the industrialized world concerned the appropriate environment for the corresponding institutions. Both liberals and conservatives touted the advantages of agriculture and country living, for the cult of nature and peasant lifeways belonged to the commonplaces of the era. For liberals, however, this stance was not a rejection of modernity or a retrenchment into traditional values. It was merely a rejection of certain sordid consequences of city life for the working class.

Indeed, enthusiasm for the benefits of capitalism was rarely expressed without a concomitant expression of anxiety about the pollution, noise, danger, and general inhumanity of the cities that had grown out of the unrestrained industrialization of Western societies.[58] Farm life was perceived and presented as a more hygienic, stable, and regular educational environment for children and their reform; they could live their lives at the pace of nature, isolated from the temptations of the city.[59]

Unsurprisingly, the majority of custodial child welfare institutions (such as foster families) were located in the countryside. Urban institutions would remain in the minority, even though the immense majority of children in need of assistance came from the cities and were destined to return there.[60]

Yet Quebec proved a curious exception to this pattern. The Catholic authorities were often recalcitrant to the agriculturalist ideology of the Protestant "child savers," and the idea that they strongly favoured a version of agriculturalism in matters of child welfare is largely a myth. The

Pères de Montfort congregation did, in 1884, found a nominally agricultural institution at Montfort in the Laurentians (despite the poor soil fertility in the region),[61] and this institution became the province's largest industrial school. But it was an exception (and did not, at any rate, involve much farming, given the young age of its charges). All the other Catholic reform and industrial schools would be established in cities or inner suburbs. Yet the 1873 contract entrusting the Brothers of Charity with the administration of the Montreal boys' reformatory stipulated that the friars were to establish a model farm in the country within three years. Objecting to this stipulation, the institution's director presented an argument in fourteen points, the most important of which were as follows:

> 1 I look upon the removal of our Reformatory School from the city as its utter ruin: the only revenue we derive comes from the work done in the shops, and this revenue, once taken away, it is evident that we could no longer keep our School on its present footing; the price paid for the board of our pupils would not be sufficient, as we have too many expenses for foremen and other employees in our workshops ...
> 7 The great majority of the offenders, having been brought up in the cities, return there on their discharge, without a good trade, their future is completely spoilt ...
> 9 Persons who have known the Reformatory School for several years have told us, that not one of those who were formerly employed at farm work continued at it after their discharge ...
> 12 By going to the country our expenses would be greatly increased from the distance of the markets, and our revenues consequently diminished.[62]

It was perhaps not overly surprising, then, that the most serious and systematic attempt to base the education of young offenders on farm work in this Catholic "agriculturalist" province would come from the Protestants, and that rather late in the period, with the opening of the reform school at Shawbridge in 1908.

Which Mode of Treatment?

> It is in childhood onward that evil ways must be visited and virtue taught to be loved.
> To the child all is new, his heart is ready to receive whatever is sown either good or evil. If good seed is sown it will fructify. Now, in order that

his heart may receive this good seed, the child must be properly cared for and therefore he should be entrusted to institutions where he will be taught to love virtue and honesty, he will acquire a love of labor in his youth, the most critical period of his life.[63]

If there is one constant in the history of child welfare initiatives prior to the development of child psychology, it is the idea of the "blank slate"; that is, that the mind of the child is virgin soil in which good values can be planted. This being the case, the gentleness and personalization of the treatment – far from any idea of punishment – are regarded as indispensable to its success.[64] Thus, the directors of the Montreal reformatory boasted that there were no bars on its windows and no fences around the building. The principle (if not the practice) according to which young people were entitled to special treatment before the judge precedes the establishment of youth courts by many years. In 1864, Inspector O'Neill argued:

That mode of treatment would best succeed, which would be gentle and compassionating. The proceeding of the tribunal before which the vagrant should be brought for examination, should be different from those pursued towards adult prisoners, and divested of the exposure consequent on actual crime. The detectives employed (men tender and considerate) should be a body distinct from the civic police, not alone in the duties discharged, but in the externals of dress.[65]

On a similar note, the principle that any child-specific treatment must serve to build children's motivation and self-esteem also appeared early on.[66] This emphasis on children's capacity to consider their situation and plan for the future – life skills regarded as essential by every liberal – show how much was believed to be at stake where their education was concerned. Here is Inspector Louis-Léon Lesieur Désaulniers describing the dynamic instituted in a reform school:

When occasionally it happens that some of them are so wicked and depraved as to create disorder or to rebel, they are soon brought to order. Although very strange, it is however true to state that such conduct, far from obtaining for them the sympathy of their fellow prisoners, only disgraces them the more, so that instead of having an injurious effect it leaves a beneficial impression.

The reprimands, sometimes the punishments, which some of those disobedient and unmanageable children draw down on themselves afford those who behave well a favorable opportunity of comparing their present and future positions. A little reflection soon makes them understand that a good, laborious and honest life with its rewards, is, in their present condition, the most favorable one and that it will in the future procure for them more happiness and pleasure than contrary behaviour could. They soon understand that those who behave badly incur severe punishment in the present and that they are sowing the seeds of future unhappiness and misfortune.

These children, like all children, are easily impressed, and the sight of the depravity of their companions strikes deeply and keenly on their feelings, bringing with it disgust and a desire to flee their companionship. These good intentions, cultivated by the benign influence of wise and devoted directors, soon become guiding principles. Thenceforth the children can look forward to an honest future.[67]

Hence the system of merit points, rewarding good conduct with a shortened sentence, made an early appearance at the reformatory.[68] Likewise, leisure activities (music, shows) and sports (hockey) were incorporated into the curriculum early on, right at the turn of the century.[69]

Is this to say that the correctional education or confinement of abandoned and at-risk children was just a specific instance of children's instruction in the nineteenth century? Does the emphasis on gentle treatment of children, on their education and reform, imply that these institutions are to be fundamentally situated outside the logic of punishment and incarceration? This is in large part the conclusion reached by one specialist in this field, Jeroen Dekker:

> Foucault's vision of these re-education homes as part of a *système carceral* set up to discipline children and adults is an inadequate explanation. Even French Mettray, which was intended for juvenile delinquents and which Foucault selected as the most famous of a whole string of institutions that made up this *archipel carceral*, was at heart a pedagogical institution, in which discipline was only one of the pedagogical means ... This residential re-education was a pedagogical answer to the negative effects of the modernization of Western European society in the nineteenth century, and it comprised a combination of punishment, salvation, and education. (Dekker 2001, 237)

For Dekker, Foucault's mistake is to present Mettray as a representative example of the general logic of incarceration while failing to see that the operational logic of the carceral archipelago instituted in the latter half of the nineteenth century was multifarious and changeable; that in this sense, due to the specific constraints represented by the child welfare context, Mettray was an exception.

But the education at issue here is of a very special kind, most notably because it is situated within an intellectual domain in which the abnormal is primary. The institution's young charges are not "ordinary" and the treatment they receive has little to do with the circumstances attendant upon the raising, education, and instruction of children under liberal regulation. In the eyes of the reformers and philanthropists, these children have tasted the freedom afforded by crime, or by abandonment, too young and hence anomalously. They already sit on the fringes of the world of crime abominated by Tocqueville's successors. Their "education" is therefore governed by two major constraints: total separation from the home environment and a disciplinary regime that cannot be escaped without harsh penalty.[70] What lay outside the walls of the reform and industrial schools was not ignorance, but freedom. These institutions still embodied a mode of regulation designed to combat the obverse of legality and liberal normality. They were still a place removed from the world, one where it was possible to forget what constitutes the essence of this world – freedom – for a period that might last an entire childhood.

> If the thoughts of liberty, and the desire to regain it, could be removed from the minds of a certain number of these young boys, their reform, the Directors of this institution tell us, would be an easy matter. This unfortunate idea always pre-occupies their attention, and disturbs their minds to such a degree that both day and night, they are actually dreaming of means to realize it. The inclination for work, as well as the love of right, is consequently paralyzed. Neither counsels, nor affection can eradicate this fatal thought, which governs them; it is the constant object of their desires, before which every favorable disposition, every healthy resolution, and every good purpose vanishes; it is the formidable rock on which are broken their best resolutions, and on which are stranded their best hopes; it is in a word the stumbling block to their conversion.[71]

* * *

Summing up, the evolving treatment of children at risk and young offenders illustrates a fundamental reconfiguration of the operational criteria of the social fabric in Western societies. The apprehension of the problem of juvenile delinquency initially led to an enlargement of the field to encompass all children in distress. But this implied a condemnation of working families and their childrearing practices. If children were victims, they were primarily victims of their own parents; hence, they had to be removed and either placed in foster care or institutionalized. This population of children "freed" from their families immediately began to pose a management problem. Thus arose what Dimitri Sudan (1997, 383) has called the "recurrent alternatives" in the debate over approaches to intervention: protection or sanction, private or public, closed or open setting. In large measure, these alternatives remain with us to this day.

But as soon as blame was shifted from the unfit family to the society that created it, and restoring and improving family ties became the order of the day, two new developments occurred. First, the role of the working family, and the problem of its offspring, came to be situated within a framework of integration rather than repressive control.[72] This led to new ways of regulating the lives of working families, going far beyond the logic of child welfare reform.[73] Soon, however, the problem of childhood stopped being reducible to a (manageable) symptom of a societal problem. Children's fate became integral to a relational (parent/child) process that was foregrounded as critical to the family's role in the construction of the social fabric. The individuality of children as *agents* (even though dependent) within the family and, in this capacity, as rights-holding subjects, was affirmed.[74]

By intensifying the contradictions between the necessity of treatment and the obligation to respect the integrity of the person, this development heightened the tension at the core of the liberal conception of child welfare. These were not passive or abandoned victims but people who, for the most part and as dictated by circumstances, had already exercised their freedom, either by committing a crime or by trying to survive outside the family nucleus. Thus, they constituted both a problem and a danger to public order.[75] The liberal ethic, founded on the recognition of personal rights and on the principle that free citizens are responsible for their actions, would always struggle with those fraught, complex situations in which it was necessary to punish or prevent misdeeds while simultaneously protecting a dependent population from poverty and violence. The liberal worldview, in its attempts to take charge of the thousand capillary ruptures of the social fabric represented by juvenile delinquency and children at risk, could do no better than to enact – always problematically – two contrasting registers, the penal and the charitable. Beyond the many ways in which they could be configured, these registers would endlessly stumble over the limits of punishment and treatment, vacillate between the judge and the therapist, and debate the cycle of questions raised by this approach: what to do (punishment versus protection), who should do it (private versus public), and how it should be done (confinement versus reintegration). The responses to these recurring questions would be perpetually beholden to the elites and their fears on the one hand, and the philanthropists and their fond ambitions on the other.

The Enlightenment century presided over the implementation of a new penal rationality based on proportionate sentencing. The advent of imprisonment as the preferred means of punishment made possible a de facto materialization of this modern rationality. Finally, the application of liberal penality to the whole population, without undue privileges or statutory exceptions, constitutes the last of the basic principles on which penal norms would be based for the centuries to come. The prison is a *time-based* punishment, giving it the immense advantage of being fully adaptable to the range of crimes committed while constituting an environment conducive to the offender's treatment and rehabilitation.

It might be supposed that the liberal regulation of punishment represented a mere extension and standardization of the penal rationality invented a century earlier. Imprisonment does remain (along with fines) the dominant sanction applied to wrongdoers even to this day. As well, there remains at the core of the liberal logic of punishment a faint belief – ever frustrated, ever entertained – in the possibility of reform, a hope for a future society in which crime is obviated if not unthinkable. But liberalism was also a thorough retreat from the humanist reformism of the Enlightenment. Its profound underlying rationale is predicated on the punishment of crime, an unavoidable corollary of the postulate that criminals, too, have freedom that must be preserved and reaffirmed, and that they have a responsibility whose misuse must be penalized. The ideal of reform faded away – or rather, it was increasingly shunted outside of the prisons where society had formerly attempted to enact it. It had to be acknowledged that a person's privacy was part and parcel of his freedom, even if he committed a crime. Even the best of reformative intentions could not justify the violation of that privacy. At any rate, decades of reform efforts and penitentiary building had clearly demonstrated the idiocy of the idea that criminals (and paupers) could be reformed by locking them up. Finally, the very concept of the punishment fitting the crime banished all hope of reform through incarceration, in that this principle forbade prolonged incarceration for crimes considered minor. Yet the phenomenon of recidivism showed that the length of treatment often had little to do with the gravity of the crime committed. Thus there was a basic contradiction – between the principles of punishment and the conditions for reform – nestled within the penal rationality inherited from the Enlightenment.

For this reason, the liberal regulation of punishment accomplished only that part of the Enlightenment agenda concerned with the effective sanctioning of deviance. Its biggest success was to implement a system of policing and justice that provided for maximally efficient apprehension of criminals. All the "innovations" of liberal penality, all the administrative measures intended to stimulate a desire for self-betterment in prisoners – tickets of leave, time off for good behaviour, probation, sponsorship for released prisoners, and so forth – merely confirmed that the proper locus of reform lay *outside* the prison walls.

The treatment of young offenders and children at risk was a major exception to this logic, which reigned supreme throughout the second half of the nineteenth century. The hopes of reformers came to ride on the backs of youth and children. The "reformatory," the "colony," the reform "school" – that place designated by any term other than the now pejorative "prison," in a rather vain attempt to mask its true nature – was the last refuge of the ideal of reform through confinement. Because the persons in custody were minors, it became possible to violate the sacrosanct principle of due process, indeed to justify confinement without any crime having been committed (in the case of child welfare). Where young offenders were concerned, their status as minors provided for a glaring exception to the principle of proportionality in sentencing, since young people guilty of minor offences could be locked away for long periods of time. For this to happen, the child's or adolescent's crime had to be thought of as a pretext for a custodial sentence, rather than the legitimate grounds for that sentence.

Thus, the issues surrounding the administration of juvenile delinquency instituted a seesawing motion, still present today, between the preventive necessity of improving children's living conditions and the obligation to punish their criminal acts. It left open the possibility that youth crime might reflect something other than a free and deliberate intent to do wrong; that it might constitute a symptom of a society whose imperfection makes that act conceivable. But for adults, any lingering confusion between deviance and poverty was banished. To be sure, the prisons overflowed with people from the poorest walks of life. But to admit that the constraint of poverty might explain deviance in any measure whatsoever was to deprive these poor people of that personal responsibility and freedom upon which the whole liberal social edifice rested. Willy nilly, the pauper's freedom implied the freedom to do wrong.

PART THREE

Poverty and Welfare in the Liberal Era

While the liberal regulation of crime and deviance could legitimately be entrusted to the punitive power of the state, poverty was a completely different story. The perpetration of the criminal act embodied a rejection of societal norms warranting state intervention and sanction. But poverty – as a negative state and not a premeditated act – posed a different challenge. To ignore it was a dubious option in the century of freedom and democracy, when the social inequalities revealed by the abject poverty of large segments of the population stood to be interpreted as obstacles to the common weal, rather than mere manifestations of the natural order of things.

Liberalism would have to devise a conception of poverty that could correspond to the imperatives of individual freedom, without it being necessary to bear the social consequences of that selfsame freedom; a concept that could reconcile the idea of progress with the resigned acceptance of poverty.

In order to understand how the concept of poverty took shape within the regulatory economy of the liberal world, it is first necessary to take the measure of the novelty that it constituted with respect to the earlier ideological constructs analyzed in the first part of this book. Chapter 6 undertakes to analyze the position of poverty within liberal regulation. Arising out of the intense ideological debate occurring in Europe, and secondarily in the United States, in the mid-nineteenth century, liberal thought formed the shared discursive heritage, the bedrock, on which Western elites would build social welfare systems when it came time to react to the negative impacts of competition and the free market. Each social formation would adopt a specific configuration of social welfare measures. In the case of Quebec, for example, the religious dimension was critically important for the provision of relief. It will be necessary to evaluate not only the role and status of the church but also the way it embodied the liberal logic of management of inequality, even though it appropriated this logic for its own ends. This discussion occupies chapter 7. Here again, the argument must be limited to the interpretive framework in which the specific development of welfare and care institutions took place. The primary task, in sum, will be to understand the liberal economy that allowed for the deployment in Quebec of a far-reaching welfare system established along denominational lines.

6

An Ethics of Poverty

> I feel that the past is falling, that the foundations of the old building are shaken, and that a terrible shock has changed the face of the earth. But what will rise out of the ruins?[1]

Was the nineteenth century the century of liberal charity? If the dominant historiography is to be believed – and it is more or less unanimous on this point – then that is indeed the case. Care of the poor was entrusted to private initiative, whether secular or religious, and the state refrained from intervening (except in specific cases) within this sphere of action.[2] Yet several facts call this interpretation into question. The countries undergoing the most intense processes of industrialization experienced constant and systematic state intervention; one thinks of the Poor Laws in England and much of the United States, or of various municipal or governmental initiatives in France, Belgium, and Germany.

But more importantly, and as discussed throughout this book, there was no unified "nineteenth century" in which the logic of liberalism was rolled out in a smooth, uninterrupted flow. In fact, in the field of public charity as in that of punishment, the social logic according to which these modes of regulation operated underwent profound transformations.

The basic postulate stated earlier is pertinent here: to wit, that the societal challenge posed by mass poverty during the democratic transition to capitalism cannot be cognized in terms of a gradual strengthening of the hold exerted by liberalism over society. Quite the contrary: as the concomitant and conflicting implications of democracy and capitalism made themselves felt, and as people learned to live with the new weave of the social fabric, the philosophy of welfare underwent major conceptual shifts, causing an abrupt change in the administration of poverty. Two important periods can be discerned. After the 1840s, a formalist liberal conception entailing a specific economy of relations between relief agencies (public or private) and the poor was progressively put in place. This conception, and the view of poverty that it implied, was profoundly called into question in the last two decades of the century, making room for the deployment of charitable and relief initiatives according to a different logic.

TRANSFORMATIVE CHANGE, 1840–60

In an era when capitalism was revealing its shameful face in pauperism, democracy took on the visage of popular revolution. At a time when the elites were propounding new moralistic explanations for the impoverishment of a large segment of the population, the working classes strove to politicize the social question: if poverty was a kind of degeneracy, its remedy did not lay in the inculcation of morals but in the organization of state-supported collective solidarity.[3] The workers' movements that culminated in the French Revolution of 1848, Chartism in England, and even Jacksonian radicalism in the United States were only the most vital contemporary expressions of a societal tendency that regarded the political sphere as the necessary corrective for the failings of the economy. These movements were the final avatars of the Enlightenment in that politics was, for them, nothing more than the individual will writ large. However, its role was now to support the working classes where liberal civil society failed to do so.

The putative existence of a "right to work" posited in these years rather eloquently expresses this drift of the social toward the political. The misery generated by the new industrial economy did not call for a moral reform of the "lower" classes. Quite the contrary, their morals were fundamentally healthy, and needed only an assurance of survival. "Right" here refers to the normative materialization of a system of solidarity in which the allocation of goods and services is governed by the market only to the extent that each person is assured some minimum level of access to that market in the form of employment. Poverty, then, was no longer the normal condition of life in society for the majority of the population, nor was it the natural if distressing outcome of unfitness. It was the unacceptable manifestation of an inadequately organized society.

The unfolding of democracy's social implications dealt a sharp blow to elite thinking – as brutal a blow as the awareness of mass poverty itself. It meant a radical rethinking of the basic postulates of societal organization put forward since the Enlightenment. The political demands of the working classes gave out on to a world in which the democratic polity could oppose self-interest, instead of being merely an agglomeration of individuals looking after their own interests; a world in which collective solidarity guaranteed one's survival where honest toil failed to do so. The future would be sculpted by the polity, not by the wishes and aptitudes of individuals.

The vehemence with which the dominant classes would oppose this idea of a *right* to work (or, failing that, guaranteed subsistence) is highly revealing. As early as 1839, Gérando had expressed reservations about this way of addressing the problem of poverty:

> This right [of indigence] is essentially a moral right, and as such there is something indeterminate about it. It does not merely entitle one to material assistance; it goes much further, rises higher; it is directed at the soul; it entitles one to benevolence ... The right to be assisted is different in nature from the right to have one's life, liberty, property, and honour respected; though not less sacred, it is less positive, less strict, less absolute. It is not the right to insist upon, to demand an allowance, to bring an action, to be granted this or that benefit: it is a legitimate expectation; it is a powerful recommendation, an entreaty worthy of the greatest consideration. It is not a calling in of a debt but the legitimate expectation of a service ... The rights of indigence have a generality that encompasses the entire class of persons in distress. They do not grant each indigent in particular an individual entitlement to be awarded, neither vis-à-vis an especially obligated person nor out of a naturally determined fund, the kind and degree of assistance of which he may have need, so much as the discharge of an absolute and positive debt. (Gérando 1839, 1: 468–9, 472)

In his *Discours sur le droit au travail* (1848), Adolphe Thiers specifies how the concept of right is to be construed in the liberal world:

> A right ... makes no exceptions among the classes of citizens, a right applies to all ... A right belongs to everyone; a right that belongs only to a given class is not a right at all: a right granted to one man and denied to another is not a right. (Thiers 1848, 32)

A class right, instead of organizing freedom by putting a frame around it, disrupts the free action of individuals for the benefit of some and to the detriment of others. For this reason, any legally payable welfare benefit, any "mandatory charity," is not only dangerous but also *unfair* and arbitrary. The obligation of welfare must remain a moral constraint only, something to be willed rather than coerced. To make it a legal obligation distorts the operation of freedom.[4]

Furthermore, a demand that the authorities protect certain social rights not only threatens the internal consistency, and in fact the integrity, of bourgeois law: it accentuates the "dangerousness" of the working classes. They are now to be feared not only for their alleged moral inferiority but also for their potential to revolt against their condition. Worse, the masses are now showing themselves capable of leading society's fundamental institutions astray, diverting them from their primary functions. The power of the working classes threatens not only to generate anarchy and revolution – a danger long acknowledged – but also to impart to democracy a direction contrary to the principles of social organization – freedom first and foremost – that it was thought to embody.

Under these circumstances, it is no surprise to find major reservations about the effects of democracy being added to the prevailing (and often paternalistic) contempt for the working classes. François Guizot, co-leader of the July Revolution and liberal minister under King Louis Philippe I, wrote in the aftermath of the revolutions of 1848:

> There is a sentiment, noble and beautiful in itself, which has been much and often appealed to throughout all the perturbations and convulsions of society in France; this sentiment is, enthusiasm for mankind – the enthusiasm of confidence, sympathy, and hope. This feeling reigned supreme among us in 1789, and gave its resistless impulse to that epoch. There was no virtue that was not ascribed to man – no success that was not hoped and predicted for him. Faith and hope in man took the place of faith and hope in God. The trial was not long deferred. The idol did not long retain its power. Confidence was soon convicted of presumption, and sympathy ended in social war and the scaffold ... Never did experience advance with such rapid strides to confront and overthrow pride. Yet it is to this same sentiment that our modern reformers of social order appeal. It is this same idolatrous enthusiasm for human nature that they invoke. (Guizot 1849, 70)

On the heels of Malthusianism comes a fundamental challenge to the idea that human nature is basically good.[5] It is, in fact, a challenge to the idea of progress itself,[6] a reconsideration of people's capacity to control their fates in the face of economic laws.[7] The idea that there can be a political solution to the social problem, and to the vagaries of the dominant economic system, is rejected outright; modern poverty, say these critics, is not amenable to a collective approach.

CONSTRUCTION OF THE SELF: A NEW ETHIC

> The greatness of England is now all collective: individually small, we only appear capable of anything great by our habit of combining; and with this our moral and religious philanthropists are perfectly contented ... but the only unfailing and permanent source of improvement is liberty, since by it there are as many possible independent centres of improvement as there are individuals. (Mill [1849] 1913, 55)

The community is no longer the guarantee of collective well-being or the privileged instrument by which it comes about. The state, however democratic and well intentioned, can become freedom's tomb. The only coherent response to this danger of stultifying uniformity that threatens modern societies is in the rediscovery of individuality and its implications. This is the meaning that must be given to Tocqueville's *Democracy in America* and Mill's *On Liberty*, those great nineteenth-century charters of liberal liberty. Since Rousseau and Smith, liberty had been a collective ideal, mapping out a standard route to progress for the individual. The idea was for everyone to be free in the same way, to embody the particular application of a general rule. Liberty made for better, better-accepted, more voluntary conformity, but conformity all the same.[8]

The radical departure of the mid-nineteenth century consisted of the discovery of an individuality expressed in the form of *difference*. People are different from one another, and moreover these differences create an essential distance between individuals and the whole represented by human beings living together in society. With this discovery, it became necessary to problematize the notion of the collective; its virtues had to be devalued in favour of the promotion of the self. The unbending laws of the market economy that were invoked to counter the collective demands of the dominated classes can be read as the abstract embodiment of individual differences freely expressed. Competition was no longer an unconstrained clash of identical units from which truth and progress naturally ensued. Rather, it was a healthy, novelty-creating clash of the irreducible particularities represented by different individuals, made all the richer by the fact of their difference and their autonomy. Autonomy itself had become more than the ability to live in society without assistance, to obey the rules of good social conduct without the support or protection of a superior: it was now the impetus imparting to each life its particular trajectory.

As a result, the response to workers' demands, to the rapid rise of socialism as a competing interpretation of the world, inevitably involved a reconfiguration and a deepening of the individualism postulated as central to the liberal worldview. The freedom to which everyone aspired was also a personal ethic implying both rights and duties on the part of every citizen.[9] These duties (and ethics in general) were not strict prescriptions but rather guideposts marking the boundaries beyond which freedom could not go, just as law set out a framework for social life without, in general, compelling people to perform particular acts.[10] Ethics, religion, and law were moulds in which the possibilities for individual action in the liberal world were cast.

With individual freedom nearly absolute, it was now possible for individuals to set about shaping their own futures. What Tocqueville referred to as "freedom of movement" (*liberté locomotive*) (Tocqueville [1835] 1997, 33) necessarily existed as a function of *time*, as a specific trajectory made possible only insofar as it corresponded to the personal aspirations of each individual. A human life was now tantamount to a project to be carried out, failing which that person's very humanity would be in doubt.

> What can be expected from a man whose position cannot improve, since he has lost the respect of his fellow men which is the precondition of all progress ... What course of action is left to the conscience or to human activity in a being so limited, who lives without hope and without fear? He looks at the future as an animal does. Absorbed in the present and the ignoble and transient pleasures it affords, his brutalized nature is unaware of the determinants of its destiny. (Tocqueville [1833] 1997, 32)[11]

The concept of self-help, although known and promoted much earlier, took on a specific meaning here: it was no longer a matter of simply manifesting one's independence, but rather of exploiting one's inner dynamism. This made it possible to express and actualize one's difference, one's control over the future. Samuel Smiles described the phenomenon as follows:

> Help from without is often enfeebling in its effects, but help from within invariably invigorates. Whatever is done *for* men or classes, to a certain extent takes away the stimulus and necessity of doing for themselves; and

where men are subjected to over-guidance and over-government, the inevitable tendency is to render them comparatively helpless. (Samuel Smiles, *Self-Help* (1859), quoted in Finlayson 1994, 19)

The notion of "responsibility" captures what is in play here. Constraints placed on personal freedom by others, and especially by state institutions, are not only arbitrary because they favour one class over another, not only dangerous because they arouse unreasonable expectations beyond what is supported by natural economic laws; they are also, and perhaps above all, unacceptable because they stanch the ultimate wellspring of self-realization: inner motivation. The usually sober and serious *Dictionnaire de l'économie politique* (1854) contains a curious article titled "Parasites" which expresses this sentiment with particular clarity:

> Society, which is bound to right its own wrongs, is not bound to repair those done by individuals to themselves, nor those they endure by the fault of others, or from undeserved misfortune. To transfer onto society the burden weighing on each person to protect, preserve, and develop himself would be to suppress individual dignity, freedom, and responsibility. What society owes to its members is to protect and guarantee, with all its strength, the free exercise of their rights; it need not and should not think, desire, or act for them. The more a state guarantees the liberty of its citizens, the less it is beholden to their interests, since it leaves the responsibility therefor more fully to them. If it interferes in private lives and influences the direction of private fortunes, its share of responsibility toward individuals increases to the same extent as its guardianship over them. (Renouard 1854, 327–8)

Thus, undue collective interference with personal liberty must be avoided at all costs. Society is no longer a spectrum running in an unbroken line from the individual will to the collectivity. Personal freedom can be just as threatened by democratic initiative as it formerly was by monarchic arbitrariness. This view was the genesis of the idea of "spheres" existing within a polity; that is, strictly delimited social spaces of action proper to either the state or the individual:

> Thus each man lives for himself, not in barbarian isolation but in independence and under the protection of a strong and civilized society that allows him, in matters concerning him personally, the free use of his faculties. If someone seeks to oppress him, it protects him; in any other case it allows him to use his mind and his muscles as he wishes, to acquire as much

property as he is able to, and then to use in his fashion, with the risks arising from his choice, that property which he has managed to acquire. With this measure of authority and liberty, the individual and the state both do their duty, each within a well-marked sphere. (Thiers [1850] 1880, 563)[12]

This precise definition of liberty makes it something that is both *of the essence* of any society and eminently *fragile*. The liberal of these years of flux was not a naive utopian but a skeptic worried about the future of freedom; staunchly opposed to the arbitrariness of the old world yet keenly conscious of the dangers of the new. And among these dangers, perhaps the worst was an exaggerated love for one's fellow human being.

PHILANTHROPY AS UNDUE INTERFERENCE

There is but one way of benefiting the poor, viz., by developing their powers of self-reliance, and certainly not in treating them like children. Philanthropists always seek to do too much, and in this is to be found the main cause of their repeated failures. The poor are expected to become angels in an instant, and the consequence is, they are merely made *hypocrites*. Moreover, no men of any independence of character will submit to be washed, and dressed, and fed like schoolboys; hence none but the worst classes come to be experimented upon. It would seem, too, that this overweening disposition to play the part of *ped-agogues* (I use the word in its literal sense) to the poor, proceeds rather from a love of power than from a sincere regard for the people. Let the rich become the advisers and assistants of the poor, giving them the benefit of their superior education and means – but *leaving the people to act for themselves* – and they will do a great good, developing in them a higher standard of comfort and moral excellence, and so, by improving their tastes, inducing a necessary change in their habits. But such as seek merely to *lord it* over those whom distress has placed in their power, and strive to bring about the *villeinage* of benevolence, making the people the philanthropic, instead of the feudal, serfs of our nobles, should be denounced as the arch-enemies of the country. (Mayhew [1851] 1968, 2: 264, emphasis in original)

Philanthropy – with its ages-old, oft-heard claim that ethics and good conduct can be inculcated by people who know what is good for us – thus joined the state as a source of abusive interference in the affairs of the free individual. The exacting vision of individual liberty under construction at mid-century would inevitably lead to hostility against all forms of intervention from "outside" the individual. Chapter 4 showed how the hopeful idea that convicts could be reformed faded away at this juncture. Philanthropy and its operative premises came in for similar criticism.

By now the Malthusians had become fixed in their view that excessive charitable intervention (especially on the part of the state) undermined the "moral fibre" of the poor. But the liberals had an even more fundamental critique of philanthropy; to wit, that it constituted a microcosm of arbitrariness, a little totalitarian world in which moral constraint (and its corollary, the claim to possess the truth) *took the place* of the will. We saw[13] how the same premises led to doubt about the possibility of knowing the soul of the criminal, and how much truer this was of the poor! How could anyone possibly know their interests and aspirations? Mill cautioned philanthropists to show humility when dealing with the poor:

> Human beings owe to each other help to distinguish the better from the worse, and encouragement to choose the former and avoid the latter. They should be for ever stimulating each other to increased exercise of their higher faculties, and increased direction of their feelings and aims towards wise instead of foolish, elevating instead of degrading, objects and contemplations. But neither one person, nor any number of persons, is warranted in saying to another human creature of ripe years, that he shall not do with his life for his own benefit what he chooses to do with it. He is the person most interested in his own well-being: while, with respect to his own feelings and circumstances, the most ordinary man or woman has means of knowledge immeasurably surpassing those that can be possessed by any one else. The interference of society to overrule his judgment and purposes in what only regards himself, must be grounded on general presumptions; which may be altogether wrong, and even if right, are as likely as not to be misapplied to individual cases, by persons no better acquainted with the circumstances of such cases than those are who look at them merely from without ... Considerations to aid his judgment, exhortations to strengthen his will, may be offered to him, even obtruded on him, by others; but he himself is the final judge. All errors which he is likely to commit against advice and warning, are far outweighed by the evil of allowing others to constrain him to what they deem his good. (Mill [1849] 1913, 59–60)

By the same token, philanthropy's critics also impugned the alleged altruism of charity. The act of giving can also betray a form of egocentrism, a self-interestedness more apt to satisfy the narcissistic tendencies of the elites, or even to cater to the boredom of the idle, than to truly help the poor.

> We are becoming foolishly soft, weakly tender, irrationally maudlin, unwisely and mischievously charitable. Under the specious mask of mercy to the criminal and benevolence to the wretched, we spare our own feelings at the cost of the most obvious principles of morality, the plainest dictates of prudence, the dearest interests of our country. We are king to every one except society. We find it easier and more agreeable to be generous than to be just ... In a vast proportion of cases, and among those who contribute most liberally and largely, charity is a clumsy and hollow compromise between indolence and kindness; the acting motive is the offspring of a half-awakened conscience and a more than half triumphant sloth. (Anonymous 1853, 63, 78)[14]

Powerless to comprehend the real interests of the poor, philanthropy becomes an abusive, misguided exercise in do-goodism which, far from alleviating misery, in fact provokes it.

> The extent, the thoughtlessness, the indiscriminate nature, of our benevolence, has called into existence a class – the most noxious that can infest a community – to whom charity is an ample, a regular, a luxurious livelihood: who can calculate with certainty upon this income – who *subsists* upon it, as upon any other occupation or profession. The same system not only maintains this class, it is perpetually recruiting and increasing it. (Anonymous 1853, 70–1)[15]

This recrudescence of hostility toward philanthropy led observers to two conclusions. Some went as far as to claim that any help for the poor should be considered undue and unjustifiable interference with the natural order of things. Poverty is less a problem than a *test*, a necessary ordeal, even a rite of passage allowing a person to demonstrate his value, his capacity to function in society. It is therefore a constant reminder and an essential teaching tool – in sum, the ferule threatening but also guiding free citizens, reminding them by its looming presence that life is a battle to be waged alone. Here is how the economist Antoine Cherbuliez explained the matter:

> Like all duties, the duty of providence needs a sanction, and in the natural order of things, this sanction is not lacking: it is the responsibility weighing on each family; it is the chain of cause and effect which condemns foolhardy labourers to their own or their family's suffering; it is that penalty – misery – which brings both torment and shame upon the improvident,

whose threat rings without cease in the ears of the needy, which is always there, on their heels, ready to make them atone, with privation and with physical and moral suffering, for the least act of laziness, the smallest vicious habit. (Cherbuliez 1853a, 167)

In this liberal conception, just as prison became the formal punitive sanction for misdeeds, poverty became the radical, inescapable penalty attaching to laziness or lack of foresight. At the outer bounds of this conception, some commentators drew a second conclusion: that poverty is a *social benefit*. It is the visible manifestation of the biological or natural laws according to which only the fittest survive. Social Darwinism, that perfunctory and uncritical application of Darwinian theory to human affairs,[16] was in fact just an extreme statement, or perhaps an unintentional caricature, of the liberal imperative arising in these years. Herbert Spencer was perfectly clear on this point: "The poverty of the incapable, the distresses that come upon the imprudent, the starvation of the idle, and those shoulderings aside of the weak by the strong, which leave so many in shallows and in miseries, are the decrees of a large, far-seeing benevolence." (*Social Statics* 1851, quoted in Spencer [1884] 1969, 139–40)[17]

Precisely because it is so extreme, this hysterical perversion of liberal thought – in which distress becomes not only (as in Malthus) a guarantee of public conformity but also an instrument of social progress[18] – in fact rather inadequately summarizes the challenge posed by the critique of philanthropy to the liberal philosophy of welfare. No one had ever proposed eliminating all assistance, but only that which supplanted instead of supplementing the autonomy of the citizen and producer. The idea of autonomy as an ethical imperative derived strength, it should be noted, from the fact that much of the working class bought into it. While the development of mutual aid societies can rightly be interpreted as a search for a working-class alternative to competition, it squares just as well with mid-nineteenth-century liberal conceptions of poverty. Mutualism, after all, shares with liberalism the objectives of personal autonomy and self-sufficiency in a market economy. In this regard, the care taken by members of these societies to distinguish themselves from charitable enterprises is revealing.

> The purpose of this institution, too often likened to the charitable agencies, has never been well understood, yet what a difference! [Such agencies] are, to be sure, composed of persons ... united for the sole purpose of delivering

alms into the hands of the poor; their members are all benefactors, and pity is the sentiment by which they are motivated. For our association, however, the relief granted is an acquired right ... All rights are equal, the only difference being the occurrence of misfortune ... Is this not in fact a provident association, and is it not an injustice to consider it a mere work of charity, humiliating to anyone obliged to receive the relief necessary to his survival? For us, reproach is a crime, disclosure a wrong severely punished – and why? Because the recipient does not receive anything from anybody; it is his property being returned to him, his wealth which he spends. He owes no thanks, for the contract is reciprocal. (*Préambule du règlement de la société des gantiers de Grenoble* 1823, quoted in Hatzfeld 1989, 204–5)

Mutuality was the collective, associative form of the imperative of autonomy fundamental to liberalism.[19] It is no surprise, then, to find autonomy and self-help at the core of the new economy of charity.

A SPECIFIC ECONOMY OF WELFARE

The economy of welfare emerging in the 1840s and 1850s was specific inasmuch as it entailed not the abandonment but rather the resumption, the development, and especially the recentring of welfare measures devised and put in place since the end of the eighteenth century. This recentring administered a shock to the humanist ethic that had accompanied the philanthropic reflex of the Enlightenment.[20] Much more importantly, it prefigured both a new social geography of welfare and a new practice of charity.

A New Social Geography of Poverty

If self-help became the fundamental principle by which the validity of relief would be measured, this was not only because it constituted the supreme objective of a successful intervention in working-class life, as per the philanthropic doctrine of welfare that had been well understood since the end of the eighteenth century if not earlier. It is also because this principle came to serve as the main criterion used to distinguish autonomous families, who were entitled to short-term household assistance, from paupers, whose lot was to be confined within the workhouses of the Victorian era. This principle would henceforth serve to distinguish poverty from pauperism, to assign each a territory and a topical remedy. The authorities had swiftly learned to differentiate the two, of course, but they had often drawn the line at the boundary between classes rather than attempting to judge the extent of the pauper's moral depravity. Pauperism was merely the extreme form of the working classes' deep-seated inability to either adapt to economic laws, or (as conservatives hoped) to recreate bonds of dependency. In either case, the pauperized urban masses suggested a possible future for societies. Their existence offered evidence of congenital vice among the poor to all those Malthusians searching for it, just as it suggested to liberals (e.g., Gérando) the need for organized, large-scale societal intervention in favour of *all* the poor, with private initiative and government collaborating on this work of social reconstruction.

But from the moment when personal and civic autonomy became the criterion used to classify poverty – when the urban industrial environment ceased to be a cause of poverty and instead became the dominant context for the manifestation of dependency – it became possible to imagine society as composed of two separate, coexisting worlds: that of "natural" poverty, the structural constraint inflecting the trajectory of all workers and peasants, and that of pauperism, an abject, amoral ghetto inhabited by those members of society who had failed the test of autonomy. Cherbuliez explained this separation as follows:

> That which makes modern pauperism a blot on society, that which makes it frightening and dangerous, is its ordinary alliance with a state of mindlessness and depravity in the mass of individuals, an all-too-natural effect of their agglomeration and their homogeneity. Instead of being disseminated throughout the population of a region, indigents form a separate "population unto themselves"; instead of a localized infection found in all stations of society, they form a separate class, a whole body infirm ... to destroy moral poverty would be the true means of driving physical poverty back within its normal bounds, and this is, in truth, all one may hope to obtain by the most energetic and continuous action of the most enlightened charity. When we have reached that point, we will have beaten pauperism; there will remain only a small sum of accidental misery, which would always be an evil, no doubt, but would no longer constitute a scourge. There would still be plenty of individual suffering, many miserable lives; but society's progress would no longer be halted, its economic development disrupted, its vital principle attacked by the scourge of collective poverty, which, by causing whole categories of workers to fall into savagery, gathers little by little, around the same hearths where civilization is being most actively developed, a people foreign to any civilization. (Cherbuliez 1853b, 337)[21]

Two fundamental corollaries flow from this separation:

1. On the one hand, the isolation of pauperism as an easily discernible social ill, as a separate world populated by failed citizens, allows for the "rehabilitation" of ordinary poverty as a normal or even legitimate social phenomenon. Poverty is the habitual condition of the working classes and constitutes a characteristic of their environment. It becomes unacceptable only when it reaches a degree of intensity that threatens the survival of the honest family. Poverty is an essentially human condition that renders human beings more vulnerable to life's unfortunate circumstances. The discourse of liberalism had at last learned to reconcile progress with poverty. Progress was no longer the emergence of a free people from the Egypt of ancestral poverty and arbitrariness. Instead it had become the sum of small individual victories over adversity: poverty was at once the precondition, the environment, and the fertile soil in which the possibility of a better life for all could take root.[22]

   Thus, this kind of poverty literally constituted the condition for the existence of civil society. It was not a political issue, or even really a social problem. Fundamentally, it derived from the inherent dynamics of civil society and was to be confined thereto. This explains why private charity reigned supreme in this economy of welfare. Not only because state charity was clumsy and dangerous, a pretext for demands formulated in terms of rights, but quite simply and more fundamentally because "normal" poverty, as a general rule, demands relief only in its accidental manifestations, on the surface of civil society. Honest workers and toiling peasants were members of the autonomous poor struggling to survive and, if possible, to thrive in a hard world.[23] The will was their driving force, the aspiration to a better life their sustenance. If an accident such as illness or temporary unemployment were to befall them, charity was there to fill the gap. However, an accident is by its nature unforeseeable, unique, circumstantial. Poverty, like accidents in general, was thus the concern of those most able to intervene at the right place and time – that is, neighbours, the community, or the local relief organization (itself staffed by neighbours). Private charity, whatever its forms – whether secular or religious, ethnically based or municipal, outdoor or indoor, occasional or long-term, and whether it dispensed goods or services – was the ineluctable horizon of this "normal" poverty.

> When poverty has ceased to be squalid and miserable, and when want is banished from a land of plenty, and dependence has died out with the social blunders and injustices which fostered it, humanity will remain as it was before – imperfect, feeble, subject to casualty, to misfortune, and to sorrow. In soothing, aiding, and strengthening these, benevolence will still and ever find abundant occupation; but its objects will be cases, not classes – exceptions, not rules; and its operations will be no longer carried on by machinery, relentless, ponderous, and indiscriminate; but by human creatures – watchful, tearful, considerate, and wise. (Anonymous 1853, 88)

2 On the other hand, the mass of pauperized individuals was excluded from the ordinary poverty that continued, for the time being, to bedevil the still-imperfect liberal societies. This mass of people was the precise equivalent of the more or less irretrievable criminals found in the liberal prisons – those described by Tocqueville and discussed in part 2 of this book. Political economy, so loquacious on the conditions of production and consumption, professed its powerlessness in the face of this marginal population, which had to be recorded as a liability on the balance sheet of progress.

> On the question of pauperism, political economy affords little but negative insights. It rejects state intervention as always impotent and often dangerous; it likewise rejects any system of social organization founded on the negation of property or the family, or on the right to work, as promising nothing but universal misery and societal dissolution. But the full exposition of these economic doctrines, and the refutation of errors and utopias ... in no way contain the solution to our problem. They teach us only that it remains unresolved, and prevent us from taking red herrings for solutions. (Cherbuliez 1853b, 338)[24]

But if pauperism has no solution, at least in the short term, it nonetheless demands a response. If it is not to be cured, it can perhaps at least be contained. As in the case of criminals, confinement begins to take on the hues of a segregation procedure in which the ideal of reform gives way to prophylactic isolation. Here again, the Foucauldian notion of disciplinary treatment is of no use in grasping the meaning of the institutions of confinement in the economy of relief.

> Workhouses were not instruments of disciplinary knowledge. The new hub and spokes structures were not panopticons and in their regimes disciplinary techniques played a blind, repressive role. Generally, official strategy did not positively aim to reform and remake individual paupers

> ... The aim was negatively to repress pauperism by making indoor relief thoroughly unattractive and making outdoor relief unobtainable for able-bodied men. (Williams 1981, 143)

Unlike the charitable aid dispensed by the private sector, which was sensitive to the specificities of each case, the confinement of "degraded" elements of the working classes was a systematic procedure based on the notion that anyone who willingly applied for and submitted to it must surely be unable to meet his own needs. This was the primary, fundamental criterion making the workhouse, the house of industry, or the beggars' prison more an instrument of discrimination than a place of refuge or assistance. A general distinction among those interned was established on the basis of the treatment accorded them, between the obligate dependency of abandoned children, the infirm, the elderly, or the insane, on the one hand, and the morally condemnable dependency of unemployed but able adults, on the other. But the particular circumstances of dependency were ultimately secondary to the facts of desperation and self-selection that gave rise to the institutionalization of extreme poverty. It would be another generation – not until around 1880 – before England's workhouses finally became specialized according to the *status* of those interned (Williams 1981). Moreover, despite the extreme discourse of the hard-liners of political economy, the validity of state intervention in this area was seldom challenged. A population without any great hope for reform, dangerous to the mass of honest citizens, and burdensome to administer had to be excluded, and appeals for state intervention to accomplish this were inevitable, if only for lack of something better.

> The very existence of a poor law, the very fact that there does exist a provision for all who cannot provide for themselves, is a direct incentive to pauperism, and to the neglect of social ties ... Do not think that I wish to say hard things against it. I say that for the time being it is the best, the only method of dealing with a great evil ... I look forward to a time when we shall return to the original principle of the poor law, and consider poverty a crime. (Lambert 1873–4, 471)[25]

Lambert makes clear that the "poverty" at issue here is that of pauperism, that form of extreme poverty represented by stigmatized dependency, and not the ordinary poverty in which so many people perpetually subsist. The poverty of paupers is a social crime of sorts, a violation of the conditions of life in society. It may be largely set down to a lack of foresight, an inability to provide for one's dependents, an unfitness for stable employment. It is a crime by omission, and the elites have learned to distinguish it from "true" crime of the deliberate or premeditated variety, yet it still dictates confinement for the individuals in question. Whether managed by the public authorities or otherwise,[26] the institutions in which paupers were confined gave them special visibility by virtue of their physical segregation from ordinary poverty. It now became possible, and indeed tempting, to ascribe specific characteristics, or even physical or psychological idiosyncrasies, to this population[27] – to categorize paupers as "defective, dependent and delinquent" (Wines 1888). The people living in prisons, houses of industry, asylums, and even hospitals became symptomatic of a *sui generis* social pathology on the basis of which they could be isolated from all forms of solidarity and marked as counterexamples of social normality. In this way, the problem they represented could be reduced to a localized condition of an otherwise fundamentally healthy social body.[28]

The social surveyors of the day helped add to this stigma. From Richard Dugdale's study of a distressed family (*The Jukes*, 1877) to Charles S. Hoyt's survey of American poorhouse inmates and on to Frederick Wines's classification of the "deficient" population into seven types based on data from a United States government census of penal and charitable institutions conducted in 1880,[29] scientific research proceeded to uphold and rigidify the fundamental divide between poverty and pauperism reflected in the confinement of the destitute. With this distinction in place, the stage was set for a renewal of charitable practices.

A New Practice of Charity

Charitable practices would rather strictly follow the contours of this geography of poverty – initially, the isolation of extreme cases of dependency in state- or private-run institutions and the case-by-case management of "normal" poverty to be handled by private charity. A systematic division of welfare responsibilities was taking shape, with poor families being aided by private or civil society initiative and highly dependent populations being placed in institutions.[30] The fundamental consequence was that both conservative and liberal elements of society had room to manoeuvre where the question of "accidental" poverty was concerned. Insofar as this form of poverty was a matter for the forces of civil society to handle, it made little difference whether charity was guided by a religious conception of poverty as eternal or by a philosophy of society in which poverty is a natural condition from which everyone aspires to free themselves. The liberal welfare economy was perfectly capable of accommodating either alternative, since both agreed on a depoliticized and even "desocialized" version of charity and emphasized case-by-case intervention.

Thus, the liberal conception of charity gave free rein to highly conservative initiatives for the management of poverty. For liberals, however, private charity's focus on "acceptable" poverty afforded space for a renewal of intervention methods. This renewal was based on three cardinal principles: that poverty is curable, that the cure must be based on scientific knowledge, and that a special relationship between the helper and the person being helped is necessary.

CURABILITY

> We religiously believe that the want, destitution, and misery, which so haunt and shock us in our complicated modern world, are in no way natural or necessary; that in all cases it is due and traceable, not to God's ordinances, but to some notable and palpable contravention of those ordinances; and that he who would cure it and relieve it, must first find out where that contravention has been, and how it can most promptly be amended.
> (Anonymous 1853, 82)

Without a doubt, liberalism gave up on the idea of societal reform. The fight against mass poverty, the systematic inculcation of values into the masses, was not to become a shared agenda. In this regard, the harsh critique of philanthropy's illusions, discussed earlier, was telling. But liberalism also accepted that the passage from quotidian to extreme poverty was not inevitable, that it followed neither from divine decree nor from inviolable economic laws, nor even from the people's propensity to vice. Before it passed the point of no return, the deterioration of honest poverty into shameful misery could be halted. Poverty as a native state might be unavoidable, but it need not be someone's inevitable destiny. The liberal conception of welfare harboured a continually expressed critique of the conservative vision of charity that regarded extreme poverty as a pretext for bringing back older forms of dependency. Here is one critic denouncing the philosophy of poverty underlying this form of traditional charity:

> Poverty is not looked upon as an evil remediable by the better organization of social relations, and by the reformation of individual character, but as a necessary evil, designed as aforesaid to benefit the leisurely by giving them cases by which they may perfect themselves in spiritual medicine. It is as if a schoolmaster should consider ignorance as specially designed with the final cause of the creation and perfection of schoolmasters; as if a medical man should look on sickness as a divine institution for the education of surgeons and physicians. (Lambert 1873–4, 463)

Poverty, in short, was acceptable only if it was temporary, or at least contained within limits that permitted the poor to survive. The proper response to its constant presence was not resignation but combativeness.

SCIENTIFIC CHARITY

But charity was regarded as a complex, precarious thing to be practised with restraint. It meant acting on the stochastic diversity of human beings, which might have the effect of lifting up the pauper but might also, perversely, pitch him further into the throes of dependency. More than an art of giving, charity had to be a science of poverty based on a systematic analysis of its circumstances.

> The plain truth is, that the luxury of doing good, like the luxury of growing rich, demands study, effort, industry, and caution. The profession of philanthropy, like every other, can be safely and serviceably practised only by those who have mastered its principles, and graduated in its soundest schools. It is as dangerous to practise charity, as to practise physic without a diploma. He who would benefit mankind must first qualify himself for the task. (Anonymous 1853, 81)

In the recesses of dire poverty where the threat of pauperism loomed, intervention was especially delicate in that it risked turning neediness into habit and resignation.

> When the friendly relations which ought to exist between the two classes take the loose form of indiscriminate almsgiving, it only tends to nourish into idleness the large shifty portion of the lowest poor, whose life is a chronic struggle for existence. In that life the quick transitions of hope and fear, of scarcity and surfeit, chase each other so rapidly and regularly that they blend like swift-gliding prismatic rays into a colourless homogeneity,

and thus feeling hardens into the second nature of unbroken habit.
(Anonymous 1875, 109)

Personal autonomy was the obverse of the "habits" which Tocqueville resigned himself to inculcating in the criminal classes, assuming their hearts and minds were beyond reach. The task of safeguarding or developing this capacity for autonomy necessitated a practice of charity governed by rules and procedures. If it was not to be a policy as such, liberal charity at least had to be guided by a method; the initiative of good Samaritans had to be contained within rational bounds.

RELATING TO THE POOR

The hope of scientifically valid and effective intervention in situations of poverty made it necessary to relinquish not only the nostalgia and paternalism of old times but also the class contempt often integral to the philanthropic gaze. Once its implications had dawned on benefactors, they clearly saw that the principle of self-help mandated respect for self and other on both sides of the helping relationship.[31] The new charity had to be a sort of apostolate founded on human equality, not paternalistic (if well-intentioned) superiority.

> We must go as men to meet our fellow-men; believe that they are influenced by the same motives, actuated by the same principles as ourselves. But for this we need an enthusiasm of humanity, without which we cannot undertake that work. No patronizing, no advice as from superior to inferior, no wish to press people into our system, to cut them like so many ornamental bushes into our pattern, will do. We must have the love of men, the desire for their elevation so strongly at heart, that we will be content with any means, use any tools, forward any plan which will carry out that design.
> (Lambert 1873–4, 475)

It was less a matter of organizing the "conversion" of the subordinated classes than of reinstituting a social fabric in which hierarchical relations would give ground to personal contact or even friendship, if not solidarity. The philanthropist's sentimental and romantic pity had to be supplanted by a personal, voluntary bond, akin to a contract,[32] that would break down the wall between wealth and poverty – a wall in actuality built out of nothing more than personal effort, talent, and foresight. The successful helping relationship was thus a relationship of trust rather than one of deference.

The first step towards improving the condition of the poor is to gain their confidence. Dilettante sentimentalism is as repellent as is the cynicism of official facts and figures. To gain this confidence and to inspire self-respect, the foundation of which is *independence*, and whose backbone is *self-help*, the cue must be *taken*, not *given*. (Anonymous 1875, 108, emphasis in original)

In short, the liberal conception of charity, at the moment of its fullest expression, implied a particular operation of the social bond underlying democratic capitalist societies. It cannot be likened to a mask that was worn with an intent to hide class interests or elitist bourgeois contempt. Nor was it a rejection of poverty as a problem to be solved, much less a mental artifice designed to spare the state the obligation to intervene. Instead, it was an exacting and rather paradoxical ethic which concretized, in matters of poverty, the basic principles of the liberal worldview discussed in previous chapters. It was exacting in that it took human freedom seriously. People controlled their own destiny, even if this meant that a mode of assistance as scientific as it was personalized would have to be devised. It was paradoxical in that it posited a formal equality between the parties to the helping relationship at a time when their blatant de facto inequality made such an idea vain and unproductive. Moreover, shackled as it was to the categories permitted by an individualistic view of human relations, it was simply incapable of viewing poverty as a *collective* and in fact a *political* problem. Thus it denied poverty the status of a major social issue.[33] It either swept the problem out to the periphery where the poorhouses awaited or, in its more moderate form, confined it within the dynamic of a free market in benevolence.[34]

As of the late 1860s, the emergence of the Charity Organization Societies in England and America confirmed the enduring influence of this liberal view of charity.[35] An opportune moment had arrived in which to roll out a rigorous, systematic economy of charity, with a substantial albeit circumscribed role for the state. But this situation would not last, for the hegemony of the liberal conception of poverty would be brief.

THE CRISIS OF LIBERAL CHARITY

The economy of liberalism's preferred relationship between poverty and wealth stems from the social struggles of the first half of the nineteenth century as well as from a rethinking of the philanthropic and reformist worldview flowing from the Enlightenment. It would be a gross misprision of this logic of charity to reduce it to an ideological expression of the interests of a dominant class, a mere rationalization of bourgeois egotism, much less a conservative twitch provoked by fears of revolution. To fully grasp the fragility of this charitable logic and the conditions of its decline starting in the 1880s, its internal coherence must be understood. To its proponents, this vision of welfare appeared to represent an ideal compromise between the dictates of liberty and the necessary response to its social consequences. To make poverty both an ineluctable reality and a fate to be avoided was to reduce the problem of inequality in democracy to a question of personal *responsibility*, in the two basic senses of the term: prerogative and accountability. Poverty, even when it afflicted children, the elderly, or the infirm, was thus a stigma, a symbol of one's inability to fend for himself or to plan out his life with due consideration to its vicissitudes. In the liberal conception, poverty was both a circumstance, a state of things, a general context in which the people's existence bathed, and an outcome, a consequence, an effect. A dual discourse on poverty emerged, depicting it as an inescapable reality faced by the working class, and also a condition experienced by some members of that class when they failed to surmount that reality.

The polysemy of the word poverty had several advantages. For the time being at least, it served to distinguish winners from losers, and hence to confine the social problem posed by poverty to the latter. Pauperism, initially perceived as a social hazard threatening to engulf the new industrial societies, was thus brought down to the status of a mere anomaly – serious, to be sure, but cantonned geographically and socially within the extreme fringes of urban poverty. Pauperism became nothing but the collective, socially visible, isolable sum of small individual defeats in the fight against adversity. By identifying the population of the socially unfit as a specific category, by making their horizon the walls of the institutions of confinement, and ultimately by accepting that the state should take care of this population, the way was cleared for private charity to concentrate on the "true" people, on those citizens who had not yet crossed the border into extreme poverty; in sum, those deserving of assistance.[36]

The private charity rolled out over the vast terrain of curable poverty was generally able to dispense with the state. The daily battle against want did not constitute a social problem to be handled by organized policy, since it was the regrettable but inevitable way of life experienced by the majority of workers. It thus became possible to shed the grand reformist ambitions that might otherwise have made the fight against poverty a collective issue bearing upon the fate of nations; or rather, to pare them down to the thousands of individual situations in which an individual's mores or habits had to be changed. Reform in this sense was a personal quest to right oneself, with tactical, case-based support from private charity. It was all the more likely to succeed if the support was specific, targeted, and provided by a loved one, or at least someone with intimate knowledge of the case. The "private sphere" in question was nothing more than the normal operation of civil society as applied to the issues of charity.

It is understandable that such a conception of welfare should appeal to both liberals and conservatives. It allowed for the free, private deployment of all possible forms of relief, all imaginable philosophies of assistance, provided that they respected the pauper's freedom. Poverty could be viewed as God's will and an opportunity for the rich to redeem themselves, or as a condition triggering the operation of a complex process of rebuilding the poor person's autonomy in a world of competition: both interpretive models were possible and acceptable. In a world where market logic had been reconciled with persistent poverty, there was no impediment to competition between different philanthropic aspirations, different versions of good will, provided that they were severed from their potential political implications.

How then to explain the decline of the liberal economy of charity? By noting that, starting in the 1880s, its inherent contradictions ultimately undermined its own cohesion, and also that the practice of assistance itself sharpened these contradictions. There ensued a systematic critique that would significantly modify the operative logic of welfare in Western societies.

THE CONTRADICTIONS OF THE CHARITABLE ECONOMY

That a worldview is cohesive does not imply that the practices adopted with a view to materializing it will never betray its unseen internal contradictions, and the liberal approach to poverty is a case in point. Concurrent with the deployment of this logic in Western societies, liberal charity came face to face with several major contradictions.

As discussed above, the concept of pauperism made it possible for liberals to identify those members of the poor masses who, having crossed the boundary into extreme poverty, had become irremediably dependent on assistance. Institutionalization was the usual fate reserved for this mass of "unfit" individuals. Sooner or later, however, this treatment of a sizable portion of the population was bound to collide with the core liberal values of personal freedom and progress. These people were neither criminal nor insane; neither their rights nor their intellectual capacity to live in society were doubted. On what grounds could their confinement, their exclusion from progress, be justified? A mere moral failing was surely not enough.

Another alternative, however, was to construe them as lacking responsibility for their destiny by virtue of *congenital* unfitness. Social Darwinism offered a convenient palliative for the malaise occasioned by the systematic confinement of paupers. Its thrust was to ascribe innate traits to the destitute, differentiating them not just morally but also physically, or at least mentally, from the "healthy" masses. In this way, a medical dimension was inserted at the moral border between the deserving poor and the incarcerated beggar. Paradoxically, though, this attempt at prophylaxis was expressed not in terms of therapy but mere captivity.[37] The "scientific" validation of confinement thus served to accentuate the stigmatization of the lumpenproletariat who scratched out an existence below the "healthy" strata of the working class.

But if the unfitness of this population was due to heredity, what became of the principle of responsibility, the cardinal axiom of liberal thought? The invocation of "science" came at the cost of an admission that not everyone in society is governed by that axiom. Liberal philosophy, with its emphasis on the liberation of individual potentialities, stopped at the prison and poorhouse doors. At a time when rights such as suffrage were being extended to the entire working class, paupers stared out into the sun of democracy from behind the bars of the institution.[38]

"If it was a war on poverty, it was fought by vigilantes rather than by a public militia" (Huggins 1971, 11). Liberal charity had sought to institutionalize the poorest of the poor because it wanted to monopolize the whole field of ordinary poverty, through case-by-case intervention in the many cases of accidental misfortune found among the working classes. But this was to imagine that such capillary action on civil society could suffice to make ordinary poverty acceptable. It was to imagine that charity had the luxury of intervening at the precise moment where poverty threatened to topple over into misery, where need threatened to become dependency. The militants of private charity believed, therefore, that their troops should act sporadically and temporarily to keep people from falling into crime or destitution.

[The relief agencies] preferred to work with the marginal man who might be unemployed if not given the extra push, who did not know his strengths and what facilities were open to him, who might fall into pauperism without a necessary goad ... The emphasis had always been reform and uplift ... Such organizations would not attend to programs to alleviate suffering in a depression. And working men would hardly find real relief in their offices. (Huggins 1971, 159)

What was presented as a general remedy for poverty was actually just minor, sporadic, provisional intervention. Between the homeopathic and localized action of scientific charity and the knife in the water of private benevolence – submerged as it was in an ocean of poverty – lay a thin boundary often crossed, as the founder of the Salvation Army sensed near the end of the century:

There are many institutions, very excellent in their way, without which it is difficult to see how society could get on at all, but when they have done their best there still remains this great and appalling mass of human misery on our hands, a perfect quagmire of human sludge. They may ladle out individuals here and there, but to drain the whole bog is an effort which seems to be beyond the imagination of most of those who spend their lives in philanthropic work. (William Booth, *In Darkest England* [1890], quoted in Finlayson 1994, 140)

Moreover, charitable intervention in its liberal guise partook of a logic of scarcity in an economy increasingly capable of creating abundance. The idea was not at all to provide a vital minimum allowing the poor to reckon upon a new start; it was to make it so that natural insufficiency of aid would force them to take charge of their affairs.[39] As soon as charity also took on the role of providing, however occasionally or even temporarily, for the survival of the poor as a group, this ever-parsimonious assistance was apt to appear highly insufficient. The liberal definition of good charity thus allowed for a dangerous coexistence of generosity with greed, hearty giving with sordid stinginess.

To the contradictions generated by the exclusion of a large group of poor people from civic legitimacy, as well as the incapacity of private charity to provide effective and durable relief, must be added the fundamental ambiguity of the relationship between the poor and the person charged with helping them. The idea of a possible *friendship* between donor and donee, a relationship in which power dynamics would be banished in favour of mutual collaboration, in which self-sacrifice on the part of the rich would go hand in hand with a desire for personal betterment on the part of the poor: all these aspirations may seem utterly bizarre today. Yet they were central to the liberal philosophy of assistance. Egalitarian relations became possible wherever the distance between helpers and helped had nothing to do with differences of status or class or even wealth but, essentially, with the capacity to manage one's life and make provision for its risks, a capacity evaluated in terms of one's social success. Failure and unfitness were not sources of social distance as much as pretexts for consolidating the social fabric through the organization of short-term assistance.[40] Aid was a service rendered to a friend less talented in the art of living. Thus construed, liberal charity was halfway between the paternalism of old and the solidarity of modern times. Unlike paternalism, it rejected the idea that the success of the intervention resided in renewed expression of submission to authority, in the reinstatement of ties of deference. But unlike solidarity, it denied that such assistance should be gratuitous, granted without expectations of the poor and without personal gratification for the rich – that it should simply express the obligation to act that arises from the fact of coexistence within a community.

The ambiguities of this form of assistance became even more evident when the time came to institute "scientific" needs assessment of charity candidates. This inevitable rigour, this standardization of the inquisitorial procedures integral to the welfare process, would further the professionalization of welfare practice and ultimately lead to modern social work (Lubove 1965). Not content with denying the power dynamics inherent in the de facto inequality between giver and receiver, liberal charity had the additional task of reconciling friendship with science, volunteerism with the existence of a class of salaried professionals. Under these circumstances, it is hardly surprising that the history of private charity should be one of constant tension between the contrasting dictates of professionalization and volunteerism; that what purported to be friendly solicitude on the part of the rich naturally strayed into cold-hearted assessment of the poor.

Obviously, these contradictions were bound to become more flagrant as the liberal logic was enacted in the form of policy and on the terrain of practice. The episode of the Charity Organization Societies (COS) in Great Britain and America clearly illustrates this observation. Incapable of reconciling the demands of welfare coordination with the independent-mindedness of their constituent associations, caught between the imperatives of professionalization and the desire to infuse relations between rich and poor with a renewed sense of humanity, the COS failed miserably. At best they succeeded in raising the ire of a large part of the charitable intelligentsia[41] and many of the poor as well (Humphreys 1995).

However, it would take more than the development of internal contradictions within liberal discourse for this vision of charity to wind up looking like a vast hypocritical deception or even an enterprise of domination and exploitation – it would take an abrupt confrontation with the facts.

THE RUDE SHOCK OF REALITY

Beyond its own contradictions, the liberal worldview was confronting a reality increasingly hostile to it, at three complementary levels.

1 The gap between the goals of liberal welfare policy and its tangible results could hardly have been wider. Recall that the idea was to help the deserving poor while institutionalizing the most dependent paupers, particularly those fit adults who "refused to work." The demarcation between the two groups was essentially a function of the person's moral capacity to get out of poverty. The population of the workhouses and beggars' prisons was thus depicted as an aggregate of unfit and incapable individuals, and these institutions as the only feasible housing solution for them.

    The historiography has long since shown, however,[42] that the clientele of these institutions was utterly at odds with the image projected by liberal discourse.

    > The dependent poor were not degraded; they were unlucky. It is important to expose the fallacy that paupers and other dependents were a lumpen proletariat, for by making them outcasts this idea has served to fragment the working class by encouraging the working poor to despise and resent the dependent poor, to object to social welfare and, thereby, to oppose their own best interests. (Katz 1983, 218)

    Institutionalization actually took a variety of forms. Long-term placement primarily applied to children, widows without familial support, the infirm, those with incurable mental illness, and the elderly. This varied and shifting group constituted a dependent clientele placed in institutions by families unable to take care of them. But in many cases these individuals were placed by their families for short durations – months, weeks, or even days – and then taken home. As for able-bodied adults, most of them were excluded from welfare, setting aside the occasional short stay in an institution such as a workhouse (or later a house of refuge), the only form of support provided to men (and unmarried women) without work. Hospitals, for their part, accommodated the sick poor who had no access to a family doctor, generally for short periods. The point is that the population of these institutions was quite heterogeneous. It was not at all a coherent sociological group but a contingent and often-transitory collection of people who had fallen victim to one of the many dangers always looming over working-class and peasant families. Accidental poverty could happen to anyone, whether a member of the "good" or the "bad" poor.

The real divide was to be found within the institutions themselves, between long-term inmates who had practically lost contact with their families, and short-term inmates waiting for a parent, child, or relative to come to get them out. This fact all by itself annihilates the liberal distinction between poverty and pauperism. Interestingly, the gradual shift toward a pathological or genetic definition of these populations only confirmed the liberal illusion while changing the criteria for determination of pathology.

2 For liberals, poverty was the normal lot of the working classes; only the risk of falling into pauperism legitimized the resort to private charity. The hegemony of this economy of poverty could endure only as long as mass poverty appeared acceptable in the eyes of many observers. As the tide turned and poverty was increasingly viewed as intolerable, the whole liberal edifice started to crumble.

The economic crises of 1874 and 1893 would be decisive in this regard. These were classic crises of the capitalist cycle of production and could not be put down to natural factors, much less to the structural imprudence of the poor. They were far-reaching social crises that exacerbated the insecurity of the greatest number. At the same time, the idea that a significant stratum of the population should be spared the effects of the crises, their wealth untouched, became all the more untenable, indeed morally wrong.

What is more, the great mass of poverty engendered by the crises further exposed the haphazardness and insufficiency of private charity. The result was another empirical demonstration of the fallaciousness of liberal premises.

3 Liberal charity had always been a systematic attempt to depoliticize poverty in the emerging democratic societies. Poverty was a private matter and did not justify state interference in the freedom of rich and poor. Indeed, many workers' associations rallied to this position; they too sought affirmation of their autonomous organizing capacity and their freedom from interference by the bourgeois state. Their mutuals and cooperatives thus constituted an ambivalent response to liberalism, a translation of it into the politically committed language of the working class. But such a position assumed that working-class struggles would remain on the terrain of civil society. Inasmuch as the liberal worldview gave full latitude to the autonomy of the worker, however poor, nothing now stood in the way of affording him the capacity for political action. The extension of the franchise to the entire (male) working class was a seismic shift fully in keeping with the liberal logic of societal organization.

Widened suffrage, however, had the effect of repoliticizing poverty. There was no immanent force compelling people to vote in favour of a worldview completely disconnected from the living conditions of workers and peasants. The right to vote could be used to channel demands for change. Newly organized workers' political parties, as well as working-class pressures on the old-line parties,[43] were to have an immense impact on Western states. This factor is perhaps the most trenchant illustration of the profound crisis undergone by the liberal welfare system starting in the 1880s.

A SYSTEMATIC CRITIQUE OF LIBERAL PREMISES

Sapped by these internal contradictions, shaken by contact with unpleasant realities, the liberal conception of poverty and welfare soon drew harsh criticism, and not only from radicals. Perhaps the most corrosive critique came from the ranks of the educated petty bourgeoisie, and especially from the new social sciences developing within universities and private research associations. From Émile Durkheim to Max Weber and from Thomas Hill Green to Alfred Marshall, a new sociology and a new political economy were coming into being. Anchored in the positivism of Comte, the nascent social sciences were learning to analyze society as an organism both complex and complete, diversified but unitary. They incorporated advances in statistics, psychology, and history into their efforts to analyze society as a whole cognizable in and of itself, without being reduced to the sum of individual wills. They made it possible to conceive of the social "whole" as both a cause and an effect and, consequently, to redefine the individual as both a product and a source of the societal dynamic. This fundamental paradigm shift lent critical and scientific backing to those who would set society on pillars other than those of liberalism. It had a powerful influence on conceptions of poverty and welfare.

An initial clue to the re-evaluation of liberal thinking about poverty can be found in the discovery of the limits of self-help. Given the dim chances for anyone outside the upper strata of the working class to avoid hardship, much less to improve their lot through prudent behaviour, the liberal panacea of self-help seemed dubious in the extreme. It was a means of avoiding poverty, not of escaping it, and as such of little use to the poor masses.

> It is rash to assert that prudence is an all-powerful panacea. It can without doubt ward off certain individual risks, such as sickness, indigence in old age, etc.; but even then can only attenuate them in some cases ... But what of great disasters, famines ... floods, or, in a different connection, those industrial crises that interrupt the material life of a country, as a producer, but do not alter its needs as a consumer? Prudence can make little difference here, especially since the onset of such calamities is as sudden as their consequences are serious and generalized ...
>
> The counsel of prudence may shelter some from tomorrow's indigence, but it must not stop us from alleviating hardships which no one can foresee ... it cannot have any purchase on populations afflicted with pauperism, weakened in both will and strength, unable to work themselves back to health, powerless to carry on life's struggle. (Chevallier 1900a, 70–1)

Meanwhile, the economists John Hobson and John Robertson attempted to prove that household saving was not an unmitigated good, for it hindered household consumption as families scrimped in order to save (Finlayson 1994, 155).

More generally, an increasingly harsh critique of the inadequacies of private charity was developing. The decline of the Charity Organization Societies, their failure to coordinate private associations effectively, is symptomatic of this new look at poverty. "Scientific" charity was looking ever more like downright stinginess, its "targeted" intervention futile and insufficient,[44] its efforts to prevent poverty a stubborn refusal to help. Ultimately, what was presented as a gesture of friendship and love came to be regarded as contemptuous self-interest. Vehement critiques of the COS show the extent to which the good intentions of liberal charity were now impugned.

> Every person of intelligence and humanity who has seen the workings of Organized Charity, knows what a deadening and life-sapping thing it is, how unnecessarily cruel, how uncomprehending. Yet it must not be criticised, investigated or attacked. Like patriotism, charity is respectable, an institution of the rich and great ... White slavery recruits itself from charity, industry grows bloated with it, landlords live off it; and it supports an army of officers, investigators, clerks and collectors, whom it systematically debauches. Its giving is made the excuse for lowering the recipients' standard of living, of depriving them of privacy and independence, of subjecting them to the cruellest mental and physical torture, of making them liars, cringers, thieves. The law, the police, the church are the accomplices of charity. And how could it be otherwise, considering those who give, how they give, and the terrible doctrine of the "deserving poor"? There is nothing of Christ the compassionate in the immense business of Organised Charity; its object is to get efficient results – and that means, in practice, to just keep alive vast numbers of servile, broken-spirited people. (John Reed, introduction to Konrad Bercovici, *Crimes of Charity* [New York: Knopf, 1917], quoted in Katz 1986, 84)

This new approach to poverty was perhaps above all an effort to elucidate its *causes*. Say what one may about liberalism, it had never denied the role of the environment in the development of poverty. All the mid-nineteenth-century surveys that had stigmatized pauperism as a blot on society nonetheless stressed its partly environmental genesis. But a deep-seated belief – that the dilapidated dwellings inhabited by the poor, the epidemics by which they were decimated, were consequences of their moral and physical poverty as much as causes – withstood analysis. The environment was just another constraint that the poor had to overcome or at least control. The hard industrial context of the cities was a test of the workers' mettle more than a causal factor in poverty.[45]

Still, in the wake of surveys by Charles Booth and, at the turn of the century, B.S. Rowntree (Booth 1892; Rowntree 1901),[46] the new social science increasingly refused to emphasize moral failings as a cause of poverty; instead, it stressed income inadequacy. In so doing, it redefined working-class living conditions as objective determinants of poverty rather than mere constraints. Want, not vice or morality, became central to thinking about poverty. A decisive indicator of this change was the emergence of a new conception of unemployment as being caused by an objective lack of work, hence constituting a societal problem.[47]

Soon it was the concept of poverty itself, not just its causal factors, that cried out for redefinition. Liberals had always regarded poverty not as an objective state but as a regrettable slide into dependency. This meant that the concept had to be stretched to fit a large and heterogeneous group of people who included the working classes in general ("ordinary" poverty), the victims of accidents and other circumstances (who could be helped by charity and their own efforts to regain self-mastery), and paupers. But from the moment poverty came to be defined as mere want, a lack of income, not only did it become measurable according to quantitative criteria,[48] but, more importantly, it could now be considered to characterize a broader stratum of the population. Charles Booth orchestrated this paradigm shift in his epochal survey of poverty in London: "By the word 'poor,' I mean to describe those who have a sufficiently regular though bare income, such as 18 sh. to 21 sh. per week for a moderate family, and by 'very poor' those who from any cause fall much below this standard (Booth 1892, quoted in Himmelfarb 1991, 104).[49]

Below a certain objectively measurable living standard, poverty was once again a specific social *state*, and hence a social *problem*. It was no longer an existential condition of the masses or a case of accidental misfortune. Furthermore, unacceptable poverty was no longer confined to a destitute subgroup of the poor. Booth, for example, established four categories of poor people in London, these together accounting for 31 percent of the city's population. In its new meaning, poverty was a problematic condition afflicting a large portion of the working class, not just the most dependent and unfit. With its complex causality, poverty was measurably and identifiably a workers' problem, one that was now visible to all members of society; a problem collectively understood as a lack of resources, full stop. Liberalism had succeeded in depoliticizing working-class poverty both by individualizing its most widespread form and by reserving a collective interpretation for its most extreme form. Now, the collective element of poverty was recolonizing the public mind.

POVERTY AS A COLLECTIVE PROBLEM

A new economy of poverty, and of the social relations underlying it, was in gestation. It was not merely that the dominant philosophy of welfare was being reconfigured in response to the radical critique discussed above. The new approach to poverty was also, if not first and foremost, an approach to how the polity should be organized. It amounted to one of the possible modalities for the definitive integration of the working classes, and in particular the industrial class, into the democratic capitalist logic of regulation.

The Nation as Family

A holistic conception of society was taking hold, and an initial indication of its increasing influence was the exacerbation of national tensions caused by the Franco-Prussian War of 1870. The nation came to be regarded as much more than the abstract sum of political wills: it formed a quasi-organic entity unto itself. Beyond divisions of class, gender, or ideology, it embodied the specificity proper to the societal whole that it constituted. From this perspective, poverty was both a shameful stain and an obstacle to competition among nations. Winston Churchill remarked:

> It is here that you will find the seeds of imperial ruin and national decay – the unnatural gap between rich and poor, the divorce of the people from the land, the want of proper training and discipline in our youth, the awful jumbles of an obsolete Poor Law, the constant insecurity in the means of subsistence and employment ... Here are the enemies of Britain. Beware lest they shatter the foundations of her power. (Winston Churchill, *Liberalism and the Social Problem*, 1909, quoted in Finlayson 1994, 118)

On this view, organic society was akin to a large family. Counter to the liberal idea of citizenship – a privilege to be earned if one was to gain respect (and hence entitlement to relief) – there developed an idea of a kind of solidarity that precedes any social relation, a quasi-immanent collective identity said to form the very substance of that social relation. It is prior to the tangible interactions between individuals and entitles everyone to collective solicitude. The cynical rigour of Social Darwinism was no longer valid in this context, as explained in the article on "Welfare" or "Relief" (*Assistance*) in the *Dictionnaire de l'économie politique*:

> There is no need to spend time combating yet another distressing doctrine such as this; we must forget that humans belong to a species for whose improvement selection is necessary, and regard them rather as members of a single family to whom we are bound by certain moral duties. (Chevallier 1900a, 70)[50]

Promotion of the Working Class

If poverty was a scourge on the working class and not the embodiment of its flaws, then an opportunity had arisen to implement general, sustainable, systematic policies of support. It has often been correctly remarked that most of the early state social policies, starting with Bismarck's social laws of the 1880s, were explicitly directed at workers, and often came in response to organizing by workers' parties or unions. In parallel, women's associations went beyond a concern with charity to propose family support measures, including workplace protection laws for women and financial assistance to needy mothers.[51]

At the same time, the mutualist model, systematized by and reliant on the resources and power of the state, suggested a promising compromise between the virtues of providence and the need to help the poorest workers. The same was true for old-age support policies, family allowances, and unemployment insurance. These policies were explicitly directed at the working class with a view to the restoration of national unity. The consequence was that the old liberal phobia deriving from Malthus, to the effect that monetary aid (especially if guaranteed and long-term) "demoralized" workers and led to laziness, began to fade away.[52]

The other major consequence was a re-evaluation of the state's role in welfare provision, guided by a new spirit strikingly described by Joseph Chamberlain:

> Because state Socialism may cover very injurious and very unwise theories, that is no reason at all why we should refuse to recognize the fact that Government is the only organization of the whole people for the benefit of all its members, and that the community may – ay, and ought to – provide for all its members benefits which it is impossible for individuals to provide by their solitary and separate efforts ... it is only the community acting as a whole that can possibly deal with evils so deep-seated ... Now government is the organized expression of the wishes and the wants of the people, and under these circumstances let us cease to regard it with suspicion.
> (Chamberlain, quoted in Finlayson 1994, 162–3)

Historians – too often heedful of the call of teleology – have often come to view this emerging "social service state"[53] as a welfare state in embryo.[54] This is to misunderstand that in the organicist conception undergirding social policy in this era, the state was but one of the associative modalities whereby society organized itself, and not always the most important one.[55] More germanely, it is to forget how well this policy fit into a world in which the ethical imperatives and exclusions proclaimed by the liberal worldview had been preserved, even if reinterpreted in the light of the ongoing transformations.

Ethics as Condition and Horizon

Thus, the approach to poverty emerging in the late nineteenth century led to the sharp decline of moral deficiency as a putative causal factor in poverty. As for "pauperism," its pathologization deprived the moral objurgations of much of their relevance, as attested by this description of the characteristics of pauperism written in 1900:

> [Pauperism], being hereditary misery and entailing deprivation, for several successive generations, of the things most necessary to existence, manifests itself also in the physique through racial degeneracy, anemia, maladies of exhaustion, and declining strength. (Chevallier 1900c, 450)

For the eugenicist, the moral dimension was not at all the main determinant of personal destiny; it was only a symptom of an underlying physical condition. Here, for example, is Albert Regnard describing criminals and beggars:

> I do not know if there exists a physical type of a murderer, a thief, or a loafer. But I do know that there exists a moral type, since all these people, hereditary degenerates for the most part, are called by their nature to homicide, theft, or idleness. Since the moral is, moreover, the product of the physical, and in fact the brain itself, this type is as genuine, as undeniable as could be; it need not bear concomitant outward marks in order for us to confirm its existence ... Abnormal, *atypical* individuals not made for life in society – and that is man's natural condition – are divided into three categories: those who kill, those who steal, and those who, though they neither kill nor steal, wish to get along in utter idleness. (Regnard 1898, 35; emphasis in original)

It might of course be claimed that this language is itself tainted with secular moralizing.[56] But, apart from the fact that this eugenicist "ethics" operates very differently, the medicalization of a fringe of the "deficient" population, in parallel with the acknowledgment that the working class possesses certain rights in the area of welfare, deprives the ethical imperative of its status as a criterion for matching the needs of the poor to the welfare they may or may not deserve.[57] Ethics, however, has not thus withdrawn from the domain of regulation into that of personal choice; it still has a bearing on people's duties toward each other.[58] What has happened is that the ethical imperative has moved out of the religious sphere to which it was largely confined under the liberal mode of regulation, and now takes the form of a *collective* injunction to do good. Ethics is and always has been an injunction to conform. But this injunction changes shape in step with the margin of autonomy left to the individual under a given regulatory logic. From the vantage of the Enlightenment, freedom is the ideal context for the practice of virtue, that cardinal force that forms its necessary obverse; without virtue, freedom would degenerate into unbridled passion and finally anarchy.[59] For example, Adam Smith's beloved laissez-faire would be inconceivable without the ethical basis that he developed in *Theory of Moral Sentiments* (1759). In the mid-nineteenth century, ethics becomes both a framework for behaviour and a way to self-affirmation, primarily because differences among talents can be enacted only against a backdrop of shared values. Religion becomes the primary bulwark of the self-discipline that precedes action.

> When [the Republicans] attack religious beliefs, they follow their passions and not their interests. Despotism can do without faith, but not liberty. Religion is much more necessary in the republic that they advocate than in the monarchy that they attack ... How could society fail to perish if, while the political bond grows loose, the moral bond does not become tighter? And what to do with a people master of itself, if it is not subject to God? (Tocqueville [1840] 2012, 2: 478)

The liberal worldview construed ethics not only as a behavioural frame of reference but as an *impulse* underlying and driving every action. As Mill later explained, there is nothing passive about ethics: it encapsulates the very dynamic of competition in that it allows for confrontation between different private ethics. Christian ethics, although necessary, were insufficient by virtue of being merely reactive.[60] Other ethics were necessary in order to reconcile basic values with the diversity essential to liberal regulation.

> I believe that other ethics than any which can be evolved from exclusively Christian sources, must exist side by side with Christian ethics to produce

the moral regeneration of mankind; ... in an imperfect state of the human mind, the interests of truth require a diversity of opinions. (Mill [1849] 1913, 45)

The autonomy demanded of individuals assisted by liberal philanthropy had not been, therefore, a set of stereotyped or normalized behaviours but a source of motivation, a dynamism proper to the individual that proved his capacity to organize his life and thereby entitled him to aid as necessary.

The logic developing in the late nineteenth century was much more exacting. The working classes, now well integrated into the nation, still had to prove their capacity for autonomous action, but also had to observe strict conformity to a set of moral precepts governing private behaviour and rendering it socially validated. The various evangelistic groups of this period, as well as the moral lobby groups (e.g., feminist groups), had a much more intransigent definition of ethics, as witness the revival of campaigns against prostitution and alcoholism and in favour of "normal" sexuality. The bona fide missionary enterprises represented by these morality campaigns were in perfect concordance with the standardization of welfare for the family or the working class. They were in fact the translation of these measures into ethical terms and responded to the imperative of preserving order in the nation through collective discipline. This ethics of behavioural conformity was fundamentally different from liberal ethics, even though it acknowledged important components of it (such as personal freedom and autonomy). The ethical order undergirding the welfare state would be built on the debris of this ethics, not as an outgrowth of it.

> The activists were concerned to promote the enlightenment, cultivation and improvement of the people (symbolized by an improved sexual morality), in order to cement the two great modern classes into a "new" national community under the leadership of the middle class, which deserved and had earned the right to rule. At the core of this strategy was a dual environmentalism, a socio-economic strategy and a moral reform strategy. The socio-economic strategy laid the basis of what by the early twentieth century was coming to be called "welfare" ... The dimensions of moral regulation of the working class were concerned with the surveillance of youthful sexualities, primarily of females and, more generally, with making the working-class family correspond ever more closely to the middle class' own myth of the family. (Hunt 1999, 190)

In case it is not obvious, what this implied was a partial return to the reformist ideals of the early nineteenth century. Ethical conformity to basic values, unlike liberal restraint, entailed an intrusion into personal freedoms. In liberal regulation, poverty was what pushed the poor into the arms of charity, always leaving them at least a formal option of declining this fate. The new moralists, on the contrary, did not hesitate to use legal or police power to force the violent or deadbeat father, the negligent mother, the prostitute, the drunkard, etc., to conform to societal precepts. Under the banner of this moral imperative could be found evangelists of the social gospel, partisans of Catholic social teaching, hygienists, eugenicists, and others intervening in social affairs. The integration of the working class had come at a price: the ethical conformity that made the nation strong. But this ethics, even as renewed to suit the tenor of the times, could not be applied to all.

The Residuum

The 1880s are often considered the time when the welfare state first appeared on the horizon, with the adoption of the first social policies in favour of workers, the recognition of the state's right to play a large-scale role in welfare provision, and the critique of some of the most fundamental premises of liberal charity. However, historians adopting this gradualist chronology have tended to observe a prudish silence on the treatment of the poorest citizens, the lumpenproletariat subsisting under the newly respectable strata of the working class. The enduring discourse of exclusion against this population is set down either to the eugenicist fringe or to a form of proto-fascism arising out of corporatist ideology.

Quite the contrary, the systematic exclusion of the poorest and most dependent was a central aspect of the new economy of poverty being instated at this time. Still and always, the discourse promoting the interests of the working class stopped at the doors of the institutions of confinement.

The social surveyors who did so much to renew the definition of poverty are quite clear on this point. Charles Booth: "To the rich the very poor are a sentimental interest; to the poor they are a crushing load. The poverty of the poor is mainly the result of the competition of the very poor. The entire removal of this very poor class out of the daily struggle for existence I believe to be the only solution of the problem" (Booth [1892], quoted in Hennock 1976, 76).[61] This population, now tagged with the epithet "residuum," was meticulously excluded from social legislation covering workers. More specifically, the aid provided to it took the form of institutionalization, which developed during this period at an even faster pace.

The discourse on the socially "unfit" also took on an increasingly medicalized connotation under the influence of eugenics.[62] Eugenics furthered and modified the liberals' Social Darwinism by accentuating the divide between the working class and the incurably unfit, but also by recognizing the need for comprehensive and decent treatment of the latter.

If their exclusion was allowed and even promoted, it was with full acknowledgment of the need to care for them, or at least to provide them with decent institutionalized circumstances. The most notable transformation in this regard was perhaps the disappearance of the principle of "less eligibility," whose purpose had been to make these institutions a deterrent as much as a locus of custody.[63] These institutions no longer had to illustrate the perils of dependency by their menacing existence; no longer would they serve as a deterrent to the "honest" poor at whom new welfare (and insurance) policies were now directed. Their role was simply to provide a place for the destitute to live out their waning days.

As a corollary, the "residuum" stopped being a source of fear. For one thing, welfare policy measures targeted at the working classes seemed sufficient to diminish the size of this mass of social outcasts; for another, this group was now seen as constituting a minimal part of the population. Pauperism was becoming an epiphenomenon: "The numbers of the indigent have decreased, but ... there are, upon this limited expanse, more impenetrable areas, poverty more serious and less curable" (Chevallier 1900c, 454).

Likewise, the fear – not to say the paranoia – once provoked by beggars was on the wane (except as regards the young, unemployed homeless referred to as "tramps," who still worried the authorities[64]). The same was true of alcoholism, formerly the scourge of the working class, capable of dragging upstanding workers and their whole families down the slope of decadence: "alcoholism only strikes the refuse of the population, those degenerate individuals who gradually disappear because of it; they must be grieved and succoured, but we must not believe all is lost because two or three drunkards were seen rolling around in the street" (Regnard 1898, 39).[65] In short, institutionalization remained the primary solution envisaged for the residuum. According to the prevailing institutional dynamic, facilities would specialize according to the various manifestations of deficiency. The era would also be fertile in projects for *new* institutions of confinement, providing, for example, non-punitive work or nighttime housing for beggars, or asylums for drunkards, drug addicts, and consumptives.

* * *

The end of the century found the French spiritualist philosopher Jules Lagneau providing the students in an ethics course with a veritable compendium of liberal values on poverty and welfare:

> There is no such thing as a right to benevolence: it is obligatory, but no one is entitled to demand it. While the state does well to organize welfare, to make it the focus of a public service, no one may claim from the state anything more than respect for his civil rights ... It would be a danger to any state and to civilization itself, were the opinion to catch on among those who suffer that society is responsible for their suffering and that it is mandatory and possible for it to make that suffering cease ... Society is not the cause of ills whose source is found in moral imperfection, and in the inevitable laws of nature ... The struggle for existence is eternal among human beings, and for that very reason – in the words of the Gospel – the poor will always be with us. We are bound to come to their aid, not with general and constantly applied measures, artificial remedies whose only result would be to increase public misery while factitiously alleviating the effects of the abiding causes that maintain it ... Only the progress of science and industry on the one hand, and ethics on the other, can resolve the social problem of poverty in a natural, durable, progressive way, and the true benefactors of humankind are not those who practice benevolence blindly and systematically, nor those who wish to eliminate poverty through the artifice of legislation – which can only displace or aggravate it and only at the cost of hindering liberty and thus making social activity less fruitful, less productive – but the learned men who get to the heart of nature, the industrialists who exploit it, the thinkers who discover and disseminate true ideas capable of making men wiser, more prudent, stronger, so that they can withstand all the inevitable suffering and not deliberately and needlessly create more, by overexciting their appetites, their needs, their ambitions; by letting themselves be tricked by the coarse and chimerical ideal of happiness served up by an over-active imagination. (quoted in Hatzfeld 1989, 93–4)

This worldview, in which the individual is free and responsible for himself – in which the power of the collectivity is both a danger and a world of possibilities, in which the future presents itself as both a threat and an opportunity – possessed the immense power to interpret and give meaning to the world under construction for over a century. It constituted a reading of both history and the future whose self-evidence was bolstered by the institutions created under its aegis. An often-harsh critical discourse challenged some of the main pillars of liberalism, thereby rehabilitating the values of collective solidarity and the hope of changing the world for the better. But too often, the schools of thought that devised these critiques yielded only pale substitutes for what they criticized. Catholic social teaching, reform movements based on the new social sciences, corporatism – even cooperativism – never really questioned the imperative of freedom on which liberalism had been built (although its concept of freedom was, of course, quite peculiar). Nevertheless, all the far-reaching currents of the time – the adoption of state social measures systematically directed at the working classes, the rise of temperance movements and other moral crusades, the definition of poverty as a social problem implicating the whole nation – undermined the liberal logic of regulation that had underlain welfare efforts in the second half of the nineteenth century. By the time of the First World War, the liberal worldview found itself increasingly stretched between the principles it persisted in defending and the welfare practices that continued to diverge from those principles.

This lengthy exposition has provided the background necessary to understand the case of Quebec, and the very peculiar way in which liberal regulation would be constructed in that province.

7

Church and Religion in the Charity Economy

> I refuse ... to discuss the history of religion in the nineteenth century using the admittedly common concepts of secularization and institutional renewal. Far from seeing instances of *survivance* or awakening – that is, a few new branches managing to grow on an apparently old, dead trunk that nonetheless continues to fill out the landscape and at times produce new shoots – I want to try to elucidate the new religious economy using the concepts proper to it. (Despland, 1998, 17)

Any Quebec-based research on the institutions of social regulation has to grapple with the role that the Catholic Church played in the implementation, development, and administration of these institutions. That role was of course central, but our recent historiography of the administration of social problems in the province has largely reached unanimity on a much starker version of the story. In this account, the Church's dominant role in Quebec reflects the dominance enjoyed by a conservative elite in continual reaction against modernity. This elite is said to have held the Quebec public hostage by taking control over welfare and education. The depiction is a caricature, no doubt, yet it gives an idea of the broad-brush interpretation too often applied to the Church's presence in our history.[1]

The truth is that the Church's importance in Quebec – as a national monument, an institution of power, a belief system – has been such that one could claim with only slight exaggeration that our historiography has yet to take the measure of it. Historians have in general gravitated toward one of three analytical strategies. The first, part of a long historiographic tradition, views the Church as the most important institution in our national history. For better or worse, it has steered the collective destiny of the French Canadians (or the Quebecers, as they are now called) according to its own values, especially during that long and crucial period running from the Rebellions of 1837–38 to the Quiet Revolution of the 1960s.[2] The second strategy, adopted by much revisionist historiography since the 1960s, has striven to demonstrate that the Church's domination certainly did not prevent, and at times even abetted, the modernization of Quebec; that the province's history was forged almost in spite of the Church, or at least that this institution's pervasive influence over social affairs coloured the modernization process with particular hues.[3] The third strategy consists of recent work devoted to producing an "internal" history of religion and the Church. This approach dispenses with the monolithic analysis of the early interpretive tradition. It has shown the depth and diversity of the currents running through the institution as well as the complexity of churchgoers' attitudes throughout Quebec's history.[4]

Moreover, when it comes to assessing the multifaceted nature of the Church's impact on the evolution of Quebec society, it is notable how these impacts tend to be gauged (apart from a few exceptions) according to several allegedly irreducible dichotomies: most notably, ultramontanism versus liberalism and church versus state. These are said to help pinpoint the Church's position with respect to the issues surrounding the transition to modernity.

The first dichotomy, illustrated by a debate (well publicized in its day) between Louis-Antoine Dessaulles and Mgr Ignace Bourget, the Bishop of Montreal, serves to differentiate the Church from the essential values idealized by liberals: free will, democracy, secularism, and so forth. In this way, the issues essential to the transition to modernity are brought down to a conflict between two more or less irreducible ideologies, whose contrasting readings of reality form the bedrock of a centuries-long fight that marks the construction of contemporary Quebec. Ultramontanism becomes the privileged expression of the "great refusal" voiced by the elites with redoubtable constancy in their fight against modernity.[5]

The second dichotomy reiterates the first but extends its logic to the political sphere. Here the Church is no longer just a discourse but also a power rising up, as an equal, to confront the liberal democratic state.[6] Thus it constitutes an essential counterpower, pitting an alternative vision of community against modern politics and building a corresponding empire in the fields of charity and education. In so doing, it is said to have delayed the free expression of modern democratic culture in Quebec until the liberating apotheosis of the Quiet Revolution. From the "Catholic Program" of the 1870s – the official political agenda of the Catholic Church in Quebec, taken up by the ultramontane wing of the Conservative Party – to the 1949 conflict between Archbishop Joseph Charbonneau and Premier Maurice Duplessis over the asbestos miners' strike, Quebec's history is read as the long and turbulent cohabitation of an impossible couple, oscillating between open hostility and cozy complicity.

The idea here is obviously not to deny the crucial importance of the Catholic Church in the implementation of Quebec's modern network of charitable and educational institutions, much less to ignore the deep conservatism of the dominant elements of the Catholic hierarchy and much of its base. The idea is rather to clarify the context and the conditions of possibility of this hegemony, to avoid both explanatory red herrings and facile analytical shortcuts. It is less a matter of finding traces of modernity in Church discourse than of situating the Church within the regulatory economy being rolled out in Quebec after 1850. The Church in Quebec, like all the institutions foundational to our contemporary history, acted durably, in its own way and alongside other forces, to bring about the transition to the modern world. The fact that it succeeded in imbuing this transition with particular tones attests to its strength and influence, but it also indicates the multiplicity of possible readings of modernity by its historical protagonists. The Catholicism of the day was very much a part of the liberal universe, not its obverse, and that is how it must be studied.

RELIGION IN THE LIBERAL SPACE: THE ABUSES OF FREEDOM

A process of secularization does not imply that religion is being suddenly and dramatically moved to the margins. Religion can remain quite buoyant and vibrant, revival activity and church growth can continue. But at the same time other values, activities, and forms of knowledge can arise, not necessarily challenging religion and church directly, but competing with the church and the clergy for authority and influence in society. Also church growth and religious change can mask the degree to which religion and the churches were making accommodations with these new forces. Such accommodation may have significantly undermined the supernatural aspects of the faith. Indeed there was a significant amount of secularization from within religion and the churches. (Marshall 1993–94, 80)

The implementation of liberal regulatory logic in the nineteenth century was bound to have a profound impact on the Church. It posed a radical challenge to the dynamics of belief and faith, forcing them to come to grips with a world humming with the rhythms of freedom (Gauchet 1997; Chadwick 1975). Furthermore, power and communities in this new world were not organized as before, and the Church would be forced to adapt to a new logic thereof.

This process has often (especially since Weber) been described in terms of "secularization," or the rise of a specifically modern rationality. The transformation of old religious beliefs and institutions is often portrayed – once again under the nefarious influence of gradualism – as a slow "dissolution" of the old into the new until it vanished almost entirely; a long process of destruction and reconstruction.[7]

This interpretation is of course buttressed by the conservative discourse of nineteenth-century church leaders themselves. The Church is described with distressing regularity as the last bastion of mores inherited from tradition, forming a kind of moral lacquer impermeable to the abuses of modernity.

> These fine virtues have already come under dire and tragic attack. They must fight to stay alive, not only against the tendencies of the original debasement, but also against the influence of too numerous and bewitching examples. They run the risk of becoming denatured through contact with another Society, whose habits, if not its principles, differ to a certain extent from what has to date formed the character of Canadian families strongly imbued with the spirit of our forefathers. Pleasure and morals are not always allies; quite often, it must be said, they are at war. More than ever, pleasure claims to rule the world; it offers itself in the form of diversions and license which, if we wish to give in to them, must bend the strictness of our old ways …
> Let us be proud enough to insist on not being beaten in the contest of morals. A people who renounce their virtuous ways, give up on life itself. Quite the contrary, may our moral character proclaim the existence in our race of a special vitality, which, instead of being denatured through assimilation of foreign elements, seeks to make its action felt on all that surrounds it. (Raymond 1865, 12–13)[8]

Yet in this area as elsewhere, the historian would do well to notice the profound disruptions characteristic of the nineteenth century. The shock of the revolutions had quickly consigned the old (intellectual and institutional) ways of living one's faith to the past (except in the minds of those for whom the past remained the only place to live). In short order, Catholicism – like other denominations and religions for that matter – had to come up with a religious response to the challenge posed by the new hegemony of liberalism. Even the harshest, deepest rejectionism now had to be expressed in terms that acknowledged and grappled with the inexorable transformation taking place. It does not clarify matters to interpret the rigid reaction that constitutes conservatism (which appeared in various guises throughout the nineteenth century and found renewed vigour during the turn-of-the-century crisis of liberalism) as some sort of dead-end nostalgia. Like radical liberalism and indeed socialism, it is the reconstruction of past values as dictated by the needs of the present and the future, the only difference being that this reconstruction wears the veil of loyalty to the past.

The recent historiography of religions in the nineteenth century has elucidated the complex dialectic binding religion to modernity. Denis Pelletier's critique of traditional French historiography, for example, applies equally well to Quebec.

> When Catholicism is considered of a piece with the forces of reaction – often a legitimate position – it becomes an obstacle to the transformation of French society ... It is too schematic, but one might say that social history theses address the fact of religion within a first part devoted to a tableau of the society, as only one component of this tableau – generally a retrograde component destined to be marginalized – and then proceed to limit its role to that of an impediment to the dynamic of economic and social transformation that constitutes the core of the demonstration. (Pelletier 1999, 37)[9]

In fact, religion occupies an utterly central position in the democratic transition, for those who celebrated that transition just as much as for those who feared it. For where was the new freedom-loving society to find its ethical and moral underpinnings, if not in the pre-existing bedrock of religion? Tocqueville, as noted above, strikingly addressed this fundamental issue:

> Despotism can do without faith, but not liberty. Religion is much more necessary in the republic that they advocate than in the monarchy that they attack, and in democratic republics more than in all others. How could society fail to perish if, while the political bond grows loose, the moral bond does not become tighter? And what to do with a people master of itself, if it is not subject to God? (Tocqueville [1835] 2012, 2: 478)[10]

Of course, freedom's reign opened up the prospect of a world that might reject religious precepts, but this was no cause for worry: "unbelief is an accident; faith alone is the permanent state of humanity" (Tocqueville [1835] 2012, 2: 482). Nevertheless, religion, in liberal discourse, was relieved of its privileged relationship to transcendent truth. If it was still undeniably necessary, that necessity was predicated on the needs of society rather than any kind of ontological rightness: "If it is very useful to a man as an individual that his religion be true, it is not the same for society. Society has nothing either to fear or to hope concerning the other life; and what is most important for society is not so much that all citizens profess the true religion but that they profess a religion" (Tocqueville [1835] 2012, 2: 473).

Religion became a form of inner policing that kept people on the straight and narrow in a new world that offered men and women almost limitless possibilities. As they hurtled into the future, nothing but religion could tell them when to stop, if not where to go.

> Thus the human mind never sees a limitless field before it; whatever its audacity, it feels from time to time that it must stop before insurmountable barriers. Before innovating, it is forced to accept certain primary givens, and to subject its boldest conceptions to certain forms that retard and stop it. (Tocqueville [1835] 2012, 2: 474)[11]

It is clear that no principled opposition between Catholicism and democracy could exist under such conditions. Indeed, what has been called "early social Catholicism" was not based solely on certain Catholic thinkers' espousal of democratic values. It also ensued from a logic which, at the core of liberal thought itself, caused Catholicism to be taken up as a privileged ethical route to the new world.

> The Catholic system is admirable in its wisdom concerning ... the people's misery especially ... Let it alone, and you will see that it can adjust to the demands of the new society. But be patient: give it the time to find its bearings, to sound out the new terrain, on which we have walked for under a century, which is nothing in matters of social renovation. Catholicism is conservative by nature, and as such cannot be the advance guard of the political movement. Do not perturb it with unnatural associations of ideas, and you will see that it will not seek refuge among the stragglers. Study Catholicism well ... and you will see that it is the religious system most favourable to the people ... the most democratic system that exists, or ever has existed in the world. (Parent [1852b] 1975, 314–15)[12]

At mid-century, when aspirations toward a world of freedom were attempting to fit within the moral guideposts provided by religion, when the attempted divorce between modernity and faith had yet to be sanctioned by the stern rebuke of the *Syllabus* (Catholic Church [1864] 1998), an optimistic reading of Catholicism's active role in democracy was still possible.

> Are we not seeing unequivocal signs of renewal in the clergy? Do you not see it testing its mettle in this atmosphere of liberty and social progress, which, until recently, had seemed to elicit from it such profound horror? What has happened is that it has felt, and it has seen, that religion, the daughter of heaven, could have no better companion in its earthly pilgrimage than liberty, equally the daughter of heaven. (Parent [1848] 1975, 204–5)[13]

That being the case, the task at hand was to rethink the relationship between the civil and the religious, between faith and politics, along new lines. As a first step, the old ties that bound the Church to monarchic power had to be cut so that a virtuous complementarity between the religious and temporal spheres could be established.[14] The Church's place was, to be sure, within civil society, but its role was as a buttress to it; or, to use a different metaphor, as a seamstress for the social fabric in those places where it was most likely to be pulled apart by the abuse of freedom.

> The priest, who is the organ, the living expression of spiritualism, must be allowed to play a very important role in human society; but ... he must not usurp ... the role of civil power, which is specially charged with temporal affairs, with the material interests of society. These two powers, embodiments of the two constituent principles of human nature, must collaborate in steering and guiding humanity along the path of improvement and well being. (Parent [1848] 1975, 209)[15]

This was the setting for the rise of ultramontanism, and its peculiar history must be understood in part as a response to the conundrum of how and where religion was to fit into the new order. In its early manifestations, the ultramontane reflex manifested itself at times as a departure from established thinking (Hugues-Félicité Robert de Lamennais), or at other times as supreme loyalty to old-fashioned values (Louis de Bonald). In the gap opened up by the successful revolutions, at a time when old values had to be harnessed in the service of a different future, faith could appear in the guise of an instrument of liberation or a protector of tradition. It was only when liberalism, in deploying its disruptive possibilities, made it particularly difficult to reconcile faith and progress that ultramontanism took a definitive, uncompromising turn toward reaction. In this regard, 1848 is the pivotal year, with revolution sweeping across Europe and working class demands (in England and France especially) gaining traction.

But it would be a mistake to get caught up in the discourse of reaction and disruption. To have influence, the ultramontanes often had to borrow the words, the methods, and even the values of the world they prided themselves on rejecting. Thus, ultramontanism, even in its most radically conservative formulations, must be seen as a complex dialectic in which the proclaimed rejection of the new is melded with its often unconscious acceptance. For although the values of that world had to be openly rejected, such rejection could be expressed only by assimilating its language – an ad hoc accommodation of the kind on which the best intentions have often foundered.

Ultramontanism was the moment when religion tipped over into conservatism, adopting as its mission that of bolstering tradition in the face of inexorable progress. Such a choice did not prevent it from being integrated into secular society – quite the contrary. If the Church could not be the moral herald of progress, it would be the champion of resignation and sacrifice in the face of its excesses. Étienne Parent, writing in 1848, gave voice to this modulation of the discourse of faith:

> From the bosom of France ... came a young clergy, full of fire and science, virtues and love, holding the cross in one hand and the Gospel in the other, offering humankind one more demonstration of its assured salvation: in the Gospel, the divine and imprescriptible law of universal brotherhood; in the cross, an example of devotion and resignation; devotion for the great and the fortunate of this world, resignation for the many who suffer: devotion on one hand, resignation on the other, which are the two indispensable conditions of social regeneration, and without which humankind can only look forward to an unending series of fruitless struggles, paid for in the blood of its noblest children; devotion and resignation, which only the preacher of the Gospel can inspire, for he alone addresses that part of man which is capable of them, and he alone presents a goal and an end worthy of the sacrifice demanded. (Parent [1848] 1975, 220-1)

The "reformist" tendency of one variant of liberalism proved remarkably accommodating to this conservative vision of the clergy as the bearer of tradition and authority, bringing the message of resigned submission to the masses.

> The old institutions of a country, its religious beliefs especially ... are to a people what physical constitution, habits, and way of life are to an individual: in a word, they are its life. And to think that there are men, so-called patriots, willing to do away with all of that under the pretence of reform and progress! Unhappy wretches! That way lies destruction and death, yet they do not see it. Let us reform without destroying; let us advance, but without letting go of the guiding thread of tradition. (Parent [1852b] 1975, 315)[16]

Thus, whether inspired by faith in a democratic future or, contrariwise, spurred to action by the spectre of decadence and broken traditions, those pondering religion's place in the new world agreed that it had to be deeply, actively, and militantly integrated into civil society. Ultramontanism was a particularly striking example of this phenomenon.[17]

The Church, in its more or less radical rejection of certain proclaimed values of modernity, could transform this rejection into the power and capacity to act only insofar as it was able to express it in the terms of modernity itself. Put another way, the new power of the Church – even more remarkable in that it had been sapped by several decades of English domination – can only be understood in terms of its capacity to use the very terms of liberalism to grasp the urgent needs generated by the transition to the modern world. Viewed thus, the Church is not the obverse of the new world but the peculiar form taken by that world in Quebec.

Even accepting this, it is still possible to fall back on the traditional interpretation according to which Quebec society rapidly fell under the backward-looking domination of a clergy who rejected modernity, and in so doing shut down the horizons of those whom they had under their sway. This caricature does not lack for adherents.

> In Quebec, a highly religious and predominantly Catholic society, it was the priest who represented the full flowering of humanity, and who was, therefore, a leading part of the authoritative mixture. Generally speaking, the clergy received the ultimate honour of being deferred to and obeyed. For the rest of the population, the lesser degrees of honour or good reputation were accorded in proportion as the individual embodied the religious virtues most perfectly represented by the priest; just as in a militaristic society a man is

honoured for displaying the virtues of a soldier ... A man's good name in a religious society depends ultimately on the judgment of the religious authority. (Knopf 1979, 324)[18]

Instead we must strive to comprehend why someone like Lamennais's disciple Jean-Jacques Lartigue, the Bishop of Montreal, termed a "Christian liberal" by vexed Sulpicians,[19] would feel so deeply horrified upon discovering, in the thick of the Rebellions of 1837–38, all the potentially revolutionary power of the people's striving for democracy. He who denounced the "shackles of civil power which hold our Church in thrall" now found himself confronted with a democratic power that threatened to engulf and annihilate all other forms of power – even the power of God:

> If all power comes from the people, then it is clear that the power of the Church, which is independent of the people, must not be legitimate; and that one ceases to be Catholic or even Christian as soon as one wholeheartedly embraces the maxim that the people is the source of all power. It must also follow, not only that there is no divine right, or power emanating from God, since all legitimate power has the people as its source; but also, that there is no God at all – for how can one imagine a God with no power over man his creature? (Lartigue 1838)[20]

In these crucial moments of revolt, Lartigue had made his choice. But does choosing authority, tradition, faith, and immanence necessarily mean simplistically rejecting the modern world? Does it not in fact obligate the church member – perhaps more than ever – to maintain an active presence in civil society? The means whereby control was acquired over the institutions for the regulation of poverty will serve to illustrate this seeming paradox.

THE CHURCH AS ASSOCIATION

In the beginning was freedom. For religion and the Church to renew themselves in the new society predicated on freedom, they would have to find and exploit a space in which to operate – a space opened up, as it happened, by that selfsame freedom. In Canada, the Catholic Church existed in a kind of suspended animation. It enjoyed the freedom-by-default of a de facto church in contradistinction to the de jure privileges of the Anglican Church, and such a space did not exist. This explains why the ultramontane discourse began as a discourse of *liberation*: in

Europe from the Gallican yoke, in Canada from a Protestant state that still recognized only one established church.[21]

Mgr Lartigue was not long in grasping this fact. He deplored that in Canada, "where the legal establishment of our holy religion would appear to assure us the greatest benefits, the shackles of civil power hold our Church in thrall under the pretext of protecting it" (quoted in Chaussé 1985, 119).[22] Entrenched in its Gallican tradition and steadfastly allied with the state in the preservation of the old world, the Church was ill prepared to confront the challenges of the new society. Thus, the initial manifestation of the spirit of freedom in the religious sphere took the form of a no-holds-barred struggle to free the Church from the shackles of the meddlesome state. The growing recognition accorded various corporate powers after the late 1830s – first the Sulpicians and soon a host of religious associations – was only the first manifestation of what could be called a Catholic social space under construction within bourgeois civil society.

In 1848, several years after England granted ministerial responsibility to the colony, thus consecrating colonial autonomy over domestic policy, the Parliament of the Province of Canada adopted freedom of worship as its fundamental principle for the organization of religious affairs:

> Whereas the recognition of legal equality among all Religious Denominations is an admitted principle of Colonial Legislation; And whereas in the state and condition of this Province, to which such a principle is peculiarly applicable, it is desirable that the same should receive the sanction of direct Legislative Authority, recognizing and declaring the same as a fundamental principle of our civil polity: Be it therefore declared and enacted ... That the free exercise and enjoyment of Religious Profession and Worship, without discrimination or preference, so as the same be not made an excuse for acts of licentiousness, or a justification of practices inconsistent with the peace and safety of the Province, is by the constitution and laws of this Province allowed to all Her Majesty's subjects within the same.[23]

This act marks the official end of any privileged relationship between a given religion and the state, and in this respect constitutes an essential transformation of the Canadian political arena. The Catholic Church becomes, with respect to the political sphere, a social body like any other, having no special privilege vis-à-vis the other religious denominations.[24] In one stroke, the Church has both become free and been inscribed into an official logic of competition.[25]

The freedom granted to religious organizations had two implications. First, it consecrated liberal competition[26] among them, and the Catholic Church, however reluctantly, would have to live with it. With freedom of action came competition, and hence all manner of proselytism, a phenomenon that would be particularly vexing to Monseigneur Bourget. A corollary was that adherence to that free association of civil society which the Church had become was no longer predicated on any particular political legitimacy. Ineluctably, a space of potential freedom converted loyalty to any religion from an act of civic submission to a voluntary affiliation that might be revoked at any time. The challenge posed for the Catholic Church was that religious freedom changed the conditions under which religious constraints could be imposed in modern society.[27]

Second, freedom of worship consecrated the principle of *separation* between religion and politics, hence the state. This freedom vis-à-vis the state would long remain a source of confusion in clerical discourse. Initially, it fit perfectly with the context in which the religious elites intended to strengthen their hold on civil society. As the philosopher Joseph-Sabin Raymond, superior of the Séminaire de Saint-Hyacinthe, stated on the eve of Confederation: "We have freedom: let us use it for the cause of good" (Raymond 1865, 53).[28] But it could also be interpreted as a rivalry, or a competition rather, between two powers in society. This discursive shift is perceptible in ultramontanism, where the separation is depicted as being between two *parallel* worlds: the world of temporal power and the world of religion. In this conception, the state and the church become "the sovereigns of two distinct societies" (Laflèche 1889, 33), two ideally complementary poles of a power-sharing arrangement based on a division between the worlds of morality and matter. Many historians have viewed this rather hysterical, utopian discursive shift as the ultimate expression of the Catholic religious ideal developing in nineteenth-century Quebec. But it could also be regarded as a particularly acute form of the kind of distrust of the state that sits at the heart of the late nineteenth-century liberal worldview.[29]

If freedom of worship gave churches room to manoeuvre within society, and if the new legal recognition granted to incorporated religious associations provided further validation of that freedom, then the question of how these associations were to relate to the political sphere now required an answer. The temptation was great to make religion the spiritual equivalent of civil society, leaving the narrowly defined political sphere to the state. Greater still, perhaps, was the temptation to posit religion as the dominant force (or the one called upon to dominate) in society, reigning over these separate spheres of activity. After all, as Mgr Raymond stated, "faith, of necessity, intermingles with all matters intellectual and social. It decidedly must not be considered a separate order of things, governing purely spiritual affairs, expressing the immediate and direct relationship of man to God, and without connection to the sundry theories of science, or influence over temporal society" (Raymond 1865, 53).

But the ultramontane confusion between freedom *vis-à-vis* the state and influence *over* the state would be short-lived. Laurier's celebrated 1877 speech on political liberalism clarified the issues for much time to come. This liberalism, at a far remove from the radicalism of the Red Party, was no longer a philosophy borne by a certain idea of desirable change. It was merely the necessary context and precondition for action by members of civil society. It delimited a political space in which religion as a specific structure of social organization had no officially privileged place. Beyond debate over the content of liberty, this speech affirmed, in soberer terms, what the 1852 act had stated: that the Catholic Church, as a constituted religious entity, enjoyed the freedom to exist in civil society. It had no rights over and above those of other creeds, nor could it presume to encroach on the prerogatives of the state. All it had to rely on was its intrinsic strength: "Can you find under the sun a happier country than ours, where the Catholic church is freer, and enjoys greater privileges? Why then do you try to claim rights incompatible with our state of society, to expose the country to agitation, the consequences of which it is impossible to foresee?" (Laurier 1877, 27).[30]

The essence of the conflict has to do with incompatible agendas. The liberal regulating system needed to reconfigure the place of religion and its organizational structures so as to make allowance for the interaction of competing freedoms.[31] Catholicism, however, is a hierarchical organization, an authority structure whose members had not taken kindly to the Church's historic loss of hegemony. The freedom *of* the Church had no necessary correlate of freedom *within* the Church.[32] One would be deeply mistaken to regard the Church as just another associative manifestation of the new freedom posited as the basis of modern society. It bore within it a heritage of tradition and authority. Although free to operate in modern society under the banner of freedom of worship, this heritage nonetheless stood in profound contradiction to certain liberal values.

Consider, for example, the concepts of truth and freedom of conscience. If freedom was something to be cherished, this was because it allowed the adherents of the "true religion" to live more at ease with the rejection of freedom's radical implications. Thus, the freedom espoused by Catholicism has little to do with the deep-seated libertarian impulse of someone like Mill or, in Quebec, Dessaulles (Lamonde 1994). For those who believe that truth is revealed, it may appear as a right possessed, or a heritage claimed, but never as the contingent outcome of a clash among competing opinions.[33] By a paradoxical twist, official freedom of conscience, although a precondition for the development of the Catholic Church in liberal society, had to be condemned as a necessary evil, a tactical compromise, or even a surrender of basic principles.

> Considered from the absolute standpoint, freedom of worship is an evil; since it conduces to error and causes souls to be lost, it must be condemned if it is presented as an abstract principle, claimed as a natural right of man. Today, as in the past, it would be desirable for society to recognize only the one true religion. But since the public mind does not allow freedom of worship to be questioned in certain countries, without detriment to society and to the Church itself, it is permissible to tolerate such freedom, to defend it and to swear by its observance in those constitutions wherein it is a fundamental law, and this by virtue of the principle that tolerance of an order of things in which evil is to be feared from one standpoint, is permitted, if that order is a greater good when considered from a different point of view. (Raymond 1869, 17–18)[34]

Thus, for ultramontane Catholicism, the margin of freedom opened up by liberal democracy is not at all a locus of debate, a field on which ideas can square off within a public space transparent to itself, so to speak. Reason, like faith, is a limiting constraint, not the condition for the production of truth.

> Freedom of thought must necessarily be limited by reason and faith, those sacred barriers which it is never permitted to cross. Barred within this enclosure, the human mind never ceases to enjoy great freedom of study, exploration, speculation, and discussion. (Antoine Gibaud [1864], quoted in Rajotte 1991, 89)[35]

Truth and religious belief are first and foremost a matter of authority, and for this reason the Church cannot, in a democracy, be transformed into a democracy itself; it will not allow persons or ideas to gain ascendancy within the organization as a function of their ability to win a popularity contest.[36]

Torn between resigned acceptance of these and other implications of modernity, on the one hand, and the manifest advantages afforded by the space of temporal freedom that modernity had opened up, on the other, some elements of the clerical elite, at the outer bounds of utopian fancy, would come up with a specifically Catholic mode of social management in modern society. But while liberalism potentially left plenty of room for religious initiative in civil society, the outright invasion of social space by institutions partaking by and large of a *religious* dynamic still demanded some form of legitimation. If Catholicism were to have a major role in organizing the space of social regulation, it would have to begin with a critique of "legal charity."

A CRITIQUE OF THE CHARITABLE STATE

On the banks of the Saint Lawrence, [charitable works] have grown and developed, and have come to the aid of the needy classes without the government having to resort to special taxes or mandatory contributions; in a word, the whole apparatus of legal charity. The French Canadians, drawing on the soundest traditions of Old France and the fecund principles of self-government, understood that to fulfil its sublime mission, Christian charity needed only one thing: freedom! (Lallemand 1895, 13)

As discussed in chapter 6, the liberal regulation of charity was based on a thorough rethinking of the state's responsibilities in this area. The critique of the utopia held out by philanthropists left the state with the obligation to intervene, at best, in the most extreme cases of poverty; "ordinary" poverty would be the province of civil society.

For religious charity, this was an ideal setting in which to acquire newfound legitimacy. In Quebec, the organization of the first modern institutions of regulation by the Catholic Church and other religious denominations was in fact contingent upon the rise of a liberal discourse that denounced any intrusion by the state into this field. There is a remarkable parallel here between mainstream liberal discourse and the most radical, ultramontane tendencies of Catholicism. "The primary end of society is conservation; the secondary end is well-being ... What do the direct responsibilities of political power reduce to? The protection of life and property" (Beaudry 1862).

The state is incapable of ministering to the poor not only because this role does not correspond to its primary purpose, but also, and perhaps especially, because the technocratic indifference of the public servant, the blind and mechanical meting out of charity without the sensitivity of the humanitarian, will inevitably humiliate and abase the poor:

> A tax for the poor! But by what right, in the first place, does the public officer demand of me, and compel me to contribute in the name of Justice what I owe to charity alone? A tax for the poor! But, where it has been adopted, does it obviate the scourge of poverty, does it prevent the poor from dying of hunger? ... The poor tax! But in dealing with the heart, it is utterly impotent and even fatal. How can the official who earns his own bread by distributing the bread of others, find the time, the thought, the courage, the grace, to afford the poor whom he relieves, the counsel, or the reprimand calculated to enlighten the soul, or to heal its evils? Every thing about your public official, is hard and chilling: his look, his tone, his heart. (Chandonnet 1864, 50–1)[37]

After the 1840s, this discourse, drawing inspiration from the conservative critique of legal charity set out in earlier times by Alban de Villeneuve-Bargemont,[38] became systematic and deeply rooted. The dire counterexample brandished by such authors was, of course, the British workhouse, that emblematic monument created by the Poor Laws.

> Imagine one of these unfortunates, his soul broken by pain, pulverized by the blows of hardship, for whom life has held nothing but bitterness; imagine also that decrepit eighty-year-old who has never known any law but that of his own perverse and corrupt proclivities, whose life is a tissue of horrors, as he reaches the end of a career whose every moment has been marked by a crime. Imagine both of them, being received at the workhouse, entrusted to the care and keeping of a public servant, receiving charity only because the law commands it. (Beaudry 1862)

As in the case of child protection and young offender initiatives, the argument postulates that only private charity, as an outgrowth of civil society, is truly capable of providing for the welfare of the poor. Is charity not, after all, a way of weaving the social fabric that makes social relations possible? The state can establish the legal conditions for the expression of these relations, but cannot supplant them.

But a question persists: was there a way to organize charity, beyond the personal relationship implied by the charitable act, that would be consistent with the fundamental precepts of liberal civil society while giving the Church stable control over the practice of charity? The lively mid-century debate over the suitability of allowing charitable associations to incorporate tells us much about the importance of the issues raised by this question.

FREE ENTERPRISE IN CHARITY AND RELIGION: A LIVELY DEBATE (1852–54)

In 1852, the reform government tabled a bill to allow for the voluntary incorporation of charities,[39] subject to certain limitations on the right of ownership and the objects of the association. For several years, and in Lower Canada especially, a sizeable number of charitable and religious associations had been petitioning for such a measure.[40] These demands drew increasingly sharp opposition from Upper Canadian radical MPs, and especially their leader George Brown, who regarded these incorporations as an underhanded attempt to create monopolies beholden to the Catholic clergy. The government responded by proposing legislation simplifying the incorporation procedure, thus obviating incessant debate in the House of Commons. The idea was to do for charities what had just been done for for-profit companies: adopt an expedited procedure allowing any group to become a broadly autonomous body enjoying the corporate privileges of ownership and self-perpetuation.[41]

The important debate provoked by this bill provides something approaching a play-by-play account of the perfect concomitance between the implementation of the liberal logic of poverty regulation and the possibility of religious institutions' gaining control over it. Brown was quick to recognize, in these incessant demands for incorporation, an attempt by the Catholic clergy to perpetuate its hegemony in Lower Canada through the establishment of perpetual institutions. For him, these corporations were the opposite of freely organized charity:

> Upper Canada, it is true, was not covered with institutions to relieve her people from the duties of consanguinity or friendship, and of neighbourhood – thank God that she was not! It is not by the cold, heartless intervention of legal corporations – but by the hand of private benevolence, by the genial warmth of personal kindness in the domestic abode, that distress and poverty ought to be relieved.[42]

In a long, well-documented speech, the member for Quebec City, Joseph Cauchon, rebutted Brown. Statistics in hand,[43] he undertook to show that the greatest poverty is found in capitalist countries like England, not those living under the Papist "yoke," as Brown had insinuated. Cauchon also sought to prove that such poverty is not caused by religion or race but by the inequalities arising out of industrial growth.[44] Furthermore, why should solidarity between giver and receiver be restricted to a relationship of individual to individual? Couldn't associations and congregations also take on that role?

> The beggar-monk takes only what is given to him ... and when the husband and father who has given him a portion of his bread falls ill, not only does the same monk feed him, but he also administers remedies, sits by him night and day, offer words of consolation, encourages and fortifies him in his suffering. He attends his last breath and closes his eyes; he is his friend for all time ... Can you blame [the poor man] in every case for preferring him to your poor laws, which parch his soul, which decree that charity is a social crime?[45]

For the great evil is not to be found in private associational or congregational charity but in the legal, official charity offered by the state:

> What is pauperism, which weighs so heavily on the English people? It is the law substituted for charity, for the Gospel; it is tax as a replacement for love of one's fellow men. We tax ourselves to rid ourselves of the poor man, to distance him from us as a hideous object, which wounds the eyes and offends the nose.[46]

Cauchon garnered powerful support from Upper Canada. John Rolph, the member for Norfolk County and William Lyon Mackenzie's erstwhile lieutenant during the Rebellions, expressed with special clarity what stands as the fundamental mission statement of private charity in the liberal regulating system:

> Let there be the same liberty for christians and their associations as for lawyers and for doctors, for merchants and for painters and their respective associations ... It is the want of generality which is objectionable; the refusing to religious classes the civil rights of the lay people; the assumption that a religious association, because it is such, must not have the full measure of equal civil rights; the attempts, by indirect means, to impose disabilities on such associations and exclude them from legitimate fields of christian exercise and usefulness; the erection of a Parliamentary standard about religious classes, instead of leaving them to the moral laws of Providence and the judgment

of a christian people ... The less we interfere with those moral laws which have been framed with striking adaptation to the physical condition of man, the better. Even if some religious associations make a headway, in opposition to our wishes and opinions, we are not to legislate them down. If one church, under equal civil and religious rights, attains a pre-eminence over others, the case must be met, not by the arm of power, but by a christian spirit of emulation in increased and better directed moral efforts to decide the contest ... The most progressive countries are decentralizing, and the less we interfere with these benevolent institutions and leave them free under free laws, the more diffused will be their usefulness.[47]

In these arguments, freedom of worship is closely associated with the rights of charitable associations. It is not so much that religious freedom implies a certain philosophy of charity; it is rather that both this freedom and the right to associate freely in the interests of helping the poor derive from a single discursive and symbolic universe: the world that has invented the free market ought to allow good intentions to compete freely within a market of their own. Let people judge charitable initiatives, like opinions, according to what they propose to deliver and what they actually do deliver, and let those initiatives adjust their course in order to remain relevant. Hence, Rolph saw no difference between religious emulation among believers, charitable emulation among good Samaritans, wealth emulation among property owners, or even talent emulation among painters. Is it such a coincidence that denominational freedom and equality were first recognized in Canada during the same parliamentary session in which this fundamental debate took place?[48]

The eventuality of this freedom being deployed along essentially denominational fault lines did not elude everyone. Two years after this debate,[49] certain legislators pointed to the dangers implicit in such a divide being instated among charitable institutions; to wit, this exchange in the Commons:

> MR. ALLEYN Charity should be general and not bounded by sectarian feelings, but, if these gentlemen choose to put their hands into their own pockets and ask an act of incorporation, shall we refuse it? It would be desirable to have general institutions, but we must take people as we find them.
> MR. BROWN It is not what people ask us, but what we ought to do that is the question! It is on us that the responsibility rests, if we grant improper things! Do we not help directly to excite and keep alive those sectarian feelings by encouraging such institutions, and voting away the public money

to sustain them? The moment they get their charter, the promoters of these schemes come to us for a grant out of the public chest ... Where two or three general institutions would be sufficient, by this system we have to support ten or twenty out of the public purse. The evil is increasing year by year, and will be perfectly ruinous before long.

MR. MACKENZIE We meet here, Protestants and Catholics, on common ground, we transact business together without ever thinking of asking whether the man we deal with is a Protestant or a Catholic. But the moment a man gets sick, the first question must be, what is his religion, and if he did not happen to have any, what was the religion of his father or his mother ... We have a penitentiary, where the diseased in mind if not in body go. But we do not require a Catholic penitentiary and a Protestant penitentiary. Why, then, should you have sectarian hospitals and other institutions to divide the people into great classes hating each other for the love of God?[50]

Yet the very principle of charitable freedom, leaving the welfare of the poor to the forces of civil society, made resistance to denominational fragmentation difficult or even impossible – short of acknowledging that the treatment of poverty was a collective responsibility of the nation and the state. And this, as we have seen, was out of the question.

But was the religious charity that came into being during the liberal era so different from other forms of private charity?

RELIGIOUS CHARITY

It might be claimed that religious charity – by virtue of its ends, its means, and its underlying philosophy – differs profoundly from "liberal" charity, from the charity of the philanthropist who, having given up on the utopian idea of reforming the masses, strives to instill in the poor classes – or at any rate, in those of their members who are not beyond redemption – the self-mastery and the moral fibre that will make of them good citizens, skilled producers, and informed consumers all at once. The proponents of Christian charity were themselves quite assiduous in denouncing this "cold" scientific philanthropy along with the bureaucratic pitfalls of state-sponsored charity.

In fact, the religious philosophy of charitable action[51] must be understood as a particularly dynamic and eloquent version of the conservative tendency, analyzed in an earlier section, that blossomed in the nineteenth century in reaction to the most radical elements of liberalism. This tendency rested on a set of postulates that were held to be a strong corrective to the idea of progress through individual autonomy so central to the liberal experience of the world. Religious charity proved a good fit with this conservative worldview, often giving it its most sophisticated interpretation and constituting, at least in the domain of interest here, its most powerful and durable expression.

The Inherent Vice of Humanity

The first postulate of religious charity is the rejection of a naive, Rousseauist version of humanity's fundamental goodness. The Jansenist (or Calvinist) version of human nature lay dormant but deeply rooted in the minds of many contemporary observers, and made a powerful resurgence in sharp reaction to the great continental revolutions. The pessimistic words of the liberal Protestant François Guizot are revealing of this mindset:

> There is in our nature a vice, in our condition an evil that eludes all human effort. The disorder is within us, and even if any other source dried up, it would grow out of us and our will. Suffering, unequally apportioned suffering, is in the providential laws of our fate ... being free, we can create, and indeed do unendingly create evil ... Man's liberty is stronger than the institutions of society. Man's soul is greater than the things of this world. There will always be more desires in him than social science can resolve or satisfy, more unhappiness than it can prevent or cure. (Guizot [1838] 1882a, 31)

This observation does not entail rejection of the principle of human perfectibility so seminal to ultramontane activism. It simply reveals a facet of the vision of the future, in a world bent on progress, that haunted conservatives of all stripes: namely, that evil is not what a world in progress leaves behind; that it actually resides within us and is always apt to emerge from our weaknesses and our cupidity alike; that evil can be provoked, stimulated by the modern world, and that for this reason it is essential for the relentless march of civilization to be guided by strict and rigorous moral discipline.[52]

The conservative mindset, which fed on the liberal dynamic while claiming to reject it, was a mindset of *resistance*. It was in desperate quest of stable guideposts to rein in men and women now free, thanks to the perpetual flight into the future touched off by liberalism, to make their own choices. Lamennais, writing before he broke with the Catholic hierarchy with his publication of *Words of a Believer*, describes what the conservatives were up against:

> The character of democracy is that of continual mobility; everything is in ceaseless motion, everything changes, with frightening speed, in step with passions and opinions. Principles, institutions, laws: nothing is stable; time's power to establish, to destroy, or to modify is not felt. Men are driven and goaded by an irresistible force; whatever they find on their road is trodden underfoot. They advance, return, advance again, and the whole social order becomes, for them, a kind of stopping place before they move forward again. The public powers do not give the impetus, but receive it ... Democracy, in a great people, would unfailingly destroy Christianity, for a supreme and unwavering authority in the religious order is incompatible with an endlessly varying authority in the political order. Christianity preserves all, by making all constant; democracy destroys all, by making it variable. (Lamennais 1825, 34–5)[53]

What could be more normal than that this resistance should at times degenerate into idealization of the past, nostalgia for times gone by? Why should anyone be surprised that this impulse to conserve should be transfigured, at moments of extreme anxiety in the face of the revolutionary course of events, into hysterical rejection of the present? The radical modernity of the conservative tendency, and the often remarkable efficiency of its achievements, should not be taken less seriously for that.[54]

If the idea was to find solid bedrock on which to build human freedom, how could one fail to turn to religion? It presented itself, after all, as the ultimate expression of transcendence, as the outcome of a search for a meaning not altered by the course of things and time. For these thinkers, religion ought to hold the honour of giving the new era its moral centre, or at least of tempering its enthusiasm. If liberalism is the art of separation, then it surely allowed for a division of labour between the moral and the social, the religious and the secular.

> From one endeavour to another, on certain specific days, a truth emerges and rises so high that it shines brightly and commands respect. The separation of the spiritual from the temporal has had this luck ... May the two powers, instead of stooping to collect up, for a few days, some scraps from the old confusion, fully accept, in law and in fact, their mutual lack of jurisdiction; may each be firmly established within its own sphere, and proudly profess its respective principle: the Catholic Church, its infallibility in the religious realm; the State, freedom of thought in the social realm. (Guizot [1838] 1882b, 68–9)

Here again we find the regulative character of religion dear to Tocqueville and, in Quebec, to Parent. But religious charity was not just a moral bulwark against the abuses of the modern world. It was also a refuge, a sphere in which people could rediscover the joys of submission, the necessity of sacrifice, the benefits of true authority. Chateaubriand wrote: "Can a political State, in which some individuals have millions in income while others die of hunger, survive when religion no longer holds out the hope of another world to explain the sacrifice?" (Chateaubriand [1849–50] 1860, 359).[55] The Church became the defender and guarantor of social ethics in the new era, and it was thus pointless to imagine an exclusively civic ethics freed from the various interpretations imparted by particular religions. Quite the contrary, freedom of worship, far from denying the need for a religious ethics, entailed it.

> A government, some might say, could concern itself not at all with religious doctrines and yet punish flagrant immorality. There are, in society, general ideas about justice and injustice, good and evil: these, together with the power of the sword, suffice to maintain civil order. I reply: these ideas do not suffice. The facts show the invasion of private and public mores by immorality to an extent which makes one fearful for the future ... Let it be believed that religion is indifferent to the good of society; let anti-Christian doctrines develop totally unhindered, and you will see for how long morality is maintained, or whether the distinction between justice and injustice, between honesty and dishonesty, will always remain based on principles accepted by all. You will see that there will be no other motives for men than their always mutually opposed self-interest, that disorder will become permanent, regular government impossible, and that the final result of all this will be a great deal of human bloodshed during a long and awful period of anarchy. (Raymond 1869, 14–15)

Through a fascinating semantic shift, the staking out of ethics as the quintessential territory of religion transmuted into religion's incursion into the realm of the social. If ethics are fundamental to successful sociability, and if the canons of this ethics can be based only on religion, then the whole of civil society becomes the target of this new moral apostolate.

> The separation of the Church from social life, should it be successfully consummated, would be even graver than the separation of Church and State ... Our duty is therefore to devote ourselves without hesitation to these workers' questions, whose importance grows every day, and to address them without bias or prejudice; the existing order is not, at bottom, more Christian than any of the socialist systems. (Bourgeois, *Le Catholicisme dans la vie sociale*, 1867, quoted in Duroselle 1951, 668)

Precisely because it must, with all speed, ensure the moral health of the liberal world – a world distrusted by many of its members – the Church has a pressing duty to *infiltrate* that world. It no longer has the leisure to present itself solely as the material expression of divine transcendence, for it now has the additional duty of seeing to the moral survival of people living with freedom and its consequences. This duty is what Frédéric Ozanam, in a striking phrase, terms the necessity of "going over to the barbarians":

> [We must] go over to the barbarians, the camp of the kings, the statesmen of 1815, in order to reach the people. And when I say, we must go over to the barbarians, I am asking … that we look after the people who have too many needs and not enough rights, who rightly demand a larger role in public affairs, guarantees of work and protection from poverty; who have bad leaders but, being unable to find good ones, should be held responsible neither for the *History of the Girondists*, which they do not read, nor for the banquets at which they do not dine. We may not convert Attila and Gaiseric, but we may perhaps, God willing, vanquish the Huns and the Vandals. (Ozanam to A.M. Foisset, February 1848, quoted in Duroselle 1951, 296)

Paradoxically, the religious renaissance and its attendant onrush of fervour culminated in something resembling a secularization of the Church; as it acted to fulfill its perceived moral responsibilities, it became enmeshed with the affairs of civil society. The church's incursion into the social partakes of that logic whereby the living world must be reconstructed before the Kingdom of God can be reached.

> Where progress trumpeted the inevitable Kingdom, preoccupation with the souls of the poor became less. Religious leaders turned their attention more and more to social adjustment – to make the community more like the imagined Kingdom. And the churches themselves, where they met the poor, exerted greater energy in nonreligious programs to attract and aid the poor. (Huggins 1971, 51)[56]

Lacking the standing to constitute a sort of transcendent inner lining for political affairs, as they had in the past,[57] the churches turned to the task of occupying the social sphere. This was the new reality they faced as they stared into the modern world. That meant not only taking charge of people's moral education, but also working to right injustices against them.

The Church and Its Poor

The "normal" religious view of poverty is congruent with some of the basic postulates of classical liberalism as developed by Tocqueville and Mill, who had followed the path marked out by Malthus before them. For these thinkers, while poverty does afford opportunities for self-betterment, it is primarily a fact to be reckoned with because of the inequalities arising in any society based on talent and personal autonomy. Prelates such as Paul Bruchési, the Archbishop of Montreal, and other writers as well, came to the same conclusion, ascribing poverty to the natural order of things:

> Wealth has ever been the lot of the few; the indigent, the sufferers, those who often have no bread to eat, have always formed a large part of humanity. (Bruchési 1882, 18)

> Poverty ... is an evil inherent to societies, which may be tempered, softened, but not eliminated. The government, the organ and representative of society, is in every country powerless to succour, to console, to encourage those whom misfortune pursues. (*Le Correspondant*, 1844, quoted in Duroselle 1951, 159)

> Can poverty be done away with? The question is absurd, and one is amazed that after the experience of so many centuries, faced with so much evidence derived from the moral and physical constitution of the individual and of society, there are still people who ask this question, people so unperceptive that they fail to see that differences in condition and fortune flow from the nature of society itself. (Beaudry 1862)

This religious vision of charitable intervention did not hesitate, moreover, to adduce the champions of liberal economic theory, Malthus first and foremost, in its defence. Indeed, strict Malthusianism had become central to the church's philosophy of charitable intervention. Étienne Parent stated the idea with notable clarity:

> Increase the means of subsistence among the poor classes through extraordinary assistance, without simultaneously increasing the sum total of the subsistences, and you can be sure that the number of indigents will increase in the same proportion. It is sad to say, but it would be equally disastrous to ignore or suppress, the fact that in an old country covered with a large population,

especially one exposed to the fluctuations of commerce and industry, it is poverty, and poverty alone, combined with moral restraint ... which can put limits on the increase of the poor population. But then, must the poor be left to perish? No; but I say that the state and the editorialists must frankly confess their impotence in this regard, and leave the care of the poor to religion, which knows better than they do the secret of alleviating that human misery which cannot be prevented. Then let every man, in the voice of religion, alleviate as much as possible the poverty around him, and entrust the rest not to the utopians but to God, who willed it that the world be made this way. And let us not, senseless as we are, mutter against Providence. We would prefer if there were no poverty among men, a laudable wish no doubt. But if there were no poverty to be feared, tell me, who would lead men, in the absence of a nobler motive, into foresight, thrift, work, good conduct? Clearly, there is in human poverty a precious and ever-present teaching; there is good even in the evils which God sends us. (Parent [1852a] 1975, 263)[58]

The poor are the "wounded of the social order."[59] They are the victims of an unequal world, but they are also living testimony to the original sin within us; for, in Catholicism as in liberalism, poverty cannot be reduced to a mere lack. It is a function of *sin*, just as for contemporaneous liberals it is a function of moral failings and behavioural vices.

Physical suffering is merely the consequence of moral wickedness; so that, if there were no moral wickedness on the earth, there would be no physical suffering ... No sickness can have a material cause. Every sickness is a punishment, but punishment implies a moral sin. To make the punishment cease, one must erase the sin that has earned it ... Pauperism is a social sickness, and ... every sickness is a punishment. A people afflicted with this sickness is therefore guilty of some sin for which it is being punished ... Certain economists ... find the cause of pauperism in the physical order alone, in the infertility of the soil inhabited by a people, in a defective system of cultivation, in an absence of manufacturing. These causes may, no doubt, have a certain deleterious influence on the prosperity of a people living in a comparative state of inferiority, but they do not cause pauperism. (Beaudry 1862)[60]

The perversity believed to be at the root of poverty – a phenomenon nonetheless considered as inhering in the natural order of things – is precisely what makes moral intervention necessary. Poverty becomes the visible sign of a moral deficit that, for the reasons we have seen, falls primarily within the province of religion.

More extreme versions of religious discourse would even come to regard poverty as a virtue, an opportunity to achieve grace, or even to return to a state of original simplicity.

> Pauperism is neither a cancer nor a problem ... In the order of nature, since the first sin, poverty is a necessary consequence of the diversity, and variety of the talents, capacity, qualities, defects, and even of the chances, that Providence distributes at will. Man must serve man, and be served by man; and without the promptings of want, the painful but indispensable task of social service would never be carried out. In the supernatural order, pauperism is neither a cancer nor a problem; it is a grace, it is a gratuitous favour, a gift from God: a grace for the individual and for society. Poverty of spirit, genuine detachment from riches, is a grace, a precious, a necessary virtue. But real poverty, the privation and want of the gifts of fortune, is also a grace, which is occasionally superadded to the former, and which facilitates poverty of spirit, gives a free scope to virtue, and a greater assurance of salvation ...
>
> Pauperism is therefore a permanent effect of the sovereign will of God. Hence, to attempt its utter extirpation is not merely a utopian scheme, it is a crime. (Chandonnet 1864, 46–7)[61]

Poverty is a more or less indelible mark of sin, but also an opportunity for redemption, a locus of reconciliation. Although equality on earth may never come to pass, poverty remains a debt to be collected in the afterlife.

The religious discourse on poverty shares with liberal discourse this resignation before the inevitability of inequality. But it recasts the issue in terms of transcendence. Here, poverty is not only a necessary stimulus to individual action in this world, but also an opportunity for spiritual redemption. The result is a deep-seated pragmatism that is perfectly consistent with the liberal emphasis on mitigating the consequences of poverty rather than imagining that it can be eradicated. If Ozanam exhorts Christians to go over to the barbarians, it is because they have become unavoidable and must be reckoned with; it does not mean that their utopian dreams need to be taken seriously:

> "One of my good friends," says Ozanam ... "led astray ... by the Saint-Simonian theories, said to me with a tone of compassion, 'But what do you hope to do? You are eight poor young men, and you pretend to come in aid of the miseries which multiply in a city like Paris! ... We, on the contrary, are elaborating ideas and a system which will reform the world and rescue it for

ever from its misery! We will do in a moment for humanity that which you will not know how to accomplish in several ages.' You know ... what these theories have come to, which caused this illusion to my poor friend!"...

At the time when Ozanam spoke, the little company of eight who were unwilling to be nine, had swelled into two thousand [and they] had five hundred conferences in France. (Ozanam 1886, 79–80)

There is, in both the religious and temporal versions of charity central to the great mid-nineteenth-century transition, a pragmatics erected on the ruins of philanthropic dreams.

Poverty is one of those things we would like to conjure away forever ... We make strides toward this goal, and while keeping our eyes fixed on this lofty aim, which we can never attain, we pretend not to hear the cries of pain at our feet. We seem to concentrate all our efforts on the big picture and neglect the small one, where much deprivation and suffering could nonetheless be alleviated. (Beaudry 1862)[62]

All at once a fated occurrence, an unwavering indicator of moral weakness, and a source of virtue, poverty as viewed by religious charity is inevitable, yet gestures in the direction of redemption.

Caring for the Poor

One of the most striking characteristics of the Catholic charity being put in place in the nineteenth century is its approach to caring for the poor. Even if poverty was an indicator of moral weakness, even if its abolition was no longer a realistic goal, and even if it was accepted as an integral, practically immanent part of life in society, this certainly did not mean that the poor should be neglected or repressed. Resignation was not, in this instance, the mother of powerlessness or rejection. Quite the contrary: the administration of poverty ought to be incorporated into an organic vision of the social, one that would have no truck with ostracism. Liberal charity had renounced its grand philanthropic illusions of transforming the poor from within and put in their place a radical separation between the coercive confinement of extreme poverty in workhouses or beggars' prisons, and the ad hoc treatment of "ordinary" poverty by private charity, whether religious or secular. That is, liberal charity had resigned itself to making extreme poverty and consequent physical confinement the mark of social failure.

Catholic charity rejected this separation: it considered *all* forms of poverty to fall within its purview. And it likewise rejected the idea that any member of the poor should be stigmatized. The irony is that in taking this stand, it invoked the principle of freedom itself – and in particular, the pauper's freedom. Here is Monseigneur Bourget giving a lesson in liberalism to anyone tempted to sing the praises of legal or philanthropic charity:

> We do not put the poor under lock and key in order to restrain them from knocking on the doors of the rich, and we have many good reasons for this. We think that the poor man can enjoy his freedom like the rich man, as long as he does not, by his violence and other condemnable excesses, make himself a nuisance and a danger to society. We believe that immorality would find opportunities to prosper if we forced men to live apart from their wives ... It is our unwavering principle that fathers and mothers are the masters of their children; that they are charged with their proper raising; and that no one could deprive them of this right, which nature and religion grant them, over those whom they have given life. We also have reason, which shows us every day that it is by virtue of the poor that countries are populated and nations become great and powerful. In consequence, we take care of many families; far from seeking to render them barren, we seek to find within them the elements of life and prosperity. Indeed, we venerate the poor. (Bourget 1862, 5)[63]

While Catholic charity had rejected the progressive ambitions of the pioneering social Catholics, it had retained their insistence on preserving the social ties threatened by overly intense or widespread poverty. This is the deep meaning of Ozanam's dictum about going over to the barbarians. This ethos also arises out of the complex blend of sentimentality and romanticism[64] at the origin of ultramontanism, in which the poor are seen as siblings, affording humanitarians an opportunity for self-betterment, rather than as victims of the ambient immorality of modern society.

Such respect for the poor was expressed with some frequency.

> What we must also admire, in these marvelous creations of charity, is the ingenious delicacy which attends their operation, the saintly respect with which they honour the unfortunate, the motherly attentions which they lavish on the poor. Oh! but we are far from the cold liberalities of philanthropy,

or even legal charity, which haughtily toss their measly coin to the needy as one might toss an old bone to a dog barking along their path, and then walk on by, indifferent and oblivious, going about their business and their pleasure ... Faced with such mendicity in rags, the living incarnation of the God-Man who was also a man of suffering, charity bows its head; it is tempted to bow down in adoration before this denuded tabernacle of divine misery. (Gohiet 1896, 2)[65]

Expressed in this quote is, of course, the age-old notion that care for the poor affords an opportunity for one's own salvation. It is a notion fundamental to the Vincentian conception of charity, revisited and updated by Ozanam and enthusiastically promoted by Thomas-Aimé Chandonnet in Quebec:

You are members of [the Society of St Vincent de Paul], above all for yourselves, to nourish Catholic Faith in yourselves in the first place, next to nourish it and to glorify it in others. And, as nothing can be done without means, you adopt two principal and essential means: familiar gatherings of your brethren; and domiciliary visits of the poor, combined with alms ... The poor have bread, say you ... So much the better! But you yourself are the first of the poor; therefore, you must look first to yourself. (Chandonnet 1864, 25–6)[66]

But there is more. Catholic charity appears as the privileged means of crossing class barriers, even as it reproduces them. As in its liberal version, Catholic charity is an instrument for consolidation of the social fabric, through which de facto solidarity, indeed reciprocity,[67] is instituted between giver and receiver.

On the one hand, the attention we pay the poor man elevates him in his own eyes, revives his courage; the example of work prods him in his indolence, the material aid provided to him offers the means of bettering his condition, or at least encourages him to make efforts toward that end. Relations between the two poles of society are seen to be established, ties that bind them are formed, and if the levelling, the equilibrium, of which the communists dream is not established, at least there is fruitful commerce, whereby the rich man comes to the aid of the poor man to alleviate his misery and ease his lot, and often to shepherd him onto the path of honest affluence. (Beaudry 1862)

This "fruitful commerce" no longer has anything to do with the requisite deference and submission formerly demanded of the lower classes as a counterpart to the showy charity of nobles. Rather, it takes the form of generous aid arriving from the other extreme of society.[68] But make no mistake: this type of charity, this consolidation of social ties, ensues from a personal relationship whose ideal form can be enacted only through religion: the charitable bond – a private bond, need it be said – is also, and above all, quintessentially a *religious* bond:

> Purely philanthropic societies plainly lack these features of strength and endurance, because they are founded on human interests alone. One can see money being doled out, but one cannot feel the heart beating. But our kind of charity, which mixes its tears with the tears of the unfortunates whom it cannot console otherwise, which caresses and gathers in the naked foundling; which brings the counsels of friendship to timid youth; which sits with benevolence by the bedside of the sick; which listens, without evident boredom, to long, lamentable stories of misfortune ... Such charity, my friends, can only be inspired by God! (Ozanam, quoted in Bruchési 1882, 111–12)[69]

Of course, secular philanthropic initiatives such as the Charity Organization Societies also evinced this desire to draw the rich and the poor closer together. But this effort largely related to "ordinary" poverty, and it took place in a setting in which religious motives were generally subordinated to philanthropic and civic goals. For Catholics, looking after the poor was only one manifestation of the solidarity by which the religious group, and the community it constituted, had to be bound together. But the exigencies of the modern day would not countenance such solidarity being meted out in a haphazard fashion. The Church would have to build and implement a full-scale system for the delivery of Catholic public assistance.

The Poor, between the Religious Community and the Asylum

> The religious orders are the antidote to pauperism. Institutes of charity and benevolent associations are like an extension of these orders, and all converge toward the same goal ... In the solution we offer, the charity worker acts simultaneously on the cause and the effect; an intelligent worker and consummate in his art, with a perfect understanding of the nature of the individual with whom he must work, he speaks to the soul and the body. Moreover, his activity is not limited to one class of society, the poor class,

but extends to both extremes of society. In the rich it inspires and elicits charity, commiseration; in the poor, love of order, work, and economy. (Beaudry 1862)[70]

It must be understood that in this era of associations, the helping relationship central to the Catholic conception of charity is not founded on individual fellow feeling alone, but also, and perhaps above all, on the strength of communities explicitly formed, in many cases, for charitable purposes.

Nothing compares to the power of the example; a single act of virtue has greater power to render virtuous he who witnesses it than the most eloquent speeches. We are quite often recalcitrant to speech; we are always conquered by example ... But if example is so powerful even when isolated, what could be beyond the powers of a gathering of men, many of whom unfailingly distinguish themselves by their talents, their knowledge, and their virtues; who together possess all the attributes needed to win hearts? Is it not a near certainty that they will set the tone for the society in which they live? (Beaudry 1862)[71]

In Quebec and throughout the West, Catholic charity would be eminently collective. It would be enacted through the creation of both religious communities and lay groups such as the Society of St Vincent de Paul. Such collective action was particularly necessary in that the task at hand involved more than just helping the poor at home: it also entailed implementing a far-reaching network of institutions capable of looking after those whom their families could no longer maintain or support. Indeed, the great power of Catholicism at mid-century was its ability to induce an enormous number of people to devote their lives to charity work within skilfully structured hierarchical communities.[72]

These communities, on which the greatest part of the Church's charitable work depended, were highly adept at mobilizing people to take up charity as a religious vocation.[73] However, in Catholic discourse, these communities' existence was justified by arguments besides the disinterestedness of their charitable action. That action was worthy not only because of the putative superiority of religious charity over other forms, but also because it partook of the thoroughly modern rationality of liberalism. The religious communities were quite at home in the liberal economy of charity, for two reasons.

The first was that religious orders represented a splendid job opportunity for the surplus poor created by the liberal economy. A whole reserve army thereby found useful and durable employment.

> As to those poor who join a religious order, they receive their subsistence from the order to which they give their services, and that is as many fewer whom society will have to feed. Had they stayed in the world, they would quite probably have engendered whole families of poor souls, whereas in the cloister they work to alleviate poverty. (Beaudry 1862)

> For every position that becomes vacant, a crowd of applicants appears, each putting forward the best reasons for finding that he is worthy ... One seeks a way to turn back toward its source, or at least to contain within reasonable bounds, this torrent of ambitions flooding in from all around ... And that brake ... do you know where it is to be found? Above all in the halls of our monasteries and convents. All those men who, touched by grace, decide to wrap themselves in the solitude of a cloister, who withdraw from all careers, thus making room for others. All those nuns who give up marriage: are they not just as many rivals who vanish to the great relief of those girls who cannot resign themselves to the role of old maid? Is it not the case that every monastic vow is a repressed desire that will no longer bother anyone? That each vow of poverty is a voluntary renunciation in favour of those who have not the strength to be contented with their lot? ... Were all those monks to return to your midst, it would increase your already frightful numbers. How much further ahead you will be, when you see all these famished guests reclaim their seats at the banquet of our poor society, where we already complain of being so crowded. (Henriot 1892, 15–17)[74]

Such discourse might be regarded as the pragmatic opportunism of the standard-bearers of religious charity making use of any argument that came to hand. Nevertheless, this argument can be heard quite early on, from Étienne Parent among others: "It is the poor who profit from works of charity. Too, these helpful bachelors then become a salutary brake on that overpopulation which afflicts Europe today and will one day afflict our America, though that day is happily still far off" (Parent [1852b] 1975, 314).

In this way, the charitable vocation, with its characteristic virtues and enthusiasm, was asserted to also partake of an intrinsic economic rationality. An iron law of charitable labour was posited, making for a felicitous match between the demand for labour power and the personal needs of those called to the cloister.

Second, to market rationality, the restrictive logic proper to charitable action was added. Since charity obtains only in cases where self-sufficiency is clearly impossible, where personal or family autonomy is deficient or threatened, and where personal initiative cannot prevail, it must therefore be minimal[75] and parsimonious. The economy of religious charity is one of exceptional, carefully targeted, temporary, *in extremis* intervention. It is akin to a gentle push in the direction of good, one that ideally requires only limited resources.

But when asylum looms as a last resort, the need for a low-cost alternative solution becomes even more pressing. The great amount of volunteer work done by the religious orders, and by nuns in particular, resulted in substantial savings, and this fact became a staple of the economic argument for religious charity. Here is Louis-François Laflèche, the Bishop of Trois-Rivières, using a striking military metaphor to describe the volunteers ministering to the poor:

> The various religious orders of the Catholic Church are like the battalions of a great army, each having its own weapons and the requisite discipline for completing the task with which they are entrusted. There are hospital orders charged with the care of orphans and widows, the poor and the sick; teaching orders charged with the education of children and youth; penitent and contemplative orders having as their mission that of delivering God's justice through the practice of Christian mortification, and bringing His mercy to the Christian people through prayer and meditation ...
>
> If [civil society] were itself to bear the expenses necessitated by these works, it would thereby deprive itself of two valuable sources of revenue: that of spontaneous donations and offerings made to religious institutions, which would dry up after the suppression of these admirable institutions; and, no less valuable, that of the personal devotion of those who direct these institutions. It would all have to be put on the account of the State, which would pay three times as much, as France's experiences proves, and for an inferior result. (Laflèche 1889, 60–1, 64)

In this way, an argument from economic reason was added to the argument from humanitarian self-abnegation and disinterestedness. This argument would soon go far in dissuading the public authorities from intervening in the field of charity. On this point, the controversies arising from municipal attempts to levy taxes on charitable communities are particularly telling.

> The citizens should ... beg this municipality [Quebec City] to come to the aid of these Catholic and Protestant corporations, so as to give them the capacity to increase, if possible, the sum of the good that they produce already, thus discharging the municipality and the government from a host of burdensome obligations which would fall upon them, if these religious corporations did not exist. (Larue 1876, 4)[76]

Note that the principle according to which the public authorities *do* have responsibility for public welfare makes an implicit appearance in this remark. Having earlier insisted that the state ought to keep out of charity, the Church now deployed the economic argument with a view to positioning itself as a viable surrogate for the charitable functions of the state. It would continue to brandish this argument well into the twentieth century.[77]

But whatever the justification or rationalization for religious control over private charity, it is clear that it sat comfortably ensconced within the framework of liberalism. When that framework came under attack at the end of the century, what would become of religious charity? Clearly, it would have to respond.

RELIGIOUS CHARITY AND THE CRISIS OF LIBERALISM

Despite the panegyrics to the glorious advance of Catholic charity in Quebec after 1850, the meaning and direction of religious charity were increasingly being called into question.[78] The problem was that the fundamental assumptions of religious charity (its private and individual character, charitable intervention as a last resort, rejection of state interference) – which it shared with classical liberalism – were increasingly being challenged by both the new social sciences and the reform movements (radical or otherwise) that proliferated within this domain of social regulation. Three basic phenomena need to be considered here: the Church's de facto control over social welfare, the ways in which this control was challenged, and the tensions provoked by these challenges within the Church itself.

Above I examined the context for the development of a powerful network of charitable institutions under the tight control of the Church. This network did not come into being overnight, however, but as the result of a thirty-year process, during which the Church gradually solidified its power.[79] The few religious congregations founded in Quebec in the 1840s (the Sisters of Providence, the Sisters of Mercy) or imported from France (the Sisters of the Good Shepherd, later the Brothers of Charity) grew relatively slowly during the ensuing two decades. Not until the 1870s did Quebec religious communities enjoy the critical mass necessary to support a genuine expansionist thrust. Moreover, the principle of a strictly denominational network was far from garnering unanimous approval in the years before Confederation, as witness the debate surrounding the Montreal House of Industry (Chureau 1996) and the institutions responsible for juvenile delinquency and child welfare.

In this connection, Confederation does seem to have been the decisive turning point, for with it came a clear devolution of welfare responsibilities to the provinces. The Church now faced a relatively weak, poorly funded interlocutor, one that was well disposed to give away some of its health and welfare responsibilities to an organization powerful and well structured enough to do the hard work. Far from constituting an obstacle, the principle of liberal charity afforded an ideal ideological context for this arrangement. The extreme ultramontane radicalism of the early years of Confederation only exemplifies an exceptional conjuncture in which the Church would succeed in imposing an enduring denominational logic on the health and welfare system.[80]

The Church did, after all, have much to boast about. By century's end, its tight-knit network of institutions was caring for children, the elderly, widows, the sick, the insane – even female prisoners and young offenders. These institutions were at times heavily subsidized by the state,[81] but above all they functioned as a safety net around the great Catholic family, taking charge of individuals from broken or temporarily distressed families. The Church had even succeeded in taking full advantage of the charitable fervour of its lay members: the Ladies of Saint Anne and the Society of St Vincent de Paul had built essential linkages between parish life and the health and welfare network.[82] Add to this the home visits made by certain female religious communities (the Grey Nuns, the Sisters of Providence) and the result is a remarkable, tightly integrated network for the regulation of poverty and illness, operating under the authority of the bishop. In the specific conjuncture of Quebec, the Church had not only built and developed this network but also taken control over its administration.[83]

Under these circumstances, the triumphalism to be heard from turn-of-the-century religious figures is understandable: continuing in its age-old tradition, the Church had succeeded in offering complete coverage of nearly the full range of human afflictions.

> Is there any affliction that is not alleviated? Is there a work of goodness that has not its apostles and its protectors? From the moment he enters this life, from the cradle to the school, from school to apprenticeship, from apprenticeship to the workshop and from the workshop to the household; if misfortunes bedevil him, if he wants bread, or even if he is guilty of wrongdoing: at every hour of his existence, in his agony and at his death, the pauper has asylums that minister to him, guardian angels who call him their brother, mothers who afford him all the compassion and kindness of the noblest and most generous heart. (Bruchési 1882, 78)

In this idyllic tableau, nothing appeared to threaten the salutary complementarity between the goals of the Church and the principles of liberal charity.

THE CHURCH CHALLENGED

Chapter 6 described how the crisis of liberalism led to a new way of conceptualizing society in which liberal postulates faded from prominence; how it caused the analytical parameters applicable to poverty and pauperism to be redefined for the benefit of the working classes; and how it provided a new and firmer basis for the exclusion of those members of the lumpenproletariat considered unfit or deficient, who were neglected by reformers and radicals as the able-bodied working class was rediscovered. This crisis, reaching its peak after the 1870s, was evident in Quebec as well, although here it took some rather specific forms.

Toward a Science of the "Social"

> Whilst the solution to all the big questions of interest to a people can be found in philosophy and in the holy books, it is understandable that the diversity and complexity of modern constitutions dictated that the study of political and social questions be made into a veritable science – whence political or social economy. (lecture by Amédée Robitaille at the Union commerciale, in *Courrier du Canada*, 2 February 1884)

By the late nineteenth century, the society born out of the industrial and democratic revolutions could no longer be construed as the sum of individual wills. Nor could it be reduced to a compact community of the faithful making up a single unit in the eyes of the one true God. It was now to be construed as a complex organism with a peculiar texture all its own, arising out of the intermixing and melding of countless social groupings. Sociology had discovered the fundamental "social fact" constituted by social groupings and regularities which, when properly measured, can help make sense of – or even perpetuate – the social fabric. Fresh from his time frequenting Henri de Tourville's *Science social* group in Paris and absorbing the influence of Frédéric Le Play, the young Léon Gérin made this ringing statement: "Social truths have now become as self-evident as scientific truths" (Gérin 1886).[84] The unit of meaning in the new, reconceptualized society is no longer the individual but the group or cluster.

> Society remains, for us, the disorderly crowd, from which a thousand confused noises arise; the chaotic mass, in which a thousand unanalysed phenomena take place ... All around the family – the primary and ever-necessary cluster – a number of auxiliary clusters are established: the workshop, the school, the church, the market, associations of all sorts, satisfying needs for which the family cannot provide ... Just say the magic word, *cluster*, and this confused mass, this shapeless assemblage, falls to pieces, and, like the cleaved mineral, forms into regular crystals. (Léon Gérin, "La Science sociale," *La Presse*, 30 June 1886)

The new science was one in which delicate balances were struck among men and women clustered into associations, corps, classes, and other entities. This being the case, the individual too now had to be reconceptualized as being constituted, and in large part *determined*, by the dynamic of interaction among these clusters.

> The more numerous the clusters, the harder it is to keep the balance among them from being upset. And yet the happiness and strength of the nation are tied to the preservation of this balance. The stability of the social body hinges on the stability of its constituent clusters. Society will prosper if each of these clusters retains its specific function and relative importance. Let any one of these necessary clusters break down, and suffering will inevitably result. (Gérin, "La Science sociale," *La Presse*, 30 June 1886)

In Quebec, these matters were the subject of lively debate in certain scholarly circles.[85] But this initial attempt at a Quebec "sociology" would gain few adherents in the short run, at least among francophones; it appears to have been crowded out by the dominant liberal Catholic orthodoxy, in which the individual was the central construct.[86] Yet this new vantage on society would lead to a reconsideration of the conditions of reproduction of the working class, by far the most numerous grouping in society.

Rediscovering and Protecting the Working Class

> At this time in the world's history, when careful observers and honest thinkers in every land are coming more and more to realize what is meant by the interdependence of society; when those who study city life are each day more fully persuaded that ordinary urban conditions are demoralizing and that no portion of the community can be allowed to deteriorate without danger to the whole ... it is opportune that the citizens of Montreal should, for a time, cease discussing the slums of London, the beggars of Paris and the tenement house evils of New York and endeavor to learn something about themselves and to understand more perfectly the conditions present in their very midst. (Ames [1897] 1972, 7)

Rediscovering society also meant learning to measure its parameters systematically. In this regard, the enterprise of Booth and Rowntree (see chapter 6) was taken up by the Montreal businessman Herbert Brown Ames, who embarked on a systematic sociological study of Saint-Henri, one of the city's poor neighbourhoods. But, at this historical juncture, a study of the working class and its living and working conditions was obliged to suspend judgment on the moral causes of poverty, ultimately casting doubt on the whole liberal discourse on this subject.

> Few are the families that will admit to a stranger that drink, crime or voluntary idleness is the cause of their misery, though in 7 per cent of the cases visited, drunkenness was clearly at the bottom of the trouble. Still it is the belief of the investigator that the undeserving among the poor form a far smaller proportion than is generally imagined. (Ames [1897] 1972, 75)

Like Booth in England, Ames concluded that the true cause of poverty is to be looked for in the deficient operation of the economy:

> As to the causes of poverty, chief among them is insufficient employment. Few are the families where nothing is earned, although there are such

subsisting more or less worthily upon charity. Almost without exception each family has its wage-earner, often more than one, and upon the regularity with which the wage-earner secures employment depends the scale of living for the family. (Ames [1897] 1972, 72)[87]

Behind this observation lurks, here as elsewhere, a new understanding of the worker. The problematic fact of involuntary unemployment opened up room for objective thinking about the condition of the working class as a whole. Voluntarism, personal autonomy, home economy, the ability to plan: these features of the liberal ideology no longer sufficed to explain what observers were seeing. It was as a *class*, as a constituent grouping of the polity, that workers now captured the interest of reformers. Even the most moderate or liberal of these reformers, albeit not daring to question the fundamental laws of the capitalist economy, argued that these laws should be softened by welfare measures responsive to the conditions of working-class life.

We cannot interfere with the inscrutable law of supply and demand to raise the workingman's wages. We may feel, I know I do, that the pittance for which many toilers slave is far from sufficient or right. But wages will ever rest at the mark just above the requirements of absolute subsistence. We can, however, aid in making the workingman's hard-earned dollar bring him the fullest return, we can assist in making it possible for him to secure for himself a place fit to be called a home wherein he may bring up his children in health, in privacy and in comfort. To this end scientific knowledge and business experience are both requisite. (Ames [1897] 1972, 114)

Others would of course take this reformist thrust further, going so far as to challenge the very logic of the system. In an interesting lecture on the problem of the unemployed, presented in the late 1890s to the Montreal Local Council of Women, Helen R.Y. Reid insisted that workers should be regarded not only as producers but also as *consumers*:

If the demand for goods were regular, this under-use of labour and capital would not occur. The demand means not only the desire to own, to have, to consume, but it means the power to gratify the desire. Thousand of people wish to consume within legitimate and reasonable limits but are unable to do so from lack of this power ... A market demand sufficiently great and constant to keep in employment all willing labour together with a more natural distribution of the power to consume among those who have the desire to consume, would seem to offer an effective mode of deliverance from this industrial trouble. (Reid 189?, 6)

Drawing on the work of the economist John Hobson, Reid took issue with the emphasis on the "moral improvement" of the working classes:

> It has often been stated that no radical improvement in industrial organization, no work of social reconstruction, can be of any real avail, unless it is preceded by such moral and intellectual improvement in the condition of the mass of workers as shall render the new machinery effective. Is it not clear, however, that little moral or intellectual education can be effectively brought to bear upon the mass of human beings, whose whole energies are necessarily absorbed by the effort to secure the means of bare physical support? (Reid 189?, 16)[88]

The necessity of attending to the real needs of the working class achieved a broad consensus among reformers of all stripes, left and right. In certain conservative circles, this necessity increasingly took the form of a desire to "protect" the worker – from himself if need be.

> It is incumbent on the government and those interested in resolving this important issue to seek the best means of protecting the worker and his family from the two big threats to him, not to mention from the inevitable accidents to which he is exposed; to wit, the worker must be protected from his own spendthriftiness and lack of foresight, or what I would unhesitatingly call his liberality. (speech by J.A. Chapleau, *La Presse*, 2 November 1888)[89]

Thus, one finds in Quebec a rather faithful version of the European and American reform discourse that called for state policies in support of the working class, whether in the form of pensions, insurance, family allowances, or housing.[90]

The Case of the Disabled Worker: Misfortunes of the Lumpenproletariat

Likewise, one finds in Quebec the systematic confinement of those working class discards who are seen as the "dependents, defectives and delinquents" of society. Ames, for one, unceremoniously excluded them from his study:

> The submerged tenth of society, "the dependents, defectives and delinquents," those who have fallen below the level of decent subsistence, who could not, without outside help, survive through the rigors of a Canadian winter, such would I ... exclude. These latter are fit subjects for state care and for charitable effort, and do not come within the limits of the present study. (Ames [1897] 1972, 102)

The delicate equilibria that allow society to survive would, it was felt, inevitably be upset by the presence of these abject persons in its midst.[91] Reid, who propounded an economy focusing on the consumer needs of the working class, was unsparingly harsh in her description of "superfluous" labourers:

> In consequence of the conditions of his life, the value of the casual labourer's work tends to decline. Intermittent work breeds irregular habits, carelessness and a host of other evils and a sure and ofttimes swift degeneration from casually-employed to unemployable, unfit and superfluous follows ... This lowest class consists of those who are permanently unemployed, because through some physical or moral defect they are economically worthless. They include all the vagrant class, the shiftless nomads of the lower strata of society, the tramps and paupers, vagabonds and rogues, all of whom live more or less by lying and begging. Each one of these represents a commercial deficit or dead loss to the community and in the mass constitutes one of the greatest social evils to present and future generations. (Reid 189?, 2)[92]

Public Assistance and a New Vision of the State

Private charity under the liberal mode of regulation was founded on the capacity of private initiative, organized in the form of associations or otherwise, to come to the aid of the "deserving" poor on an ad hoc basis. The state could be left to take charge of certain extreme cases, such as mental patients, vagrants, and so on. In this way, the "freedom to give" was established as the basis for thousands of charitable initiatives taking shape in the nineteenth century. From the 1870s on, this freedom began to appear anarchic, ineffective, and expensive. In the United States and England, the Charity Organization Societies emerged as an organizational response designed to consolidate private charity while avoiding state interference (Humphreys 1995). It was fundamentally a matter of perpetuating the values of liberal charity while providing for a degree of planning thereof. Planning also entailed the implementation of a system for investigating welfare claimants so as to eliminate fraud.

This need for organization and systematic investigation implicitly called into question the values of spontaneity and humanitarian solidarity portrayed as central to the liberal act of charity.[93] Each case would still be considered on its individual merits, but charity was now to become a predominantly standardized operation instead of a genuine reflection of the social fabric between rich and poor. The adoption of formalized investigative procedures and the critique of "sentimentality" on the part of good Samaritans spurred on this transition. In Quebec and elsewhere, the putative dysfunctionality of long-standing practices of private charity was increasingly criticized.

> Evidences ... are not lacking to prove that this benevolent work frequently overlaps with a tendency to pauperize the recipients. This is a result that should be guarded against with the greatest care. I am strongly of the opinion that our great weakness in the work of assisting the worthy poor lies in lack of organized effort among the charitable bodies. Some Central Charity Board, upon which representatives of every race and creed might sit, should be here established. (Ames [1897] 1972, 78)[94]

Another proponent of organized charity, Francis McLean, cited the Society of St Vincent de Paul as a model, with particular reference to its investigative procedures:

> Upon the Catholic side the world-wide traditions of the St Vincent de Paul Society have effectually prevented its degenerating along the line of officialism even under the pressure of local conditions. The steady, sure methods of personal visitation before relief, of ability to order relief at any time, of secrecy so far as the applications are concerned, excepting at the conference meetings, are followed in Montreal, as elsewhere. (McLean 1901, 143–4)[95]

The Montreal Charity Organization, founded under McLean's impetus in 1899, in fact represented an important moment: despite Catholic misgivings (to which I return), coordination of relief for the "deserving" poor was the new order of the day, and all the various organizations involved, both religious and secular, would be called on to cooperate.

Perhaps ironically, this rationalization of relief afforded an opportunity for certain observers to reconsider some liberal dogmas about state-run charity, its putative ineffectiveness first and foremost:

We must all sympathize with the unwillingness to introduce a poor law, though it is a great mistake to suppose that public charity regularly and justly administered demoralizes or degrades more than private charity, which through ignorance and want of time for the examination of cases, must often be dispensed with a lavish and capricious hand ... To voluntary effort, and especially to that of the churches, we must look for the relief of the indigence which shrinks from sight and would never ask for public relief, yet is often accompanied by the keenest suffering ... Responsibility in the last resort must rest somewhere, and it can scarcely be thrown even on the most devoted volunteers. (Smith 1889, 4)

Ultimate state responsibility for dire poverty, enacted in England by the Poor Laws and in France as well, began to appear to a number of Quebec observers as an inescapable necessity. Dr Georges Villeneuve, medical superintendent at the Saint-Jean-de-Dieu asylum, made the following remarks:

I mean by public assistance the action whereby the public authorities, whether the state or the city government, directly or through the agency of constituted or representative bodies, see to the alleviation of human suffering and infirmity in all their forms, where they are found together with indigence. In this sense, there is no genuine public assistance in the Province of Quebec other than that provided to the indigent insane ... All other charitable works ... were founded and are carried on by religious congregations or philanthropic societies ... As admirable as this action by religious or private charity may be, it has not succeeded in alleviating human misery in all its aspects, for its initiative has been directed at the most urgent efforts, such as hospitals; the most indispensable ones, such as orphanages; the most desirable ones, such as institutions for the deaf and the blind, and so forth. The result is that cases not falling into these categories have remained outside their sphere of action, or, exhibiting special features or being of a difficult nature, could not receive from private concerns a solution that was the duty of the state. (Villeneuve 1904, 425)

McLean expressed a similar view. In a speech to the 28th National Conference of Charities and Correction in Chicago in 1901, the director of the Montreal Charity Organization Society issued a harsh diagnosis of the state of Montreal's charities:

Subtract the almshouse, subtract any form of public institution or aid for dependants or for defectives excepting the insane and a small fraction of the idiotic, and you have the conditions existing in Montreal ... In other words, neither the city nor province, either by the maintenance of public institutions or by reasonable grants to private institutions, assumes or pretends to assume any responsibility beyond the care of all delinquents, the care of the insane among the defectives and orphaned children among the dependants ... To begin with, the absence from the tax rates of compulsory benevolence has not in any way increased the generosity of the community at large with reference to charities organized into societies or institutions. In Montreal, as elsewhere, the supporters of one society are generally the supporters of a dozen others; and no institution can boast of a genuinely popular support ... The absence of governmental responsibility has even prevented the placing of any effective settlement laws on the statute books of the province. This has added even more to the unjust burdens borne by the city institutions ... Thus the simple absence of governmental responsibility works toward an unjust squandering of private charitable resources. (McLean 1901, 140–1)

A curious irony had led this vehement partisan of private charity to lament the non-existence of a Quebec equivalent of the Poor Laws. Far from representing an abuse of power or an unjustified encroachment on private initiative, government assumption of responsibility for the most destitute citizens[96] would relieve the private institutions of a burden. They could then concentrate on the groups regarded by their managers as their true clientele; namely, those "honest" families needing only temporary or contingent support. McLean argued that the absence of an official institution for the mentally ill and the incapacitated placed such a heavy burden on the existing institutions that they were incapable of distinguishing among or classifying applicants for relief:

In a community where there is even an almshouse, it is perfectly possible for an old people's home maintained by private funds to exercise discrimination in admitting only the comparatively respectable poor. With no public institution as a place for final refuge, the usual standards have to be done away with. New differentiation and classification are nowhere better illustrated than in private charitable institutions. But place the public burden upon private charity, and these two of its shining excellences are crushed under the weight without at the same time its satisfactorily performing the additional duties. (McLean 1901, 142)[97]

Francophone charities were similarly sensitive to the problem. Starting in the 1890s and throughout the next decade, the liberal paper *La Patrie* campaigned for the city to set up an almshouse:

> In the United States, the unfortunate are not permitted to go hungry; in every city there is a shelter for those who have none. Are we Montrealers insensitive to misery and suffering? We need an almshouse, an asylum to rid the streets of the infirm of all sorts, who beg and display their lamentable misfortune on the pavement. We must offer refuge to the penniless, to those homeless who need a place to eat and sleep. (*La Patrie*, 18 January 1901)

Clearly, the people referenced by such pleas are those who were unable to find refuge in the existing charitable institutions and were reduced to begging on the streets. One finds in this argument an admixture of disdain for the incapacitated and insane, along with pity for these irretrievably disadvantaged souls. It was an attitude thoroughly typical of the philanthropic view of the lumpenproletariat.

> Who are these vagrants, for the most part? The underprivileged, to put it plainly: squalid vagabonds, abandoned women, or workworn and diseased elders who exhibit, nay, who distastefully parade their lamentable destitution, their abject misery, their crying distress along our streets, under the sun or by the light of electric lamps. (*La Patrie*, 4 May 1901)[98]

But there is also, in this position, an implied criticism of religious institutions for their alleged inability – Catholic propaganda notwithstanding – to alleviate all varieties of suffering.

> We know that the charity organizations ... will do whatever they can to provide shelter, food, and fuel to all those who lack them. But will they, with their limited resources, be equal to such a huge and demanding task? Probably not. Is it not time for the municipal authorities to think seriously about doing something for the poor? To date, all the city has done is to jail a number of people who have found themselves homeless, or to offer a few others a night's hospitality in one of our police stations ... Private initiative – the devotion of a class of citizens and a few admirable but insufficiently endowed societies – has thus far been alone in working to alleviate grievous misfortune and desperate poverty ... We would like to see reasonable and even generous provision made for the poor [in the municipal budget].
> (*La Patrie*, 6 December 1907)[99]

Fundamentally, what was at stake went far beyond the insufficiencies of the private welfare system. Looming on the horizon was an embryonic acknowledgment of *societal responsibility* for the poorest citizens.

It is the age of banquets, luncheons, subscriptions – in a word, appeals to public charity. It is the cold season, and the season when work is least plentiful. What these appeals all amount to is public mendicity. They are supplemented by the private mendicity in which the mutual aid societies, the St Vincent de Pauls and so on and so forth, are obliged to engage. Public and private charity both will always exist. But it seems to us that if a different kind of social organization were placed on a firmer footing, on broader and more Christian foundations, we would see fewer of these appeals to private charity, which is indeed their negative side. The state, i.e., the citizenry as a whole, should take better care of the underprivileged, give them larger and more liberal subsidies. (*La Patrie*, 22 December 1904)[100]

A semblance of an almshouse for beggars and destitute citizens did in fact come into existence in 1903. This institution was partially subsidized by the city, although its governance remained strictly private. Not until 1912 did Montreal get a wholly municipal institution, the Refuge Meurling (in fact funded by a private bequest).[101] Apart from such timid and laggard measures and an increase in municipal subsidies toward the end of the decade, very few initiatives were taken to systematize aid to Montrealers living in extreme poverty. Why? Because that was the domain of the Church.

THE CHURCH AND THE CRISIS OF LIBERAL CHARITY

Catholic charity had melded willy-nilly with the liberal system and had come to constitute a deeply conservative version of it. In most Western countries, the Church had cannily reinterpreted some key axioms of liberalism – individual responsibility, private organization of relief, moralistic assessment of personal merit, consolidation of the social fabric through voluntary charity – as religious values. In so doing, it had succeeded in developing a remarkable network of welfare institutions embedded within the society-wide system of free enterprise. In a sense, the turn-of-the-century crisis of liberal regulation, arising as a consequence of workers' and socialist struggles as well as the development of social science, was ipso facto a crisis of religious charity. Increasingly insistent calls for government intervention, strident criticism of private charity, and arguments for better coordination of welfare services were heard. The Church's response took three forms. Initially it reacted vehemently against this criticism, proudly pointing to the extensive institutional infrastructure that it had built up at great expense over the preceding decades. At a second stage, it directed its efforts toward identifying a new basis for Catholic charity. Finally, it began evincing some openness to change, particularly as regards the role of the state.

The Power of the Fait Accompli

December 1899 saw the founding of the Montreal Charity Organization Society, with the enthusiastic support of a sizeable group of mainly anglophone philanthropists.[102] A few weeks earlier, Paul Bruchési, the Archbishop of Montreal, had been asked by Lady Julia Drummond to participate in the association. The bishop responded at once, writing on 20 November: "You know that there is among the Catholics, thanks to the many asylums and hospices directed by our nuns, and to the Societies of St Vincent de Paul, a bona fide network of benevolent works" (*La Patrie*, 22 November 1899).[103]

The bulk of the bishop's reply, however, constituted a stirring plea for keeping the religious principle central to charitable efforts. For this reason, he took issue with a provision of the association's draft by-laws that condemned religious proselytism:

> The concept of charity that I am permitted to infer from your draft differs in its essence from that which inspires and guides us Catholics, in our devotion to the poor. It is one thing to give them bread, clothing, firewood and money – but it is not the only thing. Their moral conduct, the performance of their duties, their return to religion, if they have strayed from it: these things are, in our view, of the highest importance. We make this the object of our zeal – and how can it be achieved if charity is to be kept strictly separate from the religious question, and if it is asserted as a precept that we must keep exclusively to the neutral ground of philanthropy? (*La Patrie*, 22 November 1899)

The Catholic response to the reform aspirations expressed in this instance by a portion of the Montreal elite clearly came from an awareness of the great gains made by Catholic charity in the previous half-century. In Montreal, liberal charity had been deployed along strictly denominational lines, and the result was, on the Catholic side, a remarkably well-organized, hierarchical system that had nothing to envy the Protestant elites' efforts at coordinating their own network.[104]

But resistance to the reformers was also a function of the peculiar features of Catholic charity. Catholic relief rejected the radical distinction often made between the "deserving" poor, the honest working family in difficulty, and what Ames termed (following the example of other authors) the "submerged tenth" of society. For Catholics, beggars represented the most desperate charity cases but not some irredeemable social residue. To reformers obsessed with the potential for dissembling beggars to obtain alms on false pretences, Bruchési responded:

> If we are at times deceived when we give alms, if it happens that we come, in sympathy, to the aid of persons claiming to be poor indigents, there is nothing surprising about it; and all the measures we may put in place will not succeed in shielding our good faith from all deception. (Bruchési to Drummond, *La Patrie*, 21 February 1898)

This vision of aid to beggars had won the day at a debate on the subject held several months earlier at the Union catholique, one of the ultramontane literary associations that proliferated during the latter decades of the century. The recorder, B.-A.T. de Montigny, echoing Bourget's defence of the pauper's freedom, had stated:

> I believe that any law limiting the freedom to beg would be an infringement of social liberty ... Thanks to the institutions which look after the needs of the greatest number of needy, only a very small proportion of the poor hold their hands out to us. Let us be happy, then, to give them the alms and to derive, at this low price, all the benefits resulting from the practice of charity. (*La Patrie*, 21 February 1898)[105]

From here it was but a short step to making the freedom to beg a right – a step readily taken during this debate by the president of the Union catholique, Albert de Lorimier:

> It is indisputable that man has an imprescriptible right to his subsistence. Now, if man has a right to his subsistence, he has a right to alms. And if you are entitled to alms, you are entitled to ask them ... It seems quite clear, then, that one cannot, in principle of sound philosophy, punish the indigent for begging in cases of urgent need, without doing injury to that freedom which is most essential to human life. (*La Patrie*, 22 February 1898)

Catholic charity had set up institutions for the victims of broken or distressed families. The beggar was only the extreme example of this fragility. The alms given to him were complementary, and quite secondary, to the charity systematically provided by the Society of St

Vincent de Paul for families living in their own homes, as well as to the kind of charity that took the form of housing for the homeless. Nothing in this justified ministering to a particular class, albeit the working class, or to a stigmatized fringe of social rejects. This is the solid bedrock upon which Catholic charity would be able to endure through time and changes.

A Renewed Church?

But not all Catholics felt this high degree of satisfaction with the charitable achievements of their church. Some showed awareness of the challenges posed by the crisis of liberalism and by the rise of the most eloquent embodiment of this crisis: a combative labour movement. Could it be, they wondered, that the Church could no longer make do with an ad hoc approach to giving? Some observers argued that the Church should devise a bona fide *agenda* for secular society, one that could provide a suitable response to the aspirations of the working masses:

> The success of socialist ideas does not derive solely from the fact that they flatter the passions ... but they present themselves as a solution, a total system; they respond to the difficulties of the social problem and, albeit impracticably ... put forward a theory that appears as the revelation of a renewed society. We present nothing comparable ... For their part, the economists have a theory, a very simple system: to wit, that liberty which lets each man struggle as best he can and gives him responsibility for his actions under an inflexible law, a law higher than all human schemes. Being what it is, with its appalling inequalities between the worker and the man who puts him to work, this law will never be accepted by the people. I believe in a Christian political economy which is not that of the economists, much less that of the socialists; but nowhere do I see its formulas and its laws. (Armand de Melun to Édouard Le Camus, 25 July 1871, quoted in Duroselle 1951, 656)[106]

The ultramontane church had claimed to be building a community more or less divorced from secular affairs, striving for the transcendence of future salvation. It had left to others the job of structuring people's aspirations for earthly happiness, their hopes for improvement of everyday living conditions. With the *Rerum Novarum* encyclical of 1891, the Church served notice that Catholicism would become not only a transcendent religion but also an agenda for a society centred around the Catholic community. *Rerum Novarum* is the Catholic version of the organic vision of the social that the reformers and the new social sciences were setting up against liberal individualism. In the process, Catholic thought rediscovered natural law and the concept of an inherent right to a social minimum.

> If a family perchance is in such extreme difficulty and is so completely without plans that it is entirely unable to help itself, it is right that the distress be remedied by public aid, for each individual family is a part of the community ... for this is not usurping the rights of citizens, but protecting and confirming them with just and due care. (Catholic Church [1891] 1942, 12)[107]

Ultramontanism's reticence about democracy is of course still evident in this encyclical; note, for example, its corporatist reconfiguration of the principle of political representation[108] as well as the deeply hierarchical, paternalistic worldview running through it:

> Leo XIII's strategy: to show governments that they would do well to collaborate with the Church and its services. Catholic doctrine in fact reinforces the principles of authority and obedience within society. It is the only bulwark of public morals, and hence of the social order, and it opposes egalitarian ideologies by affirming, alongside the equality of all human beings as regards their nature and purpose, the inequality of right and power emanating from the Creator of nature himself ... The people are not directly concerned by a dialogue taking place among the powers responsible for their supervision. (Vaucelles 1995, 194)

Leo XIII's encyclical thus does two things at once: it constitutes a conservative version of the critique of liberalism taking shape from the late nineteenth century onward, and it serves as a formal acknowledgment of the legitimacy of working class needs. It is an ambiguous discourse, in which resignation in the face of the earthbound sinner's unfortunate fate is mixed with hope for material and moral improvement in the lives of the masses. In a series of lectures given by Father François Gohiet in Quebec City to present the *Rerum Novarum* doctrine to workers, this ambiguity is clearly apparent. Poverty, for example, is portrayed as inherent to the human condition:

> And so the elimination of poverty in this world is a vain hope..Yes, there will always be tears, whimperings, misery, disease, sorrow, travails of the heart which nothing can console, at the top of society as at the bottom; and, at the final end, the horror of death! Laud progress as we may, gather useful

inventions, extend the conquests of civilization, nothing will serve: there will always be suffering on earth! ... We can hope for an order of things in which everyone's condition is raised. But is it not wiser to trust in Providence, to inure one's heart to resignation and patience, and to calmly await the Good Lord's heaven? (Gohiet 1892, 56)[109]

But something else is taking shape as well, a foretaste, perhaps, of the earthly happiness that could at least ease the pain of having to wait for the afterlife:

It is desirable, and even legitimate, that even the material happiness of this life shine ever brighter on every human being under the sun ... A modicum of happiness, which of course does not exclude work and hardship, but which gives us the idea that the possession of happiness, that small joy, is possible, we can desire it, seek it, provided that we always govern the tendencies of our souls according to the great maxim of the Gospel: Seek first the Kingdom of Heaven and its justice ... My brothers, unless we be pessimistic, let us admit that it is joy which preponderates and abounds in this life. (Gohiet 1892, 68)

One notable feature of this discourse is how it rehabilitates the state and acknowledges its capacity, indeed its obligation, to intervene to help workers.[110] In his preface to Gohiet's above-cited pamphlet on the labour question and Catholicism, Joseph-Jules Fillâtre, Vice-Rector of the University of Ottawa, exclaimed:

Many have pushed the fear of the state too far, and have denied it the rights necessary to its ends, indeed to its existence. Why should the state not possess the power to punish public abuses of which workers are the perpetrators, or the victims? Why should it not be allowed to protect the weak in this area, as it does in others? (Fillâtre, in Gohiet 1892, 10)[111]

All these factors, then – the expression of an organic vision of society concretized by the grouping of individuals into large associations,[112] the recognition of the collective rights held by the working class, and a renewed openness to corrective intervention by the state – underlay the new inscription of the Church within society. There is in this development a profound continuity with the ultramontane ideal, for the Church is still imagined as an autonomous social body. But this Catholic entity, its gaze turned heavenward, no longer has the luxury to assume its transcendence with respect to the state or modernity. It must increase its hold on the faithful by mobilizing them around social issues essential to the protection of workers. It must also recognize the legitimacy of state regulatory power in this area, and even encourage the use of that power.[113] *Rerum Novarum*'s exhortation to activism will, in the long run, allow the Church to gain a new anchorhold in civil society, in collaboration with the state. The result will be to open up new possibilities in the fight against poverty.

The Quebec Charitable Network: The Beginnings of a Social Policy?

What was the real impact of *Rerum Novarum* in Quebec? The text of the encyclical admits that its effects would not likely be felt for a number of years, and one is indeed struck by the limited extent of Quebec initiatives indicating that the message had been heard – that the Church was becoming open to social intervention on behalf of workers. The most frequently cited examples are Archbishop of Quebec Louis-Nazaire Bégin's mediation in the 1900 shoemakers' strike and the founding of the Workers' Federation of Chicoutimi and Marie Gérin-Lajoie's Fédération nationale Saint-Jean-Baptiste (Hébert 1997).[114]

The dense network of Catholic welfare institutions was indeed experiencing tensions, but they had very little to do with *Rerum Novarum* and its new social ideology. The hierarchy and relief staff were too busy at the parish level to pay much attention to these lofty sentiments. If there were tensions, they flowed from the fact that Catholic charity was insufficiently endowed (largely by sporadic donations from wealthy individuals) and in danger of being overwhelmed by the burgeoning demand for relief. The provincial government and municipalities were, for their part, only too happy to let the Church shoulder most of the welfare burden, including the direst cases, and this exacerbated the problem.

Thus it is not surprising to find an increasing number of voices issuing pragmatic calls for state intervention. It is not so much a discourse promoting systematic protection of workers by the state as it is an appeal from the existing institutions for help from the authorities. Already, in the cases of mental illness, child welfare, and juvenile delinquency, the state was systematically funding the housing of these populations in institutions managed, in the overwhelming majority of cases, by religious communities. Even some of the most radical ultramontane elements expressed – in private, at any rate – their approval of increased state intervention. Father Villeneuve, for example, confided to a French friend:

that the Canadian clergy was losing its social influence because it remained too far behind the current ... He said that the Canadian worker is content, that he lives in a comfortable house. But he wanted to see official charity in Canada, in the same way that it exists in the United States. The state, he said, should look after all cases of urgent distress, drawing up a list of the sums spent on this and, at year's end, being reimbursed by the wealthy. Thus are the selfish rich – concluded Villeneuve, speaking bluntly – forced to give to the poor. (Georges Goyau to Jean Brunhes and his brothers, 19 April 1893, quoted in Poulat 1977, 142)[115]

As the city of Montreal increased the budget allocated to support charitable institutions, certain clergy members were quick to stress the advantages of such funding. In 1910, this position gained influential support from Monseigneur Bruchési:

Everywhere, in all civilized countries, three great works occupy governments and public corporations. And these three works are those of material progress, education, and philanthropy. The obligations incurred for the support of these three works are, moreover, spread out over all the citizens ... Could it be that care for the poor and the sick, the foundling, and the orphan are not worthy of our attention? If we want to be just, we will do what is done everywhere else – in Saint-Boniface, Baltimore, or New York, for example ... Here, our various institutions, with their exceptionally economical methods, make do with fifteen cents a day per patient. By providing for our charitable works, the distasteful habit of panhandling would be eliminated wherever our nuns are found. (Bruchési, quoted in *La Patrie*, 29 December 1910)[116]

Thus, at the turn of the twentieth century, a novel collaborative arrangement was coming into view, in which the state acted as the funding agency and the Church as the administrator of institutional charity. Further to preliminary steps taken by the City of Montreal,[117] this major compromise became an enduring fact with the Public Assistance Act of 1921.

* * *

In conclusion, the Western approach to poverty that materialized in the nineteenth century partook of the liberal logic of regulation and led to a profound depoliticization of the social question at mid-century. Social inequalities, most blatantly poverty, were accepted as the ineluctable horizon of modern societies. At the same time, they represented an essential spur to individual initiative. In the liberal ethos, poverty was said to manifest itself as a sporadic reflection of the precariousness of life in liberal society. When it took the extreme form of pauperism, those affected could seek refuge in special institutions. Confinement therein became a stigma, and also a sign that the individuals in question were unfit, incapacitated, and/or failing to thrive in society. In keeping with this logic, most Western states implemented a national or municipal system to take care of extreme poverty and left the administration of ad hoc charity to the workings of civil society.

Religious charity constituted a particularly interesting variant of this economy of charity – not a rejection of it, as some might assume. When the administration of "ordinary" poverty became the province of civil society, a broad, infrapolitical arena of intervention opened up, to be occupied by whatever organizations had the capacity to deliver public assistance successfully. The Catholic Church, its fervour heightened by ultramontane militancy, stepped confidently into the breach. But in doing so, it appropriated the reconstruction of the social fabric implied by the act of charity for its own ends. The charitable dimension of social relations was thus re-embedded into a strategy of community-building centring around religious faith and rooted in the privileged space of the parish. No wonder, then, that attempts to repoliticize the social question, to mobilize the public authorities in support of society's most destitute citizens, would meet with fierce resistance not only from liberals but also from the religious elites. The "freedom to help" acquired by the churches under the system of liberal regulation was not to be relinquished without a fight. At a deeper level, however, all of society's elites, whether religious or secular, saw eye to eye on how welfare should be administered. There might be programmatic differences between Catholic charity and secular philanthropy; there might even be fierce ideological rivalry between the theocratic ideal of the ultramontanes and the libertarian agenda of radical liberalism. One side might deplore the putative impotence of an ideal of civic philanthropy in which religion is only a tool for instilling moral conduct and not a supreme objective; the other might express fears that religious charity would be used as a pretext for proselytism. But both sides agreed that poverty is not a condition but a transitory state, a manifestation of the natural inequalities found in any society, and that it is all too often a consequence of rashness or vice. And this meant that the poor, whether seen as members of a spiritual community or of the polity, had only one option when reeling from life's blows: to appeal to the charity of the rich, be it meted out by philanthropists or nuns.

Throughout the West, religious charity would find the means to prosper on the fertile soil of liberal values. Only at the end of the nineteenth century was the liberal model to undergo the shock of what must be described as a radical repoliticization of the social question, with the collective needs of the working class garnering broad if often timid support and workers' organizations stepping up their agitation for change. At that point, both liberal philanthropy and religious charity had to adapt their methods to reckon with a welter of legislative provisions enacted for the protection of the working class: old-age pensions, medical coverage, workers' compensation, mother and child welfare policies, unemployment insurance, public hygiene measures, and early attempts at worker housing policies. As to the people considered unfit, incapable, or deficient, those who lived in dire poverty and were ignored by social solidarity, confinement and exclusion (softened to a minimal degree by medicalization) would continue to be their lot.

The Quebec case veers away from this historical narrative in two deeply complementary respects. First, the Catholic Church capitalized on the enactment of official religious freedom in the province to build a remarkable network of institutions founded on both parish-level sociability and the work of the rapidly expanding religious orders. Spurred on by the spectre of Protestant proselytism and by its own ultramontane tendency, the Church managed not only to wield increasingly tight control over the Catholic faith community but also to isolate its members from the wider society by imposing a strict confessional logic on the institutions from which they received basic social and educational services. The Church, having succeeded in forging a religious identity out of the tattered remains of the French Canadian national identity left behind by the Rebellions of 1837–38, was able to consolidate a tight-knit Catholic spiritual community under its leadership.

The radical division of civil society along confessional lines would have been impossible without a second essential factor: the weakness of the colonial state. Even after the establishment of responsible government in 1848, most policy measures were heavily influenced by pervasive ethnic and regional tensions, impeding the construction of a general polity. Confederation concentrated the tools of economic policy in the hands of the federal government, but at the cost of devolving social policy responsibilities to provincial governments that often lacked the resources to take them on. In 1867, the rapidly expanding Catholic Church stood face to face with a provincial government only too happy to entrust many of its regulatory powers to a body with a proven track record in the area of charity.

As a result, the Church – often to the great chagrin of the Protestant elites – successfully consolidated its dominion over much of the province's social welfare system. The notable fact here is not the diversity and breadth of the charitable initiatives undertaken under its auspices, for similar vibrancy was observable in most Western states. Rather, it was that the Church succeeded in occupying the *lion's share* of the charitable field; the state being unable, or lacking the political will, to develop a parallel secular system. And by the turn of the century, when governments in the West were finally ready to implement progressive social policy, it was too late for Quebec. The Church had near-total control over social welfare. Spurred on by its new social doctrine, it was now reaching out to the working class on its own terms, outside the scope of state influence. The extreme timidity of the social measures undertaken by the Quebec government,[118] along with its systematic refusal to enact or even debate the great social laws passed in Europe and certain American states – and perhaps even more importantly, the extremely weak reform animus on the part of certain Quebec liberals – greatly enhanced the Church's capacity for organized resistance.

When Quebec, like other governments, finally reached the point where the public coffers had to be tapped for systematic welfare provision, nothing better could be found than the Public Assistance Act of 1921, which provided majority public funding for the Church's charities and left the administration thereof in its hands. This is how a paradox too seldom mentioned by our historiography, obsessed as it is with religious conservatism, found expression: to wit, that it was the remarkable resilience of religious charity that allowed for a profoundly liberal form of poverty regulation to subsist in Quebec, long after the heyday of this model was past. Cozily sheltered from incursions by the nascent welfare state, it would endure for much of the twentieth century.

Conclusion

A set of basic hypotheses underlies the analysis I have undertaken in this book, and it is now time to make their implications explicit. Crime, poverty, even Quebec, have only served as pretexts (or a chosen field) for addressing a question of great import: in what sense can it be said that the epochal aspirations to freedom awakened by the democratic revolutions of the late eighteenth and early nineteenth centuries were in fact fulfilled, yet at the same time asphyxiated? The revolutions had led men and women to believe in a future in which space and time might, if only partially, come under their control; in which horizons of possibility would open up to a hitherto unequalled extent; in which societies would be regulated *by* freedom, not in spite of it.

Anyone wishing to explore this question must take a careful look at how freedom was enacted in the burgeoning nineteenth-century societies, what that freedom entailed, and the various modes according to which it was envisioned. Furthermore, if one is to take the measure of freedom's influence as an idea, one must analyze how societies putatively founded on the bedrock of freedom dealt with the age-old societal dysfunctions of crime and poverty, for an understanding of these phenomena can delimit and define the version of social harmony that was desired at any given historical juncture – by mapping out its negative space, as it were. Starting from that fundamental analysis, this book has gone on to look at what it teaches us specifically about the history of Quebec.

FREEDOM AS HORIZON AND LIMIT

Another important observation must be made when attempting to answer this question. I contend that we must cease to regard liberalism as bounded within the narrow, well-structured confines of an ideology, even a dominant one – even an ideology said to have extended its hold over Western minds until it reached an apotheosis in the late nineteenth century. Liberalism was not just an intellectual product selected from among a range of options made available by democracy and the free market of ideas. The nineteenth century, in the aftermath of the Revolutions, gave us liberalism as a kind of universal language or common sense,[1] a set of basic values that was to form the foundation of societies to come. Individual freedom became a cultural substrate that could underlie a wide array of interpretations, generate a web of mutually irreconcilable aspirations, and accommodate a great variety of readings of the past (as premises for an argument about the present and the future). Freedom replaced an older substrate composed of radically different ideals – honour, deference to authority, hereditary status, distrust of the unknown – that had underlain the societies of the past.

When, under the impetus of Enlightenment ideas, the Revolutions sent the old world hurtling into a logic of free markets and democracy, they opened the Pandora's box of an indeterminate future, a future subordinate to reason and the desires of men and women. In the process, they gave scarily concrete form to the notion that the configuration of future societies would be beholden to those desires – an idea that indeed became the ethical foundation of the world under construction. The self – a harmonious whole arising organically out of the construction of one's memory, the tangle of one's personal aspirations, and the unhindered exploitation of one's talents and inclinations – was a brand-new idea that gained near-universal acceptance. Even more incredibly, it was now generally accepted that the aggregate of all these freely constructed selves might unite in solidarity, forming a virtuous and coherent collective. The freedoms enjoyed by individuals, when conjugated in the plural, would actually *constitute* society.

It is this aspiration, made thinkable by the Revolutions, that I have termed liberalism. For make no mistake: if any name was to be given to the motive force behind this sudden upwelling of human possibilities, this desire to build the new world, that name had to be liberty. With the defeat of arbitrary rule, domination, and dependency, freedom formed and delimited an as-yet empty space in which people could develop initiatives, express desires, act according to their wishes and, in general, mark the passage of time with their own imprint.

The primacy of freedom was accompanied by a new relationship to self and Other in which the individual capacity of willing would take centre stage. From now on it would be generally acknowledged that the decisions and acts that shape our world, that impel it in a given direction, emanate from something other than fate, force of circumstance, conformity to tradition, or the will of the gods. So overwhelmingly was this the case that even the most extreme recalcitrance to change, the most reactionary shrinking away from the implications of freedom, could only be expressed in the terms of freedom itself. History may grope toward the future, but it never goes into reverse. Conservatives were no different from radicals in that, if they wished to put limits on freedom or apply it to different ends, they had to present this agenda in terms that could rally their fellow citizens to the cause. The whole history of nineteenth-century conservatism and its various tendencies is one of an ideology attempting to survive and even evolve by devising a present and a future attractive to the many. The same is true, moreover, for those restless ideologies whose futuristic utopias reflected unbounded confidence in a form of freedom that could come about only through the action of all members of society. The nineteenth-century socialisms, whether utopian or scientific, were extravagant expressions of confidence in the future of the individual, and they succeeded – even better than a certain species of liberalism – in grasping the power of collective action, the common will, the idea of "all for one and one for all."

But the aspiration – the fundamental reflex, the deep-seated belief – embodied by the idea of freedom had to be materialized in a particular form of social organization. Of all the possibilities opened up by the Revolutions, liberal democracy and free competition in goods and ideas were to achieve undisputed hegemony. The process whereby freedom was materialized and organized has its own historicity, a history punctuated by radical disruptions. As a result, the ideal of freedom would gradually be tainted with social fear before thoroughly succumbing to it.

What the history of ideas has called (economic or political) "liberalism" is in reality an unstable, equivocal, constrained version of the ideal of freedom. Taken up as a cause by the bourgeois elites and their petty bourgeois allies, this version of liberalism succeeded in acquiring the institutional forms necessary to shore up and perpetuate its hegemony. It co-opted and diverted people's aspirations to freedom by decreeing the individual to be the sole driving force of progress, and hence the future.

Bourgeois liberalism set the individual will, and individual responsibility, within an institutional and normative context, prescribing the operative modalities of individual action and the limits within which it was to be contained. This enterprise necessitated the existence of a specific economy of individual interaction. In opposition to the Enlightenment-derived notion of uninterrupted complementarity between the individual will and the polity represented by the state, the task at hand was to place limits on the state, and hence on the possibilities for concerted action that it offered. This form of liberalism went further in that it rediscovered the virtues of pessimism: it learned to be wary of the future opened up by freedom.

The revolutions of the first half of the nineteenth century constituted a decisive turning point in this regard. They forced bourgeois liberalism to scale back its aspirations to freedom. Liberalism had to come to grips with the idea that even under a democracy, with the arbitrary exercise of royal power a thing of the past, nothing guaranteed that the collectivity would always coalesce as a virtuous amalgam of freely expressed political wills. Bad outcomes were also possible, due to the perverse effects of personal ambition, or frequentation with those harbouring incorrect ideas. This was the genesis of the core ambivalence of bourgeois liberalism that remains with us today. It is forever torn between the tenacious libertarian aspirations of its most radical elements and the fearfulness of its moderates.[2]

In short, the restrictive interpretive framework for the idea of freedom – the interpretation favoured by bourgeois liberalism – acquired hegemony. This framework in effect constituted an ethic of coexistence centring around the rights and duties of the individual, and governed by a suite of rules expressed in the terms of both law and ethics (the legal framework alone was insufficient). Once a mode of social regulation centring around the space allotted for the deployment of freedom had been established, it remained to devise a form of interpersonal relating guided by generally accepted ethical precepts and lying outside the realm of individual choice. By this route, the question of ethics, and thereby of religion, became a central problem of liberalism.

To put it differently, the liberal revolution entailed a new ethical relationship to transcendence. Religion as a dynamic of mandatory obedience to authority was, to be sure, a thing of the past; it no longer stood as the transcendent version of conformity to an established order. But, when seen through the filter of freedom, it could take the form of a commitment, an investment of the will giving out onto a lucid allegiance. Faith was an act of consent, and consent could always be withdrawn.[3] On this subject, Henri-Dominique Lacordaire wrote:

> The Church must be free because it issues from God and has its seat deep within the human conscience, where a power other than liberty itself cannot

penetrate violently without attacking God and man in their nature and relations ... The liberty of the Church is that of the soul, the liberty of the soul that of the world. (Lacordaire (1861), quoted in Bedouelle 1992, 38)[4]

But religion is also an institution that structures belief according to a hierarchical system. God is not just the reason for the existence of a faith: God is also its lawgiver, its source of authority. It was hard, if not impossible, to reconcile the imperatives of religious authority with the fact that one was no longer obliged to submit to that authority: that all faith was now voluntary. Ultramontanism was the ultimate response to the challenge faced by religious faith under liberalism. The ultramontanes did, of course, noisily proclaim their rejection of a society founded on freedom of choice and autonomy, but their militant attempts to rally people to the conservative cause of inner reform themselves betrayed a keen awareness of the fact of liberty – for if it had been possible to coerce people into religion, as in former times, such militancy would have been obviated.

Irrespective of the specific ways in which religion was embedded within the liberal mode of regulation (and these differed from one Western social formation to another), this embedding always took place according to the terms and values of liberal politics (and economics) as institutionalized in law and the state. In this specific sense, ultramontanism was not and could not aspire to the status of an agenda for society. At best it was a counter-agenda set reluctantly but inexorably within the social logic of liberalism, and within a civil society orchestrated and structured by that logic.

The liberal mode of regulation faced a major challenge in the last quarter of the century. To be sure, liberal values had become the common language of elite domination, and it is unsurprising to find them comfortably ensconced in the discourse of entrepreneurs and the petty bourgeoisie. But this hegemony was increasingly looking like an idée fixe. As bourgeois liberalism became rigidified and normalized by time and social fear, it took on the cast of a conservative leitmotif more than a language of liberation and progress. The critique of liberalism had given rise to other discourses centring around the rediscovery of the collective; those of the new social sciences, for example, or of government officials increasingly confident that they represented that part of the nation irreducible to a profusion of individualities.[5] The perceived "crisis of liberalism" put back on the agenda an idea of societal reform based on collective organization. The notions of the individual, of formal equality, and of the moral fibre that cements individual liberties were all thrown into doubt:

> It no longer suffices to tell someone: you shall not set foot on your neighbour's domain, for the question is precisely to define that domain; and it no longer suffices to profess that all men are equal, for what matters now is to know what that equality consists of, what are its conditions and whether they have been realized ... Morality, without ceasing to be individual – since what is morally good remains what is good for an individual – becomes a social thing, when considered in what is specific to it; in other words, it always encompasses a relationship to someone other than oneself. (Delprat 1908, 104)

At stake is a major realignment of the modes of insertion of the individualist ethic into the collectivity. This process would shake classical liberalism to its foundations, and lead to its demise.

CRIME AND POVERTY: PERSONAL MORALS AND COLLECTIVE CHALLENGES

Why, in a history of freedom as restricted by elite liberalism, have I given pride of place to the social phenomena of crime and poverty? Primarily because beyond what they tell us about individuals and their lives, the persistence of these two phenomena throughout the nineteenth century engendered a collective malaise. True, people had long been disturbed by the tear in the social fabric that these phenomena represented; but the malaise had been exacerbated by the great revolutions. Shouldn't the horizons opened up by freedom have led to a society in which crime was an aberration, poverty a disgrace? And didn't the fact that this hadn't happened point to a distressing gap between the ideal of freedom and its bourgeois liberal version? Certainly, the dysfunctions that still plagued society could no longer be set down to the old despotisms. The blame had to be laid on the imperfect society of the present, and hence on the broken promise of freedom. The resulting anger turned crime and poverty into political problems.

The anti-poverty policies implemented by the French revolutionaries had been the first manifestation of this concern. The thinkers of the following generation, too, had been unanimous in holding that crime and poverty cry out for state intervention,[6] especially since these problems pointed to the people's abject failure to conform to the imperatives and implications of freedom. The philanthropists mobilized around the challenge of reining in the persistence of vice, and their efforts gave rise to the early penitentiaries and other forms of asylum, in whose administration the state would play a predominant role.[7]

The bourgeois liberalism of the mid-nineteenth century arose *in opposition to* this tendency. On the strength of its acceptance of individual freedom and the full implications thereof, this strain of liberalism criticized the reformist ambitions of the philanthropists and their later drift toward advocacy of state intervention. It also moved to depoliticize the issues of crime and poverty to a remarkable extent. The process took place in two stages. In the first, these phenomena were individualized, interpreted as fortuitous and largely personal occurrences. As such, each was the responsibility of the individual concerned. Taken together, they did not amount to a societal problem around which the community as a whole, and the state representing it, ought to rally, but an essentially contingent aggregate that could best be addressed by targeted measures. In the second stage, a clear line was drawn between the two phenomena. Previously, philanthropic thinkers in the nascent democratic societies had tended to consider them complementary symptoms of a single, large-scale social dysfunction. They worried about a societal pathology whose etiology began in the major industrial centres and would eventually spread to the masses as a whole, if nothing were done. By contrast, the regulatory economy of mid-century liberalism dictated that the two phenomena be differentiated.

Crime, as a personal rejection of the norm, was ultimately nothing more than a sporadic avatar of the nefarious use of human freedom. As such, it could be punished by the law and hence by the state that administered it. All that was needed was to restructure the penal apparatus (police, courts, prisons) to incorporate punishment into a formal, systematic procedure codified by the criminal law. The idea of reform faded away, to be replaced by a managerial logic of crime epitomized by the widespread use of imprisonment.

Poverty was another outcome of freedom; however, it did not stem from wicked intentions, but rather from a deficiency of good intentions. Poverty denoted a temporary or even a chronic state in which individuals unable to make proper use of their freedom found themselves. Even in its most involuntary forms (illness, accident, infirmity, childhood, old age, etc.), poverty hinted at personal weakness, for while such situations might be unavoidable, they were said to cause poverty only in people unwilling or unable to make provision for them, whether individually or within the family nucleus. Poverty was thus a problematic occurrence flowing from the normal operational logic of civil society.

This normalization of crime and poverty did not rule out the possibility of state intervention. With their political dimensions expunged, these phenomena could very well be targeted with public funding in cases where civil society (including private charity) proved powerless or insufficient. Their most extreme manifestations – often attributed to a population that would be perpetually marginalized by attaching a stigma to it – could be entrusted to the care of the public administration (often at the municipal level). In this role, the state discharged a charitable function, filling in for private charity when it fell short, and for civil society when its capacity for self-regulation gave out. Tocqueville called this function "Christianity applied to politics."[8]

This liberal dynamic was the precondition for religious charity to spread its wings on an unprecedented scale in the nineteenth century. Once the duty of charity was largely confined to the sphere of private relations, nothing prevented charity from being organized along lines of force already present in civil society. The solidly structured churches, with their self-appointed role as guardians of the people's moral uprightness, proved well suited to this role. The Catholic Church would prove especially adept at using its newfound freedom to position charity as a central component of its rootedness in temporal affairs. The social space opened up to it (and to secular forms of philanthropy as well) was inversely proportional to the intensity of state intervention in these areas. Moreover, there was close coordination or even conjunction between religious charity and the public administration in most Western countries.

At century's end, this penal and charitable model came in for profound reconsideration. Phenomena such as crime and poverty could not elude the explanatory ambitions of the new social sciences. Criminology "discovered" the criminal personality, just as sociology penetrated the mysteries of chronic unemployment and precarious employment. Certain instances of these phenomena came to be regarded as specific, empirically observable pathologies rather than matters of morality or personal responsibility. Liberal penality and its individualist/voluntarist reading of societal dysfunctions fell into increasing disrepute.

The notion of proportionate sentencing, for example – the intimate causal connection posited between a nefarious act and a set of deserved consequences – was essentially meaningless to a science that held crime to be a pathology. Similarly, the individualist explanation of poverty could not stand up to a sociological analysis of working and living conditions among the masses. While the administration of crime was relatively impermeable to reformist designs (except in the case of juvenile offenders), the administration of poverty was a very different story. Private charity, itself increasingly "scientific,"[9] was joined by a suite of social policies directed largely at the working class: old-age pensions, unemployment insurance, placement, workers' compensation, medical care and hospitalization, worker housing. As Western governments found themselves under pressure from workers' organizations and from working-class voters who had recently acquired the franchise, the social question became thoroughly repoliticized.[10]

But the working class would not make these gains without giving something in return; specifically, its members would bear the brunt of large-scale efforts to render them "morally fit" to participate in society. How else to explain the rise of temperance and prohibition campaigns, the increasing interference by the apostles of morality in intra-familial relations, the systematic criminalization of behaviour formerly tolerated, and the activism of religious groups among the poor (the Protestant social gospel, Catholic social teaching), if not in terms of a felt imperative to revitalize the nation by inculcating public morals? After the liberal interlude came a rebirth of early nineteenth-century reform ideals and aspirations, but in a wider context in which ascendant science and bureaucracy gave good Samaritans unprecedented opportunities to interfere in working-class lives.

Furthermore, there was a limit to what the working class could expect from this effervescence of social laws. The new social state was not a welfare state, and it would not answer all needs in the same way, nor would it give them the same level of priority. "Progressive" social measures were out of the question – especially for that mass of persons considered unfit, deficient, and/or delinquent who made up what contemporaneous commentators got in the habit of calling the "residuum." The campaign of moral uplift gave notice that the state's new solicitude would be premised on adherence to the "bourgeois" rules of life in society: concerning hygiene, the obligation to look for and hold a job, proper childrearing, a decent and sober family life, and so on. In this way, the social contract with the working masses was redefined to include those persons able to follow the rules. Beyond the bounds of this well-adjusted group sat a host of misfits, who were entrusted to the care of institutions of last resort. Eugenics came along at this juncture to lend a semblance of scientific backing to this exclusion of the losers in the game of regulation.

THE SPECIAL CASE OF QUEBEC

How can the Quebec experience be situated with respect to the analysis presented thus far? As much as anywhere in the West, the United Province of Canada (Quebec's predecessor jurisdiction) came under the hegemony of liberalism, with its implications for the administration of poverty and crime. The historical transition to democratic capitalism cannot be explained as a post hoc composite of autonomous national experiences which, taken together, amount to an international trend. On the contrary, the principles and values of liberalism formed the pre-existing point of reference for all such societies, the through-line of their lived experience – including both their ideological debates and their institutional trajectory. It is time to stop the obsessive search for traces of the influence of a particular set of ideas, and to avoid the tendency to gauge their importance by the number of instances we find. Liberalism was not a product exported from one nineteenth-century Western society to another: it was the foundational logic of all these societies. Even the most cursory study of a set of political, economic, and cultural institutions, or of the discourses used to justify them, reveals the DNA of liberalism. Thus, my purpose has not been to "prove" the existence of liberal hegemony, but at best to comprehend the specific forms taken by this hegemony in Quebec.

The Catholic Church has been a formidable presence in Quebec's history, where its central role – most notably in the fields that are this study's concern – is manifest and undeniable. It was long the fashion to blame the Church for what was construed as Quebec's fraught transition to modernity. In much of our historiography, and in our collective memory especially, the grand period of Church domination from 1840 to 1960 is still viewed as a lengthy cryogenesis, a century during which the early stirrings of British-styled democracy were put on ice, not to be unthawed until the sudden arrival of modernity with the Quiet Revolution. A popular recent version thinks it has descried a backward conservatism in our elites, contrasting sharply with a Quebec working class open to the four winds of modernity. In another historical account, Catholic hegemony is served up with a revisionist sauce. Here the modernization of Quebec's institutions is said to have triumphed over the opposition of the Church's conservative tendencies, in spite of everything they arrayed against it. As a result of these positions, little has been done to evaluate how Quebec's affair with religion might have affected our history – so relieved are we to be reconciled with the "normality" of our modernization process.[11]

I take an intermediate position here. It is true that the Church's control of the Quebec charitable network was far from an indication that the province had rejected modernity. It was a specific modality of the liberal economy of charity. Only at this price could the Church solidify its hold over Quebec for the long term. But it would be deeply erroneous to deduce that the Church was just a passive channel for the implementation of the liberal logic of regulation, more or less in spite of itself. Quite the contrary, its exceptionally strong presence in this field served to strengthen that logic; conversely, the logic both preceded and helped perpetuate the domination of the Church. Solidly entrenched as it was, it was able to fend off any ideological forces or initiatives that might have attempted to alter this logic in the twentieth century.

The remarkable thing about what the Catholic Church achieved in Quebec is not how massively it rallied the people's allegiance, nor how successful and varied its enterprises were, nor even how it managed to cultivate an intense religious practice and a vibrant parish social life among the faithful. After all, many national churches did just as well, and on an even grander scale. No, what is notable and probably specific or even unique about the Church in Quebec[12] is the remarkably long-lasting control and influence it achieved. The Church must be studied in relation not only to what it accomplished but also to what other bodies were unable to accomplish because of its capacity to obstruct their efforts. It did not just blanket Quebec with hospitals, hospices, orphanages, and asylums – it took on the coordination, administration, and development of this web of institutions and did so with the knowing complicity, or perhaps the passive impotence, of the government. Moreover, it did not remain idle in the face of the many institutional and intellectual innovations arising out of the crisis of liberalism at the turn of the twentieth century: instead, it coopted and replicated them after its own fashion. Catholic social teaching allowed for the creation of near-exact replicas of structures and movements originating elsewhere (e.g., youth movements, leisure activities, charitable initiatives), often with a very short time lag. But this capacity to act and react was not merely mimetic. It also amounted to an immense power to impede or hinder the work of other bodies. Most often, the Church managed to eliminate or avert what it was unable to imitate or reproduce on its own terms.[13]

As should be clear, this hypothesis leads us directly to politics. Church domination was largely made possible by the peculiar political configuration of Quebec (and Canada), which gave the Church a unique position as regards the regulation of society. A brief explanation follows.

It is of the essence of the political sphere in a democracy to create a basic civic identity at a national scale. This identity constitutes the fundamental allegiance of every individual to the polity to which she belongs. Such a shared allegiance is the barest precondition for any entity to be conceived of as having a legitimate power of constraint over citizens. It is also at the root of power delegation and decision-making processes that allow the polity to organize itself in space and time. Of course, there can and must exist multiple forms of grouping, allegiance, and identity in a social formation: on the basis of ethnicity, gender, race, language, religion, or simply the desire to assemble around a certain activity or project. In this way, the expression of "natural" affinities or common desires serves to structure an identity, to collectively organize a belief system, to pursue an intention, or to fulfill an agenda. The political (or national) identity subsumes and transcends all these "partial" identities – not because it is more important, but by reason of its constituting a primary form of coexistence, capable of imposing its authority and even proscribing other forms of association or belonging within a given political space. This is why the democratic and liberal thinkers of the mid-nineteenth century were so distrustful of forms of association having the potential to supplant or predominate over political allegiance. Examples in Quebec would include Lord Durham's denunciation of ethnic conflict, George Brown's fear of religious power, and the government's enduring mistrust of secret societies (Fecteau 1991).

The history of Canada, and hence Quebec, is that of an unstable polity, one that could neither be built out of an ethnically homogeneous population nor transcend the diversity of ethnicities, as most Western nation-building movements of the time succeeded in doing. On the contrary, the Canadian polity could be built only by making major concessions to the partial identities whose persistence stood to impede or even halt the construction of the nation. In this connection, the political agenda of the Patriotes of Lower Canada – rejection of domination by any one religion or language – constituted a sound basis for a democratic national identity transcending all others. The Patriotes' failure was all the more disastrous for Canada's political future.

With the Act of Union of 1840, the arduous process of building a Canadian polity would come up against ethnic allegiances (e.g., bloc voting by francophone members of the Lower Canadian House of Assembly), and then the solidification of the confessional divide, particularly in the area of social services. The 1852–54 debate over charitable institutions pointed up the ambivalence, and ultimately the powerlessness of the legislators to overcome the strength of these partial identities. Confederation confirmed this political weakness by attempting to concentrate the impact of these partial identities at the periphery of the political system. The establishment of two levels of government served to centralize the powers most important to the regulation of the whole country while allowing for the expression of particularist allegiances at the provincial and municipal levels. The Fathers of Confederation hoped to check the social tensions engendered by ethnic and religious identity by placing private law, education, and a large part of the penal and charitable apparatus under provincial jurisdiction. The desired result was to dilute the federal-level impact of these tensions, or at least to allow these different local identities to counterbalance one another.

What in fact resulted was a set of provincial governments with curtailed power and weakened political legitimacy vis-à-vis the federal government, and largely at the mercy of the powerful ethnic and religious stakeholders existing on their territories. The Church seized the extraordinary opportunity offered by this political compromise. It capitalized on its already remarkable capacity for action to impose a strictly confessional approach to the resolution of social tensions, thus freeing the state (which wanted nothing better) of the heavy burden generally shouldered by public agencies elsewhere in the West, or at least significantly weakening its managerial capacity. The circumstances surrounding the inception of the reform and industrial schools in 1869 are a good example of this process, as is the abolition of the Ministry of Public Instruction in favour of a strictly confessional body in 1875. The Church even managed, a year later, to move into the penal administration (taking over the management of the women's prison), and soon the insane asylums (with the exception of the Protestant asylum in Verdun). As much as one might make of the opposition of certain radical liberals, nothing in the liberal conception of the regulation of social problems could prevent such a development – after all, the Church was as much a part of "civil society" as any other institution.

The Church, not content to multiply its charitable initiatives as elsewhere in the West, soon acquired a de facto monopoly over the charitable network (and the educational system as well).[14] The result was the near-total absence of the provincial government from the administration (if not the funding) of such initiatives.[15] Francis McLean's 1901 remonstrance (discussed in chapter 7) is as remarkable as it is revealing: he saw clearly that the situation in Quebec, in which the Church vigorously defended its monopoly on charity, deprived the poor of the public institutions and services that so many of them desperately needed. Acting alone, the Church did an inadequate and incomplete job, for despite its power and capacity for action, it did not possess the state's resources. It had to rely on the fluctuating fortunes of the religious communities, as well as the good will of the parishioners who ultimately funded these institutions through their alms and bequests.[16]

The result is utterly striking. Even the municipalities, which played a major role throughout the West in the administration of acute cases of poverty, were practically absent from this field in Quebec. The failure of Montreal's non-denominational house of industry project in the 1860s, combined with the city's contemporaneous refusal to build a house of correction, exemplify this glaring absence. Only in the early twentieth century would Montreal attempt to cover lost ground. As to the provincial government, it did provide substantial funding for certain institutions (asylums, reform and industrial schools), but it left them under the control of the religious communities. Government oversight was limited to routine inspection of publicly funded institutions in a manner that proved highly non-intrusive, not to say indulgent of aberrations. As to the rest of the network, it would be forced to make do with paltry subsidies throughout the entire period under study. The men's jail, especially in Montreal, became the default institution for the housing of chronic paupers, functioning essentially as a workhouse. This situation would be criticized for over seventy-five years before anything was done about it. Not until Montreal received a large bequest from a rich foreigner (Gustave Meurling) was a public refuge (nights only) opened in 1912 (Aranguiz 2000).

Along the same lines, the Church and the subservient local elites successfully opposed any and every attempt to "modernize" social policy, especially where it concerned worker protection and welfare – even though such policy, as enacted elsewhere, helped further the integration of the working class into the nation. In Quebec, the Church succeeded to a great extent in blocking this politicization of the social. The remarkable result was that the Church in Quebec – often more Catholic than the Pope – was also to be more liberal than the most extreme liberal denigrators of the interventionist state. Bourgeois liberalism, whose declaration of freedom of religion had ejected the Church from its Gallican past, also made possible its expansion in the heart of civil society. Liberalism would be its constant ally – even the banner under which it rallied – in the fight against expanded state intervention in social affairs.

The Church contributed to the deepening and widening of the political void in which it was ensconced. It fostered the formation of a religious identity largely congruent with the ethnic dividing lines of Quebec.[17] This community of faith and language, in addition to building its own organizational structures, superimposed itself on the polity. It engulfed civil society by confessionalizing a good part of its institutions and went on to promote a surrogate identity designed to rally the Catholic community, to mark out a future and a destiny for its members outside the political sphere. The Church, that is, successfully *transcended the political*. It made its community of faith, bolstered by a shared language, the main repository for society's aspirations – all this in a political context that was witnessing the simultaneous deployment of democratic institutions.

And the poor in all this? What became of them? They were integrated into a strictly controlled, hierarchical community of faith, and cared for as full-fledged members of that community. The Church never accepted the idea of a "residuum," an outer fringe of society in which poverty became grounds for civic exclusion. It was a membership-based community that rejected no one, as Bishop Bourget had recalled in his pastoral letter of 1862 (Bourget 1862). The Catholic charitable institutions thus came to act as a surrogate and a support for working families who fell into temporary or chronic poverty. These higher-level structures complemented the parish-level solidarity epitomized by the conferences of Saint Vincent de Paul and the Ladies of Saint Anne. Unlike the poor under the liberal model, particularly those who formed the residuum, the Catholic poor were incorporated into a community logic that afforded them partial protection. This safety net was the great strength and main justification of the Catholic institutions, which thus enjoyed the at-times fearful respect of the Quebec Catholic population for over a century.

This whole process took place at a cost of increasingly insufficient and haphazardly delivered social and medical services, which could be obtained only by those displaying at least the outward signs of religious allegiance. In this workaday system, carefully isolated and "protected" from outside currents of science or socialism, there was no available resort to the public authorities.[18] The system was part and parcel of a spiritual pursuit in which eternal salvation took precedence over earthly well-being.

In the name of the faith, with disregard for the liberal system that had nonetheless made its activity possible, the Church organized Quebec francophones not only as a community of faith but as an "organic" collective in which religious affiliation was superimposed on civic organization and the polity. The poor, as the privileged witnesses to this process, would have to enjoy their freedom, such as it was, under the terms set by an alternate collectivity that had supplanted the polity. In so doing, the Church limned a schizophrenic future for the nation, a future wrenched by dual loyalty, tossed between religious allegiance and appeals to a civic future transcending religious or ethnic identities.

In Quebec as elsewhere, the pauper's freedom was built on a denial of the existence of a political solution to the problem of social inequality. It was a pale, misleading avatar of freedom that presided over poverty by setting it up as a species of absence, of personal impotence. But in Quebec, this impoverished freedom also had to be expressed within the restrictive framework of religious identity. The welfare state would ultimately reconfigure this freedom and place it on a sounder footing. But in the early twentieth century, that was far in the future.

Notes

FOREWORD

1 An early version of this text was presented at a symposium held by the Centre d'histoire des régulations sociales (CHRS) in August 2015, and published as "Histoire politique et régulation sociale: Essai sur le parcours intellectuel de Jean-Marie Fecteau," *Bulletin d'histoire politique* 25 (1) (2016): 11–24. Sincere thanks to Bruce Curtis, Allan Greer, and Ollivier Hubert for their comments on early versions of the manuscript, and to Noémie Charest-Bourdon, Catherine Larochelle, Martin Robert, and the whole CHRS team for their comments throughout the writing process. I also thank the McGill-Queen's team of Magda Fahrni, Jarrett Rudy, and Jonathan Crago for their confidence, comments, and patience. Of course, the content of this essay is my full responsibility. The CHRS, closely tied to Jean-Marie's intellectual trajectory, exists in large part thanks to financial support from the Fonds de recherche Société et culture du Québec and the Canadian Foundation for Innovation.
2 See Fecteau (1976).
3 For an overview of the socialism and independence tendency, see Bourque and Dostaler (1980).
4 The many studies produced by members of the Centre d'histoire des régulations sociales since the original French-language publication of *The Pauper's Freedom* include the following: Aranguiz (2009); Bienvenue, ed. (2013); Bisson (2007); Cellard and Thifault (2007); Fecteau and Vaillancourt (2007); Fecteau and Harvey (2012); Fenchel (2007); Giroux (2011); Forcier (2004); Niget (2009); Ménard (2003); Nootens (2003); Perreault (2009); Petitclerc and Niget, eds. (2012); Petitclerc (2007); Thifault, ed. (2012);

Thifault (2003); Vaillancourt (2005). A full list of the publications produced by the CHRS is available online at www.chrs.uqam.ca.

5 Since 2004, professors Louise Bienvenue, Guy Cucumel, François Fenchel, Donald Fyson, Jean-Philippe Garneau, François Guérard, Thierry Nootens, Isabelle Perreault, Yvan Rousseau, Véronique Strimelle, and Marie-Claude Thifault have been or continue to be regular members of the team.

6 See, for example, Perrot, ed. (1980).

7 A portion of this book was published in English as Fecteau (1994a).

8 See in particular Poulantzas (1973); Poulantzas (1978).

9 Jean-Marie states that he based the theory chapter of his thesis on Brenner (1977), a paper he describes as "fundamental": Fecteau (1983), 14.

10 See, for example, Fecteau (1986b), 15. For an overview of economic regulation theory, see Aglietta (2000); Boyer (1990).

11 In the mid-1980s, Jean-Marie took part in the "Projet accumulation et régulation au Québec." The above-cited publication, Fecteau (1986b), was produced under the auspices of this project, as were Létourneau (1986) and Levasseur (1987). In Quebec, the regulationist approach was developed by the political scientists Gérard Boismenu and Daniel Drache and by the sociologists Paul R. Bélanger and Benoît Lévesque.

12 See Thompson (1978) and Thompson (1963) for his critique of Althusser's structuralism.

13 On the reception accorded Thompson's works in Quebec, see Fahrni (2013); Tremblay (2013).

14 This aspect was challenged in Fyson (2006). See also Fecteau (2007b); Fyson (2007), and note 20 to chapter 3 of this book.

15 See, in particular, Sewell (2005), 22–80.

16 Other works by this author that influenced Jean-Marie include Gauchet and Swain (1980); Gauchet (1997). See also Rémond, ed. (1988).

17 See, in particular, Koselleck (1985); Koselleck (1997).

18 See, for example, Louis-Georges Harvey (2005), 296. The book is a reworking of his doctoral thesis from the early 1990s.

19 An overview of these important 1990s debates can be found in Sangster (2000), among a host of publications.

20 See, in particular, Jones (1983).

21 "Space of experience" and "horizon of expectation" are well-known concepts first posited by the German historian Reinhart Koselleck.

22 Jean-Marie Fecteau, "La mémoire d'un échec: sur l'analyse des Rébellions de 1837–1838 au Bas-Canada," an unpublished paper presented at the

conference of the Institut d'histoire de l'Amérique française in October 1987 and available from the Centre d'histoire des régulations sociales. See also Fecteau (2002b).
23 See, for example, the fine study that he devoted to his colleague and friend the Marxist historian Stanley B. Ryerson: Fecteau (1996a).
24 One of the founders and the mainstay of the *Bulletin d'histoire politique* wrote, for example, that Jean-Marie was "a Foucault disciple" who had thereby "come to reject the specific field of political history, tracking power relations in all types of organizations"; see Comeau (2013). In recent years, the historiographic project of the *Bulletin d'histoire politique* has become normalized, so to speak, as an academic struggle for the autonomy of a field of historical study, which seems to me a rather circumscribed description of the initial project; see, for example, Warren and Gingras (2007). See also Anonymous (2012). Moreover, the history of ideas has become one of the main pillars of this conception of political history, as witness the editorial agenda of the journal *Mens, revue d'histoire intellectuelle et culturelle*, founded in 2000. Finally, this conception of political history has been the subject of a great deal of public comment in recent years, especially around the government's stated intent to require the teaching of national history at all levels of the Quebec school system. For an overview, see the numerous comments on this issue in the daily *Le Devoir*, http://www.ledevoir.com/dossiers/l-enseignement-de-l-history-un-issue/7 (accessed 12 April 2016).
25 On the conditions under which this new sensibility emerged, see Petitclerc (2009).
26 See also Nootens and Fecteau (2003).
27 Fecteau (1994d), 8. The italics are Jean-Marie's.
28 Among the most important studies, see Fecteau (1992a); Fecteau, Tremblay, and Trépanier (1993); Fecteau (1996b); Fecteau and Hay (1996); Fecteau, Greenwood, and Wallot (2002); Fecteau, Ménard, Trépanier, and Strimelle (1998); Fecteau (2002a).
29 See, for example, the special issue "Y a-t-il une nouvelle histoire du Québec?" *Bulletin d'histoire politique* 4 (2): 1995.
30 See, in particular, Burchell, Gordon, and Miller, eds. (1991)
31 Donzelot (1984); Ewald (1986); Procacci (1993).
32 He did mention the "remarkable evolution" of Foucault's thinking toward governmentality; Fecteau (1994d), 7. Nearly fifteen years later, Jean-Marie had come to believe that the Foucauldian approach embodied "a profound crisis in the conceptual study of the political phenomenon in the social sciences," in

part because he viewed it as incapable of taking the full institutional measure of the state; see Fecteau (2007a).

33 The same may be said of the work by Mitchell Dean devoted to the invention of the social in the United Kingdom in the context, obviously very different from that of France, of the Poor Law reform. See Dean (1991). This book also had a major impact on Jean-Marie's historiographic project.

34 The book's title is a reference to the work of E.P. Thompson.

35 For an extended discussion of the debates surrounding state formation at this time, see the important work edited by Greer and Radforth (1992), 328. Jean-Marie wrote a paper for this collection.

36 See, for example, Hunt (1999).

37 For an overview of the broad range of research objects covered by the moral regulationists, see the following special issue: *Canadian Journal of Sociology* 19 (2), 2004. See also McLaren, Menzies, and Chunn, *Regulating Lives*; Glasbeek (2006).

38 See, for example, Valverde (1991).

39 See, for example, Fecteau (1994c).

40 At the time, Jean-Marie was very interested in Michael Mann's work on the origins of social power. See, in particular, Mann (1993). Mann conceived of the social order as a "patterned mess" not easily reconcilable with the idea of the liberal rationality of government.

41 See Fecteau (2001); Fecteau (2007a).

42 See, for example, Fecteau and Harvey (2005), 11.

43 As witness the scarce attention he paid to a major work by Robert Castel (2003) that undertook a reinterpretation of the social question starting from a political analysis of wage work.

44 See, among numerous examples of the kind of work he criticized, Roy (1988); Lamonde ([2000] 2013).

45 This belief in one's inner freedom did not manifest itself as de facto recognition of such freedom for all individuals; inequality between classes, sexes, and races was very real. That said, Jean-Marie wanted to emphasize that henceforth, for all marginalized populations, the nascent struggle for recognition would invariably hinge on the idea that they too possess the fundamental attributes of the "liberal" individual. The consequence is that domination would now in general have to be justified by a belief in the dominated person's incapacity to make proper use of their inner freedom.

46 On this issue, see Bienvenue (2016).

47 The definition of liberalism used by McKay owes a great deal to the one given in Roy (2015).
48 Constant and Ducharme (2009). See in particular the introduction, which presents and discusses the main arguments and critiques of McKay's historiographic project.
49 See, in particular, Curtis (2001); Curtis (2012).
50 Jean-Marie had previously stated this criticism in Fecteau (1996b).
51 Fecteau and Vaillancourt (2006); Fecteau, Fenchel, Tremblay, Trépanier, and Cucumel (2006); Fecteau and Harvey (2012).
52 See Fecteau (2001).
53 Sweeny (2015) voices a similar opinion.
54 While Jean-Marie never had an opportunity to discuss this publication, which appeared shortly before his illness, he was well acquainted with its line of argument. He was, moreover, a member of the evaluation committee for the thesis that gave rise to this book. This part of the text is based on a few discussions that I had with Jean-Marie. It represents little more than my interpretation of the differences of perspective between the two authors.
55 For further proof of this statement, should any be needed, readers are referred to Petitclerc (2012).

INTRODUCTION

1 One might say of the analysis of liberal regulation, as an ideal for the construction of the social fabric, what Haskell said about the conventions that structured a portion of eighteenth- and nineteenth-century humanitarian discourse: "Conventions are not empirical entities that can be weighed or counted; they will not be found in the archives filed under 'C.' Controversies about them will seem frustratingly inconclusive, and the profession's favorite myth – that historians' quarrels turn on hard facts rather than imponderable issues of interpretation – will become harder and harder to sustain" (Haskell 1998b, 305).
2 Some of the hypotheses and analyses contained in this book have been published in preliminary versions, especially as regards liberalism (Fecteau 1996b), the social role of the Catholic Church (Fecteau 1995a), and the treatment of young offenders and children at risk (Fecteau 1998b).

CHAPTER ONE

1 "At the most profound level, the contradiction is *not* between structure and agency. It lies within agency itself, between its routinized, reified and

reproductive facet (and thus, by duality, one immediately has the structure) and its potentially divergent, innovative, autonom[ous], generative and perhaps revolutionary (but at least inciting) one" (Lipietz 1997, 276).

2. What this approach owes to the theory of conventions is evident. On the relationship of this theory to the concept of regulation, see Favereau (2002).

3. Despite certain differences, this approach capitalizes on the fertile thinking of the late historian Bernard Lepetit, who was one of the first to home in on the dialectical relationships between structure and time. See, for example, Lepetit (1995).

4. Rangeon (1986a) is a useful source on this historical notion of general interest.

5. He goes on to mention "the absolute necessity for a continuous action, produced by two forces, one moral the other physical, specially destined to bring back to the general point of view minds predisposed to diverge, and to impose the common interest upon individualities which constantly tend to deviate from it ... the influence exerted by the Individual upon the regulating doctrine is, normally, limited to deducing the Practical Rule applicable to each special case; the spiritual organ being consulted in all doubtful cases" (Comte [1826] 1877, 633–4, 638).

6. "Social control has been an expression of the outlook that held that the individualistic pursuit of economic self-interest can account for neither collective social behavior nor the existence of a social order and does not supply an adequate basis for the achievement of ethical goals" (Janowitz 1975, 83).

7. "Rules of conduct should not be imposed upon individuals, but rather should arise from within the social community. The same theme is repeated again and again: Laws arise out of folkways and mores. Systems of social control reflect the societies in which they are found. Laws define social standards, rights define social obligations, and both laws and rights are social creations. The principle of obedience cannot be formal and lawlike, but rather must conform to the reflexiveness of human nature, must build on genuine human feelings, and must draw upon the consciousness of social groups ... Social control is that which emotionally pulls individuals into social groups and holds them there. That inner tug is 'responsibility'" (Hamilton and Sutton 1989, 11).

8. The work of Talcott Parsons is also relevant here, as is that of Everett Hughes on the traditional society. See also Moore (1958). In addition, one might mention, as belonging to this intellectual universe, Norbert Elias's theory of the "civilizing process" attending the advent of modernity and of the procedures conducive to the "self-restraint" central to this process (Burguière 1997).

9. "A man in a political prison must be traitorous; a man in a mental hospital must be sick. If not traitorous, criminal, or sick, why else would he be there? This

automatic identification of the inmate is not merely name-calling: it is at the center of a basic means of social control" (Goffman 1961, 84). Simultaneously, in the field of criminology, "labelling theory" presented crime as a function of labelling rather than an objective reality (Becker 1963).

10 "The normal is not a mean correlative to a social concept, it is not a judgment of reality but rather a judgment of value; it is a limiting notion which defines a being's maximum psychic capacity. There is no upper limit to normality" (Henry Ey, quoted in Canguilhem 1978, 65).

11 Consequently, "life is in fact a normative activity," i.e., not a unified whole of which illness is merely a chance occurrence, but a contingent activity involving choice and exclusion: "Even for an amoeba, living means preference and exclusion" (Canguilhem 1978, 70, 76).

12 Thus, in the Foucauldian story of the prison, the institution's two-century history is not that of a recurrent failure, attesting to the vanity of attempts to curtail crime, but on the contrary the story of a success, one in which the elites successfully constructed a stigmatizing image of the criminal.

13 From this perspective, there are two ways to interpret the attitude of the dominant classes. On the one hand, much of the social control-centred analysis since Platt (1977) rather unsubtly postulates the existence of a conscious strategy of domination in which petty bourgeois professionals (doctors, psychiatrists, lawyers, social workers, etc.) serve as the principal agents or instruments of control procedures. On the other, the Foucauldian approach constitutes a more sophisticated interpretive mode in which processes of power function without the need to invoke the agents' intentionality or a predefined agenda: all they do is "objectively" serve the interests of the dominant. The instruments of social control have a function corresponding to a need inherent in the system of domination, and their fate fundamentally depends on how this need evolves. On the late-twentieth-century evolution of the prison, for example, Foucault states: "I think ... that the prison does seem to be in decline ... because basically the need for criminals has diminished in the last few years. Power no longer requires criminals" (Foucault 2009a, 22). For a classic example of this type of analysis, see Donzelot ([1977] 1997).

14 See Goffman (1961, 60–6), for example, on the inmates' reaction to the total institution.

15 "The concept of 'social control' ought to be abandoned by critical scholars in favour of one attentive to the dynamic complexity of history, struggle and change" (Chunn and Gavigan 1988, 120). Yet the recent work of McLaren, Menzies, and Chunn (2002) retains this concept.

16 "To hammer reality with the concept of 'social control' will produce neither the coherent social essence nor the unambiguous political messages that were once promised" (Cohen 1989, 356).

17 "The social control arguments work best as part of a history of the strategies, ambitions and plans of those who hoped to direct, manage and coordinate social life ... However, by remaining silent on [the] question of outcome ... much of the sociology of welfare literature goes well beyond that very particular project to create the impression that we are being told about 'how things actually were' as well as 'how some hoped things would be'" (Van Krieken 1991, 8).

18 As early as 1977, Gareth Stedman Jones could write with caustic wit, "The greatest 'social control' ... available to capitalism is the wage relationship itself – the fact that in order to live and reproduce, the worker must perpetually resell his or her labour power" (Jones 1977, 169).

19 "We remain attached to a view of human beings as the *objects*, whether passive, resistant or seduced, of control, social engineering, management and discipline" (Van Krieken 1991, 20).

20 Cohen (1985) adopts this more limited meaning.

21 By 1967, L'Écuyer could be found deploring that the word "control" was mainly being used in the coercive sense found in English and proposed (unsuccessfully) that the term "social control" be translated into French as *régulation social* (L'Écuyer 1967, 82).

22 François Dubet notes this phenomenon: "One can readily understand the success of symbolic interactionism, which devotes attention to the idea of role-taking and only has room for local-level regulation of social relations through face-to-face interaction, ultimately doing away with the idea of society altogether ... This approach reduces the institution to an emergent product of relations and strategies" (Dubet 2002, 58).

23 "It has become fashionable these days to wolf down concepts, to spit them back out like pits before they've even been digested, and to proclaim their death with one's mouth full of new notions that will soon meet the same fate. This kind of bulimia ignores the fact that the present is a montage of effects derived from tradition and from innovation, and that a field of knowledge cannot be built without memory. The notion of social control is part of the tradition that has constituted the social as an object of research and reflection" (Castel 1989, 184).

24 Garland expresses the same discomfort with the empiricist perspective: "The standard response to any wide-ranging social or historical interpretation is to point to the specific facts that don't fit, the variation that has been missed, or the further details needed to complete the picture ... But the detailed case

studies called for by this critical reaction suffer from exactly the opposite fate when they face up to their critical audience. Now the problem is not one of simplification but of significance. How does this study relate to the others that have been done, or might be done? Why should we be interested? What, in the end, does it tell us about the world in which we live?" (Garland 2001, vii).

25 "Freed of the obligation to cognize social change as a general, cumulative phenomenon inscribed in the overall thrust of history, some historians have wrongly concluded that society doesn't exist, or rather, that the societal dimension adds nothing to historical explanations. It seems to them more appropriate to consider the heterogeneity and discontinuity of forms of change as so many routes of access to social reality" (Burguière 1995, 272).

26 Myers (1999) offers a similar perspective with respect to reformatories for young offenders.

27 "Because deviance history is framed theoretically by the defense or critique of expert power controlling some peculiar and socially distinguished condition ('delinquency,' 'feeble-mindedness,' 'madness,' etc.), it fails to account for an institutional practice that was disconcertingly banal and that centered on familial expediency, not individual deviant need or threat" (Bellingham 1986, 552).

28 It is telling that the article on "regulation" in the prestigious *Encyclopedia Universalis* was written by Canguilhem.

29 Indeed, a key characteristic of regulation is the *adjustment* (automatic or otherwise) of a system or institution to a new situation. It is evident how this concept embraces the time dimension, albeit in a mechanical fashion.

30 "The concept of organization, used by politicians and sociologists to cover all manner of situations, in fact obscures the question of whether and how a variety of groups that are heterogeneous in their functions and ranked according to their status can be integrated into a totality capable of preserving its cohesiveness over time, adapting to partially unforeseen historical situations without losing its essence" (Canguilhem 1990, 712).

31 As Lipietz observes: "Canguilhem's famous definition ... 'Regulation is the adjustment, in conformity with some rule or set of norms, of a plurality of movements or acts, as well as their effects or products ...' ... posited the existence of a teleological norm or finalism which automatically led to functionalism. The 'goal' of adjustment seemed to be the cause of the existence of the regulating apparatus, the assembly of which could be confided to some human or divine architect. The theory of systems – cybernetics – had then only to describe the retroactive regulatory functions" (Lipietz 1997, 254).

32 This is why "structure" as such *explains* nothing: it merely opens horizons, or rather, puts in place what Foucault, following Marx, called "conditions of possibility" open to the contingency of human action: "Taking

into account the structural factor ... with its radical reductionism, should not lead us to neglect the abundance of facts, but rather to enlarge the breadth and number of those we should consider significant" (Gauchet 1997, 130).

33 It is no doubt essential to analyze the regularities manifested in social action, if only because such an analysis sheds light on the effectiveness of norms and institutions. But despite what a certain species of scientism might posit, this is not the only kind of analysis that can shed light on the dynamic of the social; refusals, dysfunctionalities, anomalies, and other non-recurrent "events" are equally meaningful in this regard.

34 I must take issue here with Jacques Chevallier's statement that "the paradigm of regulation is inseparable ... from the systemic approach. It emphasizes that any organized whole necessarily entertains ongoing, reversible interactions with the 'ecological environment' in which it bathes" (Chevallier 1995, 81–2).

35 In the wake of functionalism and structuralism, both based on a prior rationalization of institutional objectives or the supposedly incontrovertible fact of structural constants, to think of the societal whole in terms of regulation is thus another way of conceiving of totality.

36 Although the term is deeply polysemic, as Dubet notes: "The word 'institution' denotes so many phenomena and social facts that are so different and so vague that each reader can project onto them a particular meaning, which will vary according to the context and the needs of the argument. Durkheim, after all, defined sociology as a whole as 'the science of institutions'" (Dubet 2002, 21–2).

37 This "open" definition of the term institution allows for its insertion into the fabric of social relations, thus responding, as regards the institutions of "social control," to Bellingham's call: "For mainstream social history, the theoretical question is: did institutions have a reproductive role (not merely a symbolic one) in the development of capitalism? Is it adequate to view their operation as a separate world, a realm of real or imputed 'deviance' and its management – with no on-going structural relationship to 'normal' life? Are hermetic and inward-referencing, organizational or culturalist explanations then adequate? Such an on-going theoretical relationship, if it is valid, can only be examined in the concrete relationship of agents to clients or to clients' families" (Bellingham 1986, 539).

38 Dubet thus speaks of the "institutional agenda," a labour of socialization "situated above the diversity of groups and classes," and predicated on "the resolution of a basic paradox. In a single thrust, it socializes the individual and purports to constitute him as a subject" (Dubet 2002, 27, 35). This production of an "individual" who is both autonomous and integrated into the collectivity is central to liberal regulation as well as to what Norbert Elias terms the civilizing process.

39 On the history of this school, see Lipietz (1997), Boyer (1990), Boyer and Saillard (2006).
40 This approach, based on specific empirical hypotheses relating to the development of capitalist economies since the nineteenth century, was harshly criticized by Brenner and Glick (1991, 45–119).
41 Most historical work directly inspired by the French regulation school mainly concerns the development of the group's economic hypotheses (Clio 1995, 49–57). The concept of regulation developed here, although inspired by these authors, diverges from them in its emphasis on the global and historical dimension of the concept.
42 "That which is reproduced is precisely, and above all, the contradiction" (Lipietz 1979, 34). "There is a *unity* of 'unity' and 'struggle': struggle maintains unity and unity maintains struggle. Alceste remains misanthropic, Célimène remains flirtatious, and, while each of them satisfies his or her need for the other, they simultaneously prepare new divergences which lead to further fighting. It is this kind of unity – by which 'unity' (of the elements in relation) is maintained despite, and even because of, their 'struggle' – that the dialectician terms *regulation*" (Lipietz 1997, 262).
43 It is at once a strength and a weakness of capitalism these last two centuries that it has managed to incorporate innovation and novelty into its mode of development, which has brought about dazzling social progress but also profound upheavals. Former modes of regulation (such as feudalism), by confining the unforeseen and the novel within much narrower normative and institutional frameworks, managed to endure far longer.
44 One of the most fascinating phenomena relating to historical change has to do with the durability of certain institutions – e.g., the family and the state – which persist by adapting to changing modes of regulation. Likewise, certain normative ensembles (those of private law, for example) have experienced remarkable historical longevity. Clearly, the manner in which these institutions are integrated into the logic of a new system of social regulation, with the social relations they materialize being transformed as a consequence, means that this longevity cannot necessarily be taken at face value.
45 On the already dated historiography of this issue, see Fecteau (1986b).
46 I am thinking here of Europe, the Americas, and Australia.
47 For example, in the 1830s, Lower Canada (Quebec) experienced such impasses when Great Britain delayed ratification of reforms passed by the House of Assembly (municipal system, education, immigrant tax, etc.).
48 This by no means implies that all these phenomena must manifest themselves in the same way, at the same time, in all Western social formations. The case of slavery is typical. The implementation of a democratic capitalist logic is

everywhere predicated on the recognition of fundamental political rights and economic freedoms. But this does not mean that slavery, running counter to this logic, had to disappear at the same pace wherever it existed. For how else to explain its persistence, well into the nineteenth century, in the most politically and economically advanced nation, the United States? (For a different point of view on this question, see Boutang 1998). The same observation can be made about women's suffrage, which was not enacted in Quebec and France until the 1940s. This is precisely why a *global* analysis of modes of regulation is necessary, within each social formation and for the West in general. On the issue of slavery, see the riveting debate touched off by Haskell (1985, 339–61, 547–66): Davis (1987, 797–812); Ashworth (1987, 813–28); Haskell (1987, 829–78).

49 "Focused on questions of national difference, historical scholarship bends to the task of specifying each nation's distinctive culture, its peculiar history, its *Sonderweg*, its exceptionalism. Since every nation's history is – in fact and by definition – distinct, the move is not without reason. At its worst, however, the result is to produce histories lopped off at precisely those junctures where the nation-state's permeability might be brought into view, where the transnational forces do their most important work. The narrative field too often shrinks back on the nation; the boundaries of the nation-state become an analytic cage" (Rodgers 1998, 2).

50 I will not, in this book, address the question of whether or not Quebec is a nation. It suffices to state that despite its subordination to an imperial system and then a federal one, it constitutes a polity possessing a good measure of control over its instruments of regulation.

51 For such a comparative analysis of juvenile delinquency and child protection policies, see Dupont-Bouchat et al. 2001. On the methodological issues implicit in the comparative reflex, see also Fecteau (1998a) and the very relevant remarks of Dakhlia (1995).

52 On this issue, see the pertinent methodological remarks in Rodgers (1998).

CHAPTER TWO

1 I have deliberately refrained from using the grand syntheses of political ideas dealing with liberalism, such as that of Jardin (1985). Liberalism is not of interest as a system of argumentation or an ideology (in the sense of a more or less hermetic rational construct squaring off against other systems of ideas) but as a general way of relating to the world.

2 Ian McKay, to take one example, speaks of a liberal "order" or "project." He writes of "the enormity of what the Canadian liberal order undertook – the

replacement, often with a kind of revolutionary symbolic or actual violence, of antithetical traditions and forms that had functioned for centuries and even millennia with new conceptions of the human being and society" (McKay 2000, 630).

3 Yet it bore within itself the conditions for its own perversion – with the rise of Fascism, for example. Likewise, when global expansion is considered, nothing bars liberal mercantilist and political logic from coexisting with extreme forms of exploitation, and not only on the periphery (cf. the American example).

4 Thinking along similar lines, Jacques Le Goff writes of producing a history of "values": "It seems to me ... that it is urgent to build a type of history that has interested me for some time: a history of *values*. This term, which replaces the outmoded conception of *idées-forces*, represents those ideas that are also principles of ethics and action for any society, ideas that historians must consider when analyzing individual and collective behaviours" (Le Goff, preface to Clavero 1996, xvi).

5 The section that follows is, as will be evident, strongly inspired by the pioneering work of Thomas Haskell, in particular a paper about the origins of the humanitarian sensibility that occasioned a well-known debate. See Haskell (1985) and replies by Ashworth (1987) and Davis (1987).

6 It is of little import whether passions or interests drive this will. It suffices to say that from this point on, a debate about the motivators of this individual will and their relative validity becomes possible. On this issue, see Hirschman (1977).

7 This vision of creative liberty is not comparable to the vision of the same concept under the feudal mode of regulation. There, liberty is simply a faculty designating the absence of constraint, without this liberty becoming a value in itself: "Liberty is the natural faculty of he who does as he pleases, unless prevented from doing so by force or by law ... Liberal, from the Latin *liberalis*, denotes he who freely, without taking account of any recompense, does good and shows mercy to the needy, knowing how to act without falling into profligacy. This is why a grace performed is called a liberality." Other senses of the term denote the contrary: "The liberty sought by the heretics of our time, which they call freedom of conscience, is but the soul's enslavement" (*Tesoro de la Lingua Castellana o Española*, quoted in Clavero 1996, 77). In other words, "freedoms existed, but not individuals who could be determined by them in any respect. Human beings were not persons. They were not subjects as construed in that sense and with that scope of action. The contrary hypothesis, when it made its appearance after Hobbes, was unproblematically treated as a 'vulgar axiom'" (Clavero 1996, 178).

8 Even the discovery of truth followed this pattern founded on the creative opposition between things and people: "Truth, in the great practical concerns

of life, is so much a question of the reconciling and combining of opposites that very few have minds sufficiently capacious and impartial to make the adjustment with an approach to correctness, and it has to be made by the rough process of a struggle between combatants fighting under hostile banners" (Mill [1849] 1913, 46).

9 Understood here in the sense of Valverde (1998, 223): "Both psychology and Kantian ethics ... are technologies of ethical governance that rely on and perpetuate the fantasy of a truth about 'the self' that lies somewhere under the appearances of conduct. The content of this ethical self is freedom. In other words, the ethical self is for both of these traditions an intrinsically liberal self."

10 Haskell ascribed to it the greatest part of the causal force giving rise to new ethical principles: "The market heaps rewards on people who ... systematically take into account the most remote consequences of their actions. The discipline of the invisible hand thereby tends to expand causal horizons and set the stage for the appearance of what Nietzsche called 'sovereign individuals,' people who act out of conscience, 'think causally,' and strive to 'ordain the future in advance,' thereby expanding the boundaries of responsibility far enough potentially to include for the first time perfect strangers, people for whose suffering no one in traditional society felt responsible" (Haskell 1998a, 231).

11 MacPherson (1962) showed how property ownership had become an intrinsic part of the definition of the individual by the late seventeenth century. See also the notable synthesis by Atiyah (1979) on the contractual logic flowing from this worldview.

12 Thompson (1971) brilliantly dissected this process, in which appeals to tradition serve as a justification for revolt.

13 On this point, see Koselleck (1985).

14 "It would be easy for a contemporary mind, inescapably shaped by the liberal order, to miss what was startling, revolutionary, and endangered about the nucleus of liberalism when it first assumed its pedagogical role in northern North America, before its mid-century transition to a hegemonic ideology in the centre and its late-century transition to state hegemony from coast to coast" (McKay 2000, 631).

15 "But the self in the act of willing was seen as a new, non-transitive, causal beginning, independent of everything but the First Cause and His providential order – a very special sort of dependence that even predestinarians insisted did not dilute in the least the self's responsibility for whatever it willingly did. In the world of formalism, the self's very act was deemed voluntary insofar as will was in it, and scarcely anything other than direct physical coercion was thought capable of displacing the will and emptying an act of its voluntary character" (Haskell 1987, 874).

16 The word is used here in its general sense, extant since the eighteenth century if not earlier, of "social intercourse; interchange of ideas, opinions, or sentiments" (Webster's).

17 The indispensable thing here is duty; or, to put it differently, that the principial greatness of the deliberate act, as the essential fibre of the social fabric, becomes an ethical requirement where the construction of the future is concerned: "For Franklin and Bentham, as for James Mill and John Stuart Mill, the future is not something distant and inexorable that happens to us, regardless of our choices, but something that in large measure we are already creating, moment by moment, both by our actions and by our omissions to act in the present. So immediate is the future's relation to the present, so certain is the actor's capacity to shape it by embarking now on the preferred course of action, that the design and production of the future becomes a duty. To allow an unintended future to come about is to be careless, to betray a norm of responsibility" (Haskell 1998c, 339).

18 A different but parallel hypothesis is found in Gauchet (1997).

19 "Europe must learn that you no longer want a single unfortunate or oppressor on French soil; may this example bear fruit on earth; may it propose the love of virtue and happiness! Happiness is a new idea in Europe" (Saint-Just [1794] 1968, 206).

20 The shifting terms of the discourse in question imply the displacement of the elements of a discursive complex under the impetus of both internal contradictions and external challenges. It does not preclude the relative "transhistoricity" of ideologies as analyzed by Tort (1983, 10) but helps to follow their transformations over time, as in the case analyzed here of the liberal discourse on the state. Thus, the role and even the meaning of the basic concepts of liberalism ("individual," "progress," "liberty" or "freedom," "equality," "civil society," "state," etc.) can change in step with changes in the historical context of their use, without this discourse thereby becoming less "liberal."

21 On this specific point, the pioneering work of Polanyi (1944) remains irreplaceable. He was one of the first to show the extent to which the state and the problematics of the societal good remain an issue central to the development of capitalism, even – one might say especially – in its so-called "savage" phase.

22 As, for example, in the much-discussed phrase "intermediate bodies." On this issue, see Offe (1981) for a brilliant critique.

23 In my view, too little analysis has been devoted to what I would call the "baggage" carried by institutions; i.e., the effects deriving from the crystallization/coagulation of social relations within an organizational structure – be it the state, the Church, the trade union, or the neighbourhood bowling club – that overarches the individual and at the same time includes her (Chevallier 1981). The institution must, as noted in the previous chapter, be regarded as a

particular modality of the collective organization of individualities with respect to *time*, insofar as the institution has a duration independent of the various time scales represented by its members. It is thus a structure both abstract (immaterial) and concrete (possessing a specific effectiveness) that has its own temporality and can therefore *transmit over time* a value, a practice, or even a power dynamic. On this point, see Fecteau (1997, 143–57).

24 On this issue, see the trenchant analysis of Mann (1993).

25 Say what one may, the dichotomous vision of private and public remains central to political representations to this day. It forms the foundation for discourse on the future of society under the liberal mode of regulation, even in its welfarist form. The rethinking of the bureaucratic or ineffective state, the attribution of efficiency and effectiveness to the private sector in neoliberal discourse: all this is but the latest avatar of a world in which the state has come to represent a force oppositional to the dynamic of civil society.

26 This dichotomy, developed since Hume by the Scottish liberals, in no way implies a withdrawal of the state; on the contrary, the state may vigorously intervene to stimulate private trade, in particular by breaking up monopolies. On this essential point, see Pocock (1985).

27 For clarification of this issue, see Loschak (1986, 44–75).

28 See the arguments of Habermas (1989).

29 For this reason, efforts to reconstruct the political dynamic of the nineteenth century by adapting Habermas's concept of "public space" to that century seem to me shot through with contradictions. The democratic state, by virtue of presenting itself as the formal and structural realization of citizens' political will, tends to gobble up public space, to delegitimize forms of expression and political demands situated outside formal political institutions. The oppositional dynamic central to the formation of public space in the Enlightenment era was thus utterly disrupted by the institutionalization of liberal democracy in the nineteenth century.

30 The French word for competition, *concurrence*, has the dual meaning of opposition and confluence, just as its etymological cousin *concours* means both encounter and rivalry.

31 John Stuart Mill was doubtless one of the most eloquent proponents of this conception of the private/public divide: "In the particular circumstances of a given age or nation, there is scarcely anything really important to the general interest, which it may not be desirable, or even necessary, that the government should take upon itself, not because private individuals cannot effectually perform it, but because they will not. At some times and places there will be no roads, docks, harbours, canals, works of irrigation, hospitals, schools, colleges, printing-presses, unless the government establishes them; the public being

either too poor to command the necessary resources, or too little advanced in intelligence to appreciate the ends, or not sufficiently practised in joint action to be capable of the means" (Mill 1848, 558).

32 A growing bibliography on this issue includes Pocock (1985), Tribe (1978), Dean (1991), and Sledziewski (1989).

33 Or rather, self-interest, like the passions motivating personal behaviour, was redefined to reflect its contribution to the construction of a legitimate social order. On this point, see Hirschman (1977). The individual is the vehicle through which the essential nature of society is expressed, and liberty is the condition for its adequate expression.

34 For example, one of the first acts of the National Assembly in revolutionary France was to abolish corporate bodies and craft guilds (Le Chapelier Law of June 1791). Similar legislation abolished the Order of Lawyers (September 1790), the royal academies (August 1793), the chambers of commerce (September 1791), and the religious and charitable congregations (August 1792). Jean Le Chapelier, in the statement of principles of the June 1791 act, affirmed that "it must undoubtedly be permissible for citizens to assemble, but it must not be permissible for citizens of certain professions to assemble for their supposed common interests. There are no more corporations in the state; all that remains is the private interest of each individual and the general interest. No one is permitted to evoke an intermediate interest in the citizens, to separate them from the *res publica* by instilling in them a corporatist spirit" (quoted in Nourrisson 1920, 119–20).

35 On this issue, see Martin (1985). On a more general plane, Hegel would seek to reconcile the development of market forces in civil society (the "savage beast") with a communitarian ethic renewed in and by the state. See the excellent analysis by Colliot-Thélène (1992).

36 In particular, the emergence of the idea of a social minimum. On this issue, see Fecteau (1999b).

37 It then becomes possible to construe a state's intervention capacity as indicative of a *temporary* mismatch between economic logic and the needs of civil society. Intervention is a necessary evil that will be obviated once market forces complete their work of harmonizing needs with capacities.

38 On this point, see the illuminating paper by Loschak (1986).

39 In this context, the postulate of an initial social contract, or the belief in rights existing prior to the social state, becomes virtually needless (Binoche 1989); it becomes inoperative once individual liberty has been made possible by the process of harmonization through compartmentalization. This automatic harmonization itself tends, moreover, to render philanthropic efforts to transform the individual vain and utopian. It is too often forgotten that liberalism also

presented itself as an adversary to the philanthropic ambition to act on the individual *from without*. Subsequent chapters of this book describe a rapid retreat from the ideal of individual reform during this period, at least where adult males were concerned.

40 The liberals of the 1830–1850 generation were of course particularly sensitive to this eventuality. One need only think of Tocqueville and his friend Mill, to whom we owe one of the most systematic efforts to define the limits of relevant state action: "Our present civilization tends so strongly to make the power of persons acting in masses the only substantial power in society, that there never was more necessity for surrounding individual independence of thought, speech, and conduct, with the most powerful defences, in order to maintain that originality of mind and individuality of character, which are the only source of any real progress, and of most of the qualities which make the human race much superior to any herd of animals" (Mill 1848, 517).

41 The private sphere, in its inviolability, came to be defined as a negative space, as that which eludes the purchase of the state. Mill captured this moment: "Whatever theory we adopt respecting the foundation of the social union, and under whatever political institutions we live, there is a circle around every individual human being, which no government, be it that of one, of a few, or of the many, ought to be permitted to overstep; there is a part of the life of every person, who has come to years of discretion, within which the individuality of that person ought to reign uncontrolled either by any other individual or by the public collectively" (Mill 1848, 514).

42 The analysis by Ajzenstat (1984a and 1984b) of Lord Durham's and John Arthur Roebuck's conception is particularly pertinent here. What she analyzes as liberal tolerance, however, appears to me on the contrary to be a process of homogenization through elimination of the older poles of collective identification and/or those that differed from liberal-type voluntary belonging, a process forming the primary condition of the racism of that era. See Larue (1991).

43 "In democratic countries, the science of association is the mother science; the progress of all the others depends on the progress of the former. Among the laws that govern human societies, there is one that seems more definitive and clearer than all the others. For men to remain civilized or to become so, the art of associating must become developed among them and be perfected in the same proportion as equality of conditions grows" (Tocqueville [1835] 2012, 3: 902).

44 One finds here an interpretation dominant among historians of the welfare state. In its most sophisticated "neo-Foucauldian" version, it explains this expansion with reference to changes in the techniques used to manage society or the masses, rendering the "liberal" vision of social regulation obsolete and leading to new modes (statistical, actuarial, consensual) of administering large numbers of people that are conducive to state expansion (see Ewald 1986).

Here again, the expansion of the state and the public sphere appears as a gradual and relatively linear process in which society is taken in charge under the impetus of a new disciplinary logic at work as of the last third of the nineteenth century.

45 The extent of this shift can be appreciated by comparing the liberalism of Mill (1849) with that of his protégé Spencer ([1884] 1969).

46 Especially given that this period is still viewed, in Quebec historiography but not only there, as the one in which liberal hegemony was more or less unrivalled. It should be clear that beyond the routine and repetitive appearance of this discourse in the press and elsewhere, and beyond the palpable retreat of conservative discourse (except in pockets of ultramontane resistance, a matter to which I return), the critique of the fundamental postulates of liberalism posed a major challenge to the established order. This is not to deny the on-the-ground hegemony of the liberal agenda, for it was endorsed by important institutions and became integral to ordinary discourse; still, it is worth noting the ambivalence of even noisy professions of faith in the individual and progress, given the persistence of the emerging critiques. The ethic of liberty was still fundamental to these societies, but the historical form of classical liberalism was feeling the strain.

47 On the influence of genetic theories on social thought, see Rosenberg (1974). This was, moreover, the epoch in which Cesare Lombroso (1887) developed a biologically based anthropology of criminal types.

48 In allusion to legislators, Henri Marion wrote: "it is no use trying to reason with people in a state of political drunkenness" (Marion 1885, 75).

49 The political thought of John A. Macdonald in Canada was pervaded by this profound sense of doubt, this fear of a broadened democracy.

50 No surprise, then, that liberals should feel compelled, after a half-century of eclipse, to invoke theories (now validated by "science") positing *human rights* as prior to the state (Spencer [1884] 1969), or that they should now rediscover a substantive and immanent constitutional law transcending mere legislative intent (Dicey [1914] 1981).

51 For example, the idea of the necessary withering away of the state as a political expression of the collectivity is found, strikingly and almost simultaneously, in two thinkers at opposite ends of the political spectrum, Spencer and Engels:

"In a popularly governed nation, the government is simply a committee of management ... Only little by little can voluntary cooperation replace compulsory cooperation, and rightly bring about a correlative decrease of faith in governmental ability and authority" (Spencer [1884] 1969, 183, 187).

"The first act in which the state really comes forward as the representative of society as a whole ... is at the same time its last independent act as a state. The interference of state power in social relations becomes superfluous in one sphere after another, and then ceases of itself. The government of persons is replaced by the administration of things" (Engels [1878] 1939, 307).

52 Beginning in 1902, the *Revue de métaphysique et de morale* published a series of papers on this theme that clearly illustrate the phenomenon: see Bouglé (1902), Lanson (1902), Jacob (1903), and Parodi (1903).

53 One example among many: "The social group, which evolves and changes, is not by its very nature a derived synthesis, posterior to its elements, whose traits reproduce those of its elements; it is a given, primary synthesis, as necessary to its elements as they are to it, and in which, subsequently, the arrangement of the elements, the solidarity of individuals in social action, has a value of its own that cannot be derived straightforwardly from the notion of the individual" (Bernès 1901, 490).

54 "A free society is not one in which everyone, elsewise respectful of all others, listens only to himself: it is one that truly desires its own legislation, approves of its severity, and cannot therefore find it oppressive. A free society is a disciplined society. Liberty and discipline are assumed and are mutually supportive. But discipline and liberty also presuppose a degree of unanimity, a unanimity of aspirations which, in social life, is the cause of devotion and prosperity ... If the convictions of all coincide, or if, at least, they are not mutually exclusive, the society will practice its own freedom of conscience. In that case there is concord: each person approves of others' adopting and spreading convictions opposed to his own: differences of opinion are contained within bounds agreeable to all. People are free; that is, they speak and act in a manner which today's society can countenance. It is natural for this state of concord to be reflected in legislated freedom" (Martin 1905, 351, 487). The organic expression of this community is the nation.

55 This logic is particularly appreciable in the fields of insurance and workers' compensation, where an analysis of probabilities and an estimate of standard compensation partake of a logic in which individual responsibility is subsumed within the measurement of the social effect of a problem, where extremes cease to engage in creative confrontation and are reduced to the law of averages.

56 Ewald, for example, posits an identity, or at least a homology, between the logic of insurance discussed above and the birth of the welfare state.

57 More specifically, the growth of the state in Western societies occurred in two fundamentally different phases. Until the 1930s, it and the implementation of the early (e.g., Bismarckian) "social policies" were part and parcel of the expansion of a suppletive or philanthropic state. A place could be found for such interventionism in a world in which the liberal logic just discussed remained hegemonic, provided that the criteria for intervention and the areas in which it took place merely supported the development of the free market without

altering its workings. The Keynesian transformation begun in the 1930s was entirely different in scope, notably because it gave the state a comprehensive regulatory role that ultimately led to a complete remaking of social regulation.

CHAPTER THREE

1 This chapter recapitulates and updates the main points developed in a previous study (Fecteau 1989). A preliminary version was published in English (Fecteau 1994a).
2 Cunningham makes this point: "In dealing with poverty and the poor there is a limited repertoire of responses, and it is nearly always possible to find a precedent for what is at first sight novel" (Cunningham 1998, 9).
3 The same remark could be made for the age-old distinction between the "deserving" and "undeserving" poor.
4 On this score, see the fascinating study by Clavero (1996). The same critique could be applied to the mode of historical treatment of a concept such as that of exclusion and to the long-range diachronic treatment of this concept by Castel (2003).
5 At this stage of the analysis, I am dealing simultaneously with the modes of treatment of both crime and poverty. This amalgam, which may seem paradoxical with reference to today's system, in my view constitutes a basic modality of the transition at issue.
6 More specifically, the very possibility of making the individual the dynamic force of the social order does not exist in this system: "While argumentation dealt with the body and particularly the individual body, it was thus treated as an object and not a subject ... Books devoted to the body (*de corpore*) or to human beings (*de homine*) did not deal with economics and had no bearing on jurisprudence. What failed to emerge was an active category of the individual human subject, and that is not at all what was meant by a legal body ... The individual did not enjoy a space of his own and lacked the substance to define one. What we have here is an anthropology that appears misnamed in that it ignores the individually human subject ... Humans, in the generic sense of individuals, could in that situation be no more than an assemblage of legal norms which, in failing to dictate principles proper to individuals, could not form a system ... There was no common space or environment that could be determined by the individual" (Clavero 1996, 143).
7 The British hue and cry (collective prosecution) tradition and the ancestral right of citizen's arrest were only two manifestations of this type of management, which would in many cases be merely overseen by the king's local representatives.

8 This early type of intervention would, in its most extreme form, lead to the mercantilist project of "policing" the masses. It gave rise to the initial formulations of the Foucauldian concept of "governmentality" (Foucault 2009a; Burchell, Gordon, and Miller 1991), i.e., a historical approach based on the "government" of people. For a recent version of this perspective, which is often treated in a deeply gradualist fashion, see Hunt (1999).
9 On this point, see of course the classic study by Foucault (1977) but also the meticulous analysis by Spierenburg (1996b).
10 The case of houses of correction as a public approach to combatting begging and petty crime is particularly interesting. On this topic, see Innes (1987) for a highly illuminating paper.
11 The same was true of hospitals that received large, central government subsidies to take care of invalids and aging soldiers of the king's army, as in eighteenth-century France.
12 Vagrants were persons "who deserve to die because they serve no purpose in this world" (judgment against Colin l'enfant, quoted in Geremek 1976). Martin Luther was hardly more tender in his conception of a system for the institutionalized poor: "It is enough to provide decently for the poor, that they may not die of cold and hunger" (quoted in Geremek 1987, 233).
13 Dean provides a good description of the logic of confinement in which these traditional institutions operated: "The workhouse ... thus went beyond the re-formation of the social order. In doing so, however, it became less a place for the reform of individuals than the site of the metamorphosis of the idle into the industrious, or dross into sterling, as Bentham might say. It was neither a protected workshop in which the Poor learned the skills for the supersession of their condition nor a reformatory in which they became normalised individuals, but a kind of switching mechanism. In it, the Poor would remain the Poor. That was their earthly lot. They would be transformed, but not as individuals so much as categories. The mercantilist workhouse, unlike later the prison, asylum, and reformatory ... did not attempt to act on the 'soul' of the individual. It both gave rise to and was founded on the theory of associationism which sought an 'ideological' technique of power, a *semio-technique*, which would educate its objects in an orderly and respectful course of life by connecting mental representations of virtue, industry, and obedience with happiness, and vice, idleness, and insubordination with pain" (Dean 1991, 64).
14 Clearly, the role of the religious authorities in this area was not at all static. In close concomitance with the royal institutions, and especially after the Counter-Reformation, a specific dynamic of charity developed, with the founding of congregations (often composed of women) specializing in caring for the poor. The figure of St Vincent de Paul is exemplary in this regard. See Langlois (1984).

15 "It is we historians (and non-historians) who ask questions about the reality of the individual and the economy. The epoch did not pay attention to such things. These were extraneous matters; it knew of no economy other than the economy of the family and the body, both general or public as the case happened to be; there existed no subject other than the corresponding social subjects. There was only one 'oikonomia': it left no room for any others that were truly distinct, and it did not allow for the possibility of an economy determined by human beings" (Clavero 1996, 158–9).
16 See also, but in a much more gradualist and less rewarding vein, Geremek (1987) and Sassier (1990).
17 Setting aside the zeal for punishment that characterized the early years of the general hospitals and workhouses, the same situation obtained in Europe, with a few exceptions. Thus, for the British houses of correction, Innes notes an annual rate of confinement of 1–3 per thousand inhabitants (Innes 1987, 105).
18 In any event, this system came in for severe criticism in England from the late eighteenth century onward. Ontario, too, explicitly declined to import it.
19 Notably the house of correction, of which the first Quebec mention dates from 1768 (ANQ, T011–0001/2248).
20 Fyson's critique deals in particular with the argument put forward in Fecteau (1989).
21 Garneau (2002) found that the same observations apply to the colony's civil courts.
22 See, for example, Garnot (1996).
23 This idea can be expressed differently by stressing that in feudal regulation, the justice system modulates its action according to the degree of community-rootedness of the populations it regulates.
24 In this regard, I diverge radically from Fyson's conclusions: "There was in fact a state-sponsored criminal justice system in place before the Rebellions that, for all of its internal contradictions, inefficiencies, and irregularities, could and did have a significant impact on those who came in contact with it; ... both this system and the way that society at large interacted with it were not static between the 1760s and the 1820s, but evolved considerably, developing many of the traits that would later characterise the criminal justice system of the 'modern' state, such as professional police and magistrates, and bureaucratic formalism; and ... as a consequence, the period following the Rebellions did not mark as sharp a break in the nature and impact of the state in general, and the criminal justice system in particular, as has lately been assumed, although there is no denying that there were significant changes in that period as well" (Fyson 1995, 408). Fyson minimizes the remarkable continuity between the system he describes and the *old* logic of regulation. The traits of modernity

he identifies (wage work, professionalism, rootedness of the justice system in the community) are in fact not at all alien to the feudal system. To consider them forerunners of the logic to come is redolent of the teleological reflex discussed earlier.

25 While Howard became the promoter of humanitarian reform of the prison system (see Petit 1995, 5–22), it was Bentham (1791) who put forward one of the earliest theories of confinement as a "panoptic" mode of reform and punishment.

26 The idea of such an institutional amalgam was also discussed in Lower Canada. In 1807, a letter signed "The Two Friends" in the newspaper *Courrier de Québec* proposed the construction of a four-building complex on the outskirts of Quebec City, some of which would serve as houses of correction for petty criminals, the others as poorhouses (*Courrier de Québec*, 21 February 1807).

27 At the close of the eighteenth century, Benjamin Constant eloquently expressed how the democratic transition represented a break with traditional conceptions of social power: "Kings ... take power for a cause, when in fact it is an effect" (Constant 1797, 85). The point here in either case is, of course, that the principle of continuity between the governors and the governed remained intact.

28 Around the same time, William Pitt stated in the House of Commons: "Let us make relief in cases where there are a number of children a matter of right and honour, instead of a ground for opprobrium and contempt. This will make a large family a blessing, and not a curse; and this will draw a proper line of distinction between those who are able to provide for themselves by their labour, and those who after having enriched their country with a number of children, have a claim upon the assistance for support" (quoted in Dean 1991, 18).

29 "We hold these truths to be self-evident, that all men are created equal, that they are endowed by their Creator with certain unalienable Rights, that among these are Life, Liberty and the pursuit of Happiness" (United States Declaration of Independence, 1776). Article 1 of the French Constitution of 1793 states: "The aim of society is the common welfare. Government is instituted in order to guarantee to man the enjoyment of his natural and imprescriptible rights."

30 "The years of political insecurity, military crisis and recurrent economic dislocation gave incentive to develop plans of permanent socialization of the labouring classes in preference to short-term expedients of buying off 'importunity'" (Roberts 1991, 206).

31 The conservative version of this tendency called for a return to obligatory deference on the part of the poor, along with institutions that would help combat the harmful effects of industrialization, such as prison farms for adults. The radical version tried to devise new forms of socialization based on egalitarian cooperation, such as Charles Fourier's phalansteries.

32 "Not equality of conditions, but welfare in every condition: this is what the legislature must have in its sights" (Jean Charles Léonard de Sismondi, quoted in Procacci 1993, 145). In its utilitarian version, this aspiration was famously stated by Bentham as "the greatest happiness of the greatest number."

33 The same author notes, however, the particular attributes of voluntary private charity: "Private charity alone can suit the relief to the particular situation of those who invoke it; it alone is able to get down to the smallest details; it alone is capable of penetrating the secret of all necessities; it alone knows the paths that lead to hidden misfortune, and can, without wounding the unfortunate who has fallen from a situation of comfort, lift the veil under which he hides from unkind stares" (Gérando 1839, 1: 495).

34 "It is, undoubtedly, a most disheartening reflection that the great obstacle in the way to any extraordinary improvement in society is of a nature that we can never hope to overcome. The perpetual tendency in the race of man to increase beyond the means of subsistence is one of the general laws of animated nature which we can have no reason to expect will change" (Malthus [1798] 1970, 198–9).

35 On the kinship between the ideas of Burke and Malthus and on the latter's dominance over the former in conservative discourse, see McNally (2000).

36 Harsh criticism, such as the ironic remarks of William Hazlitt, was soon levelled at this view: "The common notions that prevailed on this subject, till [Malthus's] first population-scheme tended to weaken them, were that life is a blessing, and that the more people could be maintained in any state in a tolerable degree of health, comfort and decency, the better: that want and misery are not desirable in themselves, that famine is not to be courted for its sake, that wars, disease and pestilence are not what every friend of his country or his species should pray for in the first place: that vice in its different shapes is a thing that the world could do very well without, and that if it could be got rid of altogether, it would be a great gain. In short, that the object both of the moralist and politician was to diminish as much as possible the quantity of vice and misery existing in the world: without apprehending that by thus effectually introducing more virtue and happiness, more reason and good sense, that by improving the manners of a people, removing pernicious habits and principles of acting, or securing greater plenty, and a greater number of mouths to partake of it, they were doing a disservice to humanity" (Hazlitt 1819, 415–16).

37 This is the principle of "less eligibility" put into practice with the sweeping reform of the English Poor Laws in 1834. From 1815 on, under the influence of Malthusian thinking, the meaning of the workhouse test used by the laws' administrators to justify the granting of relief would change radically: "The useful work of the old test was replaced by task-work carefully contrived to be economically worthless and personally repulsive" (Mandler 1987, 141–2).

38 "Given that economic discourse had already inscribed poverty in the very operation of the distributional mechanism, it is unsurprising that the relief of poverty would call forth the wrath of the new economic god" (Dean 1991, 152). Note, however, that poverty in this connection was not a permanent state (or status) so much as an impetus to work and to observe moral conformity.
39 On this important group, see Mandler (1990).
40 "For many Englishmen, Christian political economy *was* political economy" (Mandler 1990, 103).
41 "Couched in language obliged to be conciliatory, the charitable discourse of the defenders of tradition (faith, saving souls, the edification of the poor, the virtues of humility and obedience, charity as a restorative, penitential, and redemptive practice) squared off against the philanthropic discourse of the liberals (reason, love of one's fellow men, progress, education, emancipation of the people, foresight, social science)" (Duprat 1997, 2: 1273).
42 "I cannot conceive that a sovereignly just God could have allowed such a difference to be introduced between perfect equals, had he not wanted to bind them closer together by this very inequality, affording an opportunity for the great and the rich to give free rein to a form of charity for which they would be advantageously rewarded by the services they receive from the poor" (Henri François d'Aguesseau, quoted in Villeneuve-Bargemont 1834, 2: 186).
43 In other words: "Society must become religious above all else" (Villeneuve-Bargemont 1834, 3: 137).
44 I will not concern myself here with a fourth tendency, based on conceptions of utopian socialism developing during this period that soon became marginal. The discussion is limited to the different versions of the dominant discourse on poverty and welfare.
45 Innes concludes that patterns of thought about poverty were relatively homogeneous throughout Europe at that time: "The range of efforts directed towards the poor in England did not differ greatly from that to be found elsewhere in Europe. What was different was the balance between the parts ... Although there were certainly great differences between the practices of different states ... thought and practice were also characterized by certain common features. Moreover, from their different starting points, authorities in different countries were to some extent converging on common patterns of thought" (Innes 1999, 233–4, 274–5). The same observation can be made for the nineteenth century. For a radically opposed position, see Merrien (1994).
46 So much so that Villeneuve-Bargemont did not hesitate to advocate relegating welfare recipients to the legal status of minors: "Indigent workers, who solicit or receive relief from public or private charity, tacitly declare to society that they are utterly unable to earn their own living. They ask, in reality, that others

work for them. They thus place themselves in a true state of minority which necessarily entails the renunciation of their rights as citizens and parents ... The common law can only be invoked by those members of society who remain governed by the common law. But those indigents who are granted relief are no longer governed by it; obviously, they belong to a special regime" (Villeneuve-Bargemont 1834, 3: 158). In fact, welfare recipients would be denied the franchise all through the nineteenth century.

47 "Poor law relief, or relief given indiscriminately to assert status or buy off importunity, was no true charity because it was available without certification of deservingness. It was too impersonally given to generate socially stabilizing emotions of reciprocity between giver and receiver. And it was too loosely monitored to assure the development of prudent, market-informed habit in the receiver" (Roberts 1998, 74–5). As an aside, it should be noted that two methods for controlling the distribution of relief existed as of the early nineteenth century: investigation, in the case of outdoor relief, and institutional control, as reflected in the workhouses and houses of industry.

48 Even Malthusian pessimists refrained from criticizing the operation of such "effective" charity. Malthus praised what he described as "voluntary and active charity, which makes itself acquainted with the objects which it relieves; which seems to feel, and to be proud of, the bond which unites the rich with the poor; which enters into their houses, informs itself not only of their wants, but of their habits and dispositions" (Malthus [1803] 1992, 283).

49 This type of conformity is well stated by Malthus, whom I will be forgiven for quoting one last time: "Each individual has, to a great degree, the power of avoiding the evil consequences to himself and society resulting from [the law of population], by the practice of a virtue dictated to him by the light of nature, and sanctioned by revealed religion. And, as there can be no question that this virtue tends greatly to improve the condition, and increase the comforts, both of the individuals who practise it, and through them, of the whole society, the ways of God to man with regard to this great law are completely vindicated" (Malthus [1798] 1970, 272).

50 Even the traditional private institutions doling out indiscriminate relief were targeted by the Malthusian critique.

51 Elsewhere the author specified: "We in no wise share the fright that inhabits so many minds today over the advance of what is called pauperism. We are alarmed by neither increases in the population, nor the rise of industry, nor the development of the great cities, nor inequality of conditions; but we think that the new social circumstances, born out of the progress of industry, wealth, the advancement of civilization itself, gave birth to new necessities, and impose new duties on society" (Gérando 1839, 1: lxxviii).

52 "While it was realized that misery was unequally distributed among the social strata, its concentration in urban slums was not conceived as a social pattern but rather as the stigma of an infested region in which certain maladies held sway ... Poverty and all the other aspects of social privation were accorded the same tangible status as consumption or pneumonia" (Bellingham 1983, 309).

53 Chadwick uses the terms "residuum," "refuse," and "offal" to allude to this population. On this report, see Poovey (1995, 115–31).

54 "The poor law reformers, it is evident, came in all shapes and sizes. They were utilitarians and Unitarians, Evangelicals and orthodox Anglicans, Dissenters and atheists, Whigs and Tories, manufacturers and landlords, countrymen and townsfolk, preachers and philosophers, philanthropists and politicians. They differed radically in their attitudes toward the poor, their theories of economics, their ideas about the proper role of government, their visions of a good society, their views of human nature and divine providence. But they agreed upon the urgency of the problem and the essential solution. The problem was the pauperization of the poor, the solution the removal of the poor from the fatal contamination of the pauper" (Himmelfarb 1984, 175). For a persuasive analysis of the remarkable common front formed by the elites to pass the New Poor Law of 1834, see Mandler (1987 and 1990).

55 "However poverty was viewed – as an inexorable fact of physical and human nature, as an unfortunate by-product of a particular law or institution, or as the fatal flaw of the entire system – it was seen as primarily, fundamentally, a moral problem. It was a moral problem for the poor and for society – for the poor as responsible moral agents, and for society as a legitimate moral order" (Himmelfarb 1984, 526).

56 This consensus extended as far as the most radical elements of the working classes. The socialists especially took great care to distinguish the "healthy" masses from a putatively debased "lumpenproletariat" always apt to serve the bourgeoisie. Marx, in particular, would have merciless words for this social group: "The 'dangerous class,' the social scum, that passive rotting mass thrown off by the lowest layers of the old society, may, here and there, be swept into the movement by a proletarian revolution; its conditions of life, however, prepare it far more for the part of a bribed tool of reactionary intrigue" (Marx and Engels [1848] 2013, 75–6).

57 41 Geo. III (1801), c. 6.

58 The wave of construction was set off by 45 Geo. III (1805), c. 13.

59 One anonymous correspondent, for example, deplored the establishment of soup kitchens, an initiative that tended only to "demoralize the poor; everybody was poor and nobody wanted to work" (*Le Canadien*, 5 September 1819).

60 Gérando's well-known *The Visitor of the Poor*, which would inspire generations of household relief volunteers, dates (in its original French version) from 1820.
61 "A report from the Special Committee, appointed to enquire into and report on the Establishments in this Province for the reception and care of the Insane, for the reception and support of Foundlings, and for the relief and cure of sick and infirm Poor, with the expense thereof, defrayed out of the Provincial Revenue, &c. &c.," *Journals of the Legislative Council of the Province of Lower Canada* (JLCLC), 1824, A1–9. The *Quebec Gazette* similarly denounced "the [Hôtel Dieu], which, while it evidently operates as a bounty to the vicious by relieving them from the support of their offspring, proves ineffectual for the prevention of crime" (*Quebec Gazette*, 16 February 1815, 2).
62 For example, this remark published in the *Canadian Courant* for 31 March 1819, concerning the Soeurs de l'Hôtel-Dieu de Montréal: "Sublime motives are as likely to pervade the bosom of an enlightened practitioner of the 'healing art' as to prevail in the more contracted minds of the inmates of a cloister, whose hearts may fairly be supposed to have been rendered by precept, and habit, equally impervious to the joy of actual social virtue, as to the vices, in the world."
63 "The most general and reasonable of all objections to Charitable Institutions, is founded on the uncertainty of the contributors, with regard to the real necessities of those who are relieved by their bounty ... We therefore conceive it to be one of the duties of those who have occasion to observe, and ample opportunity to assure themselves of the reality of many more scenes of distress, than it is in their power individually to relieve, to point out the proper object of charity to those, who have means of relieving them" ("Meeting, Quebec Public Dispensary," *Quebec Gazette*, 30 November 1818).
64 As proof, this caustic remark by a "Friend of Good Order" in 1821: "There are still people called constables ... who bring shame upon the people of good will ... Let us try ... to attain everyone's cherished goal, which is to no longer have to watch the big crooks chasing after the little ones" (*Le Canadien*, 3 July 1819). This critique of the policing system was especially characteristic in that it paid no attention to the genuine reforms made to this system, which are well described by Fyson (1995).
65 *Journals of the House of Assembly of Lower Canada* (JHALC), 1827, 72–3.
66 "It is not enough to punish but it ought to be an object to mend, and proper treatment may bring and has brought the most abandoned to a conviction of the happiness and ease almost infallibly attending honest conduct with common industry and thus may be reclaimed to society many of its lost and valuable members" (*Quebec Gazette*, 20 January 1823).

67 "Penitentiary Prisons: Report of the Special Committee appointed to take into consideration the Report of the Penitentiary Commissioners appointed under the Act 4th Will. IV, Cap. 10, and to whom were referred various other Papers and Documents relating to Prisons and Prison discipline," *JHALC*, 1835–6, Appendix FFF.

68 One of the main criticisms levelled at the Lower Canadian religious communities in charge of caring for the sick was their refusal to care for infectious cases on the grounds that their restrictive charters would not permit it: "The plea of charity and humanity on which all pretention to the indulgence prayed are founded, must be qualified by the consideration that the Hôtel-Dieu of Montreal ... refuses to admit infectious cases, or any that they may deem such, which greatly detracts from their pretention to usefulness" (anonymous opinion, probably by Jonathan Sewell, Chief Justice of the Province, included in a letter from Dalhousie to Bathurst, 4 May 1826, Public Archives of Canada (PAC), CO 42, vol. 209, 114).

69 "The security consistent with the safety of the Insane, their connexions and general society, can hardly ever, in the heart-rending circumstances attendant on mental derangement be enjoyed in the dwellings of private families"; "A report from the Special Committee, appointed to enquire into and report on the Establishments in this Province for the reception and care of the Insane, for the reception and support of Foundlings, and for the relief and cure of sick and infirm Poor, with the expense thereof, defrayed out of the Provincial Revenue, &c. &c.," *JLCLC* 1824, A1–5.

70 "It is believed such an Institution would be of signal Benefit to the Community, as a means of preventing the Depravation of Morals among the lower Classes by removing from among them those Persons of evil Lives who are sources of Corruption." "Petition of the Justices of the Peace for the District of Quebec," *JHALC*, 1827, 75.

71 "The experience of last winter has demonstrated to the Committee the advantage of confining all paupers who are entirely dependent upon the public charity, instead of allowing them to be fed at large" ("Second Report of the Committee for establishing a Poor House, or House of Industry in Montreal," *Montreal Transcript and General Advertiser*, 3 October 1837, 4).

72 Chief Justice's address to grand jury, Quebec City, September 1825 (*Quebec Gazette*, 10 October 1825).

73 "Continuation sur l'établissement d'Hopitaux dans la Province du Bas-Canada pour les pauvres malades," *Quebec Gazette*, 24 December 1818, 3 (my emphasis).

74 "A report from the Special Committee, appointed to enquire into and report on the Establishments in this Province for the reception and care of the Insane, for the reception and support of Foundlings, and for the relief and cure of sick

and infirm Poor, with the expense thereof, defrayed out of the Provincial Revenue, &c. &c.," *JLCLC* 1824, A1–49.

75 Garland (1985) is a rare exception.

76 Innes (1987, 70) notes the legal uncertainty surrounding the conditions of confinement in the workhouses and houses of correction prior to the democratic transition. An older method consisted of including powers of imprisonment in the founding charter of an institution of detention. This was the procedure followed in the 1820s with the founding of the first reformatory for young offenders in the United States.

77 Moreover, in the case of insanity, committal was subject to negotiation with the family, unless the person in question represented a danger to the public. On this aspect, see Nootens (2003).

78 With the important exception of abandoned children, to which I return in part 2.

79 *Quebec Gazette*, 14 October 1836.

80 Indeed, construction might begin on a project before it was entirely clear what its function was to be. In 1833, the House of Assembly of Lower Canada debated the function to be assigned to a building under construction in Montreal. While it was initially planned as a hospital, some members argued that it should instead become a house of industry or a penitentiary. On the architects' recommendation, the initially planned usage was retained (*JHALC*, 1832–1833, testimony of 6 March 1833). An anonymous author summed up this interchangeability quite nicely: "There are patients to be attended to and physicians to be trained, just as there are criminals to be punished and corrected, poor persons to be fed, and lazy persons to be put to work" (*Le Canadien*, 25 November 1833).

81 See Lea (1979) for an important but overly brief review. The problem posed here ultimately concerns the place accorded in historical studies to the critical discourse developing between 1750 and 1830 in the West. Tribe (1981) highlighted the purposiveness of the dominant analysis of this discourse in the case of the founders of political economy, and more specifically Adam Smith. This very important critique entered the historiography of social regulation with the work of Dean (1991) and Minson (1985).

82 In my view, what these institutions owed to the utopian worldview of the opening decades of the nineteenth century has too rarely been stressed. It was a time for the invention of new social models, and the philanthropists who built prisons and asylums had a great deal in common with people like Charles Fourier, Robert Owen, Louis Blanc, and Hugues-Félicité Robert de Lamennais. The main difference is that, unlike the utopian thinkers, the bourgeois elites had the means to realize their dreams – or at least the bricks-and-mortar

portion thereof. On the generativity of nineteenth-century utopian political thought, see Riot-Sarcey (1998).

83 *JHALC*, 1827, 73 (my emphasis). In a parallel petition, the justices of the peace speak of a house of correction and penitence: "it is believed such an Institution would be of signal Benefit to the Community, as a means of *preventing the Depravation of Morals among the lower Classes*" (ibid., 75, my emphasis).

84 *JHALC*, 1828–1829, 380 (my emphasis).

85 From 1815 to 1840, 39 percent of public expenditures on health and welfare took the form of subsidies to religious institutions. These institutions always housed the same type of clientele, and took them in at roughly the same pace. By way of illustration, for the nine years running from 1815 to 1823, the Hôtel-Dieu de Montréal took in an average of 13.6 patients per week. The weekly intake for the Hôtel-Dieu de Québec was 5.3 (averages calculated from statistics contained in the Report, 1824, Appendix A).

86 The funds were allocated by 10–11 Geo. V (1830), c. 23.

87 Thefts committed in a shop, on a navigable river, or in an inhabited house: 4 Geo. IV (1824), c. 4–6.

88 In terms of procedure, however, there was a notable expansion of the summary jurisdiction of justices of the peace, as shown by the ordinances carefully enumerated by Fyson (1995, Appendix 2).

89 By 58 Geo. II (1818), c. 2. In this case as in that of the payment of a salary to certain local court magistrates, the practice had been current in England since the previous century.

90 On this point, see Greer (1992).

91 Consider, for example, the statistics on crimes prosecuted before the Court of King's Bench of Quebec City. For the period 1815–19, the number of crimes against the person as a proportion of property crimes was 40 percent; by 1835–39, it was down to 11 percent.

92 Fyson (1995, 287, 319, 325–6). However, there was a slight increase in summary convictions.

93 This impasse played an important role in delaying the adoption of certain laws, such as those concerning the Montreal House of Industry. In terms of criminal law reform, *Le Canadien* had no trouble seeing the connection between the pace of adoption of the reforms and the rivalry between the two legislative bodies: "The revision of the criminal code is a big task, so big that we despair of seeing it undertaken with any hope of success, as long as a new system of government suited to the establishment of peace and security does not allow a legislature wrapped in the public's trust to direct at these improvements a level of effort which the people's branch has hitherto been obligated to employ against attempts at monopoly and despotism" (17 September 1834).

94 An example would be the law taxing ships that carried immigrants to Lower Canada, enacted in 1834 (4 Will. IV (1834), c. 31) after awaiting imperial sanction for nearly a year.

95 The justices of the peace did take on a degree of responsibility for local conflict regulation, but they proved (here as in England) to be very poor both at transmitting information to the imperial government and intervening on its behalf. The Rebellions gave striking evidence of their inadequacy. See Fecteau (2002b).

96 *Quebec Gazette*, 1 January 1818, 2.

97 "The distribution of relief to the indigent must be the work of individual charity. It is when individuals acquit themselves of this eminently religious duty that prudence can direct the choice of donations, and of the unfortunates who receive them, in such a way as to produce a salutary effect in these objects of benevolence. A government's acts of generosity in this vein nearly always have pernicious results" (*La Minerve*, 1 June 1829).

98 The important work of Duprat (1993 and 1997) in France has yielded a detailed chronicle of this movement.

99 Criticism of the Poor Law in England tended to invoke these principles; see, e.g., Mandler (1987).

100 Gérando called this "the art of creating a voluntary, immediate, and individual guardianship of the prosperous over the unfortunate" (Gérando 1832, 11).

101 This was true of the Montreal General Hospital at its inception: "No clergy or other official character are inserted as honorary governors, in order to avoid the jealousy attendant on selection" ("Memorandum about the MGH," 18 October 1821, included in a letter from Dalhousie to Bathurst, 20 April 1822, CO 42, vol. 191, 174).

102 For example, the board of the Female Compassionate Society, founded in 1820, included three francophones out of twelve members. This pattern would hold until the mid-1830s or later.

103 One thinks of the orphans' hospice opened in 1832 by the Association des dames canadiennes, and the Charitable Institution for Female Penitents founded by Agathe-Henriette Huguet-Latour in Montreal in 1831.

104 Several directors of institutions might have endorsed a remark by the directors of the Montreal House of Industry, who stated in support of their application for public funds in 1823 that funding by public subscription was "a mode altogether precarious and uncertain and incapable of giving any solidity whatever" (*JHALC*, 1823, 104).

105 *JHALC*, 1835–36, 197. The *Quebec Gazette* for 12 October 1835 argued similarly: "Societies usually have a beneficial effect in turning the public mind to matters of general interest; but they, not unfrequently, have the result of throwing the burden entirely on the revenue of the province ... Any societies

which may be formed among us for philanthropic purposes, would be more likely to succeed, if it were made part of their undertaking to guard against the recurrence of such results ... Too much has been expected from government or the Legislature. All that can reasonably be required of it is, to afford legal facilities for the inhabitants of the different localities to do, conjointly, what they cannot so well do individually. Money not derived immediately from those who reap the benefit, is not well looked after."

106 Which did not, however, totally exclude private initiative, for it would play an important role in managing institutions for young offenders, as discussed in part 2.

107 From 50 percent francophone in 1814 to 25 percent in 1834, to judge from an analysis of surnames.

108 From 1814 to 1834, the proportion of men in prison declined from 90 percent to 65 percent.

109 In 1824, 22 percent of prisoners were under the age of 25. In 1832, the proportion for the same group was 49 percent.

110 While in 1823–24, the proportion of persons incarcerated after conviction (by contrast with persons held before trial) did not exceed 20 percent, it reached 60–70 percent in 1832–34 and never declined thereafter.

111 4–5 Vict. (1841), c. 24–27. The abolition laws of 1824, cited earlier, had little impact on penal incarceration, at least in Quebec City.

112 This hypothesis is bolstered by the fact that the Montreal prison population did not undergo as abrupt a transformation as the population in Quebec City, the principal port of entry for immigrants.

113 The most telling indicator of this transformation is a comparison of penal with preventive (pre-trial) incarceration. In the Quebec City prison, incarcerations of the first type went from 10–25 percent of the total intake in 1823–25 to 65–75 percent in 1832–34.

PART TWO

1 The best known being the monumental work of Radzinowicz and Hood (1948–86).
2 Among many others, Rothman (1971), Ignatieff (1978), Melossi and Pavarini (1981), and their predecessors Rusche and Kirchheimer (1939).
3 See, in particular, Perrot (1980), and also Milo (1991). The landmark work on prisons in nineteenth-century France remains that of Petit (1990).
4 It has too seldom been noted how Foucault's "genealogical" inquiry assumes the continuity of the phenomenon through time, which is moreover of the essence of genealogy. Discontinuity (*rupture*) is, of course, a central concept in Foucault's

work, but this discontinuity is in fact his way of conceiving of the origin, the emergence of the phenomenon whose genealogy he produces. It is as if once this original discontinuity has been analyzed, dissected in its various manifestations, all that remains to be read of this phenomenon (and its underlying logic) is its unfolding through historical time. The same can be said of mental illness, the clinic, and the prison in his work (and of the welfare state in the work of his acolyte, François Ewald). It should be clear that my whole book rests on a diametrically opposed hypothesis (and philosophy of historical time).

5 See the classic study by Chevalier (1973).

CHAPTER FOUR

1 This reference to legality as a constraint on the application of treatment or punishment policies marks an important transition toward modern modes of punishment. A harbinger is found in a remark by a *Quebec Gazette* correspondent concerning the increasingly standard practice of jailing vagrants: "It seems to me that it matters not whether the legislation begins by running a muck against drunkenness in miserable wretches, their starving wives and children, already reduced to a condition when their example is rather favorable to general sobriety than otherwise or whether it is directed against witchcraft, or popery, or lewdness, or gaming, or swearing, or idleness, or laziness, or any other heinous sin or vice ... That the criminal law of England shall continue to be administered in the Province as theretofore, is good, but that innovations in matters of so much importance, if required, should have the sanction of the local legislature at least, seems to me to be indispensible to the security and welfare of the subject" (*Quebec Gazette*, 20 November 1826).

2 One can, as does Alvaro Pires, trace back to the eighteenth century the victory of "modern penal rationality" and the implementation of a problematic based on crime as an autonomous social phenomenon (see Pires [1995], and also the rest of the volume containing it, Debuyst et al. [1995]). But it is also true that this rationality left room for various ways of inscribing crime within society. The liberal regulation that I examine in what follows presented itself as one such modality and it was conditioned by a specific historical conjuncture.

3 For Foucault, for example, once the power relation expressed by confinement is put in place, the future will inevitably consist of a dreary repetition of the contradictions of the prison, pulled between its reforming intentions and its repressive reality, perpetually condemned to produce crime as much as it claims to combat it.

4 See, for example, the work of Spierenburg (1996a and especially 1996b). This gradualism is also found in Franke (1995).

5 I am thinking here of the foundational work of Rusche and Kirchheimer (1939) as well as the more recent work of Melossi and Pavarini (1981).
6 However, such studies have often stumbled into pitfalls, either by positing a mechanical analogy between punishment procedures and production techniques, or by assuming a simplistic functional relationship between the "needs" of an economy and its modes of punishment.
7 The work of Dumm (1987), despite its Foucauldian mannerisms, is a first step in this direction.
8 The "modern penal rationality" whose birth has been traced by some authors back to the eighteenth century (Debuyst et al. 1995) must in this respect be distinguished from the liberal rationalization of modes of crime management under discussion here. The latter constitutes only one possible actualization of the modern rationality in question.
9 Peter King stresses the central role of "discretion" in the old judicial system, in which, by his calculation, barely 10 percent of offences gave rise to prosecution and the working classes possessed "tremendous breadth of discretionary power" (King 2000, 357).
10 In this way, the police became an integral part of contemporary urban culture. For Quebec, Dicaire (1999) has described the process whereby the police force, instead of being a handmaiden to the justice system or the hated visage of state arbitrariness, became the indispensable instrument for front-line crime fighting that was both demanded and constantly criticized by the elites and much of the urban population. For the British case, Storch (1976) remains as relevant as ever.
11 For example, while there were only a few dozen arrests a year in 1820s Quebec City, the police made 3,437 arrests there in 1845. On this latter figure, see Dufresne (1997, 219). This statistic is merely illustrative. A systematic quantitative study of this far-reaching modernization of policing remains to be done.
12 According to Dufresne (2000), it also became possible to create a socially stigmatized category termed "crime," which would form the basis for the construction of criminological knowledge.
13 Accomplished in Lower Canada by the 1857 act that established the modern judicial map; the number of districts thereby increased from five to nineteen.
14 Inspector Wolfred Nelson voiced this concern in 1851: "As to classification, of which so much has been said, it is considered totally impracticable, for where is the line of distinction to be drawn between the traits of character, or even between the ordinary crimes of each individual inmate of a prison?" ("Report of Dr Wolfred Nelson, One of the Inspectors of the Provincial Penitentiary, on the Present State, Discipline, Management and Expenditure of the District and Other Prisons, in Canada East," *Journals of the Legislative Assembly of the Province of Canada* (JLAPC) 11 (4): 43, Appendix HH.

15 For the eloquent example of the United States, see Sutton (1988).
16 On this subject, see chapter 5.
17 On the imprisonment of women, see the cases of the United States (Rafter 1985), France (Lesselier 1982), and Ontario (Oliver 1998).
18 As for Ontario, a central prison was opened in Toronto in 1874. For the chaotic history of this institution, see Oliver (1998, 401–24).
19 In Quebec, the exponential growth in the correspondence of the Crown Law Department (succeeded by the Ministry of Justice) from 1840 to 1920 attests to this development.
20 An interesting partial exception is that of the Montreal women's prison, divided from its inception in 1876 into two sections along denominational lines. The Protestant division was administered by a salaried matron, while the Catholic division was contracted out to the Sisters of the Good Shepherd. Note, however, that the public administration was solely responsible for intake and release of prisoners, and that it closely supervised the treatment regime and any physical alterations made to the institution. For details, see Fecteau, Tremblay, and Trépanier (1993).
21 The two phenomena did, however, coexist at close quarters in the daily reality of the jailhouse. Throughout the period, inspectors and jailers complained about this unseemly cohabitation – a mixing of types no longer considered acceptable in a context of rational crime management. Inspector O'Neill stated in 1865, "It is surely time that the practice of allowing the destitute to commit themselves by the sanction of the authorities to the companionship of the criminal, were superseded by providing some benevolent institution which would rescue them from that danger." "Fifth Annual Report of the Board of Inspectors of Asylums, Prisons, &c., for the Year 1865," *Sessional Papers*, vol. III, Fifth Session of the Eighth Parliament of the Province of Canada, Session 1866, vol. 26, no. 3, SP no. 6, p. 66.
22 "Report of the Special Committee appointed to take into consideration the Report of the Penitentiary Commissioners appointed under the Act 4th Will. IV, Cap. 10, and to whom were referred various other Papers and Documents relating to Prisons and Prison discipline," *JHALC*, 1836, Appendix FFF, 9–10 (my emphasis).
23 Tocqueville argued that the improbability of prisoners' rehabilitation cast doubt on the value of any social investment whose main aim was to bring it about: "To suggest to an adult convict ideas radically different from those he had thus far conceived, to inculcate brand-new sentiments in him, to profoundly change the nature of his habits, to demolish his instincts; in a word, to turn a great criminal into a virtuous man, is assuredly such an arduous and difficult enterprise that it will only rarely be successful, and it would perhaps be unwise for

society to make this the sole object of its efforts" (Chambre des députés, 5 July 1843, in Tocqueville 1984, 2: 134). Note here that he refers to the adult criminal. The liberal approach to juvenile delinquency was different, and I return to it in the next chapter.

24 In sum, to restore someone to an honest life is to work a miracle, not to apply a therapy: "If society pardon, it restores liberty to the prisoner's person – this is all. When God pardons, he pardons the soul. With this moral pardon, the criminal regains his self-esteem, without which honesty is impossible. This is a result which society never can attain, because human institutions, however powerful over the actions and the will of men, have none over their consciences" (Beaumont and Tocqueville 1833, 56).

25 And premeditation represents the direct expression of free will.

26 The prison inspectors of Quebec likewise rejected such "sentimentalism," which they saw as obscuring the true functions of the prison: "We have little sympathy with sentimentalists, who would wish to see introduced into our gaols a system of boarding and lodging which would lead the inmates to believe that they were the guests, instead of the prisoners, of the State. We should bear in mind that those who are in gaol are sent there for their crimes, and that the duty of the Government is to punish them and to inspire them with a proper dread of our penal establishments, and not to give them a desire to return there by too good treatment." "Tenth Report of the Inspectors of Prisons, Asylums, &c. of the Province of Quebec for the Year 1879," *Quebec (Province), Legislature, Sessional Papers* (QSP), vol. 14, no. 8, p. 6.

27 However, Tocqueville's thought is not free of contradictions in this regard: during the same period, in response to criticism to the effect that solitary confinement is inhuman and leads to madness, he stated, "We want to restore the mind to righter thoughts, the soul to more honest sentiments; we want to change the vantage, so to speak, from which the prisoner gazes upon human affairs. Can we hope to make so great and so salutary a revolution in the minds of men without, at times – rarely, very rarely ... the resulting excitation producing some of the symptoms that have caused alarm?" (Chambre des députés, 26 April 1844, in Tocqueville 1984, 2: 231). Compare with the quotation in note 24 above.

28 Note the phrasing, nearly identical to that of the Patriote Amury Girod cited earlier.

29 In a fascinating paper on the role of habits in power relations, Mariana Valverde writes, "Even the most militarized and bureaucratized technologies for surveillance and discipline involved more than making individuals into perfect embodiments of a particular group *habitus*; they involved, paradoxically, the constitution of each of the persons disciplined as an individual, even as a

free, autonomous, self-governing individual" (Valverde 1998, 239). But at the core of the liberal view of the criminal, habits may also be regarded as an inferior form of behaviour, the only form available to those who have lost their self-esteem. In matters criminal, bourgeois formalism is perfectly capable of making do with passive conformity in the absence of "body-and-soul" commitment. This too, distinguishes the criminal from the honest pauper.

30 See chapter 2.

31 That is because humanitarian sentiment goes no further than the boundaries of responsibility and the will. What Wendell Philips put forward as a trait distinguishing labourers from slaves can also be applied to criminals: "There are two prominent points which distinguish the laborers in this country from the slaves. First, the laborers, as a class, are neither wronged nor oppressed: and secondly, if they were, they possess ample power to defend themselves, by the exercise of their own acknowledged rights. Does legislation bear hard upon them? Their votes can alter it. Does capital wrong them? Economy will make them capitalists. Does the crowded competition of the cities reduce their wages? They have only to stay at home, devoted to other pursuits, and soon diminished supply will bring the remedy ... To economy, self-denial, temperance, education, and moral and religious character, the laboring class, and every other class in this country, must owe its elevation and improvement" (Philips [1847], quoted in Haskell 1987, 873). I return to this essential point in part 3.

32 Here again, the need to fight the spread of crime takes precedence over the idea of reform in Tocqueville's thought: "What matters to society most of all is not that a few criminals should by chance become virtuous men; it is that the greatest number of criminals are not hardened in prison; it is that they do not come out more dangerous than they went in; it is that they do not form the kind of associations of miscreants in prison whose misdeeds are visible to all" ("Observations sur le mémoire de M. Ch. Lucas relatif au régime pénitentiaire" (1844), in Tocqueville 1984, 2: 190).

33 As in Beccaria, these authors view proportionality as having a deterrent effect on criminals; see Debuyst et al. (1995, 139).

34 Instances of speeches advocating prisoner reform can of course be found after 1850. Humanitarian solidarity and faith in the future remained central to liberalism. But one is inevitably struck by the scarcity and timidity of tangible reform measures for adult prisoners, including the often envisaged and always postponed panacea of patronage for released prisoners. The liberal era was hard for those who sympathized with the failings of convicted adults. Moreover, the same was true in the world of charity. For example, the Sisters of Mercy in Quebec always found it difficult to solicit donations to help teen mothers, whose behaviour was judged deeply immoral.

35 "Extracts from the Special Report of Inspectors of Prisoners, Asylums, &c.," *QSP*, vol. 18, no. 15, p. 138.
36 "Eleventh Report of the Inspectors of Prisons, Asylums, &c., &c., for the Province of Quebec for the Year 1880," *QSP*, vol. 15, pt. 2, p. 8.
37 "Thirteenth Report of the Inspectors of Prisons, Asylums, &c., of the Province of Quebec for the Year 1882," *QSP*, vol. 16, no. 15, pp. 15–16. In support of this caution, the inspectors quote from the speech of an unidentified Quebec City judge: "If … prompted by an exaggerated sensitiveness, a mistaken idea of philanthropy, we place these criminals in a better position than they were in before committing their crime, does not the punishment become an illusion, a mockery, I may even say a reward for crime. Let us ask ourselves whether the treatment of criminals in our gaols and penitentiaries is in the interest of society and of the state" (ibid., 16–17).
38 Given this context, it is understandable that the eighteenth-century mania for classification described by Foucault would come in for harsh criticism from specialists such as Tocqueville: "Nothing has been more fully proved than the futility of classifying prisoners for the purposes of preventing their mutual corruption" (Chambre des députés, 5 July 1843, in Tocqueville 1984, 2: 121). This was also Joseph Astor's position a generation later: "To be both fair and profitable, classification should comprise no other criterion of evaluation than the nature and worth of individual morals. Unfortunately, there are no psychologists who can feel sure enough of themselves to undertake such a triage without the constant fear of falling into arbitrariness" (Astor 1887, 35–6).
39 At the Philadelphia prison in the 1820s, isolation was seen as providing the necessary setting for the quietude and self-reflection central to the Quaker philosophy of cellular confinement.
40 The argument is eloquently reprised by Pierre Chanteret: "The benefit of the cell ought to have been extended to all, so that no camaraderie could form within the prison … Until now, the cell-confined prisoner has been kept away from good people, who could have taken an interest in his lot and instilled feelings of duty in him. On the contrary, the cell should be opened up to our benefactors, and every opportunity to effect this change for the better should be afforded them … In that case, the cellular system would lose even the appearance of isolation, and would offer the dual advantage of keeping the prisoner away from bad company and exposing him to good" (Chanteret 1876, 14, 16).
41 The recommendation reads: "The object of the sentence is inevitably sacrificed when industrial and productive employment is substituted in short terms of imprisonment, or in the earlier stages of long terms, for labor strictly penal; whilst it will be found to be a delusion to suppose that any real economy is effected by defeating the object of the sentence." "Fifth Annual Report of the

Board of Inspectors of Asylums, Prisons, &c., for the Year 1865," *SPPC*, vol. III, Fifth Session of the Eighth Parliament, Session 1866, vol. 26, no. 3, SP no. 6, p. 41.

42 Ibid., p. 72. In 1884, Inspector A.L. de Martigny was still proposing that rock-breaking be replaced by moving piles of stones around the Montreal jailyard, which "would have the advantage of fatiguing the prisoners and consequently of punishing them, and make them dread the gaol, and it would cost but little": "Extracts from the Special Report of Inspectors of Prisoners, Asylums, &c.," *QSP*, vol. 18, no. 15, p. 138, 1885.

43 "Twentieth Report of the Inspectors of Prisons, Asylums & Public Works, in the Province of Quebec for the Year 1888," *QSP*, vol. 23, pt. 2, no. 145, p. 20. Around the same time, Astor once again stated this position with eloquence: "What good result could we expect from work assigned exclusively as punishment? Its partisans defend it as a means of intimidation for future criminals and of atonement for the prisoner who suffers it. For our part, we believe there would be no other effect than to engender hatred and demoralization, to instill in convicts a disgust for occupations of all kinds ... On work alone can we base the hope of regeneration of the convict ... the idea of punishment must be associated with being deprived of it, not with being forced to do it."

44 I will not dwell on the outcome of the debate over total or partial isolation of prisoners. Suffice it to say that in North America, nocturnal solitary confinement with communal daytime work would prevail in the large majority of cases, while most countries of Western Europe would invest heavily in total solitary confinement as of the 1840s. However, this latter practice existed only in the large central prisons and was applied for relatively short periods. On this point, see Franke (1995, xi).

45 This approach, which both explains crime and provides for its punishment, depends of course on the perpetrator's understanding of the wrong he has committed. It is no surprise, then, to find that just as this model of regulation was being instated, a rigorous definition of the mental insanity defence was also being put in place with the McNaughton decision of 1843. The use of psychiatric expertise quickly became standard practice. See Moran (1981), Verdun-Jones (1981), and especially, for Quebec, Labrèche-Renaud (1991).

46 "Discouragement is impossible, however, for the law of progress is manifest. Though evil is with us for the long term, so is that protestation of the human conscience – varied in its forms, immutable in its principle, vast, universal, indefatigable, invincible – which withers and combats it" (Blanc 1845).

47 This openness to the social environment as a source and a trigger of criminality would ultimately find timid support even among certain proponents of solitary confinement: "Social organization, the insufficiency or inadequacy

of laws, must be given pride of place among the various causes of crime. These causes are poverty, child abandonment or exploitation, abuse of parental power, lack of education and instruction, and also the showy display of their wealth by the rich, inadvertently arousing a thirst for similar enjoyment in the poor man's heart ... The paths of good must be opened up to these minds perverted by the environment in which they lived or by unfortunate circumstances; hope must be permitted to enter these souls prone to discouragement and too apt to believe in the undying hostility of the honest population" (Astor 1887, 29–30). But the conclusion derived by this philanthropic version of "environmentalism" was of course the necessity of charity, not social change. I return to this point in part 3.

48 "Here is a man of misfortune, born out of the mud of our cities ... Do not forget that your social order has not extended to this unfortunate the protection to which his suffering entitles him. Do not forget that his free will has been perverted since the cradle; that crushing and unjust fate weighed upon his good will; that he has known hunger; that he has been cold; that he has not known or learned goodness" (Astor 1887, 28–9). For Astor, the will is not primary, for society is the crucible in which it is formed.

49 "The cellular system ... is nothing more than long-term entombment, a form of dreadful suffering that leads to insensibility, suicide, or madness!" (Blanc 1845, 25–6).

50 Speech by Hippolyte Carnot in the Chamber, session of 23 April 1844, in Tocqueville (1984, 2: 318).

51 It was also necessary to acknowledge that such re-education called for attention to the specifics of each case. In this, the radical critique of liberal penality stated a principle with a grand future ahead of it; namely, that of individualized treatment: "Do not subject all these rebel natures, which have resisted social education, to a uniform method of curative education ... If it is true that absolute methods of education must be rejected, and that the method must above all be adapted to the individual ... this is even truer in the case of these personalities so deeply set in their ways, which are all the more inflexible for having been forged, as it were, by prolonged and arduous struggle against the social order" (Speech by Hippolyte Carnot in the Chamber, session of 23 April 1844, in Tocqueville [1984, 2: 331]). Contrariwise, the liberal regulation of crime, beyond the functional specialization of penal institutions and the principle of proportionate sentencing, was based on standardized treatment. Classification was at best a particular enactment of this principial uniformity.

52 "Twenty-third Report of the Inspectors of Prisons, Asylums and Public Offices of the Province of Quebec for the Year 1892," *QSP*, vol. 27, pt. 2, no. 8, p. 13. The inspectors add: "Good intention is essential to reformation, for a prisoner cannot effect his reformation if the state of his mind is hostile thereto, in like

manner as a bad man cannot become good against his wish. It is not a military discipline which is needed but one of moral force" (ibid., 14–15).

53 The Irish system of penal discipline, developed by Sir Walter Crofton in the 1860s according to a model originally proposed by Alexander Maconochie, involved a sequence of stages (solitary confinement, hard labour, "intermediate prisons," possibility of parole) and the use of a "mark system" to provide incentives for good performance. In 1864, the Canadian inspectors unsuccessfully proposed the adoption of these penitentiary techniques. See "Annual Report of the Board of Inspectors of Asylums, Prisons, &c., for the Year 1864," *SPPC*, Vol. 1, Fourth Session of the Eighth Parliament, Second Session 1865, vol. 25, no. 1, SP no. 14, p. 16.

54 Garland rightly stresses the limited latitude of philanthropy vis-à-vis the penal system: "The nineteenth-century state was concerned not to monopolise care of the poor, but rather to minimise its involvement, relieving only the truly destitute, and leaving the remaining field open to charitable intervention. Philanthropy could thus have direct access to the poor ... In contrast, 'penal philanthropy' could have access to offenders only as and where authorised by the state" (Garland 1985, 126).

55 The American judge Charles Hoffman was even more caustic: "It borders on the ridiculous that in the light of all that science and medicine has revealed on the line of pathological and psychopathic states as affecting conduct ... our criminal courts still continue the farce of trying the offense and not the offender" (quoted in Rothman 1980, 72).

56 This did not, however, imply any breaking up of the cognitive category of the "criminal." Quite the contrary, the "scientific" view of crime as a curable defect had as a consequence that of throwing those possessing this defect into the stigmatized category of the unfit. Eugenics would systematize this tendency to isolate the "healthy" working classes from a defective sub-proletariat. I return to this central issue in part 3.

57 Compare with Marx's critique of bourgeois formal equality: "Right by its very nature can only consist in the application of an equal standard; but unequal individuals (and they would not be different individuals if they were not unequal) are only measurable by an equal standard in so far as they are brought under an equal point of view, are taken from one *definite* side only" (Marx 1875, 9).

58 The same can be said for the relative decline of belief in "the improving effect" of solitary confinement (Franke 1995, 301). In Quebec, allusions to intermediate prison (for recidivists) and the benefits of the cell disappear entirely after the mid-1890s.

59 It should be clear that there is no attempt here to write a "history" of the Montreal prison, but rather to situate the institution in the context just sketched

out. A more in-depth study of this prison is in progress at the Centre d'histoire des régulations sociales.
60 These remarks apparently apply to Quebec's first penitentiary, Saint-Vincent-de-Paul, whose history has yet to be written.
61 However, extensive work in 1852 turned the east wing into an exemplar of the Auburn or New York system (nighttime solitary confinement, daytime work in groups), with tiny cells looking onto a central area (no windows to the outside) and secret outer passageways for the guards. Although not a penitentiary as such, the Montreal prison thus had the dubious honour of having drawn inspiration from the two dominant penitentiary models in the West. On this issue, see Noppen (1976).
62 The Saint-Vincent-de-Paul penitentiary only opened in 1873.
63 Until 1913 it housed a much larger population than all the other Quebec prisons combined. Even the Quebec City prison, although entirely rebuilt between 1861 and 1871, was a distant second.
64 By 1876 there were 163 cells and three dormitories.
65 Similarly, some basic material improvements (e.g., steam heating in 1872, electricity in the early twentieth century) were introduced with varying degrees of success.
66 However, the construction of the imposing Bordeaux prison, which opened in 1913, caused a scandal due to the high cost of the facility; see Lafont (2003).
67 "The positivist school, with its 'scientific' approach, introduced principles of legitimacy no longer based on juridical ethics but on what was claimed to represent scientific evidence. At this point the reaffirmed abnormality of offenders provided justification for suspending the relationship between punishment and crime in order to build a new relationship between the individual and the quest for appropriate 'treatment'" (Debuyst et al. 1995, 292).
68 And science did indeed find inmates in other institutions whom it could use as guinea pigs for its experiments – but that is a whole other story.

CHAPTER FIVE

1 Mettray, too, had predecessors, in the early institutions of farm education for poor children such as the Hofwyl colony in Switzerland, founded in 1799. See Ruchat (1996) and Dekker (2001).
2 "Report of the Special Committee appointed to take into consideration the Report of the Penitentiary Commissioners appointed under the Act 4th Will. IV, Cap. 10, and to whom were referred various other Papers and Documents relating to Prisons and Prison discipline," *JHALC*, 1836, Appendix FFF, 10.

3 This optimism did not apply to girls, however: "the reformation of girls, who have contracted bad morals, is a chimera which it is useless to pursue" (Beaumont and Tocqueville 1833, 123).
4 The case of the particular treatment accorded to women will not be addressed here, for lack of space and because a comprehensive history of women's incarceration in Canada, and especially Quebec, has yet to be written. Suffice it to say that the inauguration of institutions specifically intended for women, at first largely predicated on the unsuitability of any sexual mixing in the space of the prison, would henceforth allow for treatment based on the characteristics of the feminine "soul": sharing space with the other prisoners, being initiated to "feminine" trades such as sewing and ironing, etc. Even for children, the treatment philosophy would differ greatly for girls as opposed to boys. This was true in the United States (Rafter 1985; Brenzel 1983), England (Mahood 1995), and France (Lesselier 1982). For Quebec, see Strimelle (1998).
5 Whence the continual insistence by advocates of specific institutions for young offenders on the importance of distinguishing such houses from prisons. The Quebec prison inspectors emphasized this distinction when new reformatories were opened in the province: "A Prison strictly so called and a Reformatory are two very different things. It is true that in this Province, the inmates of our Reformatories, instead of being young people entering them of their own free will or sent by their parents, are offenders under sentence of the courts; but the object, sought to be attained is not less the same in both cases, and this object is not punishment, but correction, improvement and reform. They are not establishments where punishment is inflicted and they are consequently not prisons": "First Report of the Board of Inspectors of Prisons, Asylums, &c., &c., for the Years 1867 & 1868," *QSP*, vol. 1, no. 23, p. 10.
6 See, e.g., Radzinowicz and Hood (1948–86, vol. 5), Renouard (1990), Platt (1977), P. Meyer (1983), and Rothman 1980.
7 See Hawes (1971). Beaumont and Tocqueville enthusiastically approved of this initiative: "The houses of refuge ... are, as is seen in their origin, private institutions; yet they have received the sanction of public authority. All the individuals whom they contain are legally in custody. But in approving of the houses of refuge, government does not interfere in their management and superintendence ... Thus left to themselves, and subject to the control of public opinion alone, the houses of refuge prosper" (Beaumont and Tocqueville 1833, 110–1).
8 "Instead of stepping up police action or brute force to redress the moral disorders identified, it was suggested to alter course and focus on consciences by means of a special form of education that would aim for such regeneration" (Ruchat 1993, 32).

9 Katz (1968, 19–112), Rothman (1971, 230–6), Stack (1979–80). Dekker (2001, 5) identifies two different currents in this movement: "The Evangelical philanthropists wanted to save the child from a life of sin; the modern philanthropists wanted to raise it to become an emancipated and self-reliant citizen." It is not clear, however, that these goals were contradictory. I return to this important point.

10 This was a core idea of the Napoleonic legislation of 1804; see Théry and Biet (1989).

11 For Lower Canada, an early statement of this growing awareness of the danger that neglected children might represent is found in the pages of *La Minerve*: "At present, in the absence of any system, a large number of children are being raised in such a fashion as to become a blot on society, and perhaps the terror of the forthcoming generation. One look at the behaviour of these miserable youths and it is clear that we must have public institutions to accommodate them, regardless of the cost" (*La Minerve*, 28 July 1836, quoted in Lapointe-Roy [1987, 212–14]).

12 One example would be the work of Benjamin Appert in 1820s France; see Petit (1994, 79–90).

13 For the English case, see King and Noel (1994).

14 See Ruchat (1993 and 1996).

15 "Child control reforms are not in any meaningful sense expressions of social or economic instrumentalities but rather are primarily institutional and political in nature" (Sutton 1988, 245).

16 "Annual Report of the Board of Inspectors of Asylums, Prisons, &c., for the Year 1864," Canada, Parliament, *Sessional Papers of the Province of Canada* (SPPC), vol. 25, Fourth Session of the Eighth Parliament, Second Session 1865, pt. 1, no. 14, p. 80.

17 At the risk – always perceived, always avoided by methods I shall review – that a basic contradiction in philanthropic discourse would poke through: "Philanthropists did a pedagogic Jekyll and Hyde by hailing the family as the ideal place to raise children and at the same time creating the re-education home where children were to be re-educated outside the family, torn away from their parents and siblings" (Dekker 2001, 39).

18 For the American case, see Sutton (1988); for France, see Gaillac (1991) and Carlier (1994). For a comparative analysis, see Dupont-Bouchat et al. (2001).

19 Bellingham raises an important point in this regard. He shows that the first placement initiatives for "foundlings" arising in the 1840s actually housed children given up by impoverished families who could not afford to keep them. Despite the philanthropists' contempt-ridden discourse, these children were institutionalized with some complicity on the part of the families, in that

abandonment was precisely the pretext for the intervention. But, as it was extended to *negligent* or unfit families, intervention became increasingly invasive, since it operated with a more exacting definition of family ties: "The blood tie was formally and openly rivaled by another, equally valid or even more valid symbolism of loving conduct that might supplant the claims of blood kin, who cease to be symbolically 'real' for failure to satisfy a code for conduct" (Bellingham 1990, 151).

20 For example, this cry of exasperation from MP William Dunlop during a legislative debate on the question in 1843: "There was, in his opinion, in the present day, altogether too much of that maudlin sentimentality abroad in the world, which extended charity to vice at the expense of honesty and industry, ... which sympathized with crime, and neglected the really honest man ... He thought the best punishment was to tie them up and give them a good thrashing; he would whip them and send them to bed. It was really too absurd to talk of a moral school for such characters. He would be glad to see a house of correction in the rear of each prison, where they would be taken, tied up, and treated in the way he had pointed out": Canada, Legislature, Legislative Assembly, *Debates of the Legislative Assembly of United Canada* (DLAUC), 1843, p. 383. Note the extent to which this speech corresponds to the liberal conception of adult crime regulation analyzed in the preceding chapter.

21 "Fifth Annual Report of the Board of Inspectors of Asylums, Prisons, &c., for the Year 1865," SPPC, vol. 26, Fifth Session of the Eighth Parliament, Session 1866, pt. 3, no. 6, p. 39.

22 For a detailed analysis of the implementation of these institutions, see Fecteau et al. (1998). See also Joyal (2000).

23 "Fifth Annual Report of the Board of Inspectors of Asylums, Prisons, &c., for the Year 1865," SPPC, vol. 26, Fifth Session of the Eighth Parliament, Session 1866, pt. 3, no. 6, p. 38.

24 Monseigneur Ignace Bourget, who served as Bishop of Montreal from 1840 to 1876, seems to have made special provision to bring in the Brothers of Charity from Belgium to administer Canada's largest reform school, the Institut Saint-Antoine, starting in 1873. For an in-depth analysis of this institution, see Ménard (2003). For the girls' school, see Strimelle (1998).

25 Joyal (2000, 44–5) offers a detailed analysis of these amendments.

26 In practice, however, children would to a great extent be placed in one or the other of these schools on the basis of age, with the youngest going to the industrial school. This division was especially obvious when the two institutions were housed in the same building and administered by the same congregation, this being the Sisters of the Good Shepherd in the girls' case. On this point, see Strimelle (1998).

27 On this point, see Clapp (1998) for a fine, detailed study.
28 The development of a more activist feminism and the reaffirmation of the working family have been the subject of an extensive literature in recent years; see, e.g., Gordon (1994), Pedersen (1993), Ross (1993), Bock and Thane (1991), Comacchio (1993), and the major work by Skocpol (1992).
29 Particularly after the great surveys of Le Play; see, e.g., Le Play (1884).
30 Note that the change in how the working family was viewed in no way implies that they had hitherto accepted their children's confinement without resistance. As Brother Hermias, director of the Montreal Reformatory, explained: "Experience has shown more than once that parents in no way concerned about the real interests of their children, but moved by false caring or self-interest, will have recourse to all sorts of expedients, put forward a thousand and one specious reasons, for having their child pardoned. It is useless to show them their mistake: that the child is not really corrected, that his character is not sufficiently tempered, that he does not work conscientiously, that a longer stay would probably insure his perseverance along the path of good, that we cannot vouch for his future good conduct, etc. Nothing will do. The father or mother insist, put pressure on one or another influential personage, and finally achieve their goal"; "Forty-fourth Report of the Inspectors of Asylums, Reformatory Schools and Industrial Schools of the Province of Quebec for the Year 1913," *QSP*, vol. 48, pt. 4, no. 12, p. 10. On this point, see Myers (1999).
31 The discourse of eugenics would survive this critique of confinement. In parallel with the reaffirmation of the working family (and following deeply complementary logic), the medical discourse justifying the exclusion of "hopeless cases" and deficients could be applied in support of extended confinement for extreme cases of dependency and deviance, and helps explain the maintenance (and at times, the development) of institutions of confinement for minors. Rothman has rightly noted that the new youth courts did not supplant older institutional forms of confinement: they merely extended the social safety net for children, opening up new opportunities for state intervention. On this point, see also Chunn (1992).
32 On this institution, see Rains and Teram (1992).
33 The contrast is particularly stark in this statement taken from an 1874 report by the New York Children's Aid Society: "Man must be taken for what he is. But the child may be trained to what he should be"; quoted in Bellingham (1983, 311).
34 Alexander Thomson, *Social Evils, Their Causes and Their Cure*, quoted in "Annual Report of the Board of Inspectors of Asylums, Prisons, &c., for the Year 1864," *SPPC*, vol. 25, Fourth Session of the Eighth Parliament, Second Session 1865, pt. 1, no. 14, p. 81. The inspector added: "It is a much better investment

to pay the cost for preventing a youth from becoming a thief, than, after he has become so, to bear his levies. Viewing the evil in this light, it is clearly the duty of society to call on the state to supply, by legislation, to the truant vagrant child, that place which there is either no natural parent to fill, or which the parent, by reason of his immorality or negligence, is incompetent to fill."

35 The scholarly literature, however, is not unanimous on this important point. Schlossman (1977, 211n26) dates the disappearance of the distinction between these two categories to the mid-nineteenth century, while May (1973, 23), Brenzel (1983, 45), Mennel (1973, 76), and Digneffe and Dupont-Bouchat (1983, 138), among others, claim that this basic distinction was still very much in place at that time. Of course, this does not necessarily entail an institutional separation, for a number of institutions (e.g., Mettray, the English and Quebec reform schools) could accommodate both young offenders and children abandoned by their parents.

36 It is important to note that the declaration of parental incapacity was only one strategy available at this time. The extension of compulsory power could take the form of temporary removal of children from the family, as it did in Quebec.

37 "An act for the more speedy trial and punishment of juvenile offenders," *Statutes of the Province of Canada*, 20 Vict. (1857), c. 29.

38 "An Act for establishing Prisons for Young Offenders – for the better government of Public Asylums, Hospitals and Prisons, and for the better construction of Common Gaols," *Statutes of the Province of Canada*, 20 Vict. (1857), c. 28.

39 This process would not go unchallenged, as Rothman shows by citing the remonstrance of the American lawyer Edward Lindsay in 1914: "In the case of commitment to an institution, there is often a very real deprivation of liberty, nor is that fact changed by refusing to call it punishment or because the good of the child is stated to be the object" (Rothman 1980, 232).

40 For the Quebec Protestant case, see the eloquent demonstration by Harvey (2001).

41 Also of note is the parallel case of the French public child care centres, analyzed by Luc (1997).

42 Sudan (1997, 385) makes the same remark.

43 Brace founded the Children's Aid Society, one of the first organizations of its kind, in the United States. Carpenter was among the founders of the reformatories and industrial schools in England. Demetz was the founder of Mettray.

44 Such an argument would have been difficult to defend, given the inconvenient fact that the institutions promoted by these good Samaritans were often recipients of substantial state funding.

45 On the contrary, state support was frequently acknowledged to be necessary. Inspector O'Neill: "If the vagrant is to be reclaimed and the public spared the injury and cost of his misdeeds, some organized agency for the purpose

is requisite. This must necessarily be a state institution. The support desirable from private beneficence is too uncertain to base on it the maintenance of a permanent undertaking": "Annual Report of the Board of Inspectors of Asylums, Prisons, &c., for the Year 1864," *SPPC*, vol. 25, Fourth Session of the Eighth Parliament, Second Session 1865, pt. 1, no. 14, p. 82.

46 Or, to quote Brace: "Each poor, deserted, unfortunate little creature in the streets is an individual like no other being whom God has created ... The pledge of his immortality, is his individuality ... which makes it impossible ever absolutely to include him within the machinery of a system" (Brace 1859, quoted in Schlossman 1977, 44).

47 I stress that the near-universal recognition of the essentiality of religious and moral education did not necessarily entail an institutional division along denominational lines, nor even a devolution of administrative responsibility to the religious authorities. I return to this critical issue in part 3.

48 "First Report of the Board of Inspectors of Prisons, Asylums, &c., &c., for the Years 1867 & 1868," *QSP*, vol. 1, no. 23, p. 10.

49 On the multiple forms of collaboration between the state and private philanthropy, see Valverde (1995).

50 It became necessary in this same context to separate the Catholic women's prison, entrusted to the Sisters of the Good Shepherd in 1876, from the Protestant women's prison, even though they continued to share a building!

51 "The Belgian Brothers, a holy order, have evidently not forgotten the lessons taught by the monsters of the Inquisition, and have fully sustained their devilish machinations for practicing oppression on their fellow beings"; *Montreal Daily Witness*, 3 February 1873.

52 *Montreal Daily Witness*, 19 March 1873.

53 For example, the placement of children in large-scale institutions was at times justified with reference to the family model: "The great design of the school should be to make it, as much as possible, like a family – to have the boys stand to the officers in the relation of children to parents" (Joseph Addison Allen, Superintendent of the Massachusetts State Reform School, 1861, quoted in Katz 1968, 188). The family model could equally well serve as an argument against institutionalization and in favour of outdoor relief: "The family must grow: it cannot be made in a day, nor be put together by rules and compass ... We have, at best, a make-believe society, a make-believe family, and, too often, a make-believe virtue (S.H. Howe, *Second Annual Report of the Massachusetts Board of State Charities*, 1866, quoted in Schlossman 1977, 48).

54 "An Act to empower the Managers of Industrial and Reformatory Schools, and of certain Charitable Institutions, to apprentice or place out children under their charge," Quebec (Province), *Statutes of the Province of Quebec*, 35 Vict. (1871), c. 13. However, the law only permitted industrial and reform

schools to place out or indenture children under their control, whereas it allowed other institutions, including orphanages, to "place [children] out to domestic service and indenture, bind or apprentice [them] thereto, or to any healthy trade or business, and [to] send [them] out to be nursed, supported, educated or adopted" (section 4).

55 The lay-administered Protestant institutions, on the other hand, developed an intensive practice of placement. On this point, see Harvey (2001). From the 1890s on, Ontario adopted the placement of abandoned children as standard practice.

56 On the connection between the development of the youth courts and the growing practice of placement, see Tétard (1994). A systematic study has yet to be done for Quebec.

57 The event took place under the presidency of Dr John George Adami, president of the Montreal Civic Progress League, and the vice-presidency of Thomas Gauthier, president of the Société Saint-Jean-Baptiste. The organizing committee included a cross-section of Montreal's progressive elites.

58 See Bender (1975) for an eloquent demonstration of this point.

59 This sentiment was clearly expressed in 1873 by the proponents of a Montreal Protestant industrial school: "Neither the heart of a city like Montreal, nor a less populous place like Sherbrooke, seems suitable for the retention of those youths, who, full of animal vigor, and accustomed to desperate acts, are apt to feel, whilst in the city, like the caught bird which has just been caged when it hears and sees its free fellows on the outsides of the bars" (*Montreal Daily Witness*, 1 February 1873).

60 On this point, see Holloran (1994, 266n70).

61 Burban (1997) produced an interesting analysis of this institution.

62 "Sixth Report of the Inspectors of Prisons and Asylums, etc. for the Year 1873," QSP, vol. 7, no. 5, pp. 85–6.

63 "Twentieth Report of the Inspectors of Prisons, Asylums & Public Works, in the Province of Quebec for the Year 1888," QSP, vol. 23 (1890), pt. 2, no. 145, p. 85.

64 This is, in my view, one of the main characteristics of the liberal approach, as opposed to the idea of the fundamentally bad child who needs correction in order to be saved. This latter notion was basic to the older way of thinking, whether Catholic or Protestant.

65 SPPC, vol. 25, Fourth Session of the Eighth Parliament, Second Session 1865, pt. 1, no. 14, p. 82. As a result, the cellular system, while important to liberal penal thinking, was not generally recommended for children, except perhaps for short periods: "We are of opinion, that young offenders, instead of being shut up every evening in cells similar to those in which convicts are confined in the penitentiary, might, with greater advantage, sleep in ordinary dormitories, in such a manner as to habituate them to family life": QSP, vol. 1, no. 23, p. 10.

66 Even Tocqueville, so reluctant to accept this principle for adults, admitted its importance in the case of children: "the high opinion instilled into the child, of his own morality and social condition, is not only fit to effect his reformation, but also, the best *means* to obtain from him entire submission" (Beaumont and Tocqueville 1833, 119).

67 "Twentieth Report of the Inspectors of Prisons, Asylums & Public Works, in the Province of Quebec for the Year 1888," QSP, vol. 23 (1890), pt. 2, no. 145, p. 84.

68 On this point, see Ménard (2003).

69 Certain Protestant organizations, such as the YMCA, were probably also influential in this regard; see Macleod (1978) and, more generally, Mjagkij and Spratt (1997).

70 Beyond formal homologies, the fate of children in reform institutions thus has to be distinguished even from the boarding school system, which partakes of a logic of complementarity between the family and the institution that is itself integral to a service relationship. For example, in the Quebec industrial schools for non-criminal abandoned children, running away was punishable by confinement in a reform school. In the case of the boarding school, expulsion was the worst punishment that could be applied to a runaway.

71 "Sixth Report of the Inspectors of Prisons and Asylums, etc. for the Year 1873," QSP, vol. 7, no. 5, p. 65.

72 Weinberger (1994) raises this point, although she does not identify the changes in society's views of the family underlying the phenomenon.

73 Aid to needy mothers, family allowances, even old-age pensions were thus conceived as elements of a *family* policy (not merely a policy on children). For an analysis of the changes undergone by this discourse in Quebec, see Quesney (1998).

74 On this point, see Boli-Bennett and Meyer (1978).

75 The perception of this danger, and the denunciation of unfit families, led to the adoption of the first policies for intervention in the cases of young offenders and children at risk. It matters little that, at this juncture, their own families often placed these children in institutions; I return to this essential point. For an excellent analysis of the discrepancies between philanthropic discourse and actual familial attitudes, see Bellingham (1990) and, for Quebec, Myers (1999).

CHAPTER SIX

1 Ozanam to Fortoul and Bluchard, 15 January 1831 (Ozanam 1886, 18).

2 For two examples of this interpretation in Quebec, see Lapointe-Roy (1987) and D'Allaire (1997).

3 One of the main critics of Malthusianism, William Hazlitt, had early on shown sensitivity to the impact of structural insecurity on the situation of the poor and the issue it represented: "What has been most grievous to [the poor] of late years is that no man, however hardworking ... could be sure that insecurity and poverty would not overtake him. It is this that sometimes drives a poor man to spend on drink the money he sorely needs for bread, because, alas! to the labouring poor it is often more important to forget the future even than to satisfy their present wants. The extravagance and thoughtlessness of the poor arise, not from their having more than enough to satisfy their immediate needs, but from their not having enough to ward off impending ones – in a word, from desperation. This sense of insecurity presses hardly less than hunger itself ... some kind of reform is necessary. Otherwise a national bankruptcy becomes inevitable, or even a revolution" (Hazlitt 1807).

4 "The liberal position on law rigorously distinguishes it from ethics. Better, it makes this distinction, and hence the limitation of the sphere of law, the condition of possibility for the coexistence of different freedoms. It is because we have the possibility of distinguishing between two orders of social obligations, of delimiting their respective spheres, that a free life in society is possible. The creation of law as a selection or limitation starting from a set of natural obligations must itself be accomplished with respect for the principle of the coexistence of freedoms" (Ewald 1986, 61).

5 "We know the course of human nature when left to its own devices: revoltingly naked selfishness, squabbling, brutality, and bad examples for the private man and the family; debauchery, stultifying folly, and frequent crimes for the public man and society" (Gasparin 1846, 50).

6 And particularly the progress to be expected from philanthropy: "While much remains to be perfected, or to be extended, little remains to be invented ... While it is possible to improve the organization of the forms of charity practised in older times, to deploy them on a wider scale, there are few new ones to be employed, if we are to remain within the bounds of common sense. When we say that there are few new ones, we do not mean none at all ... but we say that there are few, and this makes sense when one thinks of all the establishments that humanity and religion have created over the centuries" (Thiers [1850] 1880, 465).

7 Looking back on the events of 1848, Adolphe Blanqui (1849) contended that it is a vain hope that politics can ever trump the operation of the marketplace.

8 Natural law, whether in its optimistic humanitarian version or its pessimistic Malthusian one, constituted the highest expression of this compelled conformity.

9 During this era, Comte developed the notion of social duty: "Duty ... determines one's place in the social body and binds all its members together; it is

the counterpart, at the individual level, of the laws that govern society. Thus the natural basis of individual sociality becomes the open and boundless field of a pedagogy of the citizen" (Procacci 1993, 305).

10 This is what is meant by the formalism of liberal law, as opposed to more active forms of normative and legislative intervention in the life of the citizen. On this point, see Fecteau (1994b).

11 Gérando makes essentially the same point when he stresses hope as the driver of the poor man's motivation: "Only he who has a future knows how to plan for it; to the present hardship, setbacks add the loss of prospects and expectations ... Prudence, which foresees perils, needs to be entertained in the mind of man by the hope of success. To be provident only out of fear is a sad and depressing situation. Make it so that, for the poor man, existence has a certain price, if you want him to be concerned about the means of preserving it! Show him some favourable prospects, if you want him to think of tomorrow!" (Gérando 1839, 1: 342–3).

12 Again it was Mill who mapped out the "sphere" of action left to the state (Mill 1848, 5: 936–71).

13 See chapter 4.

14 This hostility toward philanthropy is found at both ends of the political spectrum, from Balzac to Marx and Engels: "Modern philanthropy is the bane of society" (Balzac [1845] 1915, 102); "human misery itself, infinite abjectness which is obliged to receive alms, must serve as a *plaything* to the aristocracy of money and education to satisfy their self-love, tickle their arrogance and amuse them ... charity has long been *organized* as entertainment" (Marx and Engels [1844] 1975, 257).

15 "The practice of charity is incompatible with the full responsibility of the pauper – that is, with the full sanction of the duties of providence – and this sanction must be established as a direct function of the level of activity carried out by charity and the scope it gives to its works ... Assistance and responsibility are two mutually exclusive ideas, the one being the implicit negation of the other" (Cherbuliez 1853a, 167).

16 Darwin himself always rejected this misappropriation of Darwinian thought. See the convincing demonstration of this assertion by Tort (1983, 166–97).

17 "Is it not manifest that there must exist in our midst an immense amount of misery which is a normal result of misconduct, and ought not to be dissociated from it? There is a notion, always more or less prevalent and just now vociferously expressed, that all social suffering is removable, and that it is the duty of somebody or other to remove it. Both these beliefs are false" (Spencer [1884] 1969, 83).

18 This idea is to be distinguished from the Catholic notion of the inevitability of poverty, to which I return in chapter 7.

19 While workers generally tend to focus on solidarity as the key to mutual aid, the elites of the day mainly picked up on the preventive and voluntary dimensions of the mutualist ethos. This ambiguity would be central to the development of mutualism in the century to come.

20 "Thus, a dual process occurred within the space of a decade, in which the conduits of philanthropy came into increasing disrepute and it was confined to the sphere of private action. Whether well- or ill-intentioned, positive or negative in its effects, its interventions were henceforth perceived as strictly private, voluntary practices, as opposed to those of the enlightened legislator or the competent administrator. This led around 1840 to the destruction of the ethical model that had been so powerful in the eighteenth century: that of the citizen as friend of man and the 'philanthropic statesman'" (Duprat 1997, 1: 1249).

21 It should be noted that the industrial world was no longer perceived as a cause of pauperism in this connection; on the contrary, it was pauperism that was considered an obstacle to economic development.

22 "Poverty, whatever can justify the designation of 'the poor,' ought to be a transitional state to which no man ought to admit himself to belong, tho' he may find himself *in* it because he is passing *thro'* it, in the effort to leave it. Poor men we must always have, till the Redemption is fulfilled, but *The Poor,* as consisting of the same individuals! O this is a sore accusation against society" (Coleridge [1831], quoted in Dean 1991, 146).

23 "Poverty ... is the natural, the primitive, the general and the unchangeable state of man ... as labour is the source of wealth, so is poverty of labour. Banish poverty, you banish wealth" (Chadwick [1836], quoted in Poovey 1995, 188).

24 "It will take centuries perhaps to raise the class with whom we have to deal out of their present condition. But when we have learnt how to do so, then we shall have solved the question of pauperism. Now we are dealing with the poisoned river; we must cut off the poisonous supplies. And any measure taken to raise the whole tone of the class in which pauperism exists, is, if a wise one, more efficacious than twenty measures to remedy the evils of pauperism in its development" (Lambert 1873–4, 471).

25 Better still, the harsh administrative model of the Poor Laws served as a stick with which to beat the destitute back into the ranks of the honest poor. This was the spirit of the Goschen Minute of 1869 in England, specifying the status of the Poor Laws: "Well-organized charity would assist the deserving poor by encouraging them to maintain themselves; a strict poor law would deal with the undeserving poor in such a way as to try to jolt them into the ranks of the deserving" (Finlayson 1994, 92).

26 Depending on the country and the extent of pauperism, state intervention to help these populations could take the form of a law mandating state custody (the Poor Laws in England and the United States, public assistance and beggars'

prisons in France) or a practice of systematic funding of private institutions (Australia, the Netherlands, Belgium).

27 "The nineteenth-century poor law differentiated various kinds of indigence which were to be rewarded and punished in different ways" (Williams 1981, 38).

28 "Whether the people who mean no harm, but are weak in the essential powers necessary to the performance of one's duties in life, or those who are malicious and vicious, do the more mischief, is a question not easy to answer" (Sumner 1883).

29 The seven categories were the blind, the insane, prisoners, deaf mutes, idiots, paupers, and homeless children. For a careful study of these surveys, see Katz (1983, 93–156).

30 It need hardly be specified that this model existed in a number of significantly different variants. Private charity could in some cases take charge of dependent populations, with or without state funding; or, the caregiving responsibility could be entrusted to an institution, such as the Church in Quebec, powerful and stable enough to take on the role for an extended period. See chapter 7.

31 This was the logic behind the establishment of the first "settlements," where young bourgeois men and women moved into poor districts to offer services to the destitute. On this issue, see Lubove (1962) and Davis (1967).

32 William Graham Sumner clearly grasped the abrupt change implied by this new relationship: "It is out of the question to go back to status or to the sentimental relations which once united baron and retainer, master and servant, teacher and pupil, comrade and comrade ... Our farther gains lie in going forward, not in going backward. The feudal ties can never be restored. If they could be restored they would bring back personal caprice, favoritism, sycophancy, and intrigue. A society based on contract is a society of free and independent men, who form ties without favor or obligation, and cooperate without cringing or intrigue. A society based on contract, therefore, gives the utmost room and chance for individual development, and for all the self-reliance and dignity of a free man ... The only social improvements which are now conceivable lie in the direction of more complete realization of a society of free men united by contract ... It follows, however, that one man, in a free state, cannot claim help from, and cannot be charged to give help to, another" (Sumner 1883).

33 For this reason, I must take serious issue with François Ewald's assessment of the place of poverty in the liberal problematic: "As attested by the scale of the philanthropic movement and the large number of books written about the problem, the liberal stance was certainly not retreat, disinterest, or disengagement. Rather, it crystallized a new experience of poverty, a new 'pathetics of misery,' a new sensibility which, far from pushing it out to the periphery of society, placed it in the centre, for much time to come" (Ewald 1986, 73).

34 Katz expresses this contradiction well: "From its inception, contradictions plagued scientific charity. Charity organization society agents and visitors were supposed to be both investigators and friends. They were to inspire confidence and radiate warmth as they intruded in the most intimate details of their clients' lives. They were to be welcome guests in the homes of people who had no choice but to receive them, if they wanted to eat or keep warm. Even more, the concept of charity organization was hopelessly anachronistic. It diagnosed the great social problem of its day as the chasm that had opened between classes, which it proposed to close through human contact" (Katz 1986, 67).

35 See Humphreys (1995). For the United States, see Katz (1986, 58–84).

36 The distinction between the deserving and undeserving poor found throughout the historiographical literature is in this sense eminently ambiguous. It primarily denotes, as if by process of elimination, those who are worthy of aid, as opposed to fraudsters and layabouts. This meaning is as old as charity and relates to the *genuineness* of the need and the necessity, for those in charge of giving assistance, to determine it. But under the domination of the liberal conception, the deserving poor are also distinguished from the extreme but involuntary poverty of the infirm, the old, and the abandoned child. The deserving poor thus become those with not only the desire for self-betterment but also the capacity to achieve it.

37 The extent to which discretion, even silence, characterized the discourse on the treatment to be applied to these marginalized populations, especially between 1840 and 1880, has too seldom been noted. More or less compulsory labour for the able-bodied, coupled with moral treatment for the mentally ill, made up the bulk of the therapeutic arsenal put forward in a discourse remarkable for its redundancies. Inside the walls of the institution, a great scientific silence was observed. "The purpose of most institutions shifted by the 1860s away from reform or rehabilitation and toward custody" (Katz 1983, 204). Theories of degeneracy would only accentuate these phenomena.

38 The English law of 1884 that extended suffrage to the whole working class explicitly excluded those who had received relief under the Poor Laws. Elsewhere, this exclusion simply took the form of electoral laws setting minimum income levels or requiring a private place of residence as voter eligibility criteria.

39 On this point, see Fecteau (1999b, 61–70).

40 It should be quite clear that enduring class contempt could put considerable distance between the nominal spirit of this philosophy of assistance and what actually happened in practice. The contemporaneous discourse of the advocates of "scientific charity" is peppered with arrogant statements or condescending remarks about the poor.

41 "I doubt ... whether the Twelve Disciples would have been able to qualify as worthy according to your system. And Christ himself might have been turned over by you to the police department as a 'vagrant without visible means of support'" (a pastor to F.C. Howe, director of the COS of Cleveland, quoted in Bremner ([1956] 1967, 54).

42 On this point, see Katz (1983) for the United States and Williams (1981) for England. For France, see the localized but revealing study by Faure and Dessertine (1991).

43 This latter was much more common in North America, at least until the emergence of the Canadian agrarian parties in the 1930s.

44 "Much of current philanthropic effort is directed to remedying the more superficial evils" (George Cadbury [1891], quoted in Finlayson [1994], 139).

45 "Because formalists perceived the causes of suffering to lie largely in the victims' own apparently unimpeded choices (ultimately, in defects of the will), the only general remedy for their misfortunes was to help them perfect the arts of self-mastery and educate them about the predictable consequences of their actions" (Haskell 1987, 874).

46 These surveys have been analyzed by Williams (1981) and Hennock (1976). For the United States, see the survey by Hunter (1904) and an analysis thereof by Bremner ([1956] 1967, 140–63).

47 On this point, see the enlightening analysis by Topalov (1994).

48 The liberals of the Charity Organization Societies clearly perceived this and deplored it: "Once the 'poverty line' has been erected, the classification of human beings becomes for the world at large a question of money income, and the remedy for poverty represents itself as the distribution of money" (Helen Bosanquet [1903], quoted in Himmelfarb 1991, 177).

49 Somewhat later, in the previously cited survey, Benjamin Seebohm Rowntree invented the concept of the poverty line.

50 The author also employed the military metaphor of an army on the march: "Is it not proper to any society, which is progressing in terms of civilization and wealth, to alleviate the misfortunes of its dispossessed? Does it not in fact have the duty to wrest them away from the enemy?" (Chevallier 1900a, 70).

51 Recent historiography has highlighted the parallel, at times contrasting, social struggles of organized workers, on the one hand, and what has been called the "maternalist" movement, on the other. See, among a spate of newer accounts, Skocpol (1992) and Bock and Thane (1991). However, both processes essentially targeted members of the working class.

52 This development was encouraged by the professionalization of welfare practice, as Katz explains: "As social workers became more self-consciously professional, they argued that the source of funds mattered less than their management and they redefined outdoor relief as a problem of

administration rather than a matter of principle. With the poor subdivided into appropriate categories, public officials could hand out relief while private agencies concentrated on casework" (Katz 1986, 156). This trend explains why the COS gradually turned into social service associations.
53 The phrase is due to Finlayson (1994, 198). Sandrine Kott uses the term "social state," while Didier Renard speaks of a "charity state"; see also Kästner (1981).
54 See, e.g., Donzelot (1984) and Ewald (1986).
55 I hope to return to this important point in a subsequent work on association.
56 Alan Hunt agrees: "The espousal of eugenics was an aspect of the secularization of moral discourses. The self-justifying appeals to God's law and God's wrath suddenly became less persuasive to the rapidly secularizing working classes and the middle class, whose religious commitment increasingly approached an occasional conformity. As religion became less self-evident, the prestige of science rose. Yet eugenics reflected a similar intellectual style to that of evangelicalism in that it acquired a categorical form in which the dictates of nature replaced the dictates of God" (Hunt 1999, 181).
57 Eugenics differed greatly from religious ethics in that its emphasis on nature's unbending laws left little room for the will.
58 One thinks of the fundamental change of ethos implied by the transition to contemporary regulation and the welfare state, which is beyond the scope of this book.
59 See Hirschman (1977) and especially the foundational work of Pocock (1985).
60 "Christian morality (so called) has all the characters of a reaction ... It is essentially a doctrine of passive obedience; it inculcates submission to all authorities found established; who indeed are not to be actively obeyed when they command what religion forbids, but who are not to be resisted, far less rebelled against, for any amount of wrong to ourselves" (Mill [1849] 1913, 47).
61 Alfred Marshall, one of the principal architects of the critique of classical liberalism, wrote with particular vehemence: "The feeling that the residuum ought not to exist, and that they will exist till the working class have themselves cleared them away ... has coloured my whole life and thought for the last ten years" (Marshall, quoted in Hennock 1976, 79).
62 "Eugenics supplied a scientific basis with which to write the old distinction between the worthy and unworthy poor into social policy" (Katz 1986, 182).
63 Beveridge offers a clear contemporaneous expression of this sentiment: "It is frankly impossible for any public committee openly to give those dependent on [the workhouse] conditions of life approaching in badness and harmfulness the condition which ... public thoughtlessness passes by as 'inevitable' for large sections of a free and independent proletariat" (Beveridge [1906], quoted in Finlayson 1994, 151).
64 See Monkkonen (1984).

65 Of course, remonstrances against alcoholism would continue, but now in the form of campaigns waged by temperance associations. Here, too, the preferred strategy would entail state intervention (prohibition).

CHAPTER SEVEN

1 In the most recent version of this interpretation (Bouchard 2008), the clerical elite, with its gaze nostalgically fixed on Old France, succeeded in repelling the democratic momentum of the working classes for over a century. From 1840 to 1960, Quebec's modernization was essentially sidelined.
2 Even recently, Roberto Perin could be found stressing the Church's historical capacity "to institutionalize French-Canadian culture ... as well as religion's role in fashioning a cohesive and self-confident identity" (Perin 2001, 102).
3 A good example is found in Rouillard (1989).
4 See, for example, Hudon (1996), Rousseau and Remiggi (1998), Ferretti (1999), and Hardy (1999).
5 At best, more recent historiography strongly nuances this view, first by indicating that ultramontanism was only one of several worldviews espoused within the Church, then by stressing its rapid retreat in the face of more modernity-friendly ideological forms, such as Catholic social teaching. See, e.g., Sylvain and Voisine (1991) and Ferretti (1999).
6 See, for example, Fahmy-Eid (1978).
7 Marshall, although quite critical of this approach, nonetheless describes the tenacious resistance of Catholicism in analogous terms: "Catholicism was better able to withstand the acids of modernity" (Marshall 1993–4, 66).
8 It should be noted that Catholicism was, for its adherents, not only a moral but also an ethnic bulwark, and that modernity was closely associated with Protestantism. This depiction of Protestantism as the Trojan horse of modern liberalism was a constant in Catholic discourse. Nevertheless, there was a close correspondence between preservation of customs and religious ethic, in that Catholicism presented itself as the one true religion.
9 Kaiser, too, stresses the adaptation of the religious response to the exigencies of modernity: "Christian initiatives that came into being as association in the early nineteenth century drew upon unabashedly new principles involving the supplanting of the society of estates by the bourgeois society and used the new possibilities offered by the evolution of social structures" (Kaiser 1999, 26).
10 "Religions give the general habit of behaving with the future in view. In this they are no less useful to happiness in this life than to felicity in the other. It is one of their great political dimensions" (Tocqueville [1835] 2012, 3: 966).

11 In Quebec at that time, Étienne Parent remarked quite similarly: "While the press, on the one hand, will keep society awake as regards material interests, the priest, on the other, will prevent it from neglecting spiritual things; they are as a dual beacon erected on the sides of the road to show which way it goes, and to point out the dangers lying to both the right and the left of it" (Parent [1848] 1975, 213).

12 "I think that it is wrong to regard the Catholic religion as a natural enemy of democracy. Among the different Christian doctrines, Catholicism seems to me on the contrary one of the most favorable to equality of conditions ... once priests are excluded or withdraw from government ... there are no men who, by their beliefs, are more disposed than Catholics to carry the idea of equality of conditions into the political world" (Tocqueville [1835] 2012, 2: 469–70).

13 From this standpoint, Parent considered the likelihood of the clergy's gaining excessive power to be small: "The clergy emanates from the people, lives and dies amidst the people; more than any other body of men, it is interested in the happiness and prosperity of the people; with our political institutions, and our social position, it is impossible for it to ever become powerful enough to have the temptation to become oppressive" (Parent [1852a] 1975, 289).

14 "In Europe, Christianity allowed itself to be intimately united with the powers of the earth. Today these powers are falling and Christianity is as though buried beneath their debris. It is a living thing that someone wanted to bind to the dead: cut the ties that hold it and it will rise again" (Tocqueville [1835] 2012, 2: 488).

15 "The hand that bears the thurible must not carry the sceptre, and vice versa. To the Church, counsel and advice; to the state, legislation and the direct government of society; it is for the Church to mark out the way and for the state to travel along it, and finally, for the people to follow them" (Parent [1852a] 1975, 246).

16 Parent's view of the role of religion led him to express strong reservations about the value of individualism as an aspiration for the masses: "Catholicism ... is association in its highest and widest expression, and this for the benefit of the poor and the weak, who can only be strong by association. By joining them in a single beam of light, association will make them stronger than the strong. I will not deny that, humanly speaking, the principle of private judgment, which is, in practice, individualism applied to moral matters, tends to increase the strength of individualities ... but that can only profit a small number of individuals, those of great mettle. Individualism is like the wind that whips up the brazier, but blows out a candle. For the masses, what is needed is the association of ideas, unity, and consequently authority" (Parent [1852b] 1975, 315).

17 Such mobilization of civil society was also evident among Protestants: "A total and interlocking system of participatory organisations, all of which ideally involved forms of joining or continuous attending, had become part of the self-definition of religion in the town. Active, committed, sustained participation in a range of organisations, some specialist and some inclusive, came to be a large and visible part of what religion was trying to generate ... during the second half of the nineteenth century" (Yeo 1976, 66).

18 Even David Marshall gives in to this simplistic interpretation: "It was not until the Quiet Revolution and Vatican II that Quebec society began to experience significant secularization pressure. Secularization in Quebec seems to be a very recent, relatively sudden and dramatic event instead of something deeply rooted in the nineteenth century" (Marshall 1993–4, 65).

19 "One does not blush at being a liberal ... but a Christian liberal" (Joseph-Vincent Quiblier, superior of the Séminaire de Saint-Sulpice, Montreal, to Joseph Carrière, superior general, 15 November 1831, quoted in Chaussé 1980, 189).

20 This excerpt is taken from an extraordinary handwritten diatribe by Lartigue against democracy (Lartigue 1838), found by Philippe Pruvost (1988) in the archives of the Archdiocese of Montreal. It deserves to be published in its entirety.

21 Westfall rightly stresses that, for the British Crown, the close union of church and state was central to a policed society, as James Knox wrote to Lord Liverpool shortly after the passage of the Quebec Act in 1774: "The National Religion of any state may be presumed to be best adapted to the Civil Constitution of the State, hence it claims the Countenance and Support of the Civil Magistrate, which should be considered not only as a Matter of Piety and Prudence, but of the utmost Necessity in a Political View, being connected with the Peace and Welfare of the Community" (quoted in Westfall 1990, 180).

22 Chaussé comments: "The Bishop of Montreal had understood that the Church, in a country with representative institutions, did not need to solicit protection from politicians; the Church possessed autonomy thanks to the authority it exerted over the faithful, who also had the capacity of electors."

23 "An Act to repeal so much of the Act of the Parliament of Great Britain passed in the Thirty-first year of the Reign of King George the Third, and Chaptered Thirty-one, as relates to Rectories, and the presentation of Incumbents to the same, and for other purposes connected with such Rectories," 14–15 Vict. (1851), c. 175. Three years later, the preamble to the act abolishing the Anglican clergy reserves stipulated: "And whereas it is desirable to remove all semblance of connection between Church and State" (*Statutes of the Province of Canada*, "An Act to make better provision for the appropriation of Moneys

arising from the Lands heretofore known as the Clergy Reserves, by rendering them available for Municipal purposes," 18 Vict. (1854) c. 2, sect. III). Obviously, in the Quebec case, the public functions assigned to the Church (notably in the areas of education and civil registration) made such separation a relative affair. Marc Lalonde states: "If one adopts a strict concept of the principles of separation of church and state, and of religious freedom and equality, it is permitted to ask whether, in Quebec, there were not so many exceptions to these principles that it would be doing them excessive obeisance to assign them the denomination of 'fundamental principle of our civil polity,' as the legislature of 1852 did" (Lalonde 1961, 99–100). But the assignment of civic responsibilities to certain religious denominations does not invalidate the observation that these laws represented a fundamental break with tradition.

24 Westfall makes an analogous observation about the Protestant churches: "The Anglican Church was now a private institution, cut off from its former ally, the colonial state. It continued, however, to define itself in public terms, holding on tenaciously to the dogma that its teachings and practices should play a major role in Canadian society." He goes on to state the dilemma thus created in terms that can equally well be applied to the Catholic experience in Quebec: "How do you construct a public religion at a private site?" (Westfall 2001, 24).

25 Giroux (1945–6, 139–41) stresses the juridical implications of this act. In the eyes of the law, the churches became voluntary associations enjoying independence from the state and operating within the framework of public law. Notably, this foundational measure instituting freedom of religion in Canada is barely mentioned in two major syntheses of Quebec Catholic Church history (Sylvain and Voisine 1991; Ferretti 1999). The now voluminous historiography of religion has yet to produce a systematic history of church-state relations for Quebec. Milot (2002) is an interesting first attempt, although for some reason it ignores the 1851 act.

26 The principle of liberal competition was in fact central to demands for freedom of religion: "The different sects would all be placed in a level in their competition with one another ... The relative standing and respectability of all the different Churches would thus depend – not upon extrinsic or adventitious circumstances – but solely upon their comparative worth and usefulness, ascertained by public opinion – unfettered by prejudice – uninfluenced by political party" (Montreal Society for the Attainment of Religious Liberty and Equality in British North America 1837, 27–8).

27 It also changed the forms taken by such constraints: "A Christian ethics made up of immutable obligations was supplanted by a notion of Christian responsibility that was always having to reinvent and account for itself" (Despland 1998, 65). Under liberal regulation, faith is primarily a matter of will and

responsibility. Here again, the basic values of liberalism constituted the unshakeable bedrock and the primary precondition for modern religious belief.

28 Also, "Thank the Heavens for the liberty they have given you; cherish it as the guardian of your religion" (Raymond 1869, 19).

29 Roberto Perin has no trouble seeing beyond the literal meaning of the ultramontane discourse on the state: "Ultramontanism was used to advance the church's claim of autonomy from the provincial state. Instead of reading this discourse literally as a bid for theocratic control, historians should see it as an argument in favour of a French-Canadian public space free from the influence of political parties" (Perin 2001, 92). Although my construction of the social space occupied by the Church differs from Perin's, I view his reading of ultramontane political discourse as fundamentally correct. See also Chalifoux (1999).

30 Lamonde ([2000] 2013) contains a rewarding treatment of the relations between liberalism and religion in Quebec.

31 As Westfall germanely asserts, freedom of religion was not a gain for the churches so much as a withdrawal of the state from the sphere of religion: "The state abandoned the church because it decided that it no longer needed the church; the state rejected the old axiom that a specific form of public religion was essential to public order because it believed on the one hand that the establishment could no longer perform its social function and on the other that it had found a new formula for creating order and happiness" (Westfall 1990, 184).

32 Laurier instinctively expressed this when he refused to define liberalism (per Dessaulles) as a liberating entity capable of penetrating even the religious sphere. This is why mature political liberalism could so easily square itself with the decline of Catholic liberalism: "I may be asked what is Catholic Liberalism. At the threshold of the question I refrain. The question is not included in my subject, and moreover is beyond my power to elucidate. But I may also say that Catholic Liberalism is not Political Liberalism" (Laurier 1877, 4).

33 Joseph-Sabin Raymond speaks of "men's right to enjoy the truth," that truth which forms a sort of rampart against error: "Do we really believe that tolerance of all waywardness, indifference as regards all religions, is an actual good for society? ... This maxim ... encompasses the idea that error is not in itself harmful ... Shame on the doctrine that preaches the freedom to err" (Raymond 1869, 13, 15). Note the striking resemblance between this rejection of truth as an outcome of freedom of thought and the contemporaneous distrust of the political freedom granted to the masses in the form of the franchise, a distrust entertained by liberals themselves, starting with Spencer.

34 Lewis Thomas Drummond, the attorney-general of Canada East, had publicly warned Catholics of the implications of freedom of religion as early as 1852: "He would tell the Catholics throughout the world, that unless they were

ready to give real religious liberty to all, they would be themselves the first to suffer from intolerance" (*DLAUC*, 1852–3, vol. XI, p. 1989). Tocqueville, always a keen analyst, likewise wrote: "I finally discover a small number of the faithful ready to defy all obstacles and to scorn all dangers for their beliefs. The latter have acted contrary to human weakness in order to rise above common opinion. Carried away by this very effort, they no longer know precisely where they should stop. Since they have seen that, in their country, the first use that man made of independence has been to attack religion, they fear their contemporaries and withdraw with terror from the liberty that the former pursue. Since unbelief appears to them as something new, they include in the same hatred everything that is new. So they are at war with their century and their country, and in each of the opinions that are professed there they see a necessary enemy of faith. Such should not be today the natural state of man in matters of religion" (Tocqueville [1835] 2012, 2: 486–7).

35 "One of the traits of religion is to never reason with men" (Lamennais, *Essai sur l'indifférence*, quoted in Despland 1998, 317).

36 This vexed relationship to truth and the free market of ideas would have a remarkably long life. Here is ultramontane ideologue Louis-Adolphe Paquet a half-century later: "Shake the dust off the manuscripts; search the memory of peoples and browse the archives of the world; draw out of the enduring shadows all that which has had a name, or spoken a language; I do not fear the light. But do not deduce from this language of facts and these revelations from the past, consequences not contained within them; do not build, on these too often dubious facts, arbitrary systems which the faith holds to be suspect, gratuitous conjectures that are condemned by infallible teaching or authorized tradition" (Paquet [1902] 1915, 177).

37 "We repudiate any government which assumes over its subjects the right of parents over their children; we repudiate it as degrading to those who suffer it … To sacrifice one's freedom, to sacrifice one's dignity for food, is to give up what a people has that is most precious, most sacred, in return for something coarse" (Beaudry 1862).

38 That critique was radical, however, in that unlike Chandonnet, it rejected *any* state intervention in this sphere.

39 *JLAPC*, "Bill to provide for the incorporation of Societies formed for Charitable and Educational purposes," 1852–53, pt. II, p. xliii.

40 Although extremely rare before 1840, such applications for private incorporation proliferated under the Union. In the case of Lower Canada, no fewer than thirty-five charitable and religious associations made such applications after 1840, fourteen of them after 1849. For an analysis of this phenomenon, see Fecteau (1992a).

41 On the act allowing companies to incorporate, see Fecteau (1992b). The later bill discussed here, of which I was unable to obtain the text, was probably intended to standardize the very limited advantages conferred upon mutual aid societies by 13–14 Vict. (1850), c. 32 ("An Act for incorporating certain Charitable Philanthropic and Provident Associations, and for the effectual protection from fraud and misappropriation of the funds of the same") and to extend them to a much wider range of charitable associations.

42 *DLAUC*, 1852–53, vol. XI, p. 1723. "In Upper Canada, there were no poor to be seen in the streets from one end to the other. The poor were relieved by individuals, and at personal sacrifice, which was the correct system" (ibid., 1724). Note that the charge of bureaucratic coldness is levelled here at the inhumanity of corporatism; no argument for or against the private or public sphere is implied. There is in these remarks a soupçon of Rousseau arguing against corporate monopoly as being inimical to civic democracy. On this point, see Fecteau (1990).

43 Cauchon refers to official British statistics as well as to the work done in France by Villeneuve-Bargemont and Louis-Mathurin Moreau-Christophe.

44 "[Cauchon] did not believe that the prosperity caused by the accumulation of capital in a few hands, was desirable. The masses were not the better off for a few men being rich. Better that there should not be so much capital in the country if the great body of the people were happier without it" (*DLAUC*, 1852–53, vol. XI, p. 1964).

45 Ibid., 1965.

46 Ibid.

47 Ibid., 1476.

48 Of course, certain legislators had perceived the potential danger of such across-the-board freedom. The Catholic MP Louis-Victor Sicotte was one who opposed the general incorporation act: "The Mormons will be able to have their holy temple and the Fourrierists their phalansteries, like the Turks their mosques. There is a big difference between tolerating sects and giving them legal existence by recognizing them as institutions. Society must not get ahead of the facts in legislation on such matters, but it must wait for events to transpire, and not sanction all possible faiths in advance with such a general legislative measure" (ibid., 1985).

49 The 1852 bill died on the order paper despite the government's efforts. While freedom of association in this area was supported by a very large majority of members, several, including Cauchon himself, expressed doubt as to the advisability of an overly general law likely to give rise to abuse on the part of ill-intentioned groups. It seemed preferable, in the case of charitable associations, to proceed on an ad hoc basis.

50 *DLAUC*, 1854–55, vol. XII, p. 3191.
51 I use the phrase "religious charity" inasmuch as the charity practised by the Protestant denominations does not (at this level of analysis and with a few exceptions to be discussed later) seem to me truly different, in either its assumptions or its methods, from Catholic charity. On the charitable action of the Protestant churches in Montreal, Harvey (2001) is useful.
52 "Today more than ever, men are greedy, ambitious, unhappy with their lot ... The most powerful and effective method of all ... is to pit, against the three great passions just mentioned, the three virtues diametrically opposed to them: against greed, voluntary poverty; against sensual pleasure, perfect continence; against insubordination, total obedience" (Henriot 1892, 18, 24–5).
53 Much has been made of the radicalization of Lamennais's thought, his enthusiastic acceptance of the ethical and religious issues of democracy. In fact, the epoch witnessed many such zigzagging trajectories between conservatism and the stirrings of liberal or even radical ideas, particularly in the aftermath of the seismic shock of 1848. Examples include François Guizot and Charles Forbes René de Montalembert in France and Étienne Parent and Joseph-Sabin Raymond in Quebec. In a few cases, such as those of Alessandro Gavazzi and Charles Chiniquy, the outcome even involved conversion to another faith.
54 It should be clear that this interpretation represents a radical departure from the historiographic current that considers nineteenth-century conservatism a mere nostalgic holdover from the *Ancien Régime*. On the complexity and profound modernity of the conservatism arising out of the revolutions, see Rémond (1969), a classic work, and Sirinelli (1995).
55 For a progressive variant of this "functionalist" view of religion, consider the following: "The working class will not accept religion, its consolations and hopes, unless religion shows itself to be full of concern for the hardships of that class, and just with regard to its legitimate desires" (*L'Ère nouvelle*, 15 October 1848, quoted in Duroselle 1951, 310).
56 "The charity-reform movement grew out of religious activity to begin with. To say that charities enunciated a Protestant ethic is merely to describe in a different way the secularization of Protestantism. Seen from one point of view, the religious impulse was losing to a social ethic, while from the other viewpoint it would appear that social institutions had vestiges of religious demands. Each view shows a different facet of the same condition" (Huggins 1971, 193). This Protestant dynamic, well described by Huggins, is quite similar to the evolution of Catholicism.
57 In my view, too little mention has been made of the degree to which this transition from the Gallican church to the "social" church entailed a decline in collusion between church and state, or at any rate a radical reformulation thereof.

The Church of the new era was a guardian of the social order without being beholden to the political order. The mid-century social Catholics were able to make this basic distinction: "What better means of making Catholicism unpopular than to enlist it, against the current movement of the suffering classes, in the unquestioning defense of what exists, in the maintenance of the social status quo. Is this not to put the means of Catholicism in the hands of egotism, to restore the sacrilegious alliance of self-interest and ideas? Is it not to renew, in the name and under the pretense of property, the deadly alliance of the throne and the altar?" (E. Rendu to F. Arnaud, 1848, quoted in Duroselle 1951, 22).

58 Traces of this Malthusian axiom can be found along a broad spectrum running from conservatism to liberalism: "The suffering caused by the pressure of population on the means of subsistence in overcrowded countries is what no kind of laws can cure, any more than they can prevent the occurrence of the accidental distress with which it is mainly the business of the charities to deal" (Smith 1889, 18); "Even if monetary equality were to be effected at some point by dividing up wealth and property into equal shares, some would see their share diminished through laziness and carelessness, while others would make theirs increase by dint of talent, labour, and effort; and the extremes of opulence and poverty would reappear after a certain amount of time" (Baillairgé 1898, 282).

59 The phrase is due to Bishop Louis-Charles Féron (1854); quoted in Duroselle (1951, 689).

60 "The hardships and the misery of the poor are invariably accompanied either by a great perversity of habits, or by a profound affliction of the soul, and both require special care" (Beaudry 1862). Around the same time, Thomas-Aimé Chandonnet exclaimed: "Why is it ... that material poverty and moral poverty, though not sisters, should be nevertheless so intimate? Why is it that the poor make an abuse of poverty itself; that the being who is disinherited by his mother earth does not always appeal to the justice and to the generosity of Heaven? Why are the poor wicked?" (Chandonnet 1864, 42–3).

61 It should be recalled that the poverty in question here is ordinary poverty. There is a notable imprecision to the era's religious discourse, in that it rarely refers to pauperism as a modern, extraordinary form of poverty. Some observers went as far as to deny its existence in Canada: "It may be happily said that pauperism, with its funereal causes and its disastrous consequences, is unknown in this country. We live in a fertile land, we have space, we enjoy freedom" (Beaudry 1862). Others noted its presence even in Quebec: "Oh, the hundreds of families whom we have seen bid adieu to Canada and take the path of exile! The hordes of beggars whom we see, at the end of each winter, rise up from all corners of the city and run to the houses of charity; and then this great tumult, this reaction, this cry of pain from out of the people's chest, it speaks loudly indeed!" (Thibault 1867, 932).

62 It is of course perfectly relevant to note the correspondence between this "realism" and the retreat of reformist ambitions from classical political liberalism: "The Liberal principle is in the very essence of our nature, in that thirst for happiness which we all feel in this life, which follows us every where to be, however, never completely satisfied on this side of the grave. Our souls are immortal, but our means are limited. We unceasingly approach toward an ideal which we never reach. We dream of the highest good, but secure only the better" (Laurier 1877, 10–11). Nothing prevented such a discourse from being coopted to religious ends: "To hear its adepts tell it, the realization of Christianity is entirely bound up with social progress and refinement; it is here below that redemption is accomplished. The Catholic clergy is entreated to end its support for the pursuit of these wonderful results, and if it is still permitted to preach resignation, it is only for a time and as a temporary indemnity, while awaiting the coming day of full and universal renewal. Without a doubt we will see all consequences conducive to the material good of peoples emerge from the Gospel doctrines, and we will contribute, as we have always done, to their application. But tomorrow as today, we will say to our brothers: look first to the kingdom of God and his justice" (Mgr Giraud, 1845, quoted in Duroselle 1951, 239).

63 Note here an explicit rejection of the English workhouses' practice of separating married couples.

64 "It seemed as though one could sense in the best-informed circles a powerful groundswell combining religious awakening, intellectual renewal upon the rubble of the Enlightenment, democratically inspired reform of political institutions, changing mores, and attention to the needs of society's poor. Little thought was given to the formidable question of power. Instead, a religious authority invested with the role of a moral beacon was imagined" (Rousseau 1993, 211). Christine Hudon trenchantly describes how the Christian brotherhoods effected a transformation of religious attitudes toward the poor during this period: "Beyond debates over grace and predestination, the Jansenists and their adversaries shared the same ideal of austerity that enduringly marked sacramental practice ... By valuing sentimental, popular, indeed populist piety, these brotherhoods and these pious works went some way toward modifying the modalities according to which the faithful expressed their faith and their Christian identity" (Hudon 1995, 479, 481).

65 Even more damagingly, to scorn the poor was to demoralize them: "The most false-hearted and pernicious enemy of the poor is discouragement ... Note that the discouragement in question here does not derive from the misery and deprivation of the poor man so much as from the scorn of which he believes himself the target, the lowliness of his condition in men's estimation. As long as he is under this impression, he is paralyzed: he is incapable of undertaking anything to improve his condition" (Beaudry 1862).

66 "The Catholic conviction that suffering offered a process of purification and conferred a special status on the sufferer tended to soften the stigma of poverty and was diametrically opposed to the Calvinist idea" (Parthun 1988, 855).

67 "Society is like any other friend: its visits and its affection must need be returned; its attentions must be reciprocated" (Chandonnet 1864, 40).

68 "Our duty as Christians is to intervene between these irreconcilable enemies, to cause the one to shed his wealth as if obeying a law, and the other to receive it as a benefit; to cause the one to stop demanding and the other to stop refusing; to make it so that equality operates insofar as possible among men" (Frédéric Ozanam, quoted in Duroselle 1951, 169).

69 "This generous devotion can only have its source in religious convictions. It is unknown to philanthropy, and this latter is likely to age considerably before it learns the first thing about it" (Beaudry 1862).

70 "Go ... into the asylums which Catholicism opens up to the poor. You will see poverty's victims there, no doubt; but there is nothing repugnant about the scene before your eyes. You will take an interest in the victims' pain. You will breathe a certain air perfumed with the fragrance of charity" (Beaudry 1862).

71 "When a whole class is suffering, it is by a class that it must be relieved; and in order that this difficult object may be effectually carried out, there must be a common organization of the whole body. Charity, like self-interest, properly understood, becomes the pursuit of a life time ... In presence of the evils which naturally afflict one portion of society, disinherited of all earthly wealth, we need a class that will give without receiving any return, who will invest their capital for heaven alone. A charity persistent as fell disease; strong as death, or rather as God himself, who is its principle; a charity whose energy is derived from a faith in Eternity: for this alone can make it endure and hold out to the very end" (Chandonnet 1864, 49–50).

72 For an exemplary analysis of this wide-ranging, female-dominated movement, see Langlois (1984). This remarkable ability to mobilize people and resources, and the formidable efficacy of the results, were not long in awakening fears among Protestants (as in the case of the Quebec reform and industrial schools) and government officials alike; as witness this 1852 memo written by someone in the French Ministry of the Interior: "A power is not shared with the Church without consequences. Its occult influences, its tenacity, its homogeneous standing militia, free of the cares that occupy lay citizens, would soon give it a total monopoly" (Duroselle 1951, 506).

73 I am only concerned here with the discourse legitimizing the communities' role within the realm of charity. The history of these religious communities, and in particular, the key role played by women in this development, is well known. See, e.g., D'Allaire (1997), Danylewycz (1987), and Laurin, Jureau, and Duchesne (1991).

74 This argument was also, at times, imbued with the lyrical accents of predestination: "There are on earth a multitude of human creatures whom God has predestined for all eternity to religious life ... privileged beings made to live in the solitude of the cloister like a fish in water ... Young men, or girls, for example ... fearing themselves too weak in the face of the world's dizzying temptations ... who now feel the need to lament their sins, to rest their weary heads and hearts on God's bosom, and to deliver their bodies to the bloody rigours of penitence ... Fervent individuals they are, and thirsty for immolation ... Such are these many human creatures for whom the world is not made, and who are certainly not made for the world" (Henriot 1892, 8–11).

75 It is striking how contemporary observers vastly underestimated the amounts of money considered necessary to resolve the "social question," particularly as the great wave of religious charity was set in motion in the mid-nineteenth century. Monseigneur Bourget wrote: "If the charitable institutions in charge of [helping the poor] could have two or three thousand louis more, all the poor would be so effectively helped that scarcely a one would come knocking at your doors, except perhaps those who, being lazy, would only receive alms on condition of doing the work for which they were deemed capable" (Bourget 1862, 5).

76 A few years later, Louis-Nazaire Bégin took up the charge: "Who has the obligation to house, feed, and care for these poor and sick? What has the city of Quebec done for these unfortunates who lack everything? So far, nothing, or nearly nothing. It has acquired the habit of letting the Hôtel-Dieu make the expenditures that it should be making, and even levying a tax on the institution" (Bégin 1892, 1–2). On the taxation of religious institutions, see Rodrigue (1996).

77 As late as 1939, Esdras Minville, in testimony before the federal Rowell-Sirois Commission, justified the Quebec "exception" on the basis of this argument: "The Church ... has at hand, even from the purely material standpoint, an organization of extraordinary breadth and extreme flexibility ... the Catholic Church should, from the beginning, have assumed in its entirety the burden of social welfare work ... The presence of the religious communities at the head of charitable and welfare institutions is responsible for an annual saving of some ten million dollars to the ratepayers of Quebec province. Such are the facts, and to our mind they constitute a sufficiently clear answer to the question asked, viz., to what degree does the Church supply services provided by law in the other provinces?" (Minville 1939, 47–9).

78 Early criticism of religious institutions was relatively rare in Quebec. The controversy over asylums in the 1880s provided one occasion for criticism: "It is well established that these nuns, wherever they have settled, have only done so by virtue of cash money, room and board, and that charity had very little to do with that ... Honourable members ... you would spare us from having to pay considerable and excessive sums to persons who will inevitably come to you

afterward and try to assuage you, telling you that (though too lavishly and generously remunerated) they only accepted this new source of revenue out of charity, devotion, and humanity. We know them well enough to be sure that they will later on be perfectly capable of telling us, that they only did this to make us Canadians happy, to be of service to us" (Le Testu, ca. 1885, 3, 7). On the asylums controversy, see Paradis (1997). Here again, the monetary argument makes an appearance.

79 Traditional historiography has not done much to establish a careful chronology of the Catholic charity network in Quebec (see, for example, D'Allaire [1997] and Lapointe-Roy [1987]). It tends to be assumed that the process set in motion by Monseigneur Bourget in the early 1840s was smooth and uninterrupted. Actually, the numbers of individuals whom Bourget brought over from France was extremely small – really just a handful.

80 The political excesses of the ultramontanes, culminating in the Catholic Program of 1871, would bring about an important clarification of the kinds of church-state relations that should be considered desirable. Although the Church occasionally flexed its political muscles in the ensuing years (e.g., the Louis Riel case, the Manitoba schools, regulation 17), it largely withdrew from the sound and the fury of the democratic arena. The year 1877 was crucial in this regard, with Laurier's speech on a "more matured and calmer" liberalism, the Conroy mission, and the bishops' pastoral letter of 11 October, which may be said to have consecrated a "new concordate" between church and state.

81 This was true of the insane asylums, the reform and industrial schools, and the Montreal women's prison, all of which received a per diem from the provincial government and, as of the 1890s, from the Montreal city government for children at risk and mental patients.

82 For an excellent local illustration of this dynamic, see Ferretti (1992); for an example of the interlinkages between the Society of St Vincent de Paul and the religious communities for the delivery of welfare services, see Divay (1999).

83 This is one of the key differences with France, Germany, and other countries in which, despite the notable development of Catholic religious communities, the government retained control over much of the welfare and health care network. For the German case, see Bueltzingsloewen (1999). A detailed history of the Quebec charity system is, to be sure, beyond the scope of this book. For that study, see the publications of the Centre d'histoire des régulations sociales at the Université du Quebec à Montréal.

84 The idea that society was amenable to scientific analysis had many variants at this juncture, of course. It is no accident that the Le Playsian tradition, the one closest to Catholicism, had pride of place in Quebec: "Le Play is to social economy as Copernicus is to astronomy, as Bichat or Claude Bernard are to medicine,

as Lavoisier is to chemistry. Like them, he is producing the impressive outline of a new science" (Léon Gérin, "La Science sociale," *La Presse*, 22 June 1886).

85 The principal manifestation of this dynamic was the Société canadienne d'économie sociale, to which Pierre Trépanier (1986a, 1986b, 1987) has devoted extensive study.

86 The newspaper *La Presse* could still be found deploring this fact in the early twentieth century: "Sociology in Canada is purely, or to a very great extent, a workers' science. Outside of a few notable figures, the workers are the only ones concerned with the serious problems which hold in thrall the most enlightened minds in every country of the world today" (*La Presse*, 13 November 1902).

87 And again: "It is evident that at least one-third of [the families of the poor] are in indigent circumstances through no fault of their own. Death or disease have so crippled the family group that it can no longer unaided keep up in the fierce struggle for subsistence. Charitable effort must come to the relief of such. With nearly two thirds of the cases, however, it is not charity that is demanded but a chance to work" (Ames [1897] 1972, 76).

88 The poet William Morris wrote: "Hopeful work and fearless rest [are] man's greatest earthly blessings ... To have space and freedom to gain these is the end of politics; to learn how best to employ them is the end of education; to learn their inmost meaning is the end of religion" (Morris, quoted in Reid 189?, 17).

89 The complex relations between workers and some elements of the Canadian Conservative Party have often been noted in the historiography of the working classes. The earliest formal recognition of labour unions, for example, was due to the Macdonald administration of 1872.

90 In Quebec, this critical tendency was largely found among a segment of the anglophone minority. The French-Canadian elites, including the few representatives of radical liberalism, were notably quiet on this point, and in fact on everything relating to social policy.

91 Even Léon Gérin's writings are tinted with Social Darwinist overtones: "Whereas in primitive lands, work – due to its inherent attractiveness and even its ease – was accessible to all, in transformed lands, on the contrary, only those individuals gifted with certain moral qualities will do the arduous work of production, and I mean those individuals who are hard-working and provident. Inequality does manifest itself among men: the line of demarcation is between the *capable* and the *incapable*" (Gérin 1886).

92 These groups might even have to be physically isolated: "If a labour colony system is to be adopted, one system of colonies should be established for the discharged prisoners, the vagrant and the loafer on the open or free principle, and another for the worthy unemployed on the principle of selection or investigation. The classes will not mix. To admit one is to exclude the other" (Reid 189?, 11).

93 In fact, needs assessment was not a late-nineteenth-century invention. From the moment when charity began to demonstrate its effectiveness, the necessity of distinguishing the "genuine" needy from the "undeserving" poor pushed relief organizations to adopt assessment procedures. The more the distribution of relief was standardized, the more these procedures were refined. Needs assessment was a feature, for example, of the systems adopted in Glasgow by Thomas Chalmers in 1819, the Society for the Improvement of the Poor in London, and Ozanam's St Vincent de Paul societies. But at this early stage, the veiled aim of the assessment was generally to create a paternalistic relationship of dependency in which the poor were forced to admit to their poverty, thereby giving the rich an opportunity to flaunt their magnanimity. By contrast, the case-by-case needs assessment emerging in the latter third of the nineteenth century was an individualized approach in which the peculiar circumstances of any given case were studied so as to provide for coordinated and efficient intervention. It became increasingly clear that assessment procedures would have to be standardized and welfare efforts planned in an organized fashion.

94 At the same time, the proponents of mutual associations often described private charity in the terms formerly employed by the latter to denigrate legal charity: "Most of the time, imprudence makes it so that the disaster is total and irreparable. Resort must be made to cold public charity, which never fails ... to rub salt into the wound and make it burn even more painfully. That is when people's thoughts turn to economy and to mutual aid societies: friends, by then it is too late" (Robillard 1897, 6).

95 Helen Reid goes further: "Too much stress cannot be laid on the right and judicious administration of charity. With regard to the unemployed, a loose system of administration is a powerful instrument of evil, and is often the means of maintaining and increasing pauperism. In this connection the work of the Charity Organization is of the first importance, as it affords the most effective way, by means of its system of case-investigation, of providing against imposture and overlapping of work" (Reid 189?, 15).

96 McLean is very clear as to the target clientele: "In any normally constituted community we do recognize a certain class of dependants and defectives whose care rightly belongs to the community at large, and whom for brevity's sake we will call the almshouse poor; that is, those who in other communities are housed in county almshouses and infirmaries and other institutions either temporarily or permanently. In Montreal there is no such public care, and more than that, as we have seen, no adequate provision for, or certainty of, indoor treatment under private auspices" (McLean 1901, 142).

97 The undifferentiated treatment of all types of poverty by private charity allows sterile and ineffective sentimentality to flood back in: "Take away the place of

final refuge – the public institution – and the poison of weakness and shuffling inefficiency and headless sentimentality, which must always be guarded against in private outdoor relief, simply runs rife; and more than that, private charity finds its interests unwholesomely centred around elemental material problems of bread and fuel" (McLean 1901, 145).

98 "Among the true poor ... there are seemingly some for whom public charity ought to have something to offer beyond the mere permission to beg alms from passersby ... The place of the old and the infirm is in hospices, that of the sick in hospitals ... Those old and sick who live in hospices and those beggars who live in hospitals do not cost the public any more than those who are on the streets, and, into the bargain, they are sheltered from the elements" (*La Patrie*, 24 March 1898).

99 The treatment of institutionalized populations was sporadically criticized in the press, often in muted terms. On children's education, *La Patrie* wrote: "Most institutions lack the means to do much for the children in their care, and the result is that the girls come out knowing a bit of sewing and how to wash floors and dishes, while the boys know something of shoe repair and carpentry" (28 December 1912). On care for the elderly, the paper opined, "it is impossible to imagine sending honest workers who have toiled all their lives [to houses of refuge]" (16 January 1913).

100 And a few years later: "The fate of the poor, the needy, and the destitute has long been given over to the charity of private citizens or religious institutions. Today, society understands that it must, for its own protection at least, concern itself with the fate of its paupers and provide for their subsistence" (*La Patrie*, 6 May 1907).

101 On the history of this asylum, see Aranguiz (2000). On Montreal's public welfare policies, see Fecteau (1995a).

102 At this founding assembly were Senator William Hingston; Herbert Brown Ames; Helen Reid; Frédéric Liguori Béique, president of the Saint-Jean-Baptiste Society; Dr Emmanuel-Persillier Lachapelle; J.D. Rolland; and William Peterson, the principal of McGill University. The women's associations were represented by Lady Julia Drummond, a Mrs Thibaudeau, and Françoise Barry. The assembly was chaired by Lady Mary Minto, the governor general's wife, and by Mayor of Montreal Raymond Préfontaine. See *La Patrie*, 13 December 1899, 6.

103 He added, cautiously: "How will this organization function? What will be the results? Experience will tell, but it is my duty to wait, I believe, before taking a more direct and active part" (*La Patrie*, 22 November 1899).

104 Indeed, several speakers at the founding assembly of the Montreal Charity Organization Society praised the Society of St Vincent de Paul for its efforts

to coordinate home visits to the poor. Raphaël Bellemare, the president of St Vincent de Paul in Montreal, attended the COS's initial organizing meetings.

105 The recorder, in good Catholic tradition, took the opportunity to criticize any institution even vaguely resembling "legal charity" or the Poor Laws: "Should charity be compelled? ... There is talk of building prisons to house all the beggars, and of levying a tax on the rich to pay for the upkeep of these institutions. And begging would be abolished; the needy would no longer be permitted to hold out their hands. With such a measure, the poor would be sated but not consoled, and the primary goal of charity – love – would not be attained. The poor will not love those who feed them, for they will know that the bit of bread which alleviates their hunger is tossed to them by law and not out of pity, sympathy, or friendship" (*La Patrie*, 21 February 1898).

106 This malaise, this sense that the future holds nothing, accentuated by the decline of liberal optimism and the rise of socialist "utopias," was discernible in Quebec: "These social authorities do nothing to coordinate their actions, to work together for the utility of the greatest number. They believe they have done enough when they have pursued their own refinement, and that of their immediate entourage, within the limited circle of the home or the shop ... Who, then, is responsible for the failure of benefactors to be inclined toward the good and the true, if not the natural educators of democracy, who instead leave the field open for the insurgent invasion of utopias and reveries?" (*La Presse*, 1 August 1895).

107 And further: "Public authority ought to exercise due care in safeguarding the well-being and the interests of non-owning workers. Unless this is done, justice, which commands that everyone be given his own, will be violated" (Catholic Church [1891] 1942, 28).

108 The encyclical puts forward a form of social organization based on guilds and on "natural" groupings in civil society.

109 Gohiet takes up here a central idea of *Rerum Novarum*: "To suffer and endure is human, and although men may strive in all possible ways, they will never be able by any power or art wholly to banish such tribulations from human life. If any claim they can do this, if they promise the poor in their misery a life free from all sorrow and vexation and filled with repose and perpetual pleasures, they actually impose upon these people and perpetuate a fraud which will ultimately lead to evils greater than the present. The best course is to view human affairs as they are and ... to seek appropriate relief for these troubles elsewhere" (Catholic Church [1891] 1942, 15).

110 "Wage workers are numbered among the great mass of the needy [and therefore] the State must include them under its special care and foresight" (Catholic Church [1891] 1942, 32).

111 In the body of the text, Gohiet adds: "Doubtless we have been paid well enough to have to fear the intervention of today's apostate governments. But once again, that is no reason to reject their intervention where they have a duty and a right to intervene. That we mistrust them, that we only call for their assistance in cases where it is indispensable, that we keep watch on them while they exercise this perilous right: this is the counsel of prudence. But let us not tell them, 'Whoa there!,' when the voice of nature and conscience cries out, 'Go! Act!'" (Gohiet 1892, 71).

112 *Rerum Novarum* identifies three major entities responsible for the "renewal" of society: the church, the state, and workers' and employers' associations.

113 A curious opuscule also titled *Rerum Novarum* proposed, in the wake of the encyclical, that responsibilities for the care of elderly paupers be transferred from the private to the public sector: "The principal objection to old age pensions is the large cost they would entail on the Government. This is a secondary consideration. The first question to determine is whether it is just and desirable to provide these pensions. The aged have to be provided for, in any case, whether by their relatives or by the Charitable Institutions, so that there would be no economic loss to the country at large, but only a shifting of the responsibility" (Guérin 1899, 43).

114 Likewise, progressives such as Gohiet seem to have been relatively marginal ecclesiastical figures in Quebec. The young Paul Bruchési did keep company with the members of the Société d'économie sociale in the 1880s, but this kind of cross-fertilization between progressives and conservatives was not the norm.

115 I thank Jean-Luc Marais of the Université d'Angers for this reference.

116 This speech had been given at the board meeting of the Hôpital Notre-Dame. *La Patrie* commented on Bruchési's remarks as follows: "Mgr Bruchési ... chiefly stressed the illogic of public bodies' levying taxes for the purposes of material progress and education while utterly neglecting to collect the levies necessary to save our philanthropic works. A 'poor tax' is urgently necessary to help the sick poor and alleviate the hospitals' burden ... Such applications to the municipal governments are not just a duty on the part of those who concern themselves with philanthropic matters, but a right. The 'poor tax' exists in all civilized countries. It should exist in Canada" (*La Patrie*, 29 December 1910).

117 Pressures on the city council were the strongest in Montreal. In 1908, the city created a public welfare department in charge of supervising the distribution of municipal assistance to institutions. In 1915 it instituted the "poor cent," a cinema tax used to fund this assistance. This model would be the one chosen for the provincial act of 1921. See Fecteau (1995a).

118 E.g., the *Manufacturing Act* of 1885 or the *Workmen's Compensation Act* of 1909.

CONCLUSION

1. I use this term in the broader sense adopted by Topalov: "A common sense or a shared language, a packaging of problems and a horizon of possibilities on which agreement is reached do not in any way entail a consensus as to the effective modalities of action, much less as to their ultimate ends" (Topalov 1999, 44).
2. Steven Seidman states this contradiction as follows: "The paradox of nineteenth-century liberalism was that although it functioned as an ideology of class domination, its universal ideals entailed a democratic polity and society that underscored the limitations of bourgeois society. In other words, to the extent that liberalism retained its ideological vitality, it projected a post-bourgeois society. Insofar as liberalism functioned as a class-bound ideology, it lost much of its legitimating power and accelerated social polarization. Instead of liberals surmounting this dilemma by elaborating a democratic program, we find that throughout the nineteenth century, liberals supported the forces of traditional conservatism" (Seidman 1983, 277–8).
3. In his study of the Catholic liberal Alexandre Vinet, Hervé Haskin captures this basic truth: "With the [religious] Awakening, Vinet discovered individualism, and a truth made itself plain to him: 'One is not born Christian, one becomes Christian.' So it was not enough to be born in a Christian country in order to be a Christian oneself" (Haskin 1992, 17).
4. Thirty years earlier, on 11 January 1831, Lacordaire had written to Eugène Janvier: "The primary virtue today is not faith, it is sincere love of liberty. We can tell anyone for whom it is dear to heart: 'You are not far from the Kingdom of God.' The world will belong to God once it belongs to liberty, and that alone, for those who believe it, demonstrates the truth of our religion" (Bedouelle 1992, 39).
5. On the rise of an ethic of the nation as a fact surpassing the mere aggregation of civic individualities, see Mann (1993).
6. François Guizot was an example of this new awareness: "Guizot is certainly one of the first authors to have perceived that, contrary to the original liberal idea, the notion of representative government and the distinction between the state and civil society strongly implied a considerable extension of the state's power over civil society. This extension had its source less in power's despotic proclivities than in 'social demand,' as we say today" (Manent 1995, 97). Bentham made the same observation in England at that time.
7. Even Tocqueville, usually skeptical of the role of the state, envisioned the elements of a "social policy":

Finally, three means of coming to the aid of the lower classes:
1. Exempt him from part of the public burdens ...
2. Put within his reach the institutions which will let him get by and help him.
3. Come to his aid and assist him directly with his needs (Tocqueville [ca. 1847] 2002, 225).

8 "The French Revolution wished ... to introduce charity into politics. It conceived the idea of duties of state toward the poor, toward the suffering citizens, a broader, more universal, nobler idea than anyone had had before ... Nothing in this, however, gives workers an entitlement over the state; nothing forces the state to take the place of individual providence, economy, honesty; nothing authorizes the state to interfere in industries, impose regulations on them, tyrannize the individual in order to better govern him, or ... save him from himself. There is only Christianity applied to politics." *Le Moniteur universel* 257 (13 September 1848), 2418.

9 Examples would include tighter coordination of services and a larger number of case studies based on poor families.

10 To liberals who feared that such benefits would only encourage vice and laziness, a reformer gave a response quite characteristic of the new spirit: "We must trust the working class: we must boldly and generously accept the proofs it gives every day of its spirit of wisdom, equity, and sacrifice ... This experience deserves to be attempted and is, after all, a risk worth running" (Delprat 1908, 111).

11 Rudin (1997) has strenuously criticized this revisionist normalization of our history; see my critical analysis of his position (Fecteau 1999c).

12 With the possible exception of Ireland.

13 Obviously, I am speaking here of the dominant elements within the Church. It was never anything like a monolithic bloc. As recent historiography has shown, the Church was shot through with contradictory currents, and conflict raged between its tendencies. It remains my view that the "progressive" elements always played a subsidiary role vis-à-vis the hierarchy and the conservative elements, which were solidly entrenched within the parish system and the network of institutions controlled by the religious communities.

14 The rare exceptions to this monopoly (technical schools, civic hospital for the contagious, etc.) barely alter the truth of this statement.

15 The Ontario example is quite different; there, the government heavily funded the whole system of charitable institutions from the 1870s on. See Valverde (1995).

16 To my knowledge (and with the exception of Cliche [1984]), no serious in-depth study has been done on the funding of charitable institutions under religious

control in Quebec, and in particular the practice of charitable bequests. For a good example of a French study of this type, see Marais (1999).
17 I am ignoring here the English-speaking (essentially Irish) Catholic component, which was marginalized to a significant degree in Quebec.
18 The mass emigration of French Canadians to the United States and western Canada would play an essential role as a safety valve, lowering the social pressure that these hundreds of thousands of poor people might have placed on Quebec's cities. Without it, the insufficiency of the private welfare system would have been even more glaring.

Bibliography

GOVERNMENT DOCUMENTS

Canada. Legislature. Legislative Assembly. *Debates of the Legislative Assembly of United Canada* (DLAUC)
Canada. Legislature. Legislative Assembly. *Journals of the Legislative Assembly of the Province of Canada* (JLAPC)
Canada. Parliament. *Sessional Papers of the Province of Canada* (SPPC)
Canada. Public Archives of Canada (PAC).
Lower Canada. Legislature. House of Assembly. *Journal of the House of Assembly, Lower Canada* (JHALC)
Lower Canada. Legislature. Legislative Council. *Journals of the Legislative Council of the Province of Lower Canada* (JLCLC)
Quebec (Province). Legislature. *Sessional Papers* (QSP)

MONOGRAPHS

Adami, J.G. 1912. *A Study in Eugenics: "Unto the Third and Fourth Generation."* Montreal, n.p.
– 1913. *Le Clergé et les études sociales.* Montreal: L'École sociale populaire.
Aglietta, Michel. 2000. *A Theory of Capitalist Regulation: The US Experience.* Translated by David Fernbach. New York: Verso.
Ajzenstat, Janet. 1984a. "Liberalism and Assimilation: Lord Durham Reconsidered." In *Political Thought in Canada: Contemporary Perspectives*, edited by S. Brooks, 239–57. Toronto: Derringfield.
– 1984b. "Collectivity and Individual Right in 'Mainstream' Liberalism: John Arthur Roebuck and the Patriotes." *Journal of Canadian Studies* 19 (3): 99–111.

Ajzenstat, Janet, and Peter J. Smith, eds. 1997. *Canada's Origins: Liberal, Tory, or Republican?* Ottawa: Carleton University Press.

Alexander, Ruth. 1995. *The "Girl Problem": Female Sexual Delinquency in New York, 1900–1930.* Ithaca: Cornell University Press.

Altermatt, Urs. 1998. "Le Cas de la Suisse catholique aux XIXe et XXe siècles." In Lagrée, *Chocs et ruptures en histoire religieuse,* 97–112.

Ames, Herbert Brown. [1897] 1972. *The City below the Hill.* Toronto: University of Toronto Press.

Anonymous. 1853. "Charity, Noxious and Beneficent." *Westminster Review* 59: 62–88.

– 1875. "Charity, Pauperism and Self-Help." *Westminster Review* 103: 107–42.

– 1912. *Exposition pour le bien-être des enfants: guide souvenir.* Montreal, n.p.

– 2012. "Éditorial: les principes du *Bulletin d'histoire politique*." *Bulletin d'histoire politique* 20 (3): 57–64.

Aranguiz, Marcela. 2000. *Vagabonds et sans abris à Montréal: perception et prise en charge de l'errance (1840–1925).* Montreal: RCHTQ.

– 2009. "Cours de justice criminelle et classes ouvrières au tournant du XXe siècle à Montréal (1891–1921)." PhD diss., Université du Québec à Montréal.

Archambault, Joseph-Papin. 1916. *Le Clergé et les oeuvres sociales.* Montreal: L'École sociale populaire.

Armstrong, George E. 1898. *Hospital Abuse.* Montreal, n.p.

Ashworth, John. 1987. "The Relationship between Capitalism and Humanitarianism." *American Historical Review* 92 (4): 813–28.

Astor, Joseph. 1887. *Droit criminel de l'emprisonnement cellulaire.* Paris: Rousseau.

Atiyah, Patrick. 1979. *The Rise and Fall of Freedom of Contract.* Oxford: Oxford University Press.

Baillairgé, Charles. 1898. *Divers ou les enseignements de la vie.* Quebec: Darveau.

Baldus, Bernd. 1977. "Social Control in Capitalist Societies: An Examination of the 'Problem of Order' in Liberal Democracies." *Cahiers canadiens de sociologie* 2 (3): 247–62.

Balzac, Honoré de. 1915. *The Country Parson.* In *The Works of Honoré de Balzac,* vol. 30. New York: McKinlay, Stone and MacKenzie.

Barret-Ducrocq, Françoise. 1991. *Pauvreté, charité et morale à Londres au XIXe siècle: une sainte violence.* Paris: Presses universitaires de France.

Beaudry, Abbé H. 1862. "Le Paupérisme." *L'Ordre,* 20 June–9 July.

Beaumont, Gustave de, and Alexis de Tocqueville. 1833. *On the Penitentiary System in the United States and Its Application in France; with an Appendix on Penal Colonies and also Statistical Notes*. Philadelphia: Carey.

Bec, Colette. 1994. *Assistance et République: la recherche d'un nouveau contrat social sous la HP République*. Paris: Les Éditions de l'Atelier.

Becker, Carl L. 2002. *The Declaration of Independence*. Birmingham, AL: Palladium Press.

Becker, Howard. 1963. *Outsiders: Studies in the Sociology of Deviance*. New York: Free Press.

Bédard, Éric. 2009. *Les Réformistes: une génération canadienne-française au milieu du XIXe siècle*. Montreal: Boréal.

Bédard, Éric, and Myriam D'Arcy. 2011. "L'Histoire nationale négligée: l'histoire du Québec n'a pas assez de place dans l'enseignement et la recherche universitaires." Montreal: Fondation Lionel-Groulx, online at http://www.fondationlionelgroulx.org/L-histoire-nationale-negligee-L.html (accessed 25 October 2016).

Bedouelle, Guy. 1992. "Lacordaire, la liberté et les libertés." In *Le Libéralisme religieux*, edited by Alain Dierkens, 31–40. Vol. 3 of *Problèmes d'histoire des religions*. Brussels: Ed. de l'Université de Bruxelles.

Bégin, Louis-Nazaire. 1892. *Les Religieuses de l'Hôtel-Dieu de Québec vont présenter au Conseil de ville une pétition pour être exemptées de payer la taxe d'eau*. Quebec, n.p.

Bélanger, Réal. 1997. "Pour un retour à l'histoire politique." *Revue d'histoire de l'Amérique française* 51 (2): 223–41.

Bellingham, Bruce. 1983. "The 'Unspeakable Blessing': Street Children, Reform Rhetoric, and Misery in Early Industrial Capitalism." *Politics and Society* 12: 303–30.

– 1986. "Institution and Family: An Alternative View of Nineteenth-Century Child Saving." *Social Problems* 33 (6): 533–57.

– 1990. "Waifs and Strays: Child Abandonment, Foster Care, and Families in Mid-Nineteenth-Century New York." In *The Uses of Charity: The Poor on Relief in the Nineteenth-Century Metropolis*, edited by Peter Mandler, 123–60. Philadelphia: University of Pennsylvania Press.

Bender, Thomas. 1975. *Toward an Urban Vision: Ideas and Institutions in Nineteenth-Century America*. Baltimore: Johns Hopkins University Press.

Bénoit, Francis-P. 1978. *La Démocratie libérale*. Paris: PUF.

Bentham, Jeremy. 1791. *Panopticon; or, The Inspection-House: Containing the idea of a new Principle of Construction ... in which Persons of any Description are to be kept under Inspection. And in particular to Penitentiary Houses, Prisons, Houses of Industry, Work-Houses, Poor-Houses, Manufactories,*

Mad-Houses, Hospitals and Schools. With a Plan of Management Adapted to the Principle. In a Series of Letters Written in the Year 1787, from Crecheff in White Russia, to a Friend in England. By Jeremy Bentham, of Lincoln Inn, Esquire. London: Reprinted and sold by T. Payne.
– 1830. Constitutional Code: for the Use of All Nations and All Governments Professing Liberal Opinions. London: Howard.
Bernès, Marcel. 1901. "Individu et société." Revue philosophique de la France et de l'étranger 52: 478–500.
Bernos, Marcel. 1991. "Ambiguïté des attitudes ecclésiastiques à l'égard de la pauvreté aux XVIIe et XVIIIe siècles." In Rémond, Démocratie et pauvreté, 277–88.
Bessière, Arnaud. 1997. "La Prison du Pied-du-Courant à Montréal (1860–1890)." Master's thesis, Université de Rouen.
Bienvenue, Louise, ed. 2013. "Des hommes, des femmes, des enfants et des murs: nouveaux regards sur les institutions de soins de santé et de charité, XIXe et XXe siècles." Special issue of Revue d'histoire de l'Amérique française 65 (2–3): 143–361.
– 2016. "L'Église et l'enfance dans les écrits de Jean-Marie Fecteau (1949–2012)." Bulletin d'histoire politique 25 (1): 53–67.
Binoche, Bertrand. 1989. Critique des droits de l'homme. Paris: Presses universitaires de France.
Bisson, François. 2007. "L'État et le placement des chômeurs au Québec: les premiers bureaux d'emploi publics, 1909–1932." PhD diss., Université du Québec à Montréal.
Blanc, Louis. 1845. Organisation du travail. Paris: Cauville.
Blanqui, Adolphe. 1849. Des classes ouvrières en France pendant l'année 1848. Paris: Académie des sciences morales et politiques.
Bock, Gisela, and Pat Thane, eds. 1991. Maternity and Gender Policies: Women and the Rise of the European Welfare States, 1880s–1950s. New York: Routledge.
Boli-Bennett, John, and John W. Meyer. 1978. "The Ideology of Childhood and the State: Rules Distinguishing Children in National Constitutions, 1870–1970." American Sociological Review 43: 797–812.
Bonaparte, Napoleon, III, Emperor of the French. 1853. The Extinction of Pauperism. Translated by James H. Causten Jr. Washington: W.M. Morrison.
Booth, Charles. 1892. Life and Labour of the People of London. London: Macmillan.
Bouchard, Gérard. 1999. La Nation québécoise au futur et au passé. Montreal: VLB.

- 2008. *The Making of the Nations and Cultures of the New World: An Essay in Comparative History.* Translated by Michelle Weinroth and Paul Leduc Browne. Montreal & Kingston: McGill-Queen's University Press.

Boucher, Adélard. 1864. "De l'influence de la charité chrétienne." *Écho du cabinet de lecture paroissial*, June, 166–7, 181–3.

- 1903. "Lettre pastorale sur la question ouvrière." In *Mandements, lettres pastorales, circulaires et autres documents publics dans le diocèse de Montréal*, edited by Gustave Lamarche, 525–37. Montreal: Archidiocese of Montreal.

Bouglé, C. 1902. "La Crise du libéralisme." *Revue de métaphysique et de morale* 10 (5): 635–52.

Bourget, Ignace. 1862. *Lettre pastorale de Mgr l'Évêque de Montréal invitant les catholiques à s'unir pour favoriser les institutions charitables de la ville et des campagnes.* Montreal, n.p.

Bourque, Gilles, and Gilles Dostaler. 1980. *Socialisme et Independence.* Montreal: Boréal Express.

Boutang, Yann Moulier. 1998. *De l'esclavage au salariat: économie historique du salariat bridé.* Paris: Presses universitaires de France.

Boutry, Philippe. 1995. "La Légitimité et l'Église en France au XIXe siècle." In Plongeron, *Catholiques entre monarchie et république*, 165–76.

Bowen, Desmond. 1988. "Ultramontanism in Quebec and the Irish Connection." In *The Untold Story: The Irish in Canada*, edited by Robert O'Driscoll and Lorna Reynolds, 295–305. Toronto: Celtic Arts.

Boyer, Robert. 1990. *The Regulation School: A Critical Introduction.* Translated by Craig Charney. New York: Columbia University Press.

Boyer, Robert, and Yves Saillard, eds. 2002. Régulation *Theory: The State of the Art.* Translated by Carolyn Shread. New York: Routledge.

Bremner, Robert. [1956] 1967. *From the Depths: The Discovery of Poverty in the United States.* New York: New York University Press.

Brenner, Robert. 1977. "The Origins of Capitalist Development: A Critique of Neo-Smithian Marxism." *New Left Review* 104: 25–93.

Brenner, Robert, and Mark Glick. 1991. "The Regulation Approach: Theory and History." *New Left Review*, no. 188, July–August, 45–119.

Brenzel, B.M. 1983. *Daughters of the State: A Social Portrait of the First Reformatory for Girls in North America, 1856–1905.* Cambridge: MIT Press.

Brown, Thomas E. 1994. "Dance of the Dialectic? Some Reflections (Polemic and Otherwise) on the Present State of Nineteenth-Century Asylum Studies." *Canadian Bulletin of Medical History* 11: 267–95.

Bruchési, Paul-Napoléon. 1882. *Conférence sur la charité*. Quebec: G. Delisle.
Brunet, Michel. 1957. "Trois dominantes de la pensée canadienne-française: l'agriculturisme, l'anti-étatisme et le messianisme." In *La Présence anglaise et les Canadiens: études sur l'histoire de la pensée des deux Canadas*, 113–66. Montreal: Beauchemin.
Bueltzingsloewen, Isabelle von. 1999. "Les Chrétiens sur le terrain médical: les hôpitaux confessionnels dans l'Allemagne du second XIXe siècle." In Bueltzingsloewen and Pelletier, *La Charité en pratique*, 65–76.
Bueltzingsloewen, Isabelle von, and Denis Pelletier, eds. 1999. *La Charité en pratique: chrétiens français et allemands sur le terrain social, XIXe–XXe siècles*. Strasbourg: Presses universitaires de Strasbourg.
Buies, Arthur. 1863. "L'Avenir de la race française au Canada." *Le Pays*, 27–31 January 1863.
– 1864. "Le Progrès." *Le Pays*, 6–13 December.
Burban, Christelle. 1997. "Les Origines institutionnelles de la protection de l'enfance au Québec: l'école d'industrie de Notre-Dame de Montfort (1883–1913)." Master's thesis, Université de Rennes II.
Burchell, Graham, Colin Gordon, and Peter Miller, eds. 1991. *The Foucault Effect: Studies on Governmentality*. Chicago: University of Chicago Press.
Burguière, André. 1995. "Le Changement social: brève histoire d'un concept." In Lepetit, *Les Formes de l'expérience*, 253–72.
– 1997. "Processus de civilisation et processus national chez Norbert Elias." In *Norbert Elias: La Politique et l'Histoire*, edited by Alain Garrigou and Bernard Lacroix, 145–65. Paris: La Découverte.
Burke, Edmund. [1790] 1955. *Reflections on the Revolution in France*. New York: Library of Liberal Arts.
Cabanis, Pierre-Jean-Georges. 1798. *Opinion de Cabanis sur la nécessité de réunir en un seul système commun, la législation des prisons et celle des secours publics*. Paris: Imprimerie nationale.
Caillé, Alain. 1986. *Splendeurs et Misères des sciences sociales: esquisse d'une mythologie*. Paris: Droz.
Canguilhem, Georges. 1978. *On the Normal and the Pathological*. Translated by Carolyn R. Fawcett. Boston: D. Reidel Pub. Co.
– 1990. "Régulation." In *Encyclopædia Universalis* 19: 711.
Careless, J.M.S. 1959. *Brown of the Globe*. Vol. 1, *The Voice of Upper Canada, 1818–1859*. Toronto: Macmillan.
Carlier, Christian. 1994. *La Prison aux champs: les colonies d'enfants délinquants dans le nord de la France au XIXe siècle*. Paris: Les Éditions de l'Atelier.
Carpenter, Mary. 1862. "On the Connexion of Voluntary Effort with Government Aid." *Transactions of the National Association for the Promotion of Social Science 1861*, 440–6.

Carré, J., and J.-P. Revauger. 1995. "Pauvreté et idéologie dans les enquêtes sociales du XIXᵉ siècle." In *Écrire la pauvreté: les enquêtes sociales britanniques aux XIXᵉ et XXᵉ siècles*, edited by Jacques Carré and J.-P. Revauger, 201–22. Paris: L'Harmattan.

Castel, Robert. 1989. "De l'intégration sociale à l'éclatement du social: l'émergence, l'apogée et le départ à la retraite du contrôle social." In *L'Éclatement du social: crise de l'objet, crise des savoirs?*, edited by Didier Le Gall, Claude Martin, and Marc-Henry Soulet, 173–84. Caen: Centre de recherche sur le travail social.

– 2003. *From Manual Workers to Wage Laborers: Transformation of the Social Question*. Edited and translated by Richard Boyd. New Brunswick, NJ: Transaction Publishers.

Catholic Church. Pope (1846–1878: Pius IX). [1864] 1998. *Encyclical Letter Quanta Cura & the Syllabus of Errors, of the Supreme Pontiff Pius IX: Condemning Current Errors. December 8, 1846.* Kansas City, MO: Angelus Press.

– Pope (1878–1903: Leo XIII). [1891] 1942. *Encyclical Letter of Pope Leo XIII on Condition of the Working Classes* (Rerum Novarum). Derby, NY: Daughters of St Paul, Apostolate of the Press.

Cavallo, Sandra. 1991. "The Motivations of Benefactors: An Overview of Approaches to the Study of Charity." In *Medicine and Charity before the Welfare State*, edited by Jonathan Barry and Colin Jones, 46–62. London: Routledge.

Cellard, André, and Marie-Claude Thifault. 2007. *Une toupie sur la tête: visages de la folie à Saint-Jean de Dieu*. Montreal: Boréal.

Chadwick, Edwin. [1842] 2002. *Report on the Sanitary Condition of the Labouring Population of Great Britain*. London: Routledge/Thoemmes.

Chadwick, Owen. 1975. *The Secularization of the European Mind in the Nineteenth Century*. Cambridge: Cambridge University Press.

Chalifoux, Eric. 1999. "Entre le gouvernement des hommes et celui des temps: le rapport au politique dans les discours ultramontain et libéral québécois, 1860–1880." Master's thesis, Université du Québec à Montréal.

Chandonnet, Thomas-Aimé. 1864. *Discourses Delivered at Notre-Dame de Québec during the Triduum of the Society of St-Vincent-de-Paul on the 21st, 22nd & 23rd December 1863*. [Quebec?: n.p.].

Chanteret, Pierre. 1876. *Du régime pénitentiaire: emprisonnement cellulaire et patronage des libérés adultes*. Paris: Mulot.

Chapais, Thomas. [1920] 1935. "Le Rôle social de l'Église." *Discours et conférences* (Quebec: Librairie Garneau) 3: 223–44.

Chartier, Roger. 1997. *On the Edge of the Cliff: History, Language, and Practices*. Translated by Lydia G. Cochrane. Baltimore: Johns Hopkins University Press.

Chateaubriand, François-René, vicomte de. [1849–50] 1860. *Mémoires d'outre-tombe*. Paris: Dufour, Mulat et Boulanger.

Chaussé, Gilles. 1980. *Jean-Jacques Lartigue, premier évêque de Montréal*. [Montreal]: Fides.

– 1985. "Un évêque mennaisien au Canada: monseigneur Jean-Jacques Lartigue." In *Les Ultramontains canadiens-français*, edited by Nive Voisine and Jean Hamelin, 105–20. Montreal: Boréal.

Cheney, R.H. 1855. "The Charities and the Poor in London." *Quarterly Review* 97: 407–50.

Cherbuliez, Antoine E. 1854a. "Paupérisme." In Coquelin and Guillaumin, *Dictionnaire de l'économie politique*, 2: 333–9.

– 1854b. "Bienfaisance publique." In Coquelin and Guillaumin, *Dictionnaire de l'économie politique*, 1: 163–77.

Chevalier, Louis. 1973. *Laboring Classes and Dangerous Classes in Paris during the First Half of the Nineteenth Century*. Translated by Frank Jellinek. [1st American ed.]. New York: H. Fertig.

Chevallier, Émile. 1900a. "Assistance." In Say and Chailley, *Nouveau dictionnaire de l'économie politique*, 1: 69–83.

– 1900b. "Hôpitaux, hospices." In Say and Chailley, *Nouveau dictionnaire de l'économie politique*, 1: 1134–40.

– 1900c. "Paupérisme." In Say and Chailley, *Nouveau dictionnaire de l'économie politique*, 2: 449–55.

Chevallier, Jacques. 1981. "L'Analyse institutionnelle." In *L'Institution*, edited by Jacques Chevallier, 3–61. Paris: PUF.

– 1995. "De quelques usages du concept de régulation." In *La Régulation entre droit et politique*, edited by Michel Miaille, 71–94. Paris: L'Harmattan.

Chunn, Dorothy E. 1992. *From Punishment to Doing Good: Family Courts and Socialized Justice in Ontario, 1890–1940*. Toronto: University of Toronto Press.

Chunn, Dorothy E., and S.A.M. Gavigan. 1988. "Social Control: Analytic Tool or Analytic Quagmire?" *Contemporary Crisis* 12 (2): 107–24.

Chunn, Dorothy E., John Mclaren, and Robert Menzies. 2002. *Regulating Lives: Historical Essays on the State, Society, the Individual, and the Law*. Vancouver: UBC Press.

Chureau, Damien. 1996. "La Maison d'industrie de Montréal (1836–1870)." Master's thesis, Université d'Angers.

Clapp, Elizabeth J. 1998. *Mothers of All Children: Women Reformers and the Rise of Juvenile Courts in Progressive Era America*. University Park, PA: Penn State University Press.

Clark, Alexander L., and Jack Gibbs. 1964. "Social Control: A Reformulation." *Social Problems* 12 (4): 398–415.

Clavero, Bartolomé. 1996. *La Grâce du don: anthropologie catholique de l'économie moderne*. Translated by Jean-Frédéric Schaub. Paris: Albin Michel.

Cliche, Marie-Aimée. 1984. "L'évolution des clauses religieuses traditionnelles dans les testaments de la région de Québec au XIXe siècle." In *Religion populaire, religion de clercs*, Bénoit Lacroix and Jean Simard, 365–90. Quebec: Institut québécois de recherche sur la culture.

Clio, Jean. 1995. "Régulation et histoire: je t'aime, moi non plus." In Robert Boyer and Yves Saillard, eds., *Théorie de la régulation: l'état des savoirs*, 49–57. Paris: La Découverte.

Cohen, Stanley. 1985. *Visions of Social Control: Crime, Punishment and Classification*. Oxford: Polity Press.

– 1989. "The Critical Discourse on 'Social Control': Notes on the Concept as a Hammer." *International Journal of the Sociology of Law* 17: 347–57.

Colliot-Thélène, Catherine. 1992. *Le Désenchantement de l'État: de Hegel à Max Weber*. Paris: Minuit.

Comacchio, Cynthia R. 1993. *Nations Are Built of Babies: Saving Ontario's Mothers and Children, 1900–1940*. Montreal & Kingston: McGill-Queen's University Press.

Comeau, Robert. 2013. "In memoriam." *Bulletin d'histoire politique* 21 (2): 13–14.

Commaille, Jacques. 1991. "Normes juridiques et régulation sociale: retour à la sociologie générale." In *Normes juridiques et régulation sociale*, edited by François Chazel and Jacques Commaille, 13–24. Paris: Librairie generale de droit et de jurisprudence.

– 1993. "Régulation sociale." In *Dictionnaire encyclopédique de théorie et de sociologie du droit*, edited by André-Jean Arnaud, 349–50. Paris: Librairie générale de droit et de jurisprudence.

Comte, Auguste. [1826] 1877. *System of Positive Polity, or, Treatise on Sociology: Instituting the Religion of Humanity*. London: Longmans, Green.

Condorcet, Jean-Antoine-Nicolas de Caritat, marquis de. [1793] c1955. *Sketch for a Historical Picture of the Progress of the Human Mind*. Translated by June Barraclough. Westport, CT: Hyperion Press.

Conrad, Christoph. 2003. "Les États-providence en comparaison: état des approches en sciences sociales et en histoire." *Histoire et Société, revue européenne d'histoire sociale*, no. 6 (April): 90–8.

Constant, Benjamin. 1797. *Observations on the Strength of the Present Government of France, and upon the Necessity of Rallying Round It*. Translated by James Losh. Bath: Printed by R. Cruttwell, for G.G. and J. Robinson.

Constant, Jean-François, and Michel Ducharme, eds. 2009. *Liberalism and Hegemony: Debating the Canadian Liberal Revolution*. Toronto: University of Toronto Press.

Conzemius, Victor. 1998. "Les Défis d'un livre: à propos des thèses de M. Altermatt." In Lagrée, *Chocs et ruptures en histoire religieuse*, 113–28.
Coquelin, Charles, and Gilbert Guillaumin, eds. 1854. *Dictionnaire de l'économie politique*. 2 vols. Paris: Guillaumin.
Corrigan, Philip, and Derek Sayer. 1985. *The Great Arch: English State Formation as Cultural Revolution*. Oxford: Blackwell.
Crowther, M.A. 1982. "Family Responsibility and State Responsibility in Britain before the Welfare State." *Historical Journal* 25 (1): 131–45.
Cunningham, Hugh. 1998. "Introduction." In Cunningham and Innes, *Charity, Philanthropy and Reform*, 1–14.
Cunningham, Hugh, and Joanne Innes, eds. *Charity, Philanthropy and Reform from the 1690s to 1850*, 15–65. London: Macmillan.
Curtis, Bruce. 1988. *Building the Educational State: Canada West, 1836–1871*. London, ON: Althouse Press.
– 2001. *The Politics of Population: State Formation, Statistics, and the Census of Canada, 1840–1875*. Toronto: University of Toronto Press.
– 2007. "Comment étudier l'état?" *Bulletin d'histoire politique* 15 (3): 103–7.
– 2009. "After 'Canada': Liberalisms, Social Theory, and Historical Analysis." In Constant and Ducharme, *Liberalism and Hegemony*, 176–200.
– 2012. *Ruling by Schooling Quebec: Conquest to Liberal Governmentality – A Historical Sociology*. Toronto: University of Toronto Press.
Dakhlia, Jocelyn. 1995. "La Question des lieux communs: des modèles de souveraineté dans l'Islam méditerranéen." In Lepetit, *Les Formes de l'expérience*, 39–61.
D'Allaire, Micheline. 1997. *Les Communautés religieuses de Montréal*. Vol. 1, *Les Communautés religieuses et l'assistance sociale à Montreal, 1659–1900*. Montreal: Méridien, 1997.
Danylewycz, Marta. 1987. *Taking the Veil: An Alternative to Marriage, Motherhood, and Spinsterhood in Quebec, 1840–1920*. Toronto: McLelland and Stewart.
Davidoff, Leonore, and Catherine Hall. 1987. *Family Fortunes: Men and Women of the English Middle Class, 1780–1850*. London: Hutchinson.
Davis, Allen F. 1967. *Spearheads for Reform: The Social Settlements and the Progressive Movement, 1890–1914*. New York: Oxford University Press.
Davis, David Brion. 1987. "Reflections on Abolitionism and Ideological Hegemony." *American Historical Review* 92 (4): 797–812.
Dean, Mitchell. 1991. *The Constitution of Poverty: Toward a Genealogy of Liberal Governance*. London: Routledge.

Debuyst, Christian, Françoise Digneffe, Jean-Michel Labadie, and Alvaro Pires, eds. 1995. *Histoire des savoirs sur le crime et la peine*. Vol. 1, *Des savoirs diffus à la notion de criminel-né*. Montreal: Presses de l'Université de Montréal.

Defoe, Daniel. 1704. *Giving Alms No Charity: and Employing the Poor. A Grievance to the Nation, Being an Essay Upon this Great Question, Whether Work-Houses, Corporations, and Houses of Correction for Employing the Poor, as now Practis'd in England; or Parish-Stocks, as Propos'd in a Late Pamphlet, Entituled, A Bill for the Better Relief, Imployment and Settlement of the Poor, &c. are not Mischievous to the Nation, Tending to the Destruction of our Trade, and to Encrease the Number and Misery of the Poor. Addressed to the Parliament of England*. London: Booksellers of London and Westminster.

Dekker, Jeroen. 2001. *The Will to Change the Child: Re-education Homes for Children at Risk in Nineteenth Century Western Europe*. New York: Peter Lang.

Delprat, G. 1908. "La Crise du libéralisme en matière d'assistance." *Revue politique et parlementaire* 55: 325–38, 58: 101–11.

Denault, Bernard, and Bénoit Lévesque. 1975. *Éléments pour une sociologie des communautés religieuses au Québec*. Montreal: Presses de l'Université de Montréal.

Desgranges, Chanoine. 1914. *L'Église et le progrès social*. Montreal: L'École sociale populaire.

Despland, Michel. 1998. *Les Hiérarchies sont ébranlées: politiques et théologies au XIXe siècle*. Montreal: Fides.

Dessaulles, Louis-Antoine. [1868] 2002. *Discours sur la tolérance*. Montreal: XYZ Éditeur.

Dicaire, Daniel. 1999. "Police et société à Montreal au milieu du XIXe siècle." Master's thesis, Université du Québec à Montréal.

Dicey, Albert V. [1914] 1981. *Lectures on the Relation Between Law and Public Opinion in England during the Nineteenth Century*. New Brunswick, NJ: Transaction Books.

Digneffe, Françoise, and Marie-Sylvie Dupont-Bouchat. 1983. "À propos de l'origine et des transformations des maisons pour jeunes délinquants en Belgique au XIXe siècle: l'histoire du Pénitencier de Saint-Hubert (1840–1890)." *Déviance et société* 6 (2): 31–165.

Divay, Stéphane. 1999. "Le Patronage Saint-Vincent de Paul de Montréal (1892–1913)." Master's thesis, Université d'Angers.

Donzelot, Jacques. [1977] 1997. *The Policing of Families*. Translated by Robert Hurley. Baltimore: Johns Hopkins University Press.

– 1984. *L'Invention du social: essai sur le déclin des passions politiques*. Paris: Fayard.

Douglas, Mary. 1986. *How Institutions Think*. Syracuse, NY: Syracuse University Press.

Dubet, François. 2002. *Le Déclin de l'institution*. Paris: Seuil.

Dubois, Pierre, and Jean Trépanier. 1999. "L'Adoption de la Loi sur les jeunes délinquants de 1908: étude comparée des quotidiens montréalais et tormentilles." *Revue d'histoire de l'Amérique française* 52 (3): 345–82.

Ducharme, Michel. 2003. "Penser le Canada: la mise en place des assises intellectuelles de l'État canadien moderne (1838–1840)." *Revue d'histoire de l'Amérique française* 56 (3): 357–86.

– 2014. *The Idea of Liberty in Canada during the Age of Atlantic Revolutions, 1776–1838*. Translated by Peter Feldstein. Montreal & Kingston: McGill-Queen's University Press.

Duchâtel, Tanneguy. 1829. *De la charité*. Paris: Mesnier.

Dufresne, Martin. 1997. "La Justice pénale et la définition du crime à Québec, 1830–1860." PhD diss., University of Ottawa.

– 2000. "La Police, le droit pénal et 'le crime' dans la première moitié du siècle: l'exemple de la ville de Québec." *Revue juridique Thémis* 34 (2): 409–34.

Dugdale, Richard Louis. 1877. *The Jukes: A Study in Crime, Pauperism, Disease, and Heredity*. New York: Putnam.

Duguit, Léon. [1908] 1922. *Le Droit social, le droit individuel et les transformations de l'État*. Paris: F. Alcan.

Dumm, Thomas L. 1987. *Democracy and Punishment: Disciplinary Origins of the United States*. Madison: University of Wisconsin Press.

Dupont-Bouchat, Marie-Sylvie, Eric Pierre, Jean-Marie Fecteau, Jean Trépanier, Jacques-Guy Petit, Bernard Schnapper, and Jeroen Dekker, eds. 2001. *Enfance et justice au XIXe siècle: essais d'histoire comparée de la protection de l'enfance, 1820–1914 (France, Belgique, Pays-Bas, Canada)*. Paris: Presses universitaires de France.

Duprat, Catherine. 1993. *Pour l'amour de l'humanité: le temps des philanthropes: la philanthropie parisienne des Lumières à la Monarchie de Juillet*. Paris: Comité des travaux historiques et scientifiques.

– 1997. *Usage et pratique de la philanthropie: pauvreté, action sociale et lien social, à Paris, au cours du premier XIXe siècle*. 2 vols. Paris: Comité d'histoire de la sécurité sociale.

Durkheim, Émile. [1897] 2005. *Suicide: A Study in Sociology*. London: Routledge.

– [1893] 1984. *The Division of Labor in Society*. Translated by W.D. Halls. New York: Free Press.

Duroselle, Jean-Baptiste. 1951. *Les Débuts du catholicisme social, 1822–1870*. Paris: Presses universitaires de France.

Engels, Friedrich. [1845] 2009. *The Condition of the Working Class in England*. Edited by David McLellan. New York: Oxford University Press.

– [1878] 1939. *Herr Eugen Dühring's Revolution in Science (Anti-Dühring)*. Edited by C.P. Dutt. Translated by Emile Burns. New York: International Publishers.

Ewald, François. 1986. *L'État providence*. Paris: Grasset.

Fahmy-Eid, Nadia. 1978. *Le Clergé et le pouvoir politique au Québec: une analyse de l'idéologie ultramontaine au milieu du XIXe siècle*. Montreal: H.M.H.

Fahrni, Magda. 2013. "Who Now Reads E.P. Thompson? Or, (Re)reading the Making at UQAM." *Labour/Le Travail* 72: 241–6.

Faure, Alain. 1991. "L'Intelligence des pauvres." In Rémond, *Democratie et pauvreté*, 219–31.

Faure, Olivier, and Dominique Dessertine. 1991. *Populations hospitalisées dans la région lyonnaise aux XIXe et XXe siècles*. CNRS, Programme Rhône-Alpes, Recherches en sciences humaines.

Favereau, Olivier. 2002. "Conventions and *Régulation*." In Boyer and Saillard, *Régulation Theory*, 312–19.

Fecteau, Jean-Marie. 1976. *Pauvres, indigents et assistés au Québec: modes successifs d'insertion de l'État dans le processus de réduction des discordances sociales*. Québec: ministère des Affaires sociales.

– 1983. "La Pauvreté, le Crime, l'État: essai sur l'économie politique du contrôle social au Québec, 1791–1840." PhD diss., Université de Paris VII.

– 1986a. "Prolégomènes à une étude historique des rapports entre l'État et le droit dans la société québécoise de la fin du XVIIIe siècle à la crise de 1929." *Sociologie et sociétés* 18 (1): 129–38.

– 1986b. *Régulation sociale et transition au capitalisme: jalons théoriques et méthodologiques pour une analyse du XIXe siècle canadien*. Quebec: PARQ (note de recherche 86–102).

– 1988. "Compte-rendu de Curtis, Bruce, *Building the Educational State: Canada West, 1836–1871*." *Revue d'histoire de l'Amérique française* 42 (2): 270–2.

– 1989. *Un nouvel ordre des choses: la pauvreté, le crime, l'État au Québec, de la fin du XVIIIe siècle à 1840*. Montreal: VLB.

– 1990. "Le Pouvoir du nombre: l'idée d'association et la transition à la démocratie au Québec au XIXe siècle." In Association française des historiens des idées politiques, *L'État, la Révolution française et l'Italie: actes du Colloque de Milan, 14–15–16 septembre 1989*, 91–107. Aix-en-Provence: Presses universitaires d'Aix-Marseille.

– 1991. "Les Dangers du secret: note sur l'État canadien et les sociétés secrètes au milieu du XIXe siècle." *Canadian Journal of Law and Society* 6: 91–112.

- 1992a. "État et associationnisme au XIXe siècle québécois: éléments pour une problématique des rapports État/société dans la transition au capitalisme." In *Colonial Leviathan: State Formation in Mid-Nineteenth-Century Canada*, edited by Allan Greer and Ian Radforth, 134–62. Toronto: University of Toronto Press.
- 1992b. "Les 'Petites Républiques': les compagnies et la mise en place du droit corporatif moderne au Québec au milieu du XIXe siècle." *Histoire sociale* 25 (49): 35–56.
- 1992c. "Manifeste." *Bulletin d'histoire politique* 1 (1): 4–5.
- 1994a. "Between the Old Order and Modern Times: Poverty, Criminality, and Power in Quebec, 1791–1840." *Essays in the History of Canadian Law*, Vol. 5, *Crime and Criminal Justice*, 293–323. Toronto: University of Toronto Press.
- 1994b. "Le Citoyen dans l'univers normatif: du passé aux enjeux du futur." In *La Condition quebécoise: enjeux et horizons d'une société en devenir*, edited by Jean-Marie Fecteau, Jocelyn Létourneau, and Gilles Breton, 83–101. Montreal: VLB Editeur.
- 1994c. "Regulating the Social." In *Radically Rethinking Regulation: Workshop Report*, edited by Mariana Valverde, 52–4. Toronto: Centre of Criminology, University of Toronto.
- 1994d. "Le Retour du refoulé: l'histoire et le politique." *Bulletin d'histoire politique* 2 (3): 5–10.
- 1995a. "Un cas de force majeure: le développement des mesures d'assistance publique à Montréal au tournant du XXe siècle." *Lien social et Politiques*, RIAC, no. 33, 105–12.
- 1995b. "La Construction d'un espace social: les rapports de l'Église et de l'État et la question de l'assistance publique au Québec dans la seconde moitié du XIXe siècle." In *L'Histoire de la culture et de l'imprimé: hommages a Claude Galarneau*, edited by Yvan Lamonde and Gilles Gallichan, 61–90. Quebec: Presses de l'Université Laval.
- 1995c. "La Quête d'une histoire normale: réflexion sur les limites épistémologiques du 'révisionnisme' au Québec." *Bulletin d'histoire politique* 4 (2): 32–4.
- 1996a. "Classes, démocratie, nation: la transition au capitalisme chez Stanley B. Ryerson." In *Stanley Bréhaut Ryerson: un intellectuel de combat*, edited by Robert Comeau and Robert Tremblay, 233–63. Hull, QC: Vents d'Ouest.
- 1996b. "Ruses de la raison libérale? Éléments pour une problématique des rapports État-individu au XIXe siècle." In *Érudition, humanisme et savoir: actes du colloque en l'honneur de Jean Hamelin*, edited by Yves Roby and Nive Voisine, 69–92. Quebec: Presses de l'Université Laval, 1996.

- 1997. "Du droit d'association au droit social: essai sur la crise du droit libéral et l'émergence d'une alternative pluraliste à la norme étatique (1850–1930)." *Canadian Journal of Law and Society* 12 (2): 143–57.
- 1998a. "La Fin des mémoires parallèles: réflexion sur le comparatisme comme dimension heuristique de l'histoire québécoise." In *À propos de l'histoire nationale*, edited by Robert Comeau and Bernard Dionne, 91–103. Sillery, QC: Septentrion.
- 1998b. "Note sur les enjeux de la prise en charge de l'enfance délinquante et en danger au XIXe siècle." *Lien social et Politiques*, RIAC, no. 40, 129–38.
- 1998c. "Notre histoire politique." *Bulletin d'histoire politique* 7 (1): 6–9.
- 1999a. "Between Scientific Enquiry and the Search for a Nation: Quebec Historiography as Seen by Ronald Rudin." *Canadian Historical Review* 80 (4): 641–65.
- 1999b. "Une économie historique du minimum: propos sur les origines de l'État-providence." *Lien social et Politiques*, RIAC, no. 42, 61–70.
- 1999c. "Entre la quête de la nation et les découvertes de la science: l'historiographie québécoise vue par Ronald Rudin." *Canadian Historical Review* 80 (3): 440–63.
- 2001. "Compte-rendu de Curtis, Bruce, *The Politics of Population: State Formation, Statistics, and the Census of Canada, 1840–1875*." *Revue d'histoire de l'Amérique française* 55 (2): 261–5.
- 2002a. "La Dynamique sociale du catholicisme québécois au XIXe siècle: éléments pour une réflexion sur les frontières et les conditions historiques de possibilité du social." *Histoire sociale* 35 (70): 495–515.
- 2002b. "'This ultimate resource ... ' Martial Law and State Repression in Lower Canada, 1837–1838." In *Canadian State Trials*, vol. 2, *Rebellion and Invasion in the Canadas, 1837–1839*, edited by E.M. Greenwood and B. Wright, 207–47. Toronto: University of Toronto Press.
- 2007a. "Écrire l'histoire de l'État?" *Bulletin d'histoire politique* 15 (3): 239–46.
- 2007b. "Primauté analytique de l'expérience et gradualisme historique: sur les apories d'une certaine lecture historienne du passé." *Revue d'histoire de l'Amérique française* 61 (2): 281–94.
- 2009. "Towards a Theory of Possible History? Ian Mckay's Idea of a Liberal Order." *Underhill Review*, http://www3.carleton.ca/underhillreview/09/fall/reviews/fecteau.htm (accessed 27 October 2016).
- 2011. "Histoire politique et histoire nationale au Québec." *Action nationale* 101 (9–10): 210–39.

Fecteau, Jean-Marie, François Fenchel, Marie-Josée Tremblay, Jean Trépanier, and Guy Cucumel. 2006. "Répression au quotidien et régulation punitive en longue durée: le cas de la prison de Montréal, 1836–1913." *Déviance et Société* 30 (3): 339–53.

Fecteau, Jean-Marie, F. Murray Greenwood, and Jean-Pierre Wallot. 2002. "Sir James Craig's 'Reign of Terror' and Its Impact on Emergency Powers in Lower Canada, 1810–13." In *Canadian State Trials*, vol. 2, *Rebellion and Invasion in the Canadas, 1837–1839*, edited by F. Murray Greenwood and Barry Wright, 323–79. Toronto: University of Toronto Press.

Fecteau, Jean-Marie, and Janice Harvey. 2005. "From Agents to Institutions: An Historical Dialectic of Interactionism and Power Relations." In *Agency and Institutions in Social Regulation: Toward an Historical Understanding of Their Interaction*, edited by Jean-Marie Fecteau and Janice Harvey, 16–29. Sainte-Foy, QC: Presses de l'Université du Québec.

– 2012. "Le Réseau de régulation sociale montréalais." In *Histoire de Montréal et de sa région*, edited by Dany Fougères, 675–715. Quebec: Presses de l'Université Laval.

Fecteau, Jean-Marie, and Douglas Hay. 1996. "'Government by Will and Pleasure instead of Law': Military Justice and the Legal System in Quebec, 1775–83." In *Canadian State Trials*, vol. 1, *Law, Politics, and Security Measures, 1608–1837*, edited by F. Murray Greenwood and Barry Wright, 129–71. Toronto: University of Toronto Press.

Fecteau, Jean-Marie, Sylvie Menard, Véronique Strimelle, and Jean Trépanier. 1998. "Une politique de l'enfance délinquante et en danger: la mise en place des écoles de réforme et d'industrie au Québec (1840–1873)." *Crime, histoire et société* 2 (1): 75–110.

Fecteau, Jean-Marie, J. Tremblay, and J. Trépanier. 1993. "La Prison de Montréal de 1865 à 1913: évolution en longue période d'une population pénale." *Les Cahiers de droit* 34 (1): 27–58.

Fecteau, Jean-Marie, and Éric Vaillancourt. 2007. "Les Sulpiciens et la charité en ville." In Dominique Deslandres et al., eds., *Les Sulpiciens de Montréal: une histoire de pouvoir et de discrétion, 1657–2007*, 241–64. Montreal: Fides.

– 2006. "The Saint-Vincent de Paul Society and the Catholic Charitable System in Quebec (1846–1921)." In *The Churches and Social Order in Nineteenth- and Twentieth-Century Canada*, edited by Ollivier Hubert and Michael Gauvreau, 195–224. Montreal & Kingston: McGill-Queen's University Press.

Fenchel, François. 2007. "Entre petite criminalité et grande misère: la prison des hommes à Montréal et sa population (1912–1940)." PhD diss., Université de Montréal.

Ferretti, Lucia. 1992. *Entre voisins: la société paroissiale en milieu urbain: Saint-Pierre-Apôtre de Montréal, 1848–1930*. Montreal: Boréal.

– 1999. *Brève histoire de l'Église catholique au Québec*. Montreal: Boréal.

Finlayson, Geoffrey. 1994. *Citizen, State, and Social Welfare in Britain, 1830–1990*. Oxford: Clarendon Press.

Forcier, Maxime. 2004. "Alcoolisme, crime et folie: l'enfermement des ivrognes à Montréal (1870–1921)." Master's thesis, Université du Québec à Montréal.

Foucault, Michel. 1963. *The Birth of the Clinic: An Archaeology of Medical Perception*. Translated by A.M. Sheridan. London: Routledge.

– 1977. *Discipline and Punish: The Birth of the Prison*. Translated by Alan Sheridan. 1st American ed. New York: Pantheon Books.

– [1961] 2006. *History of Madness*. Edited by Jean Khalfa. Translated by Jonathan Murphy and Jean Khalfa. New York: Routledge.

– 2009a. "Alternatives to the Prison: Dissemination or Decline of Social Control?" *Theory, Culture & Society* 26 (6): 12–24.

– 2009b. *Security, Territory, Population: Lectures at the Collège de France, 1977–1978*. Edited by Michel Senellart. Translated by Graham Burchell. New York: Picador/Palgrave Macmillan.

– 2010. *The Birth of Biopolitics: Lectures at the Collège de France, 1978–1979*. Edited by Michel Senellart. Translated by Graham Burchell. New York: Picador.

Fougères, Dany. 1992. "L'Encadrement juridique des infrastructures et des services publics urbains: le cas du transport en commun à Montréal (1860–1880)." Master's thesis, Université du Québec à Montréal.

Fox, Richard. 1976. "Beyond 'Social Control': Institutions and Disorder in Bourgeois Society." *History of Education Quarterly* 16 (2): 203–7.

Franke, Herman. 1995. *The Emancipation of Prisoners: A Socio-Historical Analysis of the Dutch Prison Experiment*. Edinburgh: Edinburgh University Press.

Freeden, Michael. 1994. "Les Libéraux progressistes en Grande-Bretagne." In Merrien, *Face à la pauvreté*, 71–98.

Fyson, Donald. 1995. "Criminal Justice, Civil Society and the Local State: The Justices of the Peace in the District of Montreal, 1764–1830." PhD diss., Université de Montréal.

– 2006. *Magistrates, Police, and People: Everyday Criminal Justice in Quebec and Lower Canada*. Toronto: University of Toronto Press.

– "Réplique de Donald Fyson." 2007. *Revue d'histoire de l'Amérique française* 61 (2): 294–9.

Gadille, Jacques. 1995. "Théologies et projets politiques des évêques français, de la Seconde République au Ralliement (1848–1892)." In Plongeron, *Catholiques entre monarchie et république*, 177–87.

Gaillac, Henri. 1991. *Les Maisons de correction*. 2nd ed. Paris: Cujas.

Garland, David. 1981. "The Birth of the Welfare Sanction." *British Journal of Law and Society* 8 (1): 29–45.

- 1985. *Punishment and Welfare: A History of Penal Strategies.* Aldershot: Gower.
- 1997. "'Governmentality' and the Problem of Crime: Foucault, Criminology, Sociology." *Theoretical Criminology* 1 (2): 173–214.
- 2001. *The Culture of Control: Crime and Social Order in Contemporary Society.* Chicago: University of Chicago Press.

Garneau, Jean-Philippe. 2002. "Droit, famille et pratique successorale au XVIIIe siècle canadien: les usages du droit dans la société rurale de Beaupré, en amont et en aval de la Conquête britannique." PhD diss., Université du Québec à Montréal.

Garnot, Bénoit. 1996. "L'Ampleur et les limites de l'infrajudiciaire dans la France d'Ancien Régime (XVIe, XVIIe et XVIIIe siècles)." In *L'Infrajudiciaire du Moyen Age à l'époque contemporaine: actes du colloque de Dijon, 5–6 octobre 1995*, edited by Bénoit Garnot, 69–76. Dijon: Presses universitaires de Dijon.

Gasparin, A.-E. de. 1837. *Rapport au roi sur les hôpitaux, les hospices et les services de bienfaisance.* Paris: Imprimerie royale.
- 1846. *Il y a des pauvres à Paris et ailleurs.* Paris: Delay.

Gauchet, Marcel. 1988. "Changement de paradigme en sciences sociales?" *Le Débat* 50 (3): 165–70.
- 1997. *The Disenchantment of the World: A Political History of Religion.* Translated by Oscar Burge. Princeton: Princeton University Press.

Gauchet, Marcel, and Gladys Swain. 1980. *La Pratique de l'esprit humain: l'institution asilaire et la révolution démocratique.* Paris: Gallimard.

Gérando, Joseph-Marie, baron de. 1832. *The Visitor of the Poor.* Translated by "A Lady of Boston." Boston: Hilliard, Gray, Little, and Wilkins.
- 1839. *De la bienfaisance publique.* 4 vols. Paris: Renouard.

Geremek, Bronislaw. 1976. *Les Marginaux parisiens aux XIVe et XVe siècles.* Paris: Flammarion.
- 1987. *La Potence ou la Pitié: l'Europe et les pauvres du Moyen Age à nos jours.* Paris: Gallimard.

Gérin, Léon. 1886. "La Science sociale." *La Presse*, June 22 and 30.

Giroux, Georges-Michel. 1945–6. "La Situation juridique de l'Église catholique dans la province de Québec." *Revue du Notariat* 48: 97–117, 137–52.

Giroux, Marie-Christine. 2011. *Accueillir, vêtir, nourrir, instruire, éduquer et soigner: la protection de l'enfance à l'Hospice des Soeurs Grises de Montréal (1854–1911).* Master's thesis, UQAM.

Glasbeek, Amanda. 2006. *Moral Regulation and Governance in Canada: History, Context and Critical Issues.* Toronto: Canadian Scholars' Press.

Godwin, William. [1793] 1976. *An Enquiry Concerning Political Justice and Its Influence on General Virtue and Happiness.* London: Penguin Books.

Goffman, Erving. 1961. *Asylums: Essays on the Social Situation of Mental Patients and Other Inmates*. New York: Anchor Books.

Gohiet, François. 1892. *Conférences sur la question ouvrière: données à l'église Saint-Sauveur de Québec*. Quebec: Leclerc & Roy.

– 1896. *L'Oeuvre du pain des pauvres: discours pour la bénédiction d'une statue de Saint-Antoine de Padoue, prononcé dans la basilique d'Ottawa, le 15 mars 1896*. Quebec: François-N. Faveur.

Gonthier, Dominique Ceslas. 1915. *À propos d'immunités*. Montreal: Secrétariat de l'École sociale populaire.

Gordon, Linda. 1994. *Pitied but Not Entitled: Single Mothers and the History of Welfare, 1890–1935*. New York: Free Press.

Gouin, Édouard. 1913. *Un catholique social: Frédéric Ozanam*. Montreal: Secrétariat de l'École sociale populaire.

Granatstein, J.L. 1998. *Who Killed Canadian History?* Toronto: Harper-Collins.

Greer, Allan. 1992. "The Birth of the Police in Canada." In Greer and Radforth, *Colonial Leviathan*, 17–49.

Greer, Allan, and Ian Radforth, eds. 1992. *Colonial Leviathan: State Formation in Mid-nineteenth-Century Canada*. Toronto: Univ. of Toronto Press.

Guérin, M. 1899. *Rerum Novarum: How to Abolish Poverty, How Poverty Was Abolished*. Montreal: A. Pelletier.

Gueslin, André. 1987. *L'Invention de l'économie sociale: le XIXe siècle francais*. Paris: Economica.

– 1998. *Gens pauvres, pauvres gens dans la France du XIXe siècle*. Paris: Aubier.

Guizot, François. [1838] 1882a. "De la religion dans les sociétés modernes." In *Méditations et études morales*, 2nd ed., 25–52. Paris: Didier.

– [1838] 1882b. "Du catholicisme, du protestantisme et de la philosophie en France." In *Méditations et études morales*, 55–86. Paris: Didier.

– 1849. *Democracy in France, by Monsieur Guizot*. New York: D. Appleton & Co.

Gurvitch, Georges. 1945. "Social Control." In *Twentieth Century Sociology*, edited by Georges Gurvitch and Wilbert E. Moore, 267–96. New York: Philosophical Library.

Habermas, Jürgen. 1989. *The Structural Transformation of the Public Sphere: An Inquiry into a Category of Bourgeois Society*. Translated by Thomas Burger with the assistance of Frederick Lawrence. Cambridge: Polity Press.

Hamilton, Gary G., and John R. Sutton. 1989. "The Problem of Control in the Weak State: Domination in the United States, 1880–1920." *Theory and Society* 18 (1): 1–46.

Hardy, René. 1999. *Contrôle social et mutation de la culture religieuse au Québec, 1830–1930*. Montreal: Boréal.

Harris, José. 1983. "The Transition to High Politics in English Social Policy, 1880–1914." In *High and Low Politics in Modern Britain: Ten Studies*, edited by Michael Bentley and John Stevenson, 58–79. Oxford: Oxford University Press.

Harvey, Janice. 2001. "The Protestant Orphan Asylum and the Montreal Ladies' Benevolent Society: A Case Study in Protestant Child Charity in Montreal, 1822–1900." PhD diss., McGill University.

Harvey, Julien. 1993. "L'Influence de la pensée sociale de l'Église au Québec." In Richard and O'Neill, *La Question sociale hier et aujourd'hui*, 109–28.

Harvey, Louis-Georges. 2005. *Le Printemps de l'Amérique française: américanité, anticolonialisme, et républicanisme dans le discours politique québécois, 1805–1837*. Montreal: Boréal.

Haskell, Thomas L. 1985. "Capitalism and the Origins of the Humanitarian Sensibility." *American Historical Review* 90: 339–61, 547–66.

– 1987. "Convention and Hegemonic Interest in the Debate over Antislavery: A Reply to Davis and Ashworth." *American Historical Review* 92 (4): 829–78.

– 1998a. "The Shifting Conventions of Human Agency and Responsibility." In *Objectivity Is Not Neutrality: Explanatory Schemes in History*, 225–34. Baltimore: Johns Hopkins University Press.

– 1998b. "Responsibility, Convention, and the Role of Ideas in History." In Haskell, *Objectivity Is Not Neutrality*, 280–306.

– 1998c. "Persons as Uncaused Causes: John Stuart Mill, the Spirit of Capitalism, and the 'Invention' of Formalism." In Haskell, *Objectivity Is Not Neutrality*, 318–68.

Haskin, Hervé. 1992. "Alexandre Vinet, la Belgique et la genèse du concept de séparation de l'Église et de l'État (1824–1891)." In *Le Libéralisme religieux*, edited by Alain Dierkens, 18–30. Vol. 3 of *Problèmes d'histoire des religions*. Brussels: Ed. de l'Université de Bruxelles.

Hatzfeld, Henri. 1989. *Du paupérisme à la sécurité sociale: essai sur les origines de la sécurité sociale en France*. Nancy: Presses universitaires de Nancy.

Hauriou, Maurice. 1909. "Le Point de vue de l'ordre et de l'équilibre." *Recueil de législation de Toulouse*, 2nd series, 5: 1–86.

Hawes, Joseph M. 1971. *Children in Urban Society: Juvenile Delinquency in Nineteenth-Century America*. New York: Oxford University Press.

Hazlitt, William. 1807. *A Reply to the Essay on Population: in a Series of Letters, to which are Added, Extracts from the Essay, with Notes by the Rev. T.R. Malthus*. London: printed for Longman, Hurst, Rees, and Orme.

- 1819. "On the Principle of Population as Affecting the Schemes of Utopian Improvement." In *Political Essays, with Sketches of Public Characters*, 415–24. London: printed for William Hone.

Hébert, Karine. 1997. "Une organisation maternaliste au Québec: la Fédération nationale Saint-Jean-Baptiste, 1900–1940." Master's thesis, Université de Montréal.

Hegel, G.W.F. [1820] 2002. *The Philosophy of Right*. Translated by Alan White. Newburyport, MA: Focus Pub. and R. Pullins.

Hennock, E. 1976. "Poverty and Social Theory in England: The Experience of the Eighteen-eighties." *Social History* (UK) 1: 67–91.

Henriot, Père. 1892. *Les Ordres religieux au point de vue social*. Montreal: Senécal.

Hilaire, Yves-Marie. 1991. "L'Église et les très pauvres dans la première moitié du XIXe siècle: quelques observations issues de recherches régionales." In Rémond, *Démocratie et pauvreté*, 289–94.

Hilton, Boyd. 1985a. "Chalmers as Political Economist." In *The Practical and the Pious: Essays on Thomas Chalmers, 1780–1847*, edited by A.C. Cheyne, 141–56. Edinburgh: Saint Andrew Press.

- 1985b. "The Role of Providence in Evangelical Thought." In *History, Society, and Churches: Essays in Honour of Owen Chadwick*, edited by Derek Beales and Geoffrey Best, 215–33. Cambridge: Cambridge University Press.

Himmelfarb, Gertrude. 1984. *The Idea of Poverty: England in the Early Industrial Age*. London: Faber and Faber.

- 1991. *Poverty and Compassion: The Moral Imagination of the Late Victorians*. New York: Vintage Books.

Hirschman, Albert O. 1977. *The Passions and the Interests: Political Arguments for Capitalism before Its Triumph*. Princeton: Princeton University Press.

Holloran, Peter C. 1994. *Boston's Wayward Children: Social Services for Homeless Children, 1830–1930*. Boston: Northeastern University Press.

Hordern, Francis. 1991. "Le Droit des indigents aux secours: naissance de l'assistance publique, 1880–1914." In Rémond, *Démocratie et pauvreté*, 535–49.

Hudon, Christine. 1995. "Le Renouveau religieux québécois au XIXe siècle: éléments pour une réinterprétation." *Revue d'histoire de l'Amérique française* 24 (4): 467–89.

- 1996. *Prêtres et fidèles dans le diocèse de Saint-Hyacinthe, 1820–1825*. Sillery, QC: Septentrion.

Huggins, Nathan Irvin. 1971. *Protestants against Poverty: Boston's Charities, 1870–1900*. Westport, CT: Greenwood Publications.

Humphreys, Robert. 1995. *Sin, Organized Charity and the Poor Law in Victorian England*. London: Macmillan.

Hunt, Alan. 1999. *Governing Morals: A Social History of Moral Regulation.* Cambridge: Cambridge University Press.

Hunter, Robert. 1904. *Poverty.* New York: Macmillan.

Ignatieff, Michael. 1978. *A Just Measure of Pain: The Penitentiary in the Industrial Revolution, 1750–1850.* New York: Columbia University Press.

– 1981. "State, Civil Society and Total Institutions: A Critique of Recent Social Histories of Punishment." *Crime and Justice*, no. 3, 153–92.

Innes, Joanna. 1987. "Prisons for the Poor: English Bridewells, 1555–1800." In *Labour, Law and Crime: An Historical Perspective*, edited by Francis Snyder and Douglas Hay, 42–122. London: Tavistock.

– 1996. "The 'Mixed Economy of Welfare' in Early Modern England: Assessments of the Options." In *Charity, Self-Interest and Welfare in the English Past*, edited by Martin Daunton, 139–80. New York: St Martin's Press.

– 1998. "State, Church and Voluntarism in European Welfare 1690–1850." In Cunningham and Innes, *Charity, Philanthropy and Reform*, 15–65.

– 1999. "The State and the Poor: Eighteenth-Century England in European Perspective." In *Rethinking Leviathan: The Eighteenth-Century State in Britain and Germany*, edited by John Brewer and Eckhart Hellmuth, 225–80. Oxford: Oxford University Press.

Jacob, B. 1903. "La Crise du libéralisme." *Revue de métaphysique et de morale* 11 (1): 100–20.

Janowitz, M. 1975. "Sociological Theory and Social Control." *American Journal of Sociology* 81: 82–108.

Jardin, André. 1985. *Histoire du libéralisme politique de la crise de l'absolutisme à la Constitution de 1875.* Paris: Hachette.

Jones, Colin. 1996. "Some Recent Trends in the History of Charity." In *Charity, Self-Interest and Welfare in the English Past*, edited by Martin Daunton, 51–64. New York: St Martin's Press.

Jones, Gareth Stedman. 1977. "Class Expression versus Social Control? A Critique of Recent Trends in the Social History of 'Leisure.'" *History Workshop Journal*, no. 4, 163–71.

– 1983. *Languages of Class: Studies in English Working Class History, 1832–1982.* Cambridge: Cambridge University Press.

Joyal, Renée. 1994. "L'Évolution des modes de contrôle de l'autorité parentale et son impact sur les relations entre parents et enfants dans la société québécoise." In *Entre tradition et universalisme*, edited by Françoise-Romaine Ouellette and Claude Bardeau, 245–58. Quebec: Institut québécois de recherche sur la culture.

– 2000. "L'Acte concernant les écoles d'industrie (1869): une mesure de prophylaxie sociale dans un Québec en voie d'urbanisation." In *Entre surveillance et compassion: l'évolution de la protection de l'enfance au Québec, des origines à nos jours*, edited by Renée Joyal, 35–48. Sainte-Foy: PUQ.

Kaiser, Jochen-Christoph. 1999. "Le Rôle du facteur religieux dans le travail social aux XIXe et XXe siècles en Allemagne: bilan de la recherche." In Bueltzingsloewen and Pelletier, *La Charité en pratique*, 19–32.

Kästner, Karl-Hermann. 1981. "From the Social Question to the Social State." *Economy and Society* 10 (1): 7–26.

Katz, Michael B. 1968. *The Irony of Early School Reform*. Boston: Beacon Press.

– 1983. *Poverty and Policy in American History*. New York: Academic Press.

– 1986. *In the Shadow of the Poorhouse: A Social History of Welfare in America*. New York: Basic Books.

King, Peter. 2000. *Crime, Justice and Discretion in England, 1740–1820*. Oxford: Oxford University Press.

King, Peter, and Joan Noel. 1994. "Les Origines du 'problème de la délinquance juvénile': la multiplication des poursuites contre des mineurs à Londres à la fin du XVIIIe siècle et au debut du XIXe siècle." *Déviance et Société* 18 (1): 3–29.

Knopf, Rainer. 1979. "Quebec's 'Holy War' as 'Regime' Politics: Reflections on the Guibord Case." *Canadian Journal of Political Science* 12 (2): 315–31.

Koselleck, Reinhart. 1985. *Futures Past: On the Semantics of Historical Time*. Translated by Keith Tribe. Cambridge: MIT Press.

– 1985. "'Space of Experience' and 'Horizon of Expectation': Two Historical Categories." In Koselleck, *Futures Past*, 255–75.

Koven, Seth, and Sonya Michel. 1993. "Introduction." In *Mothers of a New World: Maternalist Politics and the Origins of Welfare States*, edited by Seth Koven and Sonya Michel, 1–42. London: Routledge.

Labrèche-Renaud, Louise. 1991. "Les Racines juridiques de l'aliénation mentale et l'institutionnalisation au Québec, de 1845 à 1892." PhD diss., Université de Montréal.

Lachance, André. 1984. *Crimes et châtiments en Nouvelle-France*. Montreal: Boréal.

Laflèche, Louis-François. 1889. *Des biens temporels de l'Église et de l'immunité de ces biens devant les pouvoirs civils*. Trois-Rivières, QC, n.p.

Lafont, Jérôme. 2003. "Projet de défense sociale: ombres et lumières sur la prison de Bordeaux (1914–1921)." Master's thesis, Université d'Angers.

Lagrée, Michel, ed. *Chocs et ruptures en histoire religieuse: fin XVIIIe–XIXe siècles*. Rennes: Presses universitaires de Rennes.

Lallemand, Léon. 1895. *Les Associations charitables dans la Province de Québec*. Paris: Picard.

Lalonde, Marc. 1961. "Les Relations juridiques Église-État au Québec." In *L'Église et le Québec*, edited by Marcel Rioux, 77–100. Montreal: Éditions du Jour.
Lambert, Brooke. 1873–4. "Charity: Its Aims and Means." *Contemporary Review* 23: 462–76.
Lamennais, Hugues-Félicité Robert de. 1825. *De la religion considéré dans ses rapports avec l'ordre politique et civil*. 2 vols. Paris: Bureau du Mémorial catholique.
– 1837. *Articles du journal* l'Avenir. Paris: Daubrée.
Lamonde, Yvan. 1994. *Louis-Antoine Dessaulles, 1818–1895: un seigneur libéral et anticlérical*. Saint-Laurent, QC: Fides.
– [2000] 2013. *The Social History of Ideas in Quebec*. Translated by Phyllis Aronoff and Howard Scott. Montreal & Kingston: McGill-Queen's University Press.
Landreville, Pierre. 1983. *Normes sociales et normes pénales: notes pour une analyse socio-politique des normes*. Montreal: École de criminologie, Université de Montréal.
Landriot, Jean-François-Anne-Thomas. 1881. *La Clef du ciel ou Le Mérite dans les oeuvres par la pureté d'intention*. Montreal: Sénécal.
Langlois, Claude. 1984. *Le Catholicisme au féminin: les congrégations françaises à supérieure générale au XIXe siècle*. Paris: Cerf.
Lanson, G. 1902. "À propos de la 'crise du libéralisme.'" *Revue de métaphysique et de morale* 10 (6): 748–63.
Laperrière, Guy. 1996. *Les Congrégations religieuses: de la France au Québec, 1880–1914*. Sainte-Foy: Presses de l'Université Laval.
Lapointe-Roy, Huguette. 1987. *Charité bien ordonnée: le premier réseau de lutte contre la pauvreté à Montréal au XIXe siècle*. Montreal: Boréal.
Larkin, Emmet. 1998. "The Rise and Fall of Stations in Ireland, 1750–1850." In Lagrée, ed., *Chocs et ruptures en histoire religieuse*, 19–32.
Lartigue, Jean-Jacques. 1838. "Des doctrines du philosophisme moderne sur les gouvernements." Archives de la Chancellerie de l'Archevêché de Montréal, 901.037, 838-2.
Larue, Hubert. 1876. *The Catholic Religious Corporations of the City of Quebec and the Proposed New Taxations*. Quebec: G.T. Cary.
Larue, Richard. 1991. "Allégeance et origine: contribution à l'analyse de la crise politique au Bas-Canada." *Revue d'histoire de l'Amérique française* 44 (4): 529–48.
Laurier, Wilfrid. 1877. *Lecture on Political Liberalism Delivered by Wilfred Laurier, Esq., M.P. on the 26th June, in the Music Hall, Quebec, under the Auspices of the "Canadian Club."* [N.p.: n.p.].

Laurin, Nicole, Danielle Jureau, and Lorraine Duchesne. 1991. *À la recherche d'un monde oublié: les communautés religieuses de femmes au Québec de 1900 à 1970*. Montreal: Le Jour.

Lea, John. 1979. "Discipline and Capitalist Development." In *Capitalism and the Rule of Law: From Deviancy Theory to Marxism*, edited by Bob Fine, Richard Kinsey, John Lea, Sol Picciotto, and Jack Young, 76–89. London: Hutchinson.

Lécuyer, Bernard-Pierre. 1967. "Régulation sociale, contrainte sociale et 'social control.'" *Revue française de sociologie* 8 (1): 78–84.

Lefébure, Léon. 1889. *De l'organisation de la charité à Paris*. Paris: F. Levé.

Lepetit, Bernard. 1995a. "Histoire des pratiques, pratique de l'histoire." In Lepetit, *Les Formes de l'expérience*, 9–22.

- 1995b. "Le Présent de l'histoire." In Lepetit, ed., *Les Formes de l'expérience*, 273–98.

- ed. 1995. *Les Formes de l'expérience: une autre histoire sociale*. Paris: Albin Michel.

Le Play, Frédéric. 1884. *L'Organisation de la famille, selon le vrai modèle signalé par l'histoire de toutes les races et de tous les temps*. Tours: A. Mame et fils.

Leroy-Beaulieu, Paul. [1889] 1900. *L'État moderne et ses fonctions*. Paris: Guillaumin.

- 1891. *The Modern State in Relation to Society and the Individual*. London: S. Sonnenschein & Co.

Lesselier, Claudie. 1982. "Les Femmes et la prison, 1815–1939." PhD diss., Université de Paris VII.

Lessnoff, Michael. 1986. *Social Contract*. Atlantic Highlands, NJ: Humanities Press.

Le Testu, Jehan. n.d. [ca. 1885]. *Cri d'alarme au sujet de l'accaparement du Canada par les congrégations religieuses*. Montreal, n.p.

Létourneau, Jocelyn. 1986. *Croissance économique et régulation duplessiste: retour sur les origines de la révolution tranquille*. Quebec: Université Laval.

Levasseur, Carol. 1987. *Salariat, conflits salariaux et mouvement ouvrier: l'avènement de la société salariale et l'essor de l'État-providence au 20ᵉ siècle*. Quebec: Université Laval.

Lipietz, Alain. 1979. *Crise et Inflation: pourquoi?* Paris: Maspero.

- 1997. "Warp, Woof and Regulation: A Tool for Social Science." In *Space and Social Theory: Interpreting Modernity and Postmodernity*, edited by Georges Benko and Ulf Strohmayer, 250–84. Malden, MA: Blackwell Publishers.

Logue, William. 1994. "Les Économistes libéraux en France." In Merrien, *Face à la pauvreté*, 53–70.

Lombroso, Cesare. [1887] 2006. *Criminal Man*. Translated by Mary Gibson and Nicole Hahn Rafter, with assistance from Mark Seymour. Durham, NC: Duke University Press.

Loschak, Danièle. 1986. "La Société civile: du concept au gadget." In Jacques Chevallier, *La Société civile*, 44–75. Paris: PUF.

Lubove, Roy. 1962. *The Progressives and the Slums: Tenement House Reform in New York City, 1890–1917*. Pittsburgh: University of Pittsburgh Press.

— 1965. *The Professional Altruist: The Emergence of Social Work as a Career, 1880–1930*. Cambridge: Harvard University Press.

Luc, Jean-Noël. 1997. *L'Invention du jeune enfant au XIXe siècle: de la salle d'asile a l'école maternelle*. Paris: Belin.

Lurieu, G., and H. Romand. 1851. *Études sur les colonies agricoles*. Paris: Librairie agricole de la Maison rustique.

Macleod, David. 1978. "A Live Vaccine: The YMCA and Male Adolescence in the United States and Canada, 1870–1920." *Social History* 11: 5–25.

Macpherson, C.B. 1962. *The Political Theory of Possessive Individualism: Hobbes to Locke*. Oxford: Oxford University Press.

Mahood, Linda. 1995. *Policing Gender, Class and Family: Britain, 1850–1940*. Edmonton: University of Alberta Press.

Malthus, Thomas Robert. [1798] 1970. *An Essay on the Principle of Population: and, A Summary View of the Principle of Population*. Harmondsworth, UK: Penguin Books.

— 1992. *An Essay on the Principle of Population: or a View of its Past and Present Effects on Human Happiness, with an Inquiry into our Prospects respecting the Future Removal or Mitigation of the Evils which it Occasions*. Selected by Donald Winch using the text of the 1803 edition as prepared by Patricia James for the Royal Economic Society, 1990, showing the additions and corrections made in the 1806, 1807, 1817, and 1826 editions. New York: Cambridge University Press.

Mandler, Peter. 1987. "The Making of the New Poor Law Redivivus." *Past and Present*, no. 117, 131–57.

— 1990. "Tories and Paupers: Christian Political Economy and the Making of the New Poor Law." *Historical Journal* 33: 91–103.

Manent, Pierre. 1995. *An Intellectual History of Liberalism*. Translated by Rebecca Balinski. Princeton: Princeton University Press.

Mann, Michael. 1993. *The Sources of Social Power*. Vol. 2, *The Rise of Classes and Nation-States, 1760–1914*. Cambridge: Cambridge University Press.

Marais, Jean-Luc. 1999. *Histoire du don en France de 1800 à 1939: dons et legs charitables, pieux et philanthropiques*. Rennes: Presses universitaires de Rennes.

Marec, Yannick. 1989. "Misère, pauvreté et institutions sociales: l'exemple de Rouen au XIXe siècle." *Le Social aux prises avec l'histoire*, no. 1, 105–12.
Marion, Henri. 1885. "L'Individu contre l'État." *Revue philosophique de la France et de l'étranger* 20: 68–82.
Marks, Lynne. 1995. "Indigent Committees and Ladies Benevolent Societies: Intersections of Public and Private Poor Relief in Late Nineteenth-Century Small Town Ontario." *Studies in Political Economy* 47: 61–81.
Marshall, David B. 1993–94. "Canadian Historians, Secularization and the Problem of the Nineteenth Century." *CCHA Historical Studies*, no. 60, 57–81.
Martin, Jean-Baptiste. 1983. *La Fin des mauvais pauvres: de l'assistance à l'assurance*. Seyssel: Champ Vallon.
Martin, Jules. 1905. "L'Institution sociale." *Revue philosophique de la France et de l'étranger* 59: 346–66, 487–99.
Martin, Xavier. 1985. "Nature humaine et Code Napoléon." *Droits*, no. 2, 117–28.
Marx, Karl. [1848] 2013. *The Communist Manifesto*. New York: Simon & Schuster.
– [1875] 1966. *Critique of the Gotha Programme*. New York: International Publishers.
Marx, Karl, and Friedrich Engels. [1844] 1975. *The Holy Family*. 2nd rev. ed. Moscow: Progress Publishers.
Maurer, Catherine. 1999. *Le Modèle allemand de la charité: la Caritas de Guillaume II à Hitler*. Strasbourg: Presses universitaires de Strasbourg.
May, Margaret. 1973. "Innocence and Experience: The Evolution of the Concept of Juvenile Delinquency in the Mid-Nineteenth Century." *Victorian Studies* 17 (1): 7–29.
Mayhew, Henry. [1851] 1968. *London Labour and the London Poor*. 4 vols. New York: Dover.
McGovern, Constance M. 1986. "The Myths of Social Control and Custodial Oppression: Patterns of Psychiatric Medicine in Late Nineteenth-Century Institutions." *Journal of Social History* 20 (1): 3–23.
McKay, Ian. 2000. "The Liberal Order Framework: A Prospectus for a Reconnaissance of Canadian History." *Canadian Historical Review* 81 (4): 617–45.
– 2005. *Rebels, Reds, Radicals: Rethinking Canada's Left History*. Toronto: Between the Lines.
McLaren, John, Robert Menzies, and Dorothy E. Chunn. 2002. "Introduction." In *Regulating Lives: Historical Essays on the State, Society, the Individual, and the Law*, edited by John McLaren, Robert Menzies, and Dorothy E. Chunn, 3–22. Vancouver: University of British Columbia Press.

McLean, Francis H. 1901. "Effects upon Private Charity of the Absence of all Public Relief." *Transactions of the 28th National Conference of Charities and Corrections* 28: 139–46.

McLoughlin, William G. 1978. *Revivals, Awakenings, and Reform.* Chicago: University of Chicago Press.

McNally, D. 2000. "Political Economy to the Fore: Burke, Malthus and the Whig Response to Popular Radicalism in the Age of the French Revolution." *History of Political Thought* 21 (3): 427–47.

Melossi, Dario, and M. Pavarini. 1981. *The Prison and the Factory: Origins of the Penitentiary System.* London: Macmillan.

Ménard, Sylvie. 2003. *Des enfants sous surveillance: la rééducation des jeunes délinquants au Québec (1840–1950).* Montreal: VLB.

Mennel, Robert M. 1973. *Thorns and Thistles: Juvenile Delinquents in the United States, 1825–1940.* Hanover: University Press of New England.

Merrien, F.-X. 1994. "Divergences franco-britanniques." In Merrien, *Face à la pauvreté,* 99–138.

– ed. *Face à la pauvreté, l'Occident et les pauvres hier et aujourd'hui,* 99–138. Paris: Les Éditions de l'Atelier.

Meyer, Jean. 1983. *Le Poids de l'État.* Paris: PUF.

Meyer, Philippe. 1983. *The Child and the State: The Intervention of the State in Family Life.* Translated by Judith Ennew and Janet Lloyd. New York: Cambridge University Press.

Mill, John Stuart. 1848. *Principles of Political Economy: with Some of Their Applications to Social Philosophy.* Vol. 2. Boston: C.C. Little & Brown, 1848.

– *On Liberty.* [1849] 1913. London: Longmans, Green and Co.

Mills, Hazel. 1991. "Negotiating the Divide: Women, Philanthropy and the 'Public Sphere' in Nineteenth-Century France." In *Religion, Society and Politics in France since 1789,* edited by Frank Tallet and Nicholas Atkin, 27–54. London: Hambledon.

– 1998. "La Charité est une Mère: Catholic Women and Poor Relief in France, 1690–1850." In Cunningham and Innes, *Charity, Philanthropy and Reform,* 168–92.

Milo, Daniel S. 1991. "Périodes sans dates: les métaphores de 'Surveiller et punir.'" In *Trahir le temps: histoire,* 147–78, 252–55. Paris: Les Belles Lettres.

Milot, Micheline. 2002. *La Laïcité dans le Nouveau Monde: le cas du Québec.* Turnhout: Brepols.

Minville, Esdras. 1939. *Labour Legislation and Social Services in the Province of Quebec: A Study Prepared for the Royal Commission on Dominion-Provincial Relations.* Ottawa: King's Printer, 1939.

Minson, J. 1985. *Genealogies of Morals.* London: Macmillan.

Mjagkij, Nina, and Margaret Spratt, eds. 1997. *Men and Women Adrift: The YMCA and YWCA in the City*. New York: New York University Press.

Mondelet, D., and J. Neilson. 1835. *Report of the Commissioners Appointed under the Lower Canada Act, 4th William IV, cap. 10, to Visit the United States' Penitentiaries*. Quebec: Neilson & Cowan.

Monkkonen, Eric H., ed. 1984. *Walking to Work: Tramps in America, 1790–1935*. Lincoln: University of Nebraska Press.

Montesquieu, Charles de Secondat, baron de. *The Complete Works of M. de Montesquieu*. Vol. 2, *The Spirit of Laws*. London: T. Evans, 1777.

Montigny, B.A.T. de. 1882. "De l'utilité des corps religieux au Canada." *Revue canadienne* 18: 427–36, 477–86, 519–30.

– 1883. "Le Vagabondage." *La Thémis* 5 (4): 115–28.

Montreal Society for the Attainment of Religious Liberty and Equality in British North America. 1837. *Sequel to the Prospectus*. Montreal: Courier Office.

Moore, Barrington, Jr. 1958. "Reflections on Conformity in Industrial Society." In Barrington Moore Jr, *Political Power and Social Theory: Six Studies*, 179–96. Cambridge: Harvard University Press.

Moran, Richard. 1981. *Knowing Right from Wrong: The Insanity Defense of Daniel McNaughtan*. New York: Free Press.

Myers, Tamara. 1999. "The Voluntary Delinquent: Parents, Daughters and the Montreal Juvenile Delinquents' Court in 1918." *Canadian Historical Review* 80 (2): 242–68.

Neff, Charlotte. 1994. "The Ontario Industrial Schools Act of 1874." *Canadian Journal of Family Law* 12 (1): 171–208.

Niget, David. 2009. *La Naissance du tribunal pour enfants: une comparaison France-Québec (1912–1945)*. Rennes: Presses universitaires de Rennes.

Nootens, Thierry. 2003. "Fous, prodigues et ivrognes: internormativité et déviance à Montréal au XIXe siècle." PhD diss., Université du Québec à Montréal.

– 2007. *Fous, prodigues et ivrognes: familles et déviance à Montréal au 19e siècle*. Montreal & Kingston: McGill-Queen's University Press.

Nootens, Thierry, and Jean-Marie Fecteau. 2003. "Une nouvelle 'sensibilité historique' et ses apories." *Bulletin d'histoire politique* 12 (1): 161–9.

Noppen, Luc. 1976. "La Prison du Pied-du-Courant à Montréal: une étape dans l'évolution de l'architecture pénitentiaire au Bas-Canada et au Québec." *Canadian Art Review* 3 (1): 36–50.

Nourrisson, Paul. 1920. *Histoire de la liberté d'association en France depuis 1789*. 2 vols. Paris: Sirey.

Offe, Claus. 1981. "The Attribution of Public Status to Interest Groups: Observations on the West German Case." In *Organizing Interests in Western*

Europe, edited by Suzanne D. Berger, 123–58. Cambridge: Cambridge University Press.

Oliver, Peter. 1998. *"Terror to Evil-Doers": Prisons and Punishments in Nineteenth-Century Ontario*. Toronto: University of Toronto Press.

Ozanam, A.-F. 1886. *Letters*. Translated by Ainslie Coates. New York: Benziger Brothers.

– 1986. *Frederic Ozanam, a Life in Letters*. Edited and translated by Joseph I. Dirvin. St Louis, MO: Society of St Vincent de Paul, Council of the United States.

Pagès, Robert. 1967. "Le 'Social control,' la régulation sociale et le pouvoir." *Revue française de sociologie* 8 (1): 207–21.

Paine, Thomas. 1791. *Rights of Man: Being an Answer to Mr. Burke's Attack on the French Revolution*. 4th ed. London: printed for J.S. Jordan.

Palmer, Bryan D. 1990. *Descent into Discourse: The Reification of Language and the Writing of Social History*. Philadelphia: Temple University Press.

Paquet, Louis-Adolphe. [1902] 1915. "Sermon sur la vocation de la race française en Amérique." In *Discours et allocutions*, 163–81. Quebec: Impr. franciscaine missionnaire.

Paradis, André. 1997. "Le Sous-financement gouvernemental et son impact sur le développement des asiles francophones au Québec (1845–1918)." *Revue d'histoire de l'Amérique française* 50 (4): 571–98.

Parent, Étienne. [1848] 1975. "Du prêtre et du spiritualisme dans leurs rapports avec la société." In *Étienne Parent, 1802–1874: biographie, textes et bibliographie*, edited by J.-C. Falardeau, 201–26. Montreal: La Presse.

– [1852a] 1975. "De l'intelligence dans ses rapports avec la société." In Falardeau, ed., *Étienne Parent, 1802–1874*, 245–304.

– [1852b] 1975. "Considérations sur le sort des classes ouvrières." In Falardeau, ed., *Étienne Parent, 1802–1874*, 305–26.

Parodi, D. 1903. "Encore la crise du libéralisme." *Revue de métaphysique et de morale* 11 (2): 263–79.

Parr, Joy. 1972. "'Transplanting from Dens of Iniquity': Theology and Child Emigration." In *A Not Unreasonable Claim: Women and Reform in Canada, 1880s–1920s*, edited by Linda Kealey, 169–84. Toronto: University of Toronto Press.

Parthun, Mary Lassance. 1988. "Protestant and Catholic Attitudes towards Poverty: The Irish Community and the Development of the Saint Vincent de Paul Society in Nineteenth-Century Toronto." In *The Untold Story: The Irish in Canada*, Robert O'Driscoll and Lorna Reynolds, 853–69. Toronto: Celtic Arts.

Passy, Frédéric. 1901. "Malthus et la véritable notion de l'assistance." In *Pages et Discours*, 205–23. Paris: Guillaumin.
Pedersen, Susan. 1993. *Family, Dependance and the Origins of the Welfare State, Britain and France, 1914–1945*. Cambridge: Cambridge University Press.
Pelletier, Bastien. 2000. "Les Agents de probation à la Cour des jeunes délinquants de Montréal, 1912–1949." Master's thesis, Université du Québec à Montréal.
Pelletier, Denis. 1999. "Les Pratiques charitables françaises entre 'histoire sociale' et 'histoire religieuse.' Essai d'historiographie critique." In Bueltzingsloewen and Pelletier, *La Charité en pratique*, 33–47.
Perin, Roberto. 2001. "Elaborating a Public Culture: The Catholic Church in Nineteenth-Century Quebec." In *Religion and Public Life in Historical and Comparative Perspective*, edited by Marguerite Van Die, 87–105. Toronto: University of Toronto Press.
Perreault, Isabelle. 2009. "Psychiatrie et ordre social: analyse des causes d'internement et des diagnostics donnés à l'Hôpital Saint-Jean-de-Dieu dans une perspective de genre, 1920–1950." PhD diss., Université d'Ottawa.
Perrot, Michelle, ed. 1980. *L'Impossible Prison: recherches sur le système pénitentiaire*. Paris: Seuil.
Petit, Jacques-Guy. 1990. *Ces peines obscures: la prison pénale en France, 1780–1875*. Paris: Fayard.
– 1994. "Benjamin Appert ou les ambiguïtés de la philanthropie romantique." *Philanthropies et politiques sociales en Europe (XVIIIe–XXe siècles)*, edited by Colette Bec, Catherine Duprat, Jean-Nöel Luc, Jacques-Guy Petit, 79–90. Paris: Economica.
– 1995. "Obscurité des Lumières: les prisons d'Europe, d'après John Howard, autour de 1780." *Criminologie* 28 (1): 5–22.
– 2005. "Les Régulations sociales et l'Histoire." In *La Régulation sociale entre l'acteur et l'institution: pour une problématique historique de l'interaction*, edited by Jean-Marie Fecteau and Janice Harvey, 30–47. Sainte-Foy: Presses de l'Université du Québec.
Petitclerc, Martin. 2007. *'Nous protégeons l'infortune': les origines populaires de l'économie sociale au Québec*. Montreal: VLB.
– 2009. "'Notre maître le passé'? Le projet critique de l'histoire sociale et l'émergence d'une nouvelle sensibilité historiographique." *Revue d'histoire de l'Amérique française* 63 (1): 83–113.
– 2012. "À propos de 'ceux qui sont en dehors de la société': l'indigent et l'assistance publique au Québec dans la première moitié du XXe siècle." *Revue d'histoire de l'Amérique française* 65 (2–3): 227–56.
– Petitclerc, Martin, and David Niget, eds. 2012. *Pour une histoire du risque: Québec, France, Belgique*. Montreal and Rennes: PUQ/PUR.

Pinard, Clovis. 1857. *Bienfaits du catholicisme dans la société.* Tours: Mames.

Pires, Alvaro. 1995. "Aspects, traces et parcours de la rationalité pénale moderne." In Debuyst, Digneffe, Labadie, and Pires, *Des savoirs diffus à la notion de criminel-né*, 3–52, vol 1 of *Histoire des savoirs sur le crime et la peine*.

Platt, Anthony M. 1977. *The Child Savers: The Invention of Delinquency.* Chicago: University of Chicago Press.

Plongeron, Bernard. 1991. "Restaurer un ordre au XIXe siècle? Quand le mythe crée l'histoire." In *Lacordaire, son pays, ses amis et la liberté des ordres religieux en France*, edited by Guy Bedouelle, 383–406. Paris: Cerf.

– ed. 1995. *Catholiques entre monarchie et république: monseigneur Freppel en son temps, 1792–1892.* Paris: Letouzey et Ane.

Pocock, J.G.A. 1985. *Virtue, Commerce, and History: Essays on Political Thought and History, Chiefly in the Eighteenth Century.* Cambridge: Cambridge University Press.

Polanyi, Karl. 1944. *The Great Transformation.* Toronto: Rinehart.

Ponton, Lionel. 1993. "La Crise sociale au XIXe siècle vue par Hegel, Tocqueville et Nietzsche." In Richard and O'Neill, *La Question sociale hier et aujourd'hui*, 193–208.

Poovey, Mary. 1995. *Making a Social Body: British Cultural Formation, 1830–1864.* Chicago: University of Chicago Press.

Poulantzas, Nicos. 1973. *Political Power and Social Classes.* Translation edited by Timothy O'Hagan. London: Sheed and Ward.

– *State, Power, Socialism.* 1978. Translated by Patrick Camiller. London: NLB.

Poulat, Émile. 1977. *Catholicisme, Démocratie et Socialisme: le mouvement catholique et Mgr Benigni.* Paris: Casterman.

Procacci, Giovanna. 1993. *Gouverner la misère: la question sociale en France.* Paris: Le Seuil.

– 1994. "De la mendicité à la question sociale." In Merrien, *Face à la pauvreté*, 29–52.

Pruvost, Philippe. 1988. "La Polémique L.A. Dessaulles et J.S. Raymond ou le Libéralisme contre l'ultramontanisme." PhD diss., Université du Québec à Montréal.

Quesney, Chantale. 1998. "Pour une politique de restauration familiale: une analyse du discours de l'école sociale populaire dans le Québec de l'entre-deux-guerres." Master's thesis, Université du Québec à Montréal.

Quévillon, Lucie. 2001. "Parcours d'une collaboration: les intervenants psychiatriques et psychologiques à la Cour des jeunes délinquants de Montréal (1912–1950)." Master's thesis, Université du Québec à Montréal.

Radzinowicz, Leon, and Roger Hood. 1948–1986. *A History of English Criminal Law and Its Administration from 1750.* 5 vols. London: Stevens and Sons.

Rafter, Nicole Hahn. 1985. *Partial Justice: Women in State Prisons, 1800–1935*. Boston: Northeastern University Press.

Rains, Prue, and Eli Teram. 1992. *Normal Bad Boys: Public Policies, Institutions and the Politics of Client Recruitment*. Montreal & Kingston: McGill-Queen's University Press.

Rajotte, Pierre. 1991. *Les Mots du pouvoir ou le Pouvoir des mots: essai d'analyse des stratégies ultramontaines au XIXe siècle*. Montreal: Hexagon.

Rangeon, François. 1986a. *L'Idéologie de l'intérêt général*. Paris: Economica.

– 1986b. "Société civile: histoire d'un mot." In Jacques Chevallier et al., *La Société civile*, 9–32. Paris: PUF.

Raymond, Joseph-Sabin. 1865. *Discours sur la nécessité de la force morale*. Montreal: Plinguet.

– 1869. *Discours sur la tolérance*. Montreal: Le Nouveau Monde.

– 1877. *De l'intervention du prêtre dans l'ordre intellectuel et social*. Saint-Hyacinthe, QC: Courrier.

Regnard, Albert. 1898. *De la suppression des délits de vagabondage et de mendicité*. Paris: Librairie de la société du recueil général des lois et des arrêts.

Reid, Helen R.Y. 189?. *The Problem of the Unemployed*. Montreal: National Council of Women.

Rémond, René. 1969. *The Right Wing in France, from 1815 to de Gaulle*. Translated by James M. Laux. 2nd American ed., rev. Philadelphia: University of Pennsylvania Press.

– ed. 1988. *Pour une histoire politique*. Paris: Seuil.

– ed. 1991. *Démocratie et Pauvreté – du quatrieme ordre au Quart Monde*, 289–94. Paris: Éditions Quart Monde and Albin Michel.

Rémusat, Charles de. 1840. *Du paupérisme et de la charité légale*. Paris: Renouard.

Renouard, Charles. 1854. "Parasites." In Coquelin and Gullaumin, *Dictionnaire de l'économie politique*, 2: 323–9.

Renouard, J.-M. 1990. *De l'enfant coupable à l'enfant inadapté: le traitement social et politique de la déviance*. Paris: Centurion.

Revel, Jacques. 1995. "L'Institution et le Social." In Lepetit, *Les Formes de l'expérience*, 63–84.

Ricardo, David. [1817] 1911. *Principles of Political Economy and Taxation*. London: J.M. Dent & Sons.

Richard, Jean, and Louis O'Neill, eds. 1993. *La Question sociale hier et aujourd'hui: colloque du centenaire de Rerum Novarum*. Sainte-Foy: Presses de l'Université Laval.

Riot-Sarcey, Michèle. 1998. *Le Réel de l'utopie: essai sur le politique au XIXe siècle*. Paris: Albin Michel.

Robert, Lucie. 1989. *L'Institution du littéraire au Québec*. Quebec: Presses de l'Université Laval.

Roberts, Michael D. 1991. "Reshaping the Gift Relationship. The London Mendicity Society and the Suppression of Begging in England 1818–1869." *International Review of Social History* 36: 201–31.
- 1998. "Head versus Heart? Voluntary Associations and Charity Organization in England c. 1700–1850." In Cunningham and Innes, *Charity, Philanthropy and Reform*, 66–87.
Roberts, Wayne. 1979. "'Rocking the Cradle for the World': The New Woman and Maternal Feminism. Toronto: 1877–1914." In *A Not Unreasonable Claim: Women and Reform in Canada, 1880s–1920s*, edited by Linda Kealey, 15–45. Toronto: Women's Press.
Robillard, L.G. 1897. *Les Sociétés de bienfaisance*. Montreal, n.p.
Rodgers, Daniel T. 1998. *Atlantic Crossings: Social Politics in a Progressive Age*. Cambridge, MA: The Belknap Press of Harvard University Press.
Rodrigue, Lise. 1996. "L'Exemption fiscale des communautés religieuses." *Cahiers de droit* 37 (4): 1109–40.
Rosanvallon, Pierre. 1979. *Le Capitalisme utopique: critique de l'idéologie économique*. Paris: Seuil.
Rose, Nikolas. 1987. "Beyond the Public/Private Division: Law, Power and the Family." *Journal of Law and Society* 14 (1): 61–76.
- 1988. "Calculable Minds and Manageable Individuals." *History of Human Sciences* 1 (2): 179–200.
Rosenberg, Charles E. 1974. "The Bitter Fruit: Heredity, Disease, and Social Thought in Nineteenth-Century America." *Perspectives in American History* 8: 189–235.
Ross, Edward A. [1901] 1970. *Social Control: A Survery of the Foundations of Order*. New York: Johnson Reprint Co.
Ross, Ellen. 1993. *Love and Toil: Motherhood in Outcast London, 1870–1918*. Oxford: Oxford University Press.
Rothman, David J. 1971. *The Discovery of the Asylum: Social Order and Disorder in the New Republic*. Boston: Little, Brown & Co.
- 1980. *Conscience and Convenience: The Asylum and Its Alternatives in Progressive America*. Boston: Little, Brown & Co.
- 1983. "Social Control: The Uses and Abuses of the Concept in the History of Incarceration." In *Social Control and the State: Historical and Comparative Essays*, edited by Stanley Cohen and Andrew Scull, 106–17. Oxford: Robertson.
Rouillard, Jacques. 1989. *Histoire du syndicalisme au Québec: des origines à nos jours*. Montreal: Boréal.
Rousseau, Louis. 1993. "Impulsions romantiques et renouveau religieux québécois au XIXe siècle: quelques questions à propos de Joseph-Sabin

Raymond." In *Le Romantisme au Canada*, edited by Maurice Lemire, 199–214. Montreal: Nuit Blanche.
- 1998. "Crises, choc et révitalisation culturelle dans le Québec du XIXe siècle." In Lagrée, *Chocs et ruptures en histoire religieuse*, 51–72.
- Rousseau, Louis, and Frank W. Remiggi, eds. 1998. *Atlas historique des pratiques religieuses: le Sud-Ouest du Québec au XIXe siècle*. Ottawa: University of Ottawa Press.

Rowntree, Benjamin Seebohm. 1901. *Poverty: A Study of Town Life*. London: Macmillan.

Roy, Fernande. 1988. *Progrès, harmonie, liberté: le libéralisme des milieux d'affaires francophones de Montréal au tournant du siècle*. Montreal: Boréal.

Ruchat, Martine. 1993. *L'Oiseau et le cachot: naissance de l'éducation correctionnelle en Suisse romande, 1800–1913*. Geneva: Éditions Zoé.
- 1996. "Pédagogie de la conscience: de l'école des pauvres de Hofwyl à la colonie agricole de Serix-sur-Oron en Suisse protestante." *Sociétés et Représentations* 3: 269–76.

Rudin, Ronald. 1992. "Revisionism and the Search for a Normal Society: A Critique of Recent Quebec Historical Writing." *Canadian Historical Review* 73 (1): 30–61.
- 1997. *Making History in Twentieth-Century Quebec: Historians and Their Society*. Toronto: University of Toronto Press.
- 1999. "On Difference and National Identity in Quebec Historical Writing: A Response to Jean-Marie Fecteau." *Canadian Historical Review* 80 (4): 666–76.

Rusche, George, and Otto Kircheimer. 1939. *Punishment and Social Structure*. New York: Columbia University Press.

Sabourin, Charles. 1851. "Des institutions sociales, de leur utilité, de leurs rapports avec l'éducation physique et morale." *Le Moniteur canadien*, 7 February.

Saint-Just. [1794] 1968. "Rapport sur le mode d'exécution du décret contre les ennemis de la révolution." In *Oeuvres choisies*. Paris: Gallimard.

Saint-Pierre, Arthur. 1914. *Questions et oeuvres sociales de chez nous*. Montreal: L'École sociale populaire.

Sangster, Joan. 1996. "Incarcerating 'Bad Girls': The Regulation of Sexuality through the Female Refuges Act in Ontario, 1920–1945." *Journal of the History of Sexuality* 7 (2): 239–75.
- 2000. "Feminism and the Making of Canadian Working-Class History: Exploring the Past, Present and Future." *Labour/Le Travail* 46: 127–65.
- 2001. *Regulating Girls and Women: Sexuality, Family, and the Law in Ontario, 1920–1960*. Don Mills, ON: Oxford University Press.

Sassier, Philippe. 1990. *Du bon usage des pauvres: histoire d'un thème politique (XVIe–XXe siècle)*. Paris: Fayard.

Savard, Pierre. 1993. "*Rerum Novarum* au Canada français: des fruits tardifs et divers." In Richard and O'Neill, *La Question sociale hier et aujourd'hui*, 28–31.
Say, Léon, and Joseph Chailley, eds. 1900. *Nouveau dictionnaire de l'économie politique*. 2nd ed. 2 vols. Paris: Alcan.
Schlossman, Steven L. 1977. *Love and the American Delinquent: The Theory and Practice of "Progressive" Juvenile Justice, 1825–1920*. Chicago: University of Chicago Press.
Seidman, Steven. 1983. *Liberalism and the Origins of European Social Theory*. Oxford: Blackwell.
Sewell, William. 2005. *Logics of History: Social Theory and Social Transformation*. Chicago: University of Chicago Press.
Shore, Heather. 1999. *Artful Dodgers: Youth and Crime in Early Nineteenth-Century London*. Rochester, NY: Boydell & Brewer.
Simmel, Georg. [1908] 2001. *The Pauper*. Edited and translated by Simona Draghici. Corvallis, OR: Plutarch Press.
Sirinelli, Jean-François, ed. 1995. *Les Droites françaises: de la Révolution à nos jours*. Paris: Gallimard.
Sklar, Kathryn K. 1993. "The Historical Foundations of Women's Power in the Creation of the American Welfare State, 1830–1930." In *Mothers of a New World: Maternalist Politics and the Origins of Welfare States*, edited by Seth Koven and Sonya Michel, 1–42. London: Routledge.
Skocpol, Theda. 1992. *Protecting Soldiers and Mothers: The Political Origins of Social Policy in the United States*. Cambridge: Belknap Press of Harvard University Press.
Sledziewski, Elisabeth G. 1989. *Révolutions du sujet*. Paris: Méridiens Klincksieck.
Smith, Adam. [1759] 2002. *The Theory of Moral Sentiments*. New York: Cambridge University Press.
Smith, Goldwin. 1889. *Social Problems: An Address*. Toronto: Blackett Robinson.
Spencer, Herbert. [1884] 1969. *The Man versus the State*. Harmondsworth: Penguin.
Spierenburg, Pieter. 1996a. "Four Centuries of Prison History: Punishment, Suffering, the Body, and Power." In *Institutions of Confinement: Hospitals, Asylums, and Prisons in Western Europe and North America, 1500–1950*, edited by Norbert Finzsch and Robert Jurre, 17–35. Washington, DC: Cambridge University Press.
– 1996b. *The Spectacle of Suffering*. London: Cambridge University Press.
Stack, John A. 1979–80. "The Juvenile Delinquent and England's 'Revolution in Government,' 1825–1875." *The Historian* 42: 42–57.
Stadum, Beverly. 1992. *Poor Women and Their Families: Hard Working Charity Cases, 1900–1930*. New York: State University of New York Press.

Stansell, Christine. 1986. *City of Women: Sex and Class in New York, 1789–1860*. Urbana: University of Illinois Press.

Storch, Robert D. 1976. "The Policeman as Domestic Missionary: Urban Discipline and Popular Culture in Northern England, 1850–1880." *Journal of Social History* 9 (4): 481–509.

Strange, Carolyn. 1995. *Toronto's Girl Problem: The Perils and Pleasures of the City, 1880–1930*. Toronto: University of Toronto Press.

Strange, Carolyn, and Tina Loo. 1997. *Making Good: Law and Moral Regulation in Canada, 1867–1939*. Toronto: University of Toronto Press.

Strimelle, Véronique. 1998. "La Gestion de la déviance des mineures au Québec au XIXe siècle: les institutions du Bon Pasteur à Montréal (1844–1912)." PhD diss., Université de Montréal.

Sudan, Dimitri. 1997. "De l'enfant coupable au sujet de droits: changements des dispositifs de gestion de la déviance juvénile (1820–1989)." *Déviance et Société* 21 (4): 383–99.

Sumner, William Graham. 1883. *What Social Classes Owe to Each Other*. New York: Harper and Brothers.

Sutton, John R. 1988. *Stubborn Children: Controlling Delinquency in the United States, 1640–1981*. Berkeley: University of California Press.

Sweeny, Robert. 2015. *Why Did We Choose to Industrialize? Montreal, 1819–1849*. Montreal & Kingston: McGill-Queen's University Press.

Sylvain, Philippe, and Nive Voisine. 1991. *Histoire du catholicisme québecois: les XVIIIe et XIXe siècles*. Vol. 2, *Réveil et Consolidation (1840–1898)*. Montreal: Les Éditions du Boréal.

Tétard, Françoise. 1994. "Fin d'un modèle philanthropique, crise des patronages consacrés au sauvetage de l'enfance dans l'entre-deux-guerres." In *Philanthropies et politiques sociales en Europe (XVIIIe–XXe siècles)*, edited by Colette Bec, Catherine Duprat, Jean-Nöel Luc, and Jacques-Guy Petit, 199–212. Paris: Economica.

Thane, Pat. 1984. "The Working Class and State 'Welfare' in Britain, 1880–1914." *Historical Journal* 27 (4): 877–900.

– 1991. "Genre et protection sociale: la protection maternelle et infantile en Grande-Bretagne, 1860–1918." *Genèse*, no. 6, 73–97.

Théry, Irène, and Christian Biet. 1989. *La Famille, la Loi, l'État: de la Révolution au Code civil*. Paris: Centre Georges Pompidou.

Thibault, E.-X. 1867. "Recherches sur la vraie solution de la grande question ouvrière." *Écho du cabinet de lecture paroissial* 9: 931–8.

Thiers, Adolphe. 1848. *Discours sur le droit au travail*. Paris: Levy.

– [1850] 1880. "Rapport fait au nom de la Commission de l'assistance et de la prévoyance publiques." In *Discours parlementaires de M. Thiers*, 8: 449–592. Paris: Calmann Levy.

Thifault, Marie-Claude. 2003. "L'enfermement asilaire des femmes au Québec: 1873–1921." PhD diss., Université d'Ottawa.
- ed. 2012. *L'Incontournable caste des femmes: histoire des services de santé au Québec et au Canada*. Ottawa: University of Ottawa Press.

Thompson, E.P. 1963. *The Making of the English Working Class*. Harmondsworth: Penguin Books.
- 1971. "The Moral Economy of the English Crowd in the Eighteenth Century." *Past and Present* 50 (1): 76–136.
- 1975. *Whigs and Hunters: The Origins of the Black Act*. New York: Pantheon Books.
- 1978. *The Poverty of Theory and Other Essays*. London: The Merlin Press.

Tocqueville, Alexis de. [1835] 1997. *Memoir on Pauperism*. Translated by Seymour Drescher. London: Civitas.
- [1835] 2012. *Democracy in America*. Edited by Eduardo Nolla. Translated by James T. Schleifer. 4 vols. Indianapolis: Liberty Fund.
- [ca 1847] 2002. "Fragments for a Social Policy." In *The Tocqueville Reader: A Life in Letters and Politics*, edited by Olivier Zunz and Alan S. Kahan, 224–6. Malden, MA: Blackwell.
- 1984. *Alexis Tocqueville: écrits sur le système pénitentiaire en France et à l'étranger*. Edited by Michelle Perrot. 2 vols. Paris: Gallimard.

Topalov, Christian. 1990. "De la 'question sociale' aux 'problèmes urbains': les réformateurs et le peuple des métropoles au tournant du XXe siècle." *Revue internationale des sciences sociales*, no. 125, 359–79.
- 1994. *Naissance du chômeur, 1880–1910*. Paris: Albin Michel.
- 1996. "Langage de la réforme et déni du politique: le débat entre assistance publique et bienfaisance privée, 1889–1903." *Genèse*, no. 23: 30–52.
- 1999. "Les Réformateurs et leurs 'réseaux': enjeux d'un objet de recherche." In *Laboratoires du nouveau siècle: la nébuleuse réformatrice et ses réseaux en France (1880–1914)*, edited by Christian Topalov, 11–60. Paris: Éditions de l'École des hautes études en sciences sociales.

Tort, Patrick. 1983. *La Pensée hiérarchique et l'évolution*. Paris: Aubier Montaigne.

Tremblay, Robert. 2013. "*The Making* dans les eaux troubles de l'historiographie québécois: réception hésitante d'un livre en avant de son temps." *Labour / Le Travail* 72: 233–41.

Trépanier, Jean, and Françoise Tulkens. 1995. *Délinquance et protection de la jeunesse aux sources des lois belge et canadienne sur l'enfance*. Montreal: Presses de l'Université de Montréal.

Trépanier, Pierre. 1986a. "La Société canadienne d'économie sociale de Montréal, 1888–1911: sa fondation, ses débuts et ses activités." *Canadian Historical Review* 67 (3): 343–67.

- 1986b. "La Société canadienne d'économie sociale de Montréal (1888–1911): ses membres, ses critiques et sa survie." *Histoire sociale* 19 (38): 299–322.
- 1987. "Les Influences leplaysiennes au Canada français, 1855–1888." *Journal of Canadian Studies* 22 (1): 66–83.

Tribe, Keith. 1978. *Land, Labour and Economic Discourse*. London: Routledge and Kegan Paul.
- 1981. *Genealogies of Capitalism*. Atlantic Highlands, NJ: Humanities Press.

Tuckerman, Joseph. 1838. *The Principles and Results of the Ministry at Large: In Boston*. Boston: J. Munroe.

Vaillancourt, Éric. 2005. "La Société Saint-Vincent de Paul de Montréal: reflet du dynamisme du laïcat catholique en matière d'assistance aux pauvres (1848–1933)." PhD diss., Université du Québec à Montréal.

Valverde, Mariana. 1991. *The Age of Light, Soap and Water: Social Purity and Philanthropy in Canada, 1885–1925*. Toronto: McClelland and Stewart.
- 1995. "La Charité et l'État: un mariage mixte centenaire." *Lien social et Politiques*, RIAC, no. 33, 27–36.
- 1998. "Governing out of Habit." *Studies in Law, Politics and Society* 18: 217–42.

Van Krieken, Robert. 1991. "The Poverty of Social Control: Explaining Power in the Historical Sociology of the Welfare State." *Sociological Review* 39 (1): 1–25.

Van Leeuwen, Marco H.D. 1994. "Logic of Charity: Poor Relief in Pre-industrial Europe." *Journal of Interdisciplinary History* 24 (4): 589–613.

Vaucelles, Louis de. 1995. "La Théologie politique de Léon XIII." In Plongeron, *Catholiques entre monarchie et république*, 187–201.

Verdun-Jones, Simon. 1981. "'Not Guilty by Reason of Insanity': The Historical Roots of the Canadian Insanity Defense, 1843–1920." In *Crime and Criminal Justice in Europe and Canada*, edited by Louis A. Knafla, 179–218. Waterloo: Wilfrid Laurier University Press.

Viet, Vincent. 2003. "La Question sociale et son traitement à la fin du XIXe siècle." *Revue européenne d'histoire sociale*, no. 6, 6–21.

Villeneuve, Georges. 1904. "Les Lacunes de l'assistance publique dans la province de Québec." *Union médicale du Canada* 33: 425–35.

Villeneuve-Bargemont, Vicomte Alban de. 1834. *Économie politique chrétienne*. 3 vols. Paris: Paulin.

Villeval, Marie-Claire. "*Régulation* Theory among Theories of Institutions." In Boyer and Saillard, Régulation *Theory*, 291–8.

Walzer, Michael. 1984. "Liberalism and the Art of Separation." *Political Theory* 12 (3): 315–30.

Warren, Jean-Philippe, and Yves Gingras. 2007. "Le *Bulletin d'histoire politique* et le retour du refoulé: la lutte pour l'imposition d'un domaine de recherche dans le champ de l'histoire québécoise (1992–2005)." *Bulletin d'histoire politique* 15 (3): 25–36.

Waterman, A.M.C. 1983. "The Ideological Alliance of Political Economy and Christian Theology, 1798–1833." *Journal of Ecclesiastical History* 34 (2): 231–44.

Weinberger, Barbara. 1994. "La Police des mineurs: Manchester à la fin du XIXe siècle et au debut du XXe siècle." *Déviance et Société* 18 (1): 31–42.

Weiss, Robert. 1987. "Humanitarianism, Labour Exploitation or Social Control? A Critical Survey of Theory and Research on the Origin and Development of Prisons." *Social History* 12 (3): 331–50.

Westfall, William. 1990. "The Doctrine of Expediency: Lord Durham's Report and the Alliance of Church and State." *Journal of Canadian Studies* 25 (1): 178–90.

– 2001. "Constructing Public Religions at Private Sites: The Anglican Church in the Shadow of Disestablishment." In *Religion and Public Life in Historical and Comparative Perspective*, edited by Marguerite Van Die, 23–49. Toronto: University of Toronto Press.

Whiteford, Hamilton. 1872. "Mendicity, Repression, and Charity Organization." *Transactions of the National Association for the Promotion of Social Science*, 228–33.

Williams, Karel. 1981. *From Pauperism to Poverty*. London: Routledge and Kegan Paul.

Wines, Frederick H. 1888. *Report on the Defective, Dependent and Delinquent Classes of the Population of the United States, as Returned at the Tenth Census (June 1, 1880)*. Washington: G.P.O.

Woodroofe, Kathleen. 1962. *From Charity to Social Work in England and the United States*. London: Routledge and Kegan Paul.

Wright, David. 1997. "Getting Out of the Asylum: Understanding the Confinement of the Insane in the Nineteeth Century." *Social History of Medicine* 10 (1): 137–55.

Yeo, Stephen. 1976. *Religion and Voluntary Organizations in Crisis*. London: Croom Helm.

Index

Act of Union of 1840, 66, 142, 274
Adami, John George, 329n57
agency, 12, 20–3, 25–7, 37–45, 87–8, 264–5; of prisoners, 128–9; of workers, 178
Aglietta, Michel, xiv, 30
alcoholism, 203
Althusser, Louis, xiv–xv
Ames, Herbert Brown, 244–8, 254, 353n102
anarchism, 44, 46
Anglican Church, 215
Appert, Benjamin, 324n12
Asile des orphelins catholiques, 140
Association québécoise d'histoire politique, xviii
associations, 50, 53, 58–61; charitable, 102–3, 142, 144, 194
Astor, Joseph, 318n38, 319n43, 320n48
asylums, 14, 21, 27, 76, 104; ideal of, 97; population of, 181; proposed in Lower Canada, 93–4, 99
Asylums, 14
Auburn system, 322n61

Balzac, Honoré de, 332n14

Barry, Françoise, 353n102
Beaumont, Gustave de, 118–21, 323n7
Beccaria, Cesare, 75, 79, 317n33
Bédard, Éric, xix–xx, xxxiv–xxxv
beggars' prisons. *See* workhouses
Bégin, Louis-Nazaire, 258, 349n76
Béique, Frédéric Liguori, 353n102
Bellemare, Raphaël, 354n104
Bellingham, Bruce, 288n37, 324n19
Bentham, Jeremy, xxxv, 75, 117, 300n13, 356n6; and agency, 293n17; and panopticon, 302n25; and utilitarianism, 56, 303n32
Bismarck, Otto von, 198
Black, Henry, 104
Blaiklock, Henry Musgrave, 133
Blanc, Louis, 126–7, 309n82
Blanqui, Adolphe, 331n7
"Bloody Code," 93, 98
Board of Inspectors of Prisons and Asylums, 115
Bonald, Louis de, 212
Booth, Charles, 195–6, 202, 244
Bordeaux prison, 135, 322n66
Bourgeois, Léon, 62

Bourget, Ignace, xxxv, 207, 217, 277, 349n75, 350n79; and Brothers of Charity, 325n24; on liberalism and poverty, 234, 254
Boyer, Robert, xiv, 30
Boys' Farm and Training School (Shawbridge), 145, 155
Brace, Charles Loring, 149, 328n46
Braudel, Fernand, 32
Brenner, Robert, xiv
Brothers of Charity, 151, 155, 241, 325n24
Brown, George, 222–3, 274
Bruchési, Paul, 230, 253–4, 259, 355n114, 355n116
Bulletin d'histoire politique, xix, xxi
Burke, Edmund, 81

Cabanis, Pierre-Jean-Georges, 76
Canguilhem, Georges, 14, 23
capitalism, 30, 32, 44, 50–1, 289n43
capital punishment, 35, 93, 98–9, 104, 113
carceral archipelago, xiii, xxiii, xxix, 109–10, 115, 157
Carpenter, Mary, 149
Catholic Church: and charity, 153–5, 220–5, 235–42, 253–61, 270, 300n14; criticism of, 153, 349n78; under liberalism, 208–20, 237–9, 252, 276; in Quebec and Canada, 151, 206–8, 214–16, 241–2, 261–2, 272–3, 275–8; and working class, 256–8
Catholicism: versus liberalism, 207; and poverty, 230–6; and religious freedom, 211–12, 215–19
Catholic Program, 208, 350n80
Catholic social teaching, 46, 63, 202, 205, 271, 273, 338n5

Cauchon, Joseph, 222–3
Cellard, André, xii
Chadwick, Edwin, 90
Chalmers, Thomas, 352n93
Chamberlain, Joseph, 198
Chandonnet, Thomas-Aimé, 235
Chanteret, Pierre, 318n40
Charbonneau, Joseph, 208
Charitable Institution for Female Penitents, 311n103
charity, 68, 102, 181–2; criticized, 194–5, 248; feudal view of, 71; incorporation of charities, 222; liberal view of, 101, 165–8, 178–94, 220, 247–8; in Quebec, 92, 102–3, 222–4, 239–41, 253, 258, 261–2; religious, 70–1, 84–6, 150, 220, 225–33, 237, 252–4, 258, 260–1, 270; scientific approaches to, 183–4, state support of, 102–3. *See also* philanthropy; welfare
Charity Organization Societies, 185, 190, 194, 236, 247, 336n48; Montreal chapter of, 247–9, 253, 353n104
Chartism, 166
Chateaubriand, François-René, vicomte de, 228
Cherbuliez, Antoine, 174, 177
Chevallier, Jacques, 288n34
children, 138–61; abandoned, 71, 92, 142–3, 147, 149, 152; courts for, 144–5, 148, 312n106, 323n5; under liberal regulation, 158; in Quebec, 142–3, 153; reform of, 146–7, 156–7, 161; state responsibility for, 148–50
Chiniquy, Charles, 345n53
Churchill, Winston, 197
citizen's arrest, 299n7

classification (procedure applied to inmates), 29, 38, 87, 98, 114; advent of, 88; applied to the poor, 177, 181, 250, 336n48; difficulties of, 123, 133–4, 318n38, 320n51; mentioned by Foucault and Tocqueville, 318n38
Clavero, Bartolomé, 71
colonialism, 100
Colquhoun, Patrick, 89
Comeau, Robert, xii
communism, 45–6, 51, 62
communitarianism, 62
Comte, Auguste, 13, 193, 331n9
Condorcet, Jean-Antoine-Nicolas de Caritat, marquis de, 55, 80
Congregation of France, 102
conservatism, 46, 75
Constant, Benjamin, 39, 60, 302n27
conventions, theory of, 284n2
cooperativism, xxviii, 62, 193, 205
corporatism, 44, 46, 50–1, 62–3, 202, 205, 256
Corrigan, Philip, xxiv
Court of King's Bench, 73, 99
courts, in Lower Canada, 99
crime, 10, 30–1, 66–8, 108–9, 268; Christian view of, 82–3; cohabitation with poverty, 75–7, 87–8, 97, 109, 315n21; feudal treatment of, 68–74; liberal view of, 116–17, 135–6, 269; Malthusian view of, 81–2; scientific treatment of, 129–31; as societal dysfunction, 126–9, 31
Crofton, Walter, 321n53
Cromwell, Oliver, 40
Crown Law Department, Canada East, 115
Cunningham, Hugh, 299n2
Curtis, Bruce, xxiv, xxxii–xxxiv

Darwin, Charles, 332n16
Dean, Mitchell, 300n13
Dekker, Jeroen, 157, 324n9
Demetz, Frédéric-Auguste, 149
democracy, 31–3, 38, 56–7, 59–60, 74, 163, 168; and Catholicism, 211–15, 219, 227, 256; as constraint on liberal regulation, 97, 104, 112; and national identity, 273–4; and personal responsibility, 186–8; and revolution, 166–8, 264–5
Democracy in America, 169
Désaulniers, Louis-Léon Lesieur, 156
Desrosiers, Richard, xii
Dessaulles, Louis-Antoine, 207, 219
Dictionnaire de l'économie politique, 171, 197
Discipline and Punish, 107
Discours sur le droit au travail, 167
Division of Labor in Society, The, 62
Donzelot, Jacques, xxiii
Drummond, Julia, Lady, 253–4
Drummond, Lewis Thomas, 342n34
Dubuc, Alfred, xii
Ducharme, Michel, xxxiv–xxxv
Dufresne, Martin, 113
Dugdale, Richard, 181
Duguit, Léon, 63
Dunlop, William, 325n20
Duplessis, Maurice, 208
Durham, Lord (John George Lambton, 1st Earl of Durham), 99, 274, 296n42
Durkheim, Émile, 48, 62, 193, 288n36
Dutch Republic, 40

Eid, Nadia Fahmy, xii
Elias, Norbert, 112, 284n8, 288n38

empiricism, 19–20, 32
Engels, Friedrich, 88, 297n51, 332n14
ethics, 200–1, 266
eugenics, 133, 144, 199, 202–3, 271
Ewald, François, xxiii, 298n56, 313n4, 334n33

Fédération nationale Saint-Jean-Baptiste, 258
Fellenberg, Philipp Emanuel von, 116, 152
Female Compassionate Society, 311n102
Féron, Louis-Charles, 346n59
feudalism, 39
Fielding, Henry, 75
Fillâtre, Joseph-Jules, 257
foster care, 139, 142, 145, 152–3
Foucault, Michel, 3, 14, 19–20, 112, 121; and genealogy, 313n4; and governmentality, 300n8; on Mettray, 137, 157; on power, xiii–xiv, 28, 48, 95; on prisoner reform, 117; on prisons, 97–8, 107–9, 115, 285n13, 313n3; on structures, 287n32
Fourier, Charles, 302n31, 309n82
Franco-Prussian War, 197
freedom, 37–46, 56, 169–71, 200, 205, 263–4. *See also* agency
freedom of worship, 216–17
French Revolution, 58, 78, 295n34
French Revolution of 1848, 58, 60, 166
functionalism, 13, 15, 288n35, 345n55
Fyson, Donald, 72–4

Galarneau, Claude, xii
Garland, David, 135
Gasparin, Adrien de, 81

Gauchet, Marcel, xvii
Gauthier, Thomas, 329n57
Gavazzi, Alessandro, 345n53
Gérando, Joseph-Marie de, 85, 90, 167, 177, 307n60, 311n100
Gérin, Léon, 243
Gérin-Lajoie, Marie, 258
Gide, Charles, 62
Gierke, Otto Friedrich von, 62
Gill, Howard, 132
Girod, Amury, xxxv, 116–17, 138
Godwin, William, 80
Goffman, Erving, 14, 112
Gohiet, François, 256–7
Goschen Minute, 333n25
governmentality, xxiii, xxxiii, 48–9, 281n32, 300n8
Gramscian analysis, 15, 48
Granatstein, J.L., xix
Great Arch, The, xxiv
Green, Thomas Hill, 193
Grenon, Michel, xii
Grey Nuns, 241
Guizot, François, 168, 226, 345n53, 356n6

Habermas, Jürgen, 294n29
Hackett, William, 95
happiness, 44
Harvey, Janice, xii
Haskell, Thomas, xxvii–xxviii, 41, 44, 283n1 (introduction), 290n48, 291n5
Hauriou, Maurice, 62–3
Hazlitt, William, 303n36, 331n3
Hegel, Georg Wilhelm Friedrich, 48, 295n35
Hingston, William, 353n102
history, practice of, 9, 19–20, 32, 41, 198

History of Madness, 14
Hobson, John, 194, 246
Hoffman, Charles, 321n55
Hofwyl school, 141, 152, 322n1
hospitals, 14, 29, 181, 192; under feudalism, 72; in France, 69, 300n11; in Lower Canada, 94–6
Hôtel-Dieu de Montréal, 308n68, 310n85
hôtels-dieu, 71–2
House of Assembly (Lower Canada), 102–3, 116, 274, 289n47; debating use of building, 309n80; Girod addressing, 138
House of Assembly (United Canada), 142
houses of industry. *See* workhouses
Howard, John, 75–6, 79, 92, 117
Hoyt, Charles S., 181
hue and cry, 299n7
Hughes, Everett, 284n8
Huguet-Latour, Agathe-Henriette, 311n103
humanitarianism, 43–4, 176
Hume, David, 56, 294n26

Ignatieff, Michael, 112
Île-aux-Noix reformatory, 114, 143
illness, 30–1
individualism, 55, 57, 60, 169–70; critiqued, 62
Industrial Revolution, 57, 75, 88, 141
institutionalism, 62
institutionalization, 93–6, 188, 191–2, 202–4; criticized, 153–4. *See also* asylums; hospitals; prisons
institutions, 12, 20–1, 26–30, 50, 294n23
Institut Saint-Antoine, 325n24
insurance, 298n55

interactionism, 17–18, 20–2
isolation. *See* solitary confinement

Jacksonianism, 166
Jansenism, 226, 347n64
Jones, Gareth Stedman, xviii
judicial system, 47, 54, 72–4, 105, 112–15, 125; applied to youth, 148. *See also* courts; justices of the peace
Jukes, The, 181
July Revolution of 1830, 168
justices of the peace, 73–4, 98, 104–5, 115, 311n95

Keynesianism, 3, 51, 64, 299n57
Kingston Penitentiary, 111, 133
Knox, James, 340n21
Koselleck, Reinhart, xvii, 9, 280n21

Lachapelle, Emmanuel-Persillier, 353n102
Lacordaire, Henri-Dominique, 266, 356n4
Ladies of Saint Anne, 241, 277
Laflèche, Louis-François, 239
Lagneau, Jules, 204
Lamennais, Hugues-Félicité Robert de, 212, 215, 226, 309n82, 345n53
Lartigue, Jean-Jacques, 215–16, 340n20
Laurier, Wilfrid, 218, 350n80
Le Chapelier, Jean, 295n34
L'Écuyer, Bernard-Pierre, 286n21
legal formalism. *See* liberal penality
Legislative Council of Lower Canada, 100
Leo XIII, Pope, 256
Lepetit, Bernard, 28, 284n3
Le Play, Frédéric, 243, 326n29, 350n84

less eligibility, principle of, 121, 203, 303n37
liberalism, 195–6, 264, 272; bourgeois form of, 4, 33, 44–6, 126, 265–9, 276; and citizenship, 197; in crisis, 59–62, 192–4, 252, 267; criticized, 205; and critique of philanthropy, 173–5; defined, 3–4, 7, 23, 37–41, 45–6, 51, 290n1; misconceived, 55; and state intervention, 53–4
liberal penality, 111–13, 125–31, 135–6, 146, 161; in decline, 270; inapplicable to children, 138–9, 147–8. *See also* crime: liberal view of
liberty. *See* freedom
Lindsay, Edward, 327n39
Lipietz, Alain, xiv, 14, 30, 287n31
Livingston, David, 117
Locke, John, 51, 55
Lombroso, Cesare, 297n47
Lorimier, Albert de, 254
Lower Canada. *See* Quebec
Lucas, Charles, 123
Luther, Martin, 300n12

Macdonald, John A., 297n49, 351n89
Maconochie, Alexander, 321n53
madness. *See* mental illness
Making History in Twentieth-Century Quebec, xxi
Malthus, Thomas, xxix, 80–3, 85–7, 89, 173, 175, 198
Mann, Michael, 282n40
Marine Hospital (Quebec City), 99
Marion, Henri, 297n48
markets, 38, 40, 53, 56–7, 60, 169
Marshall, Alfred, 193, 337n61

Marx, Karl, 48, 287n32, 306n56, 321n57
Marxism, xxxvii
McKay, Ian, xxx–xxxii, xxxiv, 283n47, 290n2
McLean, Francis, 248–50, 275, 352n96
mental illness, 14, 70, 191, 309n77
Mettray farm colony, 137, 141, 143, 152, 157–8, 327n35; Demetz as founder of, 327n43
Meurling, Gustave, 276
Mill, James, 293n17
Mill, John Stuart, 39, 51, 60, 219, 230, 293n17; and ethics, 200–1; and liberty, 169; on limits of state action, 296n40, 296n41, 332n12; on philanthropy, 173; on the private/public divide, 294n31
Ministry of Public Instruction, 275
Minto, Lady Mary, 353n102
Minville, Esdras, 349n77
monarchy, 49, 51–2, 55, 70–1, 74, 171; relationship to Church, 212
Mondelet, Dominique, 116
Montalembert, Charles Forbes René de, 345n53
Montesquieu, Charles de Secondat, baron de, 78
Montigny, B.-A.T. de, 254
Montreal General Hospital, 311n101
Montreal History Group, xv
Montreal House of Industry, 241, 276, 308n71, 310n93, 311n104
Montreal prison. *See* Pied-du-Courant prison
Montreal Protestant Orphan Asylum, 140
Montreal Society for the Protection of Women and Children, 144

Moreau-Christophe, Louis-Mathurin, 344n43
Morris, William, 351n88
mutualism, 175–6, 198, 333n19

Napoleonic Code, 56, 141, 324n10
nation, 197
Neilson, John, 116
Nelson, Wolfred, 314n14
neoliberalism, 51
"new liberalism" (English movement), 62
"new societies," 33–4
New York Children's Aid Society, 153, 326n33, 327n43
New York House of Refuge, 140
Noetics, 83
Norfolk Prison Colony (Massachusetts), 132
nouvel ordre des choses, Un, xiii–xvi, xxiii, xxvi, xxxvi, xxxviii

O'Neill, Terence Joseph, 124, 141, 156, 315n21, 327n45
On Liberty, 169
Ontario Reformatory for Boys (Penetanguishene), 114
On the Penitentiary System in the United States and Its Application in France, 118
Owen, Robert, 309n82
Ozanam, Frédéric, 229, 232–6, 352n93

Paine, Thomas, 80
Paquet, Louis-Adolphe, 343n36
Parent, Étienne, 213–14, 227, 230, 238, 345n53
parole, xxix, 123, 129, 132, 134,
Parsons, Talcott, 48, 284n8
Patriotes, xxxiv, 100, 274

pauperism, 76, 88–92, 97, 101–2, 105–6, 166; in decline, 203; defined, 199; distinguished from poverty, 176–7, 179–82, 186–7; and freedom, 161. *See also* poverty; residuum
Peel, Robert, 91
Pelletier, Denis, 210
penality, liberal, 13, 125, 135; decline of, 126–31
penitentiaries. *See* prisons
Pères de Montfort, 155
Perrot, Michèle, xii–xiii
Peterson, William, 353n102
Petit, Jacques-Guy, xiv
Petite Roquette, La, 114, 141
philanthropy, 56, 79–80, 92, 184, 220, 261, 268–70; and child welfare, 148–9; and interference with personal freedom, 172–5; organization of, 102
Philips, Wendell, 317n31
Pied-du-Courant prison, 132–5
Pitt, William, 302n28
Polanyi, Karl, 32, 293n21
policing, 104, 113–15, 161, 269; in Lower Canada, 99
political economy, 77, 179, 193–4
Poor Law Amendment Act, 90–1, 282n33, 306n54
Poor Laws, 76, 165, 221, 333nn25–6, 335n38; absent from Quebec, 72; advocated, 249–50; cost of enforcing, 79; criticized, 81–2, 87, 180, 197, 223, 305n47, 311n99, 354n105; and less eligibility principle, 303n37
Poulantzas, Nicos, xii, xiv
poverty, 10, 22–3, 30–1, 66–9, 191–2, 268; Christian view of, 82–6,

230–6, 253–5; as collective problem, 166, 196–7; distinguished from pauperism, 89–91, 102, 176–8, 180–1, 186–8; feudal view of, 69–71, 74–5; and institutionalization, 76, 91, 94, 179–81; liberal view of, 175, 179, 185–9, 192–3, 196, 269; Malthusian view of, 81–2, 89, 195–6; as private responsibility, 177–8, 186–7, 270; and state responsibility, 77–80, 86–7, 102, 249–51, 258–9. *See also* pauperism; residuum
power, 20–1, 77
Prins, Adolphe, 135
prisons, 112; criticized, 131–2; as instruments of power, 14–15, 29, 95–6, 107–9; "intermediate" type, 115, 134, 321n53, 321n58; labour in, 124–7, 134; liberal view of, 124, 132–3; in Lower Canada, 92–3, 97, 104–5, 111–15, 133–5; as mainstream approach to crime management, 91; population of, 104–5, 115, 134–5, 322n63; as scientific research institutions, 94–5, 132–3, 135–6; as social prophylaxis, 94, 120–2; women's, 114, 138, 275, 315n20, 328n50, 350n81. *See also* solitary confinement
private/public distinction, 51–4, 57–9, 171–2
Procacci, Giovanna, xxiii
proportionate sentencing, 121, 131, 135, 139, 146, 270
Public Assistance Act of 1921, 259, 262

Quebec, 91–2, 150; national identity in, 273–5, 278, 290n50; as object of study, 5, 31, 33–6, 271–2; provincial government's limited power, 100, 275
Quiet Revolution, xxi, 207, 272, 340n18

Rauhe Haus, 141
Raymond, Joseph-Sabin, 217–18, 345n53
Recorder's Court, 113, 115
Red Party, 218
reform (of inmates), 67–8, 79, 91, 117, 122–3, 187; progressive view of, 127–8
Reformation, 40
reformatories, 139, 142–3, 149, 152, 161; in Canada, 114, 143–4, 148, 155–7; use of merit systems in, 129
Refuge Meurling, 252, 276
Regnard, Albert, 199
regulation: of crime, 111–12, 130, 135–6, 160–1; defined, xiii–xiv, 11–12, 23–6, 30–1; democratic capitalist form, 197; and ethics, 200; feudal form of, 68–74, 99–100, 289n43; liberal form of, 32, 34, 45, 150, 200–2, 205, 267; in Lower Canada, 66, 68, 99–100, 105, 206–8; religion as part of, 267
regulation theory, 30, 280n11, 289n41
Reid, Helen R.Y., 245–7, 353n102
Report on the Sanitary Condition of the Labouring Population of Great Britain, 90
Rerum Novarum, 62, 255–6, 258, 354n109, 355n112
residuum, 202–4, 271, 277, 306n53, 337n61. *See also* pauperism; poverty

responsibility, 42–5, 131, 171, 186, 188
Revue de métaphysique et de morale, 298n52
Ricardo, David, 39, 82, 101
Robertson, John, 194
Roebuck, John Arthur, 296n42
Rolph, John, 223–4
Ross, Edward, 13
Rothman, David, 19, 112, 132, 326n31, 327n39
Rousseau, Jean-Jacques, 55–6, 169, 226, 344n42
Rowntree, B.S., 195, 244, 336n49
Rudin, Ronald, xxi–xxii
Rush, Benjamin, 75
Ruskin, John, 117
Russell, John, 91
Ryerson, Stanley Bréhaut, xii

Saint-Just, 44
Saint-Vincent-de-Paul Penitentiary, 322n60
Sayer, Derek, xxiv
Scottish school of political economy, 56–7
Scull, Andrew, 19
secularization, 209
self-help, 170–1, 176, 184–5, 194
Sicotte, Louis-Victor, 344n48
Sisters of Mercy, 241
Sisters of Providence, 241
Sisters of the Good Shepherd, 241, 315n20, 325n26, 328n50
slavery, 34, 290n48
Smiles, Samuel, 170
Smith, Adam, 52, 55–7, 78, 200, 309n81; on liberty, 169
social control, 12–20, 23–4, 107

Social Darwinism, 60–1, 175, 188, 197, 203, 332n16; Léon Gérin and, 351n91
social defence, theory of, 120, 135
socialism, 46, 51, 61–2, 170, 210, 265; as cause of crisis of liberalism, 252; and critique of liberal penality, 126–9; excluded by Church, 255, 277
social law, 63
social sciences, 11, 13, 62, 181, 193–6, 243–5; and crime, 270–1; excluded by Church in Quebec, 277
social work, 190
societies, cohesion and change in, 10–13, 23–32, 50, 56
Soeurs de l'Hôtel-Dieu de Montréal, 307n62
solidarism, 46, 50, 62–3
solitary confinement, 123–5, 127–8, 133–4, 316n27, 329n65
Speenhamland system, 79
Spencer, Herbert, 61, 175, 297n51, 342n33
St Vincent de Paul Society, 237; in Lower Canada, 143, 241, 253–5, 277; Ozanam addressing, 235; praised, 248
suffrage, 4, 53, 59–61, 145, 188, 193, 290n48
summary prosecution, 113
Sumner, William Graham, 334n32
Syllabus, 212

Thatcher, Margaret, xxx
Theory of Moral Sentiments, 200
Thiers, Adolphe, 167
Thompson, E.P., xv, xviii, xxiv, 280n13, 282n34

Tocqueville, Alexis de, xxxv, 118, 126–8, 179, 230, 356n7; on cellular system, 123; on classification and reform, xxviii, 118–20, 184; on freedom of movement, 170; on religion, 200, 210–11, 227, 343n34; on state intervention, 270, 296n40; on young offenders, 138, 147, 330n66
Tönnies, Ferdinand, 62
Tourville, Henri de, 243
Trépanier, Jean, xii

ultramontanism, 102, 207, 212–13, 215–19, 255–7; reaction to liberalism, 267
Union catholique, 254

Vallée, Charles, 134
Van Krieken, Robert, 18
Villeneuve-Bargemont, Alban, 83, 88, 221, 304n46, 344n43
Vinet, Alexandre, 356n3

virtue, 200
Visitor of the Poor, The, 307n60

Walzer, Michael, 7
Weber, Max, 48, 193, 209
welfare, 100, 176, 197–9, 247–52, 269–70. *See also* charity
will. *See* agency
Wines, Frederick, 181
Words of a Believer, 226
workers' compensation, 298n55
Workers' Federation of Chicoutimi, 258
workhouses, 69–70, 91, 176, 179–80, 191–2, 221
working class, 166–8, 170, 177–8, 193, 271; and Catholic Church, 255–8; integration into capitalist regulation, 175, 193, 197–9, 201–2; and welfare, 245–6, 271

Young, Brian, xv